W9-CMB-114

A COMMENTARY ON OVID: *FASTI*, BOOK VI

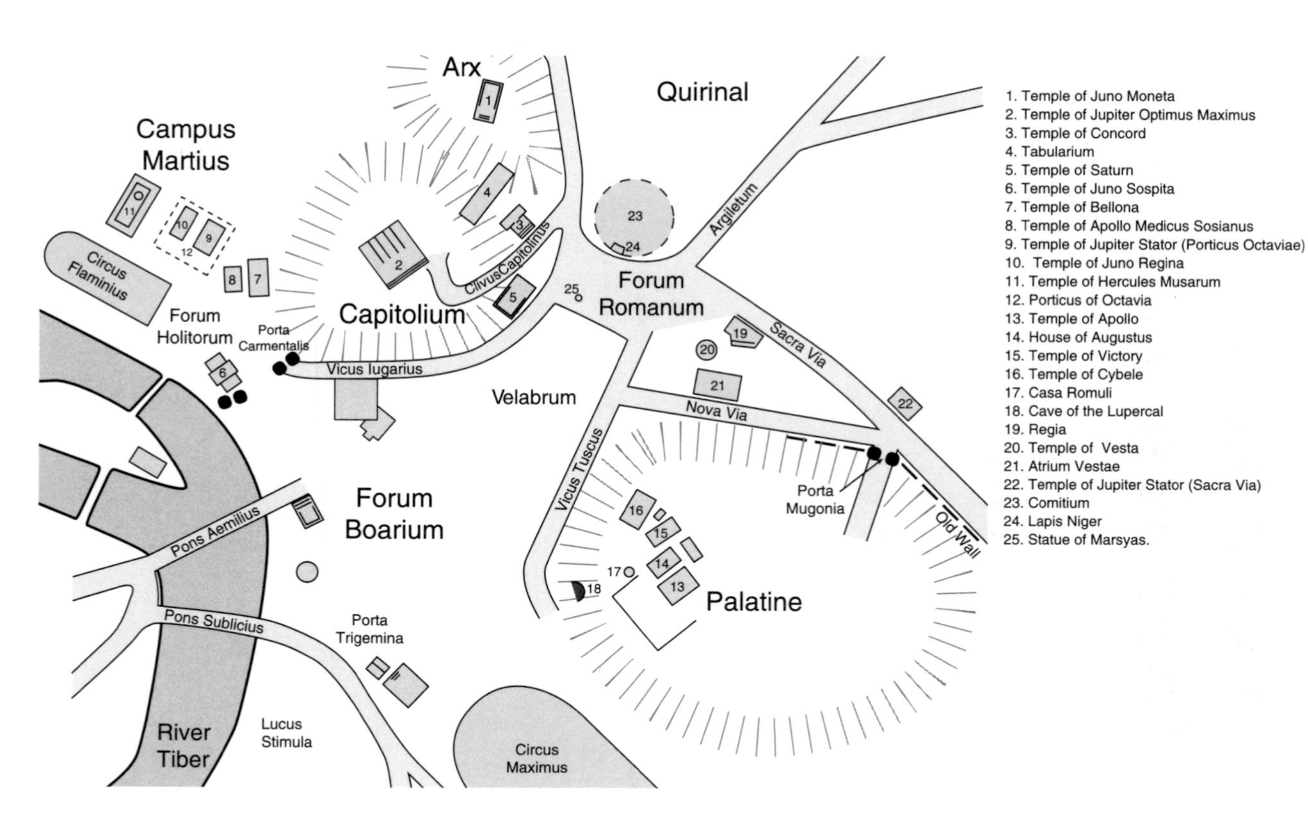

Plan 1. The City of Rome

A Commentary on Ovid: *Fasti* Book VI

R. JOY LITTLEWOOD

OXFORD
UNIVERSITY PRESS

Great Clarendon Street, Oxford OX2 6DP

Oxford University Press is a department of the University of Oxford.
It furthers the University's objective of excellence in research, scholarship,
and education by publishing worldwide

in Oxford New York

Auckland Cape Town Dar es Salaam Hong Kong Karachi
Kuala Lumpur Madrid Melbourne Mexico City Nairobi
New Delhi Shanghai Taipei Toronto

With offices in

Argentina Austria Brazil Chile Czech Republic France Greece
Guatemala Hungary Italy Japan Poland Portugal Singapore
South Korea Switzerland Thailand Turkey Ukraine Vietnam

Oxford is a registered trade mark of Oxford University Press
in the UK and in certain other countries

Published in the United States
by Oxford University Press Inc., New York

First published 2006

British Library Cataloguing in Publication Data

Data available

Library of Congress Cataloging in Publication Data

Littlewood, R. Joy.

A commentary on Ovid: Fasti book VI/R. Joy Littlewood.
p. cm.
Includes biblographical references and indexes.
ISBN-13: 978-0-19-927134-4 (alk. paper)
ISBN-10: 0-19-927134-8 (alk. paper)
1. Ovid, 43 B.C.-17 or A.D. Fasti. Book 6. 2. Didatic poetry,
Latin–History and criticism. 3. Fasti and feasts in literature.
4. Calendar in literature. I. Ovid, 43 B.C.-17 or 18 A.D. Fasti.
Book 6. II. Title.
PA6519. F6A6 2006
871′. 01–dc22

2006006158
Typeset by SPI Publisher Services, Pondicherry, India
Printed in Great Britain
on acid-free paper by
Biddles Ltd., King's Lynn, Norfolk

ISBN 0-19-927134-8 978-0-19-927134-4

1 3 5 7 9 10 8 6 4 2

Preface

Seventy years after Frazer published his monumental commentary on Ovid's *Fasti* in 1929, there appeared the first of a wave of new English commentaries: Elaine Fantham's *Ovid: Fasti Book IV*, followed in 2004 by Steven Green's *Ovid Fasti Book 1*. It is perhaps appropriate that *Fasti* 6 should come next, in order to complete the outer 'frame' for Ovid's first six books with its thematic contrasts and similarities. At least one other *Fasti* commentary is currently in preparation, and it seems likely that the end of the decade will see a complete set of six. The rediscovery of *Fasti* as an important work of Augustan literature was stimulated by the publication of a new Teubner text in 1978 by Alton, Wormell, and Courtney (*AWC*). The subsequent flow of articles and monographs included valuable surveys in the Cambridge (2001) and Brill's (2002) Companions to Ovid, and culminated in a book of twelve essays, *Ovid's Fasti: Historical Readings at its Bimillennium*, edited by Geraldine Herbert-Brown in 2002, its content ranging across Augustan politics, Roman religion, the calendar, astronomy, literary criticism, and the iconography of Augustan monuments. This concentration of scholarship on a single poem testifies to the challenge and complexity of Ovid's *Fasti*. That a poem written by Rome's most influential poet at the height of his success and simultaneously with his *Metamorphoses* should have been neglected, misjudged, and underestimated across so many years is one of the most remarkable phenomena in Western literature.

This commentary aims to highlight the essential components of Ovid's literary treatment of the Roman calendar in its context in the late Augustan Principate. The seven sections of the Introduction aim to demonstrate how contemporary political and religious changes are reflected in Ovid's *Fasti* (sections 1–2); Ovid's expansion of the elegiac genre through the antiquarian content of Book 6 (sec. 3); how the themes of *Fasti* 6 contribute to its unusual slant towards worship in times of war, balancing *Fasti* 1, a celebration of Peace (sec. 4); Ovid's narrative technique (sec. 5) and his use of Livy's histories (sec. 6); and, briefly, the textual tradition of *Fasti* 6 (sec. 7).

I am deeply indebted to a number of scholars who have generously given of their time and expertise. My first thanks must go to Robin Nisbet who, with characteristic prescience, pointed me towards Ovid's *Fasti* in the late 1970s and patiently set me on the path to appreciating this controversial and enigmatic work. It gives me great pleasure, also, to express the warmest gratitude to Elaine Fantham, Peta Fowler, Geraldine Herbert-Brown, and John F. Miller for their encouragement and valuable scholarly criticism as they read through a series of unpromising drafts. They have saved me from innumerable errors of judgement; for those which remain, I am of course entirely responsible. Sincere thanks are due to Maria Pia Malvezzi of the British School in Rome, who generously arranged many appointments for me to visit sites, museums and artefacts during my visit to Rome in September 2004, to Sylvia Diebner of D.A.I. (Rome) who spent several hours helping me to select photographic negatives, and, most particularly, to my travelling companion, Peta Fowler, who played a major part in planning the trip. This project has been enriched by the kindness of Philip Hardie, Stephen Harrison, and Gregory Hutchinson of the University of Oxford who welcomed me to their seminars and colloquia, from which a number of lively discussions have contributed to this commentary. I owe a considerable debt of gratitude to Hilary O'Shea and her colleagues at Oxford University Press for their patient guidance. I should also like to thank for their valuable contributions from widely different areas of professional expertise: Mensun Bound, Donald Hill, Andreas Löwe, and, in particular, my two sons, Cedric and Julian Littlewood. My greatest debt, however, is to my husband, John, whose wise and tactful criticism was always accompanied by loyal and unstinting encouragement.

R. J. L.

Dorchester-on-Thames

Oxfordshire

April 2005

Contents

List of figures and plans

Figures

Plans

Abbreviations

AJA	*American Journal of Archaeology*
AJAH	*American Journal of Ancient History*
AJPh	*American Journal of Philology*
ANRW	H. Temporini and W. Haase (eds.), *Aufstieg und Niedergang der römischen Welt* (Berlin and New York, 1972–)
AWC	E. H. Alton, D. E. W. Wormell, and E. Courtney, *P. Ovidi Nasonis Fastorum Libri Sex*, 4th edn. (Leipzig, 1997)
BEFAR	*Bibliothèque des Écoles Françaises d'Athènes et de Rome*
BICS	*Bulletin of the Institute of Classical Studies*
BNP	M. Beard, J. North, and S. Price, *Religions of Rome*, 2 vols. (Cambridge, 1998)
CIL	*Corpus Inscriptionum Latinarum* (Berlin, 1863–)
CJ	*Classical Journal*
CPh	*Classical Philology*
CQ	*Classical Quarterly*
CRAI	*Comptes Rendus de l'Académie des Inscriptions et Belles Lettres*
Degrassi	A. Degrassi, *Inscriptiones Italiae XIII 2: Fasti et Elogia* (Rome, 1963)
GRF	H. Funaioli, *Grammaticae Romanae Fragmenta* (Leipzig 1907; repr. Stuttgart, 1969)
HSCPh	*Harvard Studies in Classical Philology*
ILS	H. Dessau (ed.), *Inscriptiones Latinae Selectae* (Berlin, 1898–1916)
JRS	*Journal of Roman Studies*
MAAR	*Memoirs of the American Academy in Rome* (Rome, 1915–80)
Maltby	R. Maltby, *A Lexicon of Ancient Latin Etymologies* (Leeds, 1991)
MD	*Materiali e discussioni per l'analisi dei testi classici*
MDAIR	*Mitteilungen des deutschen archäologischen Instituts. Römische Abteilung*
OCD	S. Hornblower and A. Spawforth (eds.), *The Oxford Classical Dictionary* (Oxford, 1996)
OLD	P. G. W. Glare (ed.), *Oxford Latin Dictionary* (Oxford, 1982)
PCPhS	*Proceedings of the Cambridge Philological Society*
PdP	*La Parola del Passato*

Platnauer	M. Platnauer, *Latin Elegiac Verse* (Cambridge, 1951)
PIR	*Prosopographia Imperii Romani*, 2nd edn. (1933–)
Rev. Arch.	*Revue Archéologique*
REL	*Revue des Études Latines*
RhM	*Rheinisches Museum für Philologie*
Richardson	L. Richardson, *A New Topographical Dictionary of Ancient Rome* (Baltimore, 1992)
Roscher	W. H. Roscher, *Ausführliches Lexicon der griechischen und römischen Mythologie* (Leipzig, 1884–1937; repr. Hildesheim, 1965–)
Steinby	E. M. Steinby (ed.), *Lexicon Topographicum Urbis Romae*, 6 vols. (Rome, 1993–2000)
StudRom	*Studi Romani*
StudStor	*Studi Storici*
TAPhA	*Transactions of the American Philological Association*
YClS	*Yale Classical Studies*

Introduction

1. Ovid's *Fasti* in its historical context

Ovid's Augustan poetry might be said to have begun with the *Ars Amatoria*. Within the first 250 lines we find a panegyric addressed to the young Gaius Caesar setting out for Parthia with potent family backing from Augustus and Mars Ultor.[1] The poet's depiction of 'Love in the Metropolis' presents a Rome where the Pax Augusta was the only political experience of men under 30 and rising imperial monuments with their iconography of peace and plenty[2] encouraged a mood of optimism. All Rome, claimed the poet of the *Ars*, was engaged in the game of seduction: at dinner parties, among Augustus' latest monuments, even at Gaius' anticipated Parthian triumph. Ovid's *persona*, the urbane 'man about town', sprang from a social confidence engendered by his uncontroversial provincial equestrian background, a measure of financial security, and the success of his love poetry.[3] With increasing fame and widening social connections the poet appears to have been drawn into circles sympathetic to Augustus' daughter, Julia, in the power struggles which centred on a conflict of ambitions between Julia's two adolescent sons and her estranged husband, Tiberius,[4] whose 'retirement' to Rhodes in 6 BC encouraged Julia to scheme more ambitiously for a personal power base. Ovid's third wife was a regular visitor to the house of Augustus' first cousin, Marcia,[5] and her husband, Paullus Fabius

[1] Ovid *Ars* 1. 177–228.

[2] See Zanker (1988) 107–226.

[3] Three books of *Amores* and the first book of *Heroides* were written 25–15 BC. Ovid had completed revisions of both *Amores* and *Heroides* and written his *Medea*, *Ars Amatoria*, and *Remedium Amoris* by AD 1.

[4] See Levick (1972). Herbert-Brown (1994) 153–6 cites the rift between Tiberius and Julia as the reason why, in 7 BC, Tiberius dedicated Augustus' Porticus Liviae jointly with his mother, Livia, and not his wife and why Julia, in contrast to Livia, played no part in the celebrations for her husband's triumph in the same year.

[5] Ovid *P* 1. 2. 136–42. Augustus' first cousin Marcia is celebrated conspicuously in the epilogue to *Fasti* 6 as the daughter of the founder of the temple of Hercules Musarum.

Maximus,[6] a close friend of Augustus who was known to be strongly opposed to the succession of Tiberius.[7] It has been fairly observed that 'the re-emergence of accusations of immorality within the imperial household exposes not only the internal power struggles of the palace, but the fragility of imperial authority'.[8] Julia's machinations had so jeopardized dynastic harmony and stability that in 2 BC her father Augustus banished her from Rome on a charge of 'adultery'.[9] At the same time he arranged a divorce between Julia and Tiberius which effectively detached Tiberius from the prospect of succession.[10] There seemed little reason at this time for Ovid to doubt that Gaius would succeed his grandfather Augustus.

Although Ovid was sufficiently self-assured to allow his *Ars*, a mock-didactic guide to the art of seduction, into public circulation within a year of Julia's banishment, he must have been aware that his poem clashed disagreeably with the Princeps' aim to impose moral regeneration in Rome, enforced by stringent legislation.[11] The decade which had followed Augustus' leges Iuliae had seen the construction of monuments which emphasized the Princeps' control over Roman time and urban space. In the Campus Martius, near the dynastic mausoleum, a Horologium was designed so that the sun's shadow from the obelisk, which Augustus had brought from Egypt and dedicated to Apollo, bisected the Ara Pacis on Augustus' birthday, the autumnal equinox.[12] His next building project was the Forum

[6] Ovid *P* 1. 2, 3. 3, 8, 4. 6. 1–16. Ovid addresses Paullus Fabius Maximus with dignity and reserve, suggesting either that he had no wish to contaminate a good friend with his own ill repute or that Ovid's wife and Marcia shared a closer friendship than their husbands.

[7] Syme (1978) 146 describes Maximus as 'foremost among his (Tiberius') enemies.'

[8] Wallace-Hadrill (1997) 12.

[9] Adultery, in this context, implied conspiracy. A substantial bibliography on the subject is to be found in K. A. Raaflaub and L. J. Samans, 'Opposition to Augustus', in Raaflaub and Toher (1990) 417–54. See, too, R. Syme, 'The Crisis of 2 BC', *Bayerische Akademie der Wissenschaften* 7. 3, (1974) repr. in *Roman Papers III* (Oxford, 1979) 912 and *The Augustan Aristocracy* (Oxford, 1986) 91–2.

[10] Julia's involvement with Iullus Antonius and her divorce from Tiberius is discussed by Levick (1976) 44–5.

[11] Augustus' notorious Leges Iuliae were passed before his celebration of the *Ludi Saeculares* in 17 BC (Aug. *RG* 8. 5. Cf. Prop. 2. 7. 1–3, Suet. *Aug.* 34. 1).

[12] This complex was completed before 8 BC. The Ara Pacis was dedicated on Livia's birthday, 30 January 9 BC.

Augustum, dominated by the temple of Mars Ultor, which was dedicated on the eve of Gaius' campaign against the Parthians. The dynastic character of these monuments reflected a tightening of autocracy.

Responding to his personal ambitions, Ovid, now reaching the height of his poetic powers, began two intellectually ambitious works, which would reflect the spirit of the Age with the same complexity of symbolism as Augustus' newly adorned city. He appears to have worked simultaneously on his *Metamorphoses* and *Fasti*, during the years before his relegation in AD 8.[13] In the barest terms *Metamorphoses* might be described as a cosmological epic,[14] a universal history of the world from its origins to the apotheosis of Julius Caesar and the triumph of the Gens Iulia;[15] its carefully crafted epilogue foretelling the poet's own immortality suggests that Ovid considered this his greatest work. The importance which Augustus himself attached to reforming Roman religion and the calendar suggested to Ovid the idea of a poem in calendar form. The poet's 'research' into the aetiology of Roman festivals tapped into a wave of antiquarianism originating in the late Republic which was seen as a stabilizing force at a time of radical political change and as a means of restoring confidence in Roman identity.[16] If the authorial intention of the poet of the *Georgics* was to invoke a cycle of rural life which was familiar to the owners of country villas, Ovid intended his *Fasti* to bring to the official calendar a portrait of *Romanitas* in the picturesque vitality of urban and rural cults.

Ovid's subject matter, *tempora cum causis Latium digesta per annum* (*Fast.* 1. 1), inevitably evoked themes of Augustan discourse.

[13] Cross-references between the two works are discussed by Hinds (1987*a*) 10–11, 42–4, 72–7, Bömer (1988). On dating Ovid's *Fasti* see Syme (1978) 21–36, Bömer (1988) 15–17, Newlands (1995) 235–6, Holzberg (1995) 351–3, Barchiesi (1997*a*) 259–71, Fantham (1998) 1–4.

[14] See Stephen M. Wheeler, '*Imago Mundi*: Creation in Ovid's *Metamorphoses*', *AJPh* 116 (1995) 95–121.

[15] For a discussion of the implication of some of Ovid's allusions here see P. Hardie, 'Questions of Authority: The Invention of Tradition in Ovid's *Metamorphoses* 15', in T. Habinek and Alessandro Schiesaro (eds.) *The Roman Cultural Revolution* (Cambridge, 1997) 182–98.

[16] See Beard (1987) 1–15, Pasco-Pranger (2000) 275–93, who includes a bibliography on antiquarianism in her n. 23, p. 281.

Meanwhile the humour inherent in his elegiac genre permitted the poet to blur boundaries and create passages of ambiguity which, in recent decades, have provoked the suggestion that Ovid's *Fasti* may have been even more iconoclastic than his *Ars*. This seems not to have been the intention of its author, who singled out his *Fasti* with its dedication to the Princeps as the work mostly likely to demonstrate his commitment to Augustan values.

On 5 February 2 BC, Augustus accepted his most illustrious title, *pater patriae*,[17] This title, associated in Cicero's day with 'saving the lives of fellow citizens' and the oak wreath, which Augustus had been awarded in 27 BC, carried both the resonance of *patria potestas* and the distinction of being one of Rome's supreme benefactors. Celebrating the 'sacred Nones', the anniversary of Augustus receiving this 'supreme honour' (*maximus hic fastis accumulatur honor, Fast.* 2. 122), the poet elects to 'showcase' his own poetic ingenuity.[18] When his panegyric transgresses the conventional boundaries of elegiac verse,[19] in order to regain generic equilibrium, Ovid descends sharply, via Jupiter—*hominum tu pater, ille deum* (132)—to an elegiac contrast of Romulus with Augustus. At the point where he ceases to address Augustus directly and turns, instead, to apostrophize Romulus, there is a change in tone, a diminution of respect for Rome's shaggy founder, whose belligerent 'achievements' Ovid contrasts disparagingly with those of the new *pater patriae* in such lines as: *tu (Romule) rapis, hic castas duce se iubet esse maritas* (139).[20] Ovid's comparison of Romulus and Augustus has received mixed interpretation.[21] Assessing the seemliness of humour from the view-

[17] *Fast.* 2. 119–30. Augustus took particular pride in the title, the culmination of a list of honours in his *Res Gestae*, and in the unanimous chorus of approbation with which Ovid is quick to associate himself as a member of the equestrian order: *hoc dedimus nos tibi nomen eques* (*Fast.* 2. 128).

[18] See Miller (1982) 371–417.

[19] Beginning with an inflated version of the 'hundred tongues' motif, *nunc mihi mille sonos... vellem* (*Fast.* 2. 119–20), Ovid claims to be poetically dumbfounded at his madness in attempting to celebrate *maximus hic honos* in inadequate elegiacs: *quid volui demens elegis imponere tantum | ponderis?* (125–6).

[20] For the suggestion of subversive humour here, see Hinds (1992) 133 and Newlands (1995) 189.

[21] Wallace-Hadrill (1987) 228–9, Hinds (1992) 132–41, and Newlands (1995) 188–9 detect traces of anti-Augustanism. Herbert-Brown (1994) 43–63 concludes that Augustus 'would have found... the entire passage inventive, refreshing, amusing' (p. 62).

point of a different age is notoriously tricky. Considered from a literary point of view, it seems that the poet was trying to retreat from his high panegyric to generically safer ground, to a witty, elegiac contrast which exposes nothing more sinister than his delight in devising ingenious points of comparison.[22]

If Ovid knew that his humour and poetic sophistry annoyed Augustus, then it is odd that he did not make a greater effort to suppress this in *Tristia* 2, the letter defending his poetry, which he addressed to Augustus from Tomis in AD 9. In this poem Ovid represents his *Fasti* as a 'serious' work which might offer a convincing counterweight to the disgrace of his *Ars Amatoria*:[23]

> sex ego Fastorum scripsi totidemque libellos,
> cumque suo finem mense volumen habet,
> idque tuo nuper scriptum sub nomine, Caesar,
> et tibi sacratum sors mea rupit opus.
> (*Tr.* 2. 549–52)

'Six books, and another six, I wrote about the Roman calendar, the ending of each marking the end of its own month. That poem, dedicated to you, has been interrupted by my unfortunate change of circumstances.'

The tone of Ovid's 'Letter to Augustus' is difficult to assess and seemingly ambivalent. Beside passages of, apparently, grovelling self-abasement and flattery are others which seem to harbour a disingenuous wit. The poet makes light of his *error*, making out that this was a slip, a matter of poor judgement. His defence is for his poetry, his *Ars Amatoria* (with such specious arguments as illicit love being the central theme in the best literature, including Homer's *Iliad* and Virgil's *Aeneid*), which gives the impression that his open letter is really intended to persuade a wider audience that he has been unjustly punished.[24] In support of the value of his *Fasti* Ovid

[22] See particularly Hinds (1992) 81–153.

[23] The literature on Ovid's exile is extensive. A useful recent review of this is R. Verdière, *Le Secret du voltigeur d'amor ou le mystère de la relégation d'Ovide* (Brussels, 1992) and G. D. Williams 'Ovid's Exile Poetry: Worlds Apart', in B. W. Boyd (ed.), *Brill's Companion to Ovid* (Leiden, 2002) 337–81.

[24] See esp. Wiedeman (1975) 264–71, Syme (1978) 222–5, Nugent (1990) 239–57, which contains a wide bibliography on the subject, and Williams (1994) 154–209.

makes only three points, and they deserve to be taken seriously: his dedication to Augustus (*tuo... scriptum sub nomine, tibi sacratum*),[25] the number of books (*sex ego Fastorum scripsi totidem libellos*), and the untimely interruption (*sors mea rupit opus*).

First, Ovid's dedication to Augustus was no doubt absolutely true at the time when the poet was writing *Tristia* 2. The dedication of a work on religious antiquarianism to Augustus as Pontifex Maximus was appropriate and Ovid had the precedent of Varro, who had dedicated his *Antiquitates* to Julius Caesar when he was Pontifex Maximus. More importantly, however, Augustus' elevation to the office of Pontifex Maximus had been a pivotal step to his role as dynastic priest of Vesta, and Ovid's dedication of a major work on Roman religion underlined the Princeps' new role at the centre of the state cult which he had transformed (see Introduction 2). The death of Augustus in AD 14 gave Ovid a reason to rededicate his work.[26] Passing over Tiberius, who became the new Pontifex Maximus in March AD 15, Ovid dedicated his *Fasti* to Germanicus, co-heir with Tiberius' son, Drusus, and a prince with a penchant for astronomical poetry.[27]

Secondly, Ovid must have intended to complete all twelve months of the calendar. If, as some critics suggest, the high proportion of Augustan anniversaries in the second half of the year was discouraging, the poet was aware of this before he started the project.[28] The evidence of careful structure and thematic balance in the surviving six books offers some guidance across the thin ice of speculation. In AD 8, some six years into the project, it is unlikely that the poet had not sketched out a draft of the whole year, indicating, perhaps, the major passages of each month, seasonal themes, festivals which might have links to earlier months and, possibly, the direction of

[25] *Tr.* 2.551–2.

[26] Although *Fast.* 2. 3–18 has occasionally been thought to be the original dedication to Augustus which Ovid moved from Book 1, it is more probable that Ovid's promise of elevated themes simply refers to Augustus' new honour, the accolade of *pater patriae* on 5 February. See Fantham (1985) 256–8 and Miller (1991) 143–4.

[27] Germanicus' adaptation of Aratus' *Phaenomena* allowed Ovid to give him the status of a poet: *vates rege vatis habenas* (*Fast.* 1. 25). Ovid's lines on the noble pursuit of studying the constellations (*Fast.* 1. 295–310) is one of the most elevated passages in his *Fasti.*

[28] Barchiesi (1997*a*) 261, lists a daunting selection, including 12 July, birth of Divus Iulius, and Augustus' triple triumph on 9 August.

each proem. The complete absence of evidence for the later months suggests that Ovid had made little headway on the passages which constituted July–December when his flight to Tomis 'interrupted' work on his *Fasti.* During his eight years in Tomis there would have been time to complete all twelve books, for initially, during the period AD 9–14, Ovid wrote prolifically. His choice of subject matter is illuminating. In the hope of achieving his recall to Rome he expended all his literary energy on his *Tristia* and *Epistolae ex Ponto*,[29] not judging it expedient to complete the unfinished calendar poem, although it might be argued that a panegyric in celebration of the months of July and August (with September forthcoming, subject to being granted more effective research conditions) would have been more fruitful. At some point during his exile the poet evidently made a conscious decision not to persevere with the second half of the year. He imposed a careful internal structure on the six surviving books, including a set of thematic frames linking Books 1–2 with Book 6, and pointedly signposted the ending of Book 6 through a prolonged coda featuring closural themes, such as rebirth and apotheosis. *Fasti* remained, and was to remain, intentionally, a poem fractured by misfortune: a statement no less strong than the closing lines of his *Metamorphoses.*[30]

Ovid's revision of Book 1 must have begun after he received the news of the death of Augustus in AD 14. The extant version presents a cohesive impression of the new regime, with an emphasis on peace and civic order: Tiberius is addressed as *dux venerande* (1. 646) and Germanicus is promised: *saepe tibi pater est... legendus* (10); the dedication of the temple of Concordia, AD 10, is celebrated on 16 January (637–50)[31] and Livia is addressed by her new title, Iulia

[29] According to Syme's dating (1978) 37–47, Ovid's *Tristia* came out in AD 9–12, followed by the first three books of his *Letters from Pontus* in AD 12–13.

[30] In claiming that his work was interrupted, Ovid admits it was unfinished. This appears to be the poet's conscious choice, rather than simply disinclination to continue in an alien environment this quintessentially Roman work. Barchiesi (1997*a*) 262 concludes: 'The personal situation of the author invests the damaged year with at least a potential metaphorical meaning: the time of Ovid's life is severed like the structure of the poem.'

[31] Although Ovid may have incorporated the *natalis* of the Aedes Concordiae into *Fasti* 1 before Augustus' death, it is more probable that it was part of the overall revision after AD 14. On the whole question of Ovid's revision to Book 1 see Green

Augusta (536). It is clear from the poet's letters and his revised version of *Fasti* 1 that he was kept sufficiently well informed in Tomis to be able to reflect the mood of the times and write about new monuments or dynastic events. While consolidating the structure of his six books of *Fasti* with its closural coda, he added pointed subjective asides to any couplet concerned with the theme of exile.[32]

Syme's argument for Ovid's completion of *Fasti* before AD 4, that the poet would not have omitted so important an anniversary as the adoption of Tiberius on 26 June, has been successfully countered by Herbert-Brown.[33] Augustus adopted Tiberius together with the 14-year-old Agrippa Postumus, remaining son of Julia and Agrippa, on 26 June AD 4. The settlement demanded Tiberius' adoption of his nephew, Germanicus, so that he became co-heir with Drusus, Tiberius' natural son. In this way Augustus' bloodline could be—and eventually was—represented through a child of Germanicus and Agrippina, the elder Julia's daughter.[34] By introducing a reveller returning in the early hours from the festival of Fors Fortuna on 24 June, who has drunk so much that he cannot even remember that tomorrow brings the summer solstice (785–90), Ovid appears, urbanely, to gloss over an important dynastic event which might also have slipped the inebriate's mind. The ambivalence of this combination of reticence and facetiousness would seem more displeasing than entertaining, but only if Tiberius' adoption had already been designated a public holiday. Since 26 June was not marked as a public holiday in any of the official *Fasti*,[35] Ovid was not obliged to celebrate it in his calendar poem.

(2004*a*) 17–18, 32–44, who notes interesting verbal similarities between the dedication to Germanicus and *P* 4. 8. 31–4.

[32] The most direct is *Fast.* 4. 79–82, where he addresses a lament to Germanicus, 1. 482–4, 5. 652, and 6. 665–6. On a more extensive revision of Books 2–6 see Fantham (1985) 266–72.

[33] Herbert Brown (1994) 215–33. Newlands (1995) 221, finds the omission 'particularly significant'.

[34] Ironically it was Augustus' sister Octavia whose union with M. Antonius eventually produced three Julio-Claudian emperors: her daughter, Augustus' niece, Antonia Minor was the mother of Claudius, grandmother of Gaius Caligula, and great-grandmother of Nero.

[35] The earliest mention of Tiberius' adoption is an entry, dated post AD 20 by Degrassi (1963), 185, in the *Fasti Amiternini*. On this see Herbert-Brown (1994) 215–33 and this Commentary, note on line 785.

Ovid appears not to have favoured the choice of Tiberius as the next Princeps and Tiberius, like his predecessor, remained consistently obdurate to the poet's pleas for recall. Nevertheless, their mutual dislike does not figure in Ovid's exile poetry, which included reserved but respectful mention of Tiberius after he became Princeps in AD 14. Tiberius, who was known to be a connoisseur of good literature, did not suppress Ovid's books as many other books were suppressed during his Principate. Apart from the *Ars*, Ovid's works remained in Rome's public libraries after their author had left Rome.[36]

In the aftermath of the dynastic struggles, on 16 January AD 10, the anniversary of the Princeps receiving the title 'Augustus', Tiberius rededicated the newly restored Aedes Concordiae Augustae on the site of Camillus' first temple of Concord (367 BC), overlooking the Forum Romanum. The monument has a literary counterpart in Ovid's revised *Fasti* 1 in which Roman magistrates move in ordered paths, like the constellations, watched over by the cosmic god of Augustan Peace, Janus. The Aedes Concordiae and its statues, variously donated by Augustus, Livia, and Tiberius, presented to Rome a determined display of dynastic reconciliation and unity. As these symbolic fruits of the Pax Augusta were mirrored in Ovid's *Fasti*, so, for those who wished to perceive it, were the dynastic conflicts of the imperial family. In the proem to *Fasti* 6 Augustus, thinly disguised as Concordia, mediates in a dispute between Juno and her daughter, while Augustus' personal tragedy may be echoed by the grim pronouncement of Servius' statue: *voltus abscondite nostros | ne natae videant ora nefanda meae* (615–16). In Ovid's pageant of Roman festivals ancient legends gain poignancy and verisimilitude by a choice of words which may evoke fleeting images of Augustan reality. Carmentis' consoling words to her exiled son, *offenso pulsus es urbe deo* (1. 480–2), superimposes over Evander an image of the exiled poet. Ovid's description of the brutal silencing and rape of Lara (2. 608–12) elicits involuntary revulsion at the spectacle of a helpless creature tortured for unwary gossip, while the astute and morally egregious Numa outwits Jupiter's demand for a Roman life by his skill in a contest of words (3. 337–44).[37] As Ovid would

[36] See Ovid *P* 1. 1. 5–6.

[37] On the circumscription of freedom of speech in the late Augustan period see Feeney (1992).

perhaps have reassured Augustus, all this had more to do with an elegiac poet's translation of myth into terms of universal human experience than with any covert allusion to the repression of free speech or to a troubled dynasty. However, there is no doubt that the one may illuminate the other.

2. Augustus' reorganization of Roman religion and its impact on *Fasti* 6

In 29 BC Octavian ceremoniously closed the doors of the temple of Janus[38] and two years later, after much deliberation, selected for himself the title Augustus. The name was resonant of religion, of propitious augury, increase (*augere*), and prosperity.[39] This was a calculated move, both political and dynastic. Roman religion was closely bound up with political life. Divine assistance had always been routinely invoked by Rome's politicians and generals in times of crisis; distant echoes of the litany of *lectisternia*, *supplicationes*, and temples vowed which accompany Livy's military catastrophes are recurrent in Ovid's *Fasti*. In the aftermath of Actium Augustus was responding cannily to the widespread pessimism engendered by decades of civil war, reflected in Roman literature of the twenties.[40] His new title carried the promise of a new covenant which united *pax deorum*, divine favour earned by Roman *pietas*, with *Pax Augusta*: Roman peace and prosperity purchased by the victory at Actium. The conjunction of Roman *pietas* and *Victoria Augusta* hardened into a tenet of ideology, the most obvious manifestation of this being the Ara Pacis Augustae, built some twenty years later, which conveyed in simple iconography that *Victoria Augusta* was rewarded by *Pax Augusta*, and that Rome's divine parents, Venus and Mars, had engendered, respectively, two complementary paradigms of Roman virtue: Aeneas the personification of *pietas* and Romulus of heroic, martial *virtus*.

[38] *RG* 13. The ceremony was repeated in 25 BC.

[39] The religious character of this name is discussed by Ovid (*Fast.* 1. 603–16), who points out its etymological connections with religion, *augurium* (augury) and *augere* (increase and prosperity). Cf. Suet. *Aug.* 7. 2.

[40] Livy has Camillus tell the Romans after the siege of Veii and of the Roman Capitol that Roman *pietas* alone will save Rome from disaster (5. 51. 5). Cf. Hor. *Carm.* 3. 6. 1–4.

Augustus' revival of Roman religion was intended to raise public morale by advertising a continuity with the Roman republican past and Rome's age-old tradition of *pietas.* Civic religion, particularly the ritual of sacrifice, played a prominent role in Augustan Rome, and this is attested in the decoration of the great Augustan religious monuments.[41] The title 'Augustus' heralded the Princeps' intention to imprint on the outward forms of Roman cult the indelible stamp of the new regime, for 'Augustus' implied that the leader was chosen by augury and the will of the gods. The Princeps' reconstruction of Roman cult became, increasingly, consciously dynastic. Through the *Gens Iulia* Caesar and his heir traced their descent from Aeneas who had brought the Roman gods from Troy. The office of Pontifex Maximus, which had retained its republican character during the tenure of Caesar, took on the form of a hereditary priesthood, held only by the ruler, who was a descendant of Aeneas, an idea implicit in Ovid's celebration of the anniversary of Augustus' election to Pontifex Maximus on 6 March 12 BC: *ortus ab Aenea . . . sacerdos* (*Fast.* 3. 425).[42] Augustus had enhanced the outward sanctity of the office by observing scrupulously correct sacral procedure in holding the election only after the death of the previous incumbent, M. Lepidus. The passage of time made it easier for Augustus to take the unprecedented step of creating a new shrine to Vesta in his own house, instead of using the official residence of the Pontifex Maximus,[43] emphasizing the ancient sacral character of Roman kingship: the Vestal flame, reputedly brought with the Trojan Penates from the royal house of Troy, once again burned on the ruler's hearth.[44] The religious technicality which had brought this about was the rule that the Pontifex Maximus should have an official residence near the Aedes Vestae in the Forum Romanum. When Augustus' house burnt down in AD 3, it was rebuilt as an official residence, which was, legally, designated

[41] See esp. Hölscher (1999) 237–61, Scheid (1993), and Elsner (1996) 32–54, who analyses the topography of Augustus' monuments in conjunction with his *Res Gestae.*

[42] According to Dionysius (1. 70. 4) the office of high priest passed to Iulus, grandson not son of Aeneas. This hereditary office was passed down through the Gens Iulia in the administration of family cults at Bovillae and Alba Longa. See Weinstock (1971) 29.

[43] Cf. Ovid *Fast.* 3. 415–28, 4. 949–54, *Met.* 15. 864–5.

[44] For Vesta's Trojan origins see Virg. *Aen.* 2. 296, 567, 5. 744, 9. 259, Prop. 4. 4. 69. For Caesar as Vesta's priest, see Ovid *Fast.* 3. 699–700, 5. 573–6.

public property. Ovid's references to Augustus as Pontifex Maximus, which postdated this, are characterized by prayerful language and panegyrical allusions to the relationship of the Gens Iulia to the Vestal hearth.

Fig. 1 The Sorrento base: statue base with reliefs, Augustan period, from the Museo Correale, Sorrento. The theme of the reliefs are deities associated with temples restored by Augustus, in particular those associated with Augustus' new Palatine precinct. The front of the base alludes to the establishment of Vesta's hearth in Augustus' house. From the left five Vestal Virgins approach the goddess, who is enthroned on the right. The temple visible top right, with statues of a bull and a ram, may be the temple of Palatine Apollo, signifying Vesta's new location. The missing central panel may have shown a sixth Vestal and Augustus himself as Pontifex Maximus. One side panel, not shown here, depicts Diana, Apollo, and Latona with, at Latona's feet, a sibyl, symbolizing, perhaps, Augustus' transfer of the Sibylline books from the temple of Jupiter Optimus Maximus to Apollo's temple on the Palatine. The surviving part of the other side panel shows Mars Ultor accompanied by a cupid and what may be a Genius. Venus may have occupied the damaged area. (Photograph courtesy of D.A.I. Rome, Inst. Neg. 1965. 1252.)

The cult of Vesta was now celebrated in close association with Aeneas and the *sacra* brought from Troy on which the survival of Rome was believed to depend. Ovid expresses the dynastic character of Vesta's new Palatine shrine on the occasion of this new *natalis* in the Roman calendar, 28 April: *stet domus! aeternos tres habet una deos* (*Fast.* 4. 954). Ovid wrote the six-line epilogue to Book 4 not long after AD 3, when Augustus had rebuilt his house and designated it, as the residence of the Pontifex Maximus, public property. The wording here is significant because it underlines the symbolic character of topography in Roman religion. By uniting Apollo in a divine trinity with Vesta and Augustus, Ovid evokes the sacred precinct of Augustus' Palatine, the religious complex on the SW corner which included the temples of Magna Mater and Victory, which overlooked the *casa Romuli* and the Lupercal below, the House of Augustus containing Vesta's shrine,[45] and the temple of Apollo.

Since *Fasti* was a celebration of Roman religion, Ovid suggests comparisons between Augustus and Numa the priest king, the 'founder of Roman religion', whom Virgil had depicted iconographically in his pageant of heroes as the olive-crowned bearer of the Roman *sacra.*[46] At the same time, the association of 'Augustus' with augury pointed to a comparison with Romulus,[47] whose augural victory over Remus was commemorated on the pediment of the temple to Quirinus, which Augustus rebuilt in 16 BC. The existence of this comparison gave point to Ovid's humorous contrast of Augustus *Pater Patriae* with his primitive ancestor. In token of his descent from both Aeneas and Romulus, Augustus, who acknowledged himself to be *divi filius*,[48] was characteristically represented in contemporary statues either *togatus capite velato*, to perform a religious ritual for the good of his people, or, as in the Prima Porta statue, wearing a cuirass decorated with the image of Mars Ultor, receiving Crassus' standards from the Parthians, to represent Rome's vengeance on

[45] For the location of Vesta's Palatine shrine see Guarducci (1964) 158–69.

[46] *Aen.* 6. 808–9: *ille autem ramis insignis olivae | sacra ferens.* See also Littlewood (2002) 175–97.

[47] Augustus had pointedly rejected the name Romulus, Suet. *Aug.* 7, Dio 53. 16. 5–7. For this reason Ovid had the confidence to draw a strong, and witty, contrast between Augustus and Romulus in *Fasti* 2.

[48] A statue of Divus Iulius had been placed in the temple of Mars Ultor.

those who opposed her power. The dynastic character of Augustus' religious reforms may be illustrated by an examination of his high-profile construction and restoration of temples,[49] his reorganization of the urban *vici*, his institution of symbolic rituals, such as the *Ludi Saeculares*,[50] and the iconography of the later dynastic monuments such as the *Ara Pacis Augustae* (9 BC) and the *Aedes Concordiae* (AD 10).

2.1. *templorum positor, templorum sancte repostor (Fast. 2. 63)*

Under the Augustan religious revival the old cults of the Capitolium had become less important than a new group of deities with shrines centred around Augustus' Palatine home in close proximity to the *casa Romuli* and the historic cave of the Lupercal.[51] Some of these cults Augustus had inherited from his adoptive father: a temple and cult of Venus Genetrix,[52] divine ancestress of the Gens Iulia, as well as a number of cults reflecting Caesar's military success including Venus Victrix, Fortuna, and Victoria Caesaris. Augustus himself initiated new cults to abstract deities closely associated with the dynasty such as Fortuna Redux, Pax Augusta, Victoria Augusta, and, above all, in an attempt to counteract rumours of dynastic disunity, Concordia Augusta. Both Mars and Apollo were gods favoured by Caesar who had planned, but not begun, a large temple complex in honour of Mars.[53] Augustus followed his lead in vowing, early on in his career, temples to Mars the Avenger and Apollo as his ally at Actium. Mars Ultor was the patronal god of Augustus' vengeance on the murderers of his adoptive father[54] and on the Parthians who had relinquished the standards of Crassus in 20 BC. On 9 June Ovid commemorates the Roman victory of D. Iunius Brutus Callaicus over the Callici and the defeat of Crassus at Carrhae in 53 BC. The success of Callaicus is contrasted with Crassus' defeat, which is compounded by personal

[49] His *Res Gestae* testifies to his pride in restoring 82 temples (20. 4) and revitalizing membership of the priestly colleges (25).

[50] Prayers at the *Ludi Saeculares* were for Roman victory and power, but also for fertility and prosperity.

[51] Ovid describes the aition of the Lupercal in *Fasti* 2. 381–422.

[52] Dedicated on 26 September 46 BC, this was to be the centrepiece of the Forum Iulium. On Caesar's cults see Weinstock (1971) 80–132.

[53] Suet. *Caes.* 44. 1.

[54] Ovid *Fast.* 5. 569–77.

tragedy: *aquilas natumque suosque | perdidit* (6.465–6). The poet was not simply commenting on the serendipitous fortunes of war: *miscentur tristia laetis* (463); 9 June was the festival of Vesta, the most significant Augustan goddess in *Fasti* 6, and Ovid's final couplet recalls an Augustan theme associated with the temple of Mars Ultor: vengeance on the Parthians and reclamation of Crassus' standards: *'Parthe, quid exsultas?' dixit dea 'signa remittes, | quique necem Crassi vindicet ultor erit.'* (*Fast.* 6.467–8). Three portentous words closing the pentameter pointedly recall that the reclamation of the Parthian standards was one of Augustus' two canonical acts of vengeance celebrated in the Temple of Mars Ultor. The second, the defeat of Caesar's murderers at Philippi, is represented by Ovid not only as an act of filial loyalty but also as retribution for the sacrilege in killing the Pontifex Maximus, the dynastic priest of Vesta.[55] By the time the temple of Mars Ultor was dedicated in 2 BC, the surrounding Forum Augustum had become the focus of a dynastic celebration of Rome's dual ancestry. Mars stood together with Venus on the pediment of his temple, facing two lines of their descendants ranged on either side of the Forum, whose illustrious achievements were accompanied by *elogia* set underneath their statues. Whilst Divus Iulius stood beside the cult statues of Mars and Venus inside the *cella*, signifying his descent from both Romulus and Aeneas,[56] the Forum Augustum was dominated by a quadriga placed there by the senate to honour the Princeps.[57] This symbol of Triumph was an appropriate adjunct to the triumphal theme present in Mars Ultor. The iconography of both temple and surrounding Forum evoked the theme of Rome's triumph over her enemies and it was here, not at the Capitoline temple of Jupiter Optimus Maximus, that *triumphatores* now dedicated their arms[58] and where the senate met to consider the

[55] In this respect Ovid's interpretation was anachronistic. See Commentary, note on line 465.

[56] The concept of a ruler's divine descent was by no means out of keeping with the times. Its civic utility wins the approval of Varro (fr. 20, Cardauns).

[57] *RG* 35. The triumphal quadriga with four white horses was imbued with solar symbolism, which is reflected in the Augustan poets (Virg. *Aen.* 12. 161–4. Cf. the story of Phaethon which opens Ovid *Met.* 2). See also Weinstock (1971) 68–75.

[58] Suet. *Aug.* 29, Dio 55. 10. 1–5. In the rejoicing which followed the Battle of the Algidus against the Volsci and Aequi (*Fast.* 6. 721–4), Cn. Iulius (*cos.* 431 BC) dedicated the first temple to Apollo in Rome (Liv. 4. 29. 7).

merits of demands for a triumph.[59] The Forum Augustum had become 'the very performance space for the triumph'.[60] The two principal celebratory sequences, the *Vestalia* and the *Matralia*, which focus on popular and pre-Augustan elements of the two cults, both end with a coda which relates directly to the new dynasty: the return of the Parthian standards (467–8) and two Augustan monuments, Livia's Aedes Concordiae and Augustus' Porticus Liviae (637–48).

Apollo had become a god of the Iulii[61] before he was adopted as patron by Augustus, who used him as his password at Philippi[62] and attributed to him his victory over Antony and Cleopatra at Actium.[63] In 28 BC Augustus dedicated on the Palatine a temple to Apollo of unsurpassed magnificence, the iconography of which was to be interpreted in the context of Actium. Grouped together in the *cella* were statues of the triad Apollo, Diana, and Latona, who were represented as instruments of vengeance on those who flouted their power. Reliefs depicted the punishment of the children of Niobe and the Gauls expelled from Delphi, while statues of the Danaids suggested both an allegory of civil strife and, with reference to Cleopatra, foreign or Egyptian misconduct in marriage.[64] The Actium discourse was taken up again in the repetitive sequence of terracotta plaques, showing the chosen deities of the Actian protagonists, Octavian's Apollo wrestling with Antony's Hercules for the possession of a tripod. Apollo's oracular power had prevailed and, in a symbolic act, Augustus transferred to the temple of Palatine Apollo the Sibylline books from the temple of Capitoline Jupiter. Within the precinct of the temple of the divine patron of the arts was a magnificent

[59] Evidence supporting the view that Augustus discouraged the ritual of the triumphal procession is discussed by F. V. Hickson, 'Augustus Triumphator: Manipulation of the Triumphal Theme in the Political Propaganda of Augustus', *Latomus* 50 (1991) 124–38.

[60] Kellum (1997) 167.

[61] The first temple to Apollo in Rome was dedicated by Cn. Iulius (*cos.* 431 BC). Divus Iulius himself was born on the first day of the *Ludi Apollinares*, which he had subsequently financed personally in 45 BC.

[62] Val. Max. 1. 5. 7.

[63] Cf. Virg. *Aen.* 8. 704, Prop. 4. 1. 3, 4. 6. 15–18, 70, Ovid, *Met.* 13. 715.

[64] Prop. 2. 31. 3–4. Kellum (1997) 161 cites, as further evidence of the Danaids in the poetic discourse of Actium, the presence of the Danaids on the *balteus* of Pallas (Virg. *Aen.* 10. 496–9).

double Greek and Latin library where there stood a statue of Augustus himself, indicating his personal affinity with the god. Under the new regime Hercules, too, played his part as the warrior-hero of the *iuvenes*, but now his apotheosis, like that of Romulus, which signified the reward for outstanding *virtus*, was associated by the Augustan poets with the apotheosis of Augustus himself, tacitly diverting emphasis from Hercules' former association with the Princeps' opponent at Actium. Like Apollo, Hercules was incorporated into the iconography of prosperity and culture of the Pax Augusta, which made his final appearance at the end of *Fasti* 6 in the guise of Hercules Musarum, a fitting end to the first half of Ovid's *Fasti*.

Fig. 2 Fecund mother-goddess, interchangeably described as Ceres, Tellus, or Pax, from the Ara Pacis Augustae, Rome. The iconography represents the prosperity of Pax Augusta: twin babies, contented farm animals, a lapful of nuts and pomegranates, symbolizing fecundity. She is flanked by personifications of breezes bringing beneficent rain over land and sea, accompanied, respectively, by a swan and sea monster. (Photograph courtesy of D.A.I. Rome, Inst. Neg. 1986. 1448.)

The fertility of the Pax Augusta was also represented by Dionysus/Liber[65] and Ceres/Tellus, who is depicted opulently on the Ara Pacis Augustae with two babies at her breast and surrounded by symbols of the fecund earth: poppies, corn, contented farm animals, and nymphs of sea and river.[66] In his celebration of Peace in Book I Ovid gives words to the ideological message: *Pax Cererem nutrit: Pacis alumna Ceres.*[67] The month which ends with the *natalis* of the Ara Pacis Augustae begins with a proem centred on Janus, who also has joined the Augustan pantheon as a deity of Peace and civic order.[68] In Ovid's architectural structure for the first half of his *Fasti*, Janus' winter month of Peace corresponds to Juno's summer month of War. Juno's other sphere of influence, the fecundity symbolized by her goatskin, promises the abundance of the period of the summer solstice.

Close by the temple of Palatine Apollo and, incidentally, the house of Augustus with its shrine of Vesta, stood the temple of Cybele whose dynastic importance had been emphasized by her prominent role as protectress of Aeneas and his Trojans in Virgil's *Aeneid*. Cybele's temple was first constructed in 204 BC, at a time when Rome was forming diplomatic and cultural ties with Pergamum, Ilion, and Samothrace, and when the Trojan ancestry of Roman noble families, such as the *Gens Iulia*, was becoming fashionable. The ancient cult object which represented Cybele, a black stone, had been brought to Rome through the good offices of Attalus of Pergamum, as divine help from the Trojan homeland against the Carthaginian threat. As a propitious omen, it was first housed in the adjacent Aedes Victoriae. Like Vesta, Cybele's rise to prominence in Augustan religion was derived from her Trojan associations, and Cybele's temple was an integral part of a group of shrines—to Apollo and Victory, Cybele and Vesta—which offered together a clear dynastic message: they represented Victoria Augusta and the divine protection of the Gens Iulia. The sacredness of the Roman Palatine

[65] Cf. Virg. *G* 1. 7, Hor. *Carm.* 4. 15. 26.

[66] The fecund agricultural mother goddess was regarded almost interchangeably and addressed as Tellus or Ceres. Cf. *Fast.* 1. 671: *placentur frugum matres, Tellusque Ceresque.*

[67] *Fast.* 1. 704.

[68] See *Fast.* 1. 63–288.

was heightened by the founder's heroon in the shape of the *casa Romuli* and, below the hill, the Lupercal cave.

The great religious monuments of the Augustan Age illustrate a logical progression of sequential ideas. In 28 BC, Apollo's temple on the Palatine gave artistic expression to the ideology of Augustus' victory at Actium. The Ara Pacis Augustae, some twenty years later, extolled the blessings of Augustan Peace and the example of civic *pietas* passed down from Aeneas to his descendant, Augustus. The iconography of the temple of Mars Ultor, dedicated in 2 BC, reiterated the theme of Augustus' vengeance on Rome's enemies. At the same time the presence of Divus Iulius in the *cella* beside Venus and Mars was an unequivocal reminder that Rome's divine ancestry was equally the ancestry of the regnant Gens Iulia. The dynastic message was consolidated in AD 10, the *natalis* of Tiberius' rededication of the Aedes Concordiae, which overlooked the Forum Romanum, for here the message was extended to celebrate harmony within the dynasty. The temple's statuary, donated by different members of the imperial family, reflected the emphasis of Augustus' restructured religion. Apollo stands with Diana and Latona, but also with Juno. A painting of Marsyas Bound underlines his power. Present are Vesta and Mars Ultor, guardian deities of Rome. There are numerous deities associated with Peace such as Ceres, Liber, Aesculapius, and Hygeia.[69] The topography of Rome, which Livy's Camillus had so closely identified with the cult of Roman gods,[70] had now been transformed by the Augustan monuments, not only on the Palatine, but in the Forum valley and the Campus Martius. In effect, Roman religion was now inextricably interwoven with the dynasty.

2.2. *mille Lares Geniumque ducis, qui tradidit illos / urbs habet, et vici numina terna colunt* (*Fast.* 5. 145–6)

Augustus' reorganization of the cult of the Lares Compitales was a practical expedient to discourage political demonstrations centred on the neighbourhoods, which had bedevilled Roman politics since

[69] The significance of the decorative statuary in the temple of Concord has been thoroughly analysed by Kellum (1990) 276–307, who draws attention to the astrological significance of the grouping of the statues.

[70] Liv. 5. 52. 2. Cf. *BNP* 1. 167–80.

the days of Clodius' gangs. Behind this, however, there was a clear intention to attract to himself the loyalty of Rome's underclass of poor artisans, shopkeepers and freedmen. The latter, in particular, took pride in serving on boards of *vicomagistri Augustales*, who were responsible for improving local civic amenities, fighting fires and crime, and for tending the cults of the Lares Compitales. These twin 'neighbourhood gods' were sometimes known as Lares Praestites or Protectors, whose origins Ovid ascribes to Mercury's rape of the gossipy nymph Lara.[71] Not long after his election to the office of Pontifex Maximus, Augustus had subdivided Rome's new fourteen administrative *regiones* into 265 *vici* and put the cult of the Lares of each *vicus* in charge of a board of *vicomagistri Augustales*. Through their association with the Princeps each pair of Lares became known as Lares Augusti.[72] Their reorganization was completed by 7 BC and, symbolically perhaps, Augustus restored the Aedes Larum *in summa Sacra Via*, celebrating the *natalis* on 27 June.[73]

The association of Lares Augusti with Augustus and his family is apparent in the iconography of surviving compital altars. The Lares themselves are depicted singly or in pairs, dancing and holding a cornucopia. Increasingly altars also represented a Genius in the company of the twin Lares. As in private domestic religion the Genius of the *pater familias* accompanied the household Lares as an indication of his powers of generation within the family, so the Genius present with the Lares Compitales has been thought to represent the Genius of Augustus, who, from 2 BC as *pater patriae*, occupied the position of father of the Roman state.[74] This is apparent in the toast offered to Augustus by a Roman *pater familias* on the ancestral feast of the *Caristia*: *bene te, patriae pater, optime Caesar* (*Fast.* 2. 637).[75] Indisputable, however, is the outward expression of loyalty towards the dynasty of the *vicomagistri* whose altars bear the

[71] *Fast.* 2. 585–616.

[72] This is a topic which Ovid promises to mention in August (*Fast.* 5. 147–8).

[73] *Fast.* 6. 791–2.

[74] This view is supported by A. Fraschetti, *Roma e il Principe* (Rome, 1990) 204–76, Galinsky (1994) 305–13. Conversely, J. Bert Lott, *The Neighbourhoods in Augustan Rome* (Cambridge, 2004) 82–3, suggests that in later times worship of the imperial Genius became the sign of a bad emperor.

[75] Cf. Hor. *Carm.* 4. 5. 33–5.

Fig. 3 The Altar of the Lares from the *vicus Sandalarius*: stone altar, Uffizi Museum, Florence. Dedicated in 2 BC, the year when Augustus was given the title *pater patriae*, the elder Julia was exiled, and Gaius set out for his campaign against the Parthians. Gaius is probably represented by the figure on the left, at whose feet there is a sacred chicken gobbling corn auspiciously. In the centre Augustus, *capite velato*, adopts a religious pose, holding the augur's *lituus*. The female figure on the right holding a *patera* may represent Livia, but could also be the goddess Iuventas. (Photograph courtesy of D.A.I. Rome, Inst. Neg. 1965. 2155.)

iconography of the regime: oak wreaths, laurel trees, and, occasionally, a shield which recalls Augustus' *clupeus virtutis.* A particularly good, and therefore much quoted, example is the altar of the vicus Sandalarius, which depicts, on the two short sides, the twin Lares, but on the longer a group of three figures usually identified as Gaius, whose forthcoming expedition to the East is suggested by a sacred chicken propitiously gorging corn at his feet, Augustus, holding the *lituus* or augural staff, and a female figure on the right, who may represent Livia. These altars presented, simply but explicitly, for the artisans of the *vici* a basic version of the dynastic iconography which was expounded symbolically in the art of the Ara Pacis Augustae and the Aedes Concordiae for the more cultivated delectation of the educated classes.

2.3. **Symbolic ritual:** ***sacra recognosces annalibus eruta priscis (*****Fast.** ***1. 7)***

A significant example of Augustus privileging Apollo and Diana at the expense of the Capitoline deities is the *Ludi Saeculares* in 17 BC, when Augustus and Agrippa together performed solemn sacrifices prescribed by the Sibylline books, which Augustus had moved from Jupiter's Capitoline temple to the temple of Palatine Apollo. It is clear from the long extant inscription which records the sacrifices made on 31 May, 1, 2, and 3 June, that the *Ludi* and other festivities continued until 12 June.[76] This was not, of course, recorded in the Roman *Fasti* because the *Ludi Saeculares* did not recur annually. On the two previously recorded occasions when the Romans had celebrated *Ludi Saeculares*, sacrifices had been made, appropriately, to chthonic powers at times of crisis during the First Punic War (249 BC) and on the eve of the Third Punic War (146 BC). The combined evidence of the text of the inscription and Horace's *Carmen Saeculare* provide an accurate description of the deities honoured during the three days, and it is evident that Augustus' *Ludi* in 17 BC had a very different focus. Augustus' *Ludi Saeculares* honoured, not the gods of the Underworld, but goddesses associated with fecundity (Ilithyia), human life (Moirai), and fertility (Ceres and Tellus). Augustus

[76] *CIL* 6. 32323, tr. in *BNP* 2. 140–2.

himself sacrificed a white bull to Jupiter and a white cow to Juno Regina; to the Moirai he sacrificed nine female lambs and nine female goats; to Ilithyia, the goddesses who attend childbirth, twenty-seven sacrificial cakes, which corresponded to the twenty-seven youths and twenty-seven maidens who sang Horace's *Carmen Saeculare*. The games were held at the height of summer, the period of growth. This cumulative emphasis on fecundity and childbirth may reflect Augustus' recent legislation to encourage marriage and increase the Roman birth-rate. Touching the imperial family more closely, however, was the recent birth of Julia's and Agrippa's second son, Lucius Caesar, whom Augustus formally adopted with his brother Gaius (b. 20 BC) during the summer of the *Ludi Saeculares*. Augustus' Palatine deities, Apollo and Diana, *Phoebe silvarumque potens Diana*, are addressed in the opening line of Horace's invocation as well as through the extended epilogue; they receive the sacrifice which is made on the third and final day of sacrifice.

To sum up, the *Ludi Saeculares* honour deities particularly associated with Augustus' victory and with fecundity and prosperity. When Augustus sacrificed to the Moirai and to Juno Regina, he prayed for the success of the Roman legions as well as for the prosperity of the *Quirites*, reiterating, in a sense, the Augustan mantra that Victoria Augusta achieves the blessings of Pax Augusta. At the same time the birth of a new heir and Augustus' double adoption of Gaius and Lucius in 17 BC identify these *Ludi* with a further stage in Augustus' move towards a state religion which was essentially dynastic.[77]

3. Genre and antiquarianism

Ovid's development of Roman elegy[78] and the different traditions which influenced his poetic discourse have been analysed in some detail in recent publications.[79] The wide range of subject matter and

[77] See esp. Feeney (1998) 28–38 and P. J. Davis, 'The Fabrication of Tradition: Horace, Augustus and the Secular Games', *Ramus* 36: 2 (2001).

[78] For a survey of Ovid's development of the Roman elegiac genre see Harrison (2002). For analyses of Ovid's generic affiliation in his *Fasti*, see Miller (1991) 8–43, Hinds (1992), Barchiesi (1997*a*) 47–78, Fantham (1998) 4–25.

[79] For a study of Ovid's poetic discourse in the proemia of *Fasti* Books 1, 2, 3, 4, and 6, see Miller (1991) 5–43.

versatile treatment which was to characterize Ovid's transformation of Roman elegy was already evident in his three books of *Amores*. During the period of his *Heroides* and *Ars Amatoria* Ovid expanded his elegiac repertoire to include themes and characters familiar from epic and tragedy. In the *Ars* he developed a humorous extension of didactic style, which was later to reappear in his *Fasti*. Rome's religious calendar provided the poet with a wide range of material which had the potential for straining generic boundaries, because the poet's models for panegyric, hymns, and battle scenes, such as the annihilation of the Fabii at the River Cremera,[80] belonged, as a rule, to 'higher' genres. An essential dynamic of Ovid's aetiological elegy was to wrap up in humour and literary allusion both poetic and Augustan discourse. Rather than attempting to recapitulate the scholarship contained in the surveys mentioned above, this introductory section aims simply to address two issues germane to *Fasti* 6: first, whether the innovatory character of Ovid's *Fasti*, which Juno praises in her *Dichterweihe*, has to do with matters close to her own sphere of influence, *militiae labor*, a theme antithetical to elegiac verse, and secondly, to what extent the content of *Fasti* 6 demonstrates Ovid's close engagement with antiquarianism on the site of Rome.

Ovid's short programmatic proem to *Fasti* 1 alludes to five divisions of subject matter which might loosely be defined as astronomy (*signa*, 1. 2), aetiology of Roman festivals (*tempora cum causis Latium digesta per annum*, 1), dynastic anniversaries (*festa domestica*, 9), contemporary Roman religion (*Caesaris aras*, 13), and accounts of Roman ritual culled from religious archives (*sacra . . . annalibus eruta priscis*, 7). He recapitulates this, in a single succinct distich, in the proem to Book 4, halfway through the first half of the work: *tempora cum causis, annalibus eruta priscis, | lapsaque sub terras ortaque signa cano* (4. 11–12). He omits the words *sacra* and *Caesaris aras*, but Venus signals her approval of the poet's *area maior*, by touching his *tempora*[81] with a myrtle twig. For it is clear from Ovid's opening address, *alma, fave* and his promise

[80] *Fast* 2. 195–242. On this passage see Harries (1991). This passage, with its juxtaposition of military engagement with the theme of fertility (the *Lupercalia*) and the threat of extinction of the Fabii, foreshadows themes present in *Fasti* 6. See Introduction 5.

[81] This double entendre signifies both the poet's brow and the *tempora* celebrated in his *Fasti*. See Barchiesi (1997*a*) 57.

that she will be *celeberrima* in a month associated with new life that the poet is referring to her as the ancestress of the Gens Iulia whose genealogy he unrolls immediately after the proem.

In the proem to Book 6 Ovid again renews his programme, pulling together strands from his earlier proems. This is the point in Ovid's *Fasti* where he stages what appears to be a serious *Dichterweihe*, the literary consecration of the Roman *vates* in the task that he has chosen to accomplish.[82] The poet sets the scene for a divine epiphany in a remote grove with a murmuring stream and signals the literary tradition further by remarking that the goddess who now appears is not, in fact, one of the Muses who appeared to Hesiod.[83] He does, however, point out that she is one of the contestants for the Judgement of Paris, which can only serve to identify her with strife and, once Juno is named, with the antipathy to the Aeneadae which her rejection provoked. The poet is terror-struck when he recognizes the senior goddess *quae stat in arce Iovis* (18). Addressing him as 'First poet to write about the Roman calendar' (*Romani conditor anni*, 21), Juno proceeds to give Ovid her blessing to celebrate 'great matters' in the lowly elegiac metre: *ause per exiguos magna referre modos* (22).[84] In the terminology of poetic discourse her words should be interpreted: 'initiate a new type of poem by treating heroic themes in elegiac metre.' More remarkably she explains that he has won *ius numen caeleste videndi* (23), since he has decided to celebrate religious festivals in his own metre (*cum placuit numeris condere festa tuis*, 24). Before considering what is meant here by *magna*, a word should be said about Juno's preoccupation with Ovid's choice of elegiacs. The only other proem concerned with the appropriateness of this metre for Ovid's subject matter introduces Book 2, where the poet claims that for the first time he is 'sailing with a broader canvas' than before, a nautical metaphor favoured by the Latin hexameter poets,[85] and he marvels, with some pride, that his elegiac verse has

[82] This passage has been analysed in detail by Miller (1991) 35–43.

[83] *Fast.* 6. 13–14: *non quas praeceptor arandi | viderat, Ascraeas cum sequeretur oves.* It is not clear why Ovid should want to dissociate himself from Hesiod's *Theogony* and *Works and Days*, when he himself was concerned with both theophanies and festal days. See Miller (1991) 39–40.

[84] *Fast.* 6. 22.

[85] *Fast.* 2. 3–4. Cf. 1. 4, Virg. *G* 2. 41. As a metaphorical allusion to epic material in *Fast.* 2. 3–8 the poet describes spreading his sails for a seagoing voyage—which would

taken such an unexpected direction: *ecquis ad haec illinc crederet esse viam?* These misgivings foreshadow an important anniversary on 5 February. Ovid's celebration of Augustus receiving the title *pater patriae* is grandly heralded by the 'multiple tongue' topos of epic[86] followed by a show of mock terror elicited by the poet's dilemma: he cannot let the day pass without a paean of praise, *ore canenda dies* (2. 124) but he is wretchedly handicapped by the inadequacy of his elegiac metre: *quid volui demens elegis imponere tantum | ponderis* (125–6).[87]

This apologetic tone is entirely absent from Ovid's encomium celebrating Augustus' election to the office of Pontifex Maximus on 6 March.[88] The poet does not question the viability of using elegiacs to celebrate either this or, on 28 April, Augustus' creation of a shrine to the sacred flame of Vesta within his Palatine home. He does, however, begin the second passage *nunc me grandius urget opus* (4. 948), and this reflects his language in his address to Venus in the proem to Book 4, where he contrasts the love poetry which he used to write with his current, more ambitious, aspirations: *nunc teritur nostris area maior equis* (4. 10). Whilst *grandius opus* and *area maior* clearly refer to Augustan material, the two last-mentioned instances differ from the first because they commemorate religious anniversaries and therefore have their place in a work originally dedicated to Augustus as Pontifex Maximus,[89] whereas the first, Augustus' new title *pater patriae*, rewarded his political achievement. Consequently it seems possible to draw a distinction between religious material, *sacra . . . signataque tempora fastis* (2. 7), and anniversaries which, if Ovid were to elaborate, would oblige him to deal with material proper to higher genres. Following the pattern of Book 4, where Ovid's *maior area* seems to refer to Augustan themes

be unattainable for Propertius' *cumba* (Prop. 3. 9. 35–6. Cf. Ovid Ars 3. 26). See too *Fast.* 2. 863–4, 4. 18, and 729–30. On Ovid's use of the nautical metaphor see Fantham (1998) 94, 229–30 and Green (2004a) 27–31.

[86] See Hinds (1998) 35–47.

[87] An intertextual allusion to Propertius (3. 3. 15–16), who has conceived the idea of a poem about the Alban kings: *'quid tibi cum tali, demens, est flumine? Quis te | carminis heroi tangere iussit opus?'*

[88] *Fast.* 3. 415–28.

[89] *Tr.* 2. 551–2.

associated with Venus' month, we should consider whether Juno's reference to *magna* and her endorsement of Ovid's exceptional use of the elegiac metre in this connection concern a theme which is both Augustan and essential to *Fasti* 6. Balancing the theme of Peace in Janus' Book 1, the theme of War in Book 6 has different manifestations: Juno, Iuventas, and Concordia, each representing a different aspect of War, compete for the *titulus mensis*; the two major celebrations of *Fasti* 6, the *Vestalia* and the *Matralia*, honour goddesses associated with fertility but also with the survival of the Roman state and military cult. June and the period of the summer solstice was a time of both military campaigns and agrarian fertility, when goddesses of fecundity, Mater Matuta and Fortuna, were celebrated. Finally, together with seven military anniversaries, three major Republican conflicts have a place in June: the Gallic siege of 390 BC, the Second Punic War, and the Battle of Sentinum in 295 BC. It is evident, then, that Augustus' ideological tenet, that Victoria Augusta engendered Pax Augusta, expressed in Augustan ideology the range of Juno's powers in an earlier age (see Introduction 4).

To understand Ovid's interest in *sacra . . . annalibus eruta prisca*[90] we must look at the changing face of Augustan Rome, in which 'restoration of ancient ritual' masked radical change rather than representing a 'return to past values', a time which, thanks to the Pax Augusta, generated an ideal climate for antiquarian research. The move towards aetiological themes in Virgil, Tibullus, Propertius, and Ovid drew on the 'then–now' topos, a literary 'nostalgia' for Rome's legendary past. Ovid's witty version of aetiological legends is underpinned by antiquarian allusions relating to the archaic background of temples and rituals in a Rome where contemporary monuments demonstrated how much the presence and ideology of Augustus dominated civic space, the decoration of monuments, and the public calendar.[91] On several occasions the poet alludes to his own participation in the contemporary enthusiasm for Roman antiquarianism which was fed by the stimulating, and sometimes conflicting,

[90] The phrase is repeated *Fast.* 1. 7, 4. 12.

[91] See E. Buchner, *Die Sonnenuhr des Augustus* (Mainz, 1982), F. Millar, 'State and Subject: The Impact of Monarchy', in Millar and Segal (eds.), *Caesar Augustus: Seven Aspects* (Oxford, 1984) 37–60, Wallace-Hadrill (1987), Barchiesi (1997*a*) 69–73.

viewpoints of contemporary antiquarian writers.[92] At the forefront of these were M. Terentius Varro,[93] Verrius Flaccus,[94] and Dionysius of Halicarnassus,[95] whose works were newly accessible in two spacious double library complexes in the precinct of Palatine Apollo and in the Porticus Octaviae which now supplemented Asinius Pollio's library near to the Atrium Libertatis. It is probable that Ovid enjoyed research and discussion in these agreeable surroundings.

Antiquarian material provided Ovid with raw material which he could fashion into stylish passages with a complexity of allusion to such writers as Callimachus, Virgil, Horace, and, in the case of *Fasti* 6, the historian Livy. As an exponent of aetiological elegy Ovid's wide-ranging antiquarian allusions would be perceptible to the erudite reader, but, as a matter of poetic taste, subtly disguised by more dominant literary references. No reader of *Fasti*, however, should underestimate Ovid's understanding of Roman religion and its symbiotic relationship to national and civic life. And Ovid's range was wide. His calendar poem encompasses *sacra* which originated, or were thought to originate, as far back as the archaic period, votive offerings made in times of crisis during the Republic, as well as cults newly highlighted in Augustus' reformed religion and attested

[92] *Fast.* 1. 7, 289, 631, 3. 87–96, 4. 11, 6. 27–64.

[93] M. Terentius Varro died in his eighties in 27 BC. Having receiving a pardon after Pharsalus, Varro dedicated to Julius Caesar, then Pontifex Maximus, his *Antiquitates Rerum Divinarum*, a work which covered the Roman gods, priesthoods, sanctuaries, *sacra*, *feriae*, and *ludi*. See Suet. *de Grammatis* 17.

[94] Verrius Flaccus, a freedman, held a privileged position in Augustus' house as tutor to his grandsons Lucius and Gaius from 10 BC. He completed works on grammar, etymology, and Roman nomenclature as well as his *Res Etruscae* and *Res Memoria Dignae*, antiquarian studies used extensively by Pliny the Elder, Gellius, and Macrobius. Ovid's *Fasti* follows almost invariably the same notation and sequence of festivals listed in Verrius' *Fasti Praenestini*, which was eventually published in his home town of Praeneste.

[95] Dionysius Halicarnassensis, who arrived in Rome shortly after Actium, provided a 'modern', ethnographical alternative to the strongly Republican, moralizing slant of Livy's Histories. Dionysius' hypothesis, that Rome's distinction was the consequence of her Greek origins through waves of colonizing settlers after Evander, was a partisan viewpoint which stimulated antiquarian discussion, while his belief that Rome's greatness was enhanced by her ability to assimilate foreign influences focused on the historical perspective of Roman families who claimed Trojan or Etruscan roots. On Dionysius' importance in the intellectual circles of Augustus' Rome, see E. Gabba (1991).

Fig. 4 Terracotta antefix of Juno Sospita with goatskin headdress, Villa Giulia, Rome. Inv. 1029. Early fifth century BC from the sanctuary of Mater Matuta at Satricum. (Photo courtesy of D.A.I. Rome, Inst. Neg. 1968. 1.)

by the ostentatiously didactic iconography of the new Augustan monuments. In *Fasti* 6 he also gives a sharp and intelligent literary focus to the familiar figures depicted in sanctuary art across Latium and beyond. Blending the Greco-Roman literary tradition with contemporary antiquarian knowledge and personal experience, Ovid shows that he was conversant with a conglomeration of belief and with the iconography inherent in religious cult across Central Italy.[96]

In an early aetiological poem (*Am.* 3. 13) Ovid describes a visit which he made to his wife's home town to attend a festival of Juno Curitis, the tutelary deity of Falerii Veteres. His allusions offer a realistic account of the locality and the ritual, which may have been a lustration of the city of which Juno Curitis was the guardian.[97] His description of a *difficilis clivis* (6) indicates that this may have been the rural sanctuary of Juno Curitis at Celle, which has precipitous cliffs on three sides, while his allusion *densa . . . arbore lucus* (7) would refer to the grove reached by a Via Sacra, taken by the procession of girls carrying baskets at the festival described by the poet. Like Juno of Lanuvium, Juno Curitis of Celle embodied civic protection, prowess in battle, and fertility in women. Her sanctuary at Celle was adorned with fertility symbols in the form of antefixes representing Dionysiac figures, nymphs, and satyrs whose togetherness represented sexual union.[98] Similarly the awakening of fertility in springtime is evident in the Dionysiac associations which Ovid makes in his descriptions of festivals such as the *Lupercalia* in mid-February and the *Liberalia* in mid-March.[99] In this context Juno and Hercules, as a pair, usually on Etruscan bronze mirrors, had exactly the same significance and aim to promote fertility.[100] They were as united in art as they were antagonistic in Greco-Roman literature. The combination of Juno and Hercules also represented success in war. Successful conquest and the fertility of the land and of its people constituted, essentially, the prosperity of the early Italian communities. The iconography representing this was widespread in the cult centres of Central Italy, from the archaic period to the second or first century BC. Writing for an urban and literary audience, Ovid 'translated' these symbols of

[96] *Fast.* 6. 473–550.

[97] This is the view of Le Bonniec (1989) 99–109.

[98] This decoration is characteristic of other Faliscan shrines: Apollo's temple at Vignole and Lo Scasato, and in the sanctuaries of Mater Matuta at Satricum and Pyrgi, as well as in Rome itself.

[99] *Fast.* 2. 267–452 and 3. 713–90.

[100] This is particularly evident in bronze mirrors from Etruria: one example from Praeneste shows Juno and Hercules facing each other across an altar on which Jupiter is seated and on which female and male genitalia are crudely inscribed. See Pfiffig (1980) 66–7, plate 18.

religious cult into increasingly complex literary terms. The sixth book of Ovid's *Fasti* is enriched by his skill in combining literary and antiquarian allusion, which may be illustrated by three examples from his extended passage on the twin temples to Mater Matuta and Fortuna, founded by Servius Tullius (*Fast.* 6. 475–645).

3.1. Ino's Theban literary heritage and Bacchic cult in Central Italy

Ovid signals the importance of Bacchus in his story of Ino's arrival in Rome by making Bacchus his informant for the cult of Mater Matuta, his reason being that this story concerns the god's family (*si domus illa tua es*, 484). In the opening scene in the Lucus Stimulae there are many literary allusions recalling Ino's early history as a devotee of Dionysus in the palace of Thebes. Ino is threatened by Arcadian maenads who, whipped into Bacchic frenzy by Juno, try to steal her baby for their rites until she is rescued by Hercules arriving in the Forum Boarium with the cattle of Geryon. Surrounded on all sides by deities associated with fertility cult, Ino is exposed to violence, which is associated in the cult of Dionysus with sexual union and procreation.[101] Ino's apotheosis is announced by the prophetic figure of Carmentis, who is herself associated with motherhood:[102] Ino is to become Mater Matuta, a kourotrophos goddess whose care will be for the children of others. Her association with motherhood, and therefore fertility, encouraged terracotta votive offerings of anatomical female organs at the sanctuaries of Mater Matuta in the Forum Boarium, Satricum, and in Etruria. All these deities—Juno, Hercules, Ino, Melicertes, and Carmentis, in short, the dramatis personae of Ovid's exegesis—had shrines around the Forum Boarium not far from the Lucus Stimulae.[103]

[101] For violence in the cult of Dionysus see Livy's account of the Bacchanalia scandal of 186 BC (Liv. 39. 13. 10–14). Cf. the frescos on the walls of Room 5 in the Villa of the Mysteries in Pompeii.

[102] Var. *Ant.* fr. 103 (Cardauns), Plut. *Rom.* 21. 2, and Gell. 16. 16. 4, who claims that Carmentis was invoked by expectant mothers. Ovid's second January *Carmentalia* (*Fast.* 1. 617–36) deals with self-induced abortion among Roman women piqued after a restriction on their right to use *carpenta* in the streets of Rome. See Champeaux (1982) 1. 316, Green (2004*a*) *ad loc.*

[103] Juno Sospita's temple in the Forum Holitorum is not far from the temples of Mater Matuta and Fortuna.

Ovid's complex allusions to Ino's relationship to the bacchants of Thebes, to Bacchic possession, and to Bacchus himself offer a sophisticated literary counterpart to the sanctuary art and iconography associated with the pervasive cult of Dionysus in Italy. The Greek cult of Dionysus had found fertile ground in archaic Etruria, where it was adapted, as were many Greek myths, to coalesce with Etruscan religious beliefs.[104] An important aspect of the Dionysiac myth which passed from Etruria to the communities of Latium and to Rome[105] was the idea of rebirth and new life in the context of Dionysiac mysteries. It is precisely this which Ovid celebrates in his story of Ino, who is reborn as the goddess, Mater Matuta, so that she can care for new life as a kourotrophos. At the great archaic cult centre of the fertility goddess, Mater Matuta at Satricum (built 500–490 BC), acroterial statues represented Bacchus with a female consort, possibly Semele or Ariadne. The pair would appear later as Liber and Libera on the Aventine temple of Ceres, Liber, and Libera in Rome, not far from the Grove of Stimula.[106] Their union is the central focus in the frescos of the Villa of the Mysteries outside Pompeii, which illustrates the popularity of the cult in Campania.

This association with fertility cult underlies Ovid's conjunction of Bacchus with Juno, Hercules, and the kourotrophos Mater Matuta in *Fasti* 6. Dionysiac motifs—*sileni*, ivy leaves, and inebriates—are characteristically found in works of art uniting Juno with Hercules, as a sign of fertility, much as in Augustan art Liber stood for prosperity and increase. In the archaic period Juno was worshipped with Hercules in Central Italy in her capacities as both a warrior goddess and a fertility goddess.[107] A small fourth-century bronze

[104] This was associated in particular with chthonic and fertility cults. The figure of Semele or Ariadne was depicted with Dionysus in representations of the Dionysiac mysteries. In the context of fertility the two deities Juno and Hercules appear together with Dionysiac motifs. See Y. Bomati, 'Les Légendes dionysiaques en Étrurie', *REL* 61 (1983) 87–107.

[105] Livy points out in his account of the Bacchanalian scandal that the cult had found its way to Rome from Etruria, (39. 8. 3–9, 9. 1).

[106] For the identification of the statues see Lulof (1996). For the political and ideological associations of Liber in Rome, see Wiseman (1998) 35–43. The cult of Liber was not a favourite with Augustus, and his temple, destroyed before Actium, was not restored until AD 17.

[107] This is found in the conjunction of Hera and Herakles in Magna Graecia. On this subject see the chapter, 'Herakles: The Supermale and the Feminine', in Nicole

Fig. 5 Etruscan bronze mirror, Museo Archeologico, Florence. Early third century BC, from Volterra. Juno/Uni, crowned, enthroned, and regally dressed, suckles a bearded adult Hercules. Behind is Jupiter/Tinia with sceptre, pointing to an Etruscan inscription, which reads: 'This picture shows Hercules suckling.' On the left a nude couple, possibly Apollo and a maenad, look on. On the right a richly dressed woman may represent the owner of the mirror. At the top of the frame a Dionysiac figure, possibly Silenus, reclines drinking, while below, on the handle, a naked child with bulla holds an egg, symbolizing immortality. [See Pfiffig (1980) 66–71]. (Photograph courtesy of D.A.I., Rome, Inst. Neg. 1972. 257.)

Loraux, *The Experiences of Tiresias* (Princeton, 1995) 116–39 and W. Pötscher 'Der Name des Herakles', *Emerita* 39 (1971) 169–84. Since, however, most of the relevant artefacts are Etruscan, it seems likely that the association of the two deities was shows a satyr holding, on open palms, Hercules brandishing his club, and Juno armed with sword and shield.[108] Better known are a group of Etruscan bronze mirrors which depict Juno suckling Hercules, sometimes as a bearded, adult figure.[109] The representation of a woman suckling an adult male may indicate a fertility cult similar to that of Fortuna Primigenia, who was both mother and daughter of Jupiter.[110] Alternatively, the image may symbolize Juno's acceptance of Hercules into Olympus after his apotheosis: the act of suckling suggests both initiation and adoption. However, rebirth, the essence of the Dionysiac mysteries, could also be symbolized by apotheosis.

3.2. The apotheosis of Hercules and the Roman triumph

The theme of apotheosis has a significant role in Ovid's exegesis of the cult of Mater Matuta. In his brief allusion to Juno's hostility towards Hercules (*Fast.* 6. 524), Ovid describes the hero as Oetaeus, an allusion to his death and subsequent apotheosis. Soon after this Carmentis prophesies that Ino and her son Melicertes will both achieve apotheosis as guardian deities of Rome. This passage is balanced by the first *Carmentalia* in *Fasti* 1 where Carmentis prophesies the apotheosis of Hercules after his defeat of Cacus.

Apotheosis had its counterpart in the religious ritual of the triumph, and this was expressed in the iconography of chariot processions in Etruscan and Roman reliefs. Ovid's drama takes place, appropriately, in the Forum Boarium, where the Roman triumphal procession passed on its way to the Capitol. From pre-Etruscan times the Forum Boarium was associated with the Roman triumph, a religious ceremony that may have had its earliest origins in

misinterpreted by the Etruscans, who saw Hercules as Juno's male consort in a fertility cult. Douglas (1913) cites a series of illustrative examples from Etruscan art. See also Bayet (1926) 115–16, 379, Gordon (1938) 41 who cites four representations of Juno Sospita of Lanuvium with Hercules as her companion, Dury-Moyaers and Renard (1978) 188–93, Neraudau (1979) 191.

[108] A similar design occurs on an Etruscan gold ring. Both are illustrated in Roscher, 1. 2261, 2262. See Douglas (1913) 64–5.

[109] See Pfiffig (1980) 66–71, plates 18, 19, 20.

[110] The Etruscan inscription may be translated: 'This shows Hercules, son of Juno, suckling.' On this see W. Deonna, 'La Légende de Pero et de Micon et l'allaitement symbolique', in *Deux études de symbolisme religieux, Coll. Latomus* 18 (1955) 5–50. On Fortuna Primigenia as an ancient fertility cult see Champeaux (1982) 1. 39–40.

a purificatory lustration after the bloodshed of war.[111] The triumphal procession proceeded from a starting-point in the Circus Flaminius, past Bellona's temple[112] and the temple of Apollo Medicus Sosianus, which had been rebuilt shortly after Actium by C. Sosias and which was decorated with a magnificent marble frieze depicting the essential religious components of a Roman triumph.[113] From here the procession entered the Forum Boarium, eventually passing a statue of Hercules Triumphator, which stood in a group of shrines and statues to Hercules Invictus or Victor near the Ara Maxima.[114] The location, not only of Ovid's story of Ino but of the temple that Servius founded in honour of Mater Matuta and her companion goddess, Fortuna, was associated with the religious ceremonial of war.

Whilst most of the terracotta statuary now believed to have decorated Servius Tullius' archaic temple to Mater Matuta would have disappeared underground by Ovid's day, it seems in character that the aetiological poet should intend his literary allusions and highly symbolic narrative to reflect the historical and antiquarian associations of the Forum Boarium. Just as Ovid celebrates Mars' worship instead of his martial exploits in *Fasti* 3, so in the month of June the poet circumvents pure militarism by focusing on the religious ritual of war and related themes such as apotheosis. The iconography of apotheosis is strikingly present in the terracotta statuary which has been excavated from Servius' temple. For example, the acroterial statuary group from the apex of the pediment is thought to represent Hercules with Minerva introducing him to the gods on Olympus at the moment of his apotheosis.[115] In the chariot procession depicted on the terracotta plaques of the tympanum a three-horse chariot

[111] Fest. 104L.

[112] Cf. *Fast.* 6. 199–208.

[113] C. Sosius had supported the wrong side at Philippi, but was pardoned by Octavian and admitted to his political circle. In a public show of loyalty he financed the rebuilding of the temple of Apollo Medicus Sosianus, which was decorated with familiar Augustan motifs such as bucrania and laurels.

[114] Plin. *Nat.* 34. 33. See Bonfante-Warren (1970) 49–66.

[115] The ideological significance of the chariot procession in relation to Servius Tullius is analysed by Vernole (2002) 113–28 and Mertens-Horn (1996) 143–8. For an alternative identification see also Coarelli (1988) 160–82. The terracotta statues and reliefs are displayed together as part of this archaic temple in the Montemartini Power Plant in Rome.

Fig. 6 Terracotta revetment plaque, Museo Nazionale, Naples. Part of the architectural decoration of an Etruscan sanctuary at Velletri, this chariot procession bears a striking resemblance to the revetment plaques from the second phase of decoration of the Archaic temple, mid-sixth century BC, in the Forum Boarium, thought to have an ideological significance associated with triumph and apotheosis. Three-horse chariots alternate with winged, therefore supernatural, two-horse chariots accompanied by long-haired warriors in chitons. In each chariot the passenger places a hand on the charioteer's shoulder. At the front is a herald with petasus and caduceus. (Photograph courtesy of D.A.I. Rome, Inst. Neg. 1983. 2204.)

with two warriors alternates with a winged, and therefore supernatural, two-horse chariot containing a warrior behind whom stands a female divinity. The same iconography recurs in Etruscan tomb paintings and archaic reliefs found in Rome representing man's progress to immortality.[116] Ovid could not have seen this because it was buried in the fill on top of which stood the later temple complex.

[116] From the Archaic period until the fourth century BC Hercules appears frequently with Dionysiac motifs indicative of the afterlife in funerary art, mostly on sarcophagi. See J. Bayet, *Idéologue et plastique* (Rome, 1974).

Nevertheless, it might be suggested that he was tapping into an antiquarian tradition recognized in Augustan times.

3.3. Servius Tullius and the temple complex of Mater Matuta and Fortuna in the Forum Boarium: lux eadem, Fortuna, tua est, auctorque locusque, Fast. *6. 569*

The cults of Fortuna and Mater Matuta in Rome belonged to the world of women: Fortuna promoted fecundity in newly married women and Matuta watched over the care of children. As such both cults represented the civic stability which is counterpoised, on the two great literary shields of Achilles and Aeneas, with war and conquest. It might, however, be remembered that each of these two goddesses also had military or political associations. Like the goddess Juno of Lanuvium, whose powers encompassed military prowess and political organization as well as fertility,[117] Fortuna, too, was believed to bring victory in battle and support to kings. Plutarch, in his *Quaestiones Romanae*, explains that the Porta Fenestella, through which Fortuna is said to have climbed in order to share Servius' bed, was the very window at which Tanaquil persuaded the Romans to accept Servius as her murdered husband's successor.[118] Ovid alludes to the old legend that Servius was Fortuna's favourite by using the stereotyped vocabulary characteristic of erotic elegy: *furtivos timide profitetur amores* | ... *concubuisse pudet* | *arsit enim magno correpta cupidine* (*Fast.* 6. 573–5). By using erotic imagery here, as he uses Bacchic imagery in the Ino narrative, Ovid translates antiquarian material into the generically acceptable language of erotic narrative in Roman elegy. This essential facet of Ovid's aetiological technique was clearly considered appropriate, witty, and entertaining.

From the period of Plautus and Ennius, Fortuna was directly associated with military victory.[119] That the same was true of Mater Matuta is evident from statuary excavated at the archaic cult centres

[117] Ovid *Fast.* 2. 425–52. Cf. 3. 168–233. See Dumézil (1970) 291–303.

[118] See Wiseman (1998) 25–30, who prefers this to Coarelli's suggestion of a *hieros gamos* consummated by the ruler (Servius) and a temple prostitute (Fortuna).

[119] See Weinstock (1971) 112–27. Augustus' shrine to Fortuna Redux, founded 19 BC, had affinities with a set of abstract imperial deities such as Victoria Augusta and Felicitas Caesaris.

of Mater Matuta in Satricum and Pyrgi.[120] Before the capture of Veii in 396 BC Camillus vowed a temple to Mater Matuta,[121] possibly in the belief that Matuta had the power to confer victory.[122] The myth of Fortuna giving her favours to military leaders is familiar from coinage celebrating Fortuna Caesaris or Augustus' Fortuna Redux.[123] In this respect, however, Servius Tullius presented Ovid with a generic challenge. Both Livy and Dionysius regard the king's most significant achievement to be his creation by census of a centuriate assembly which enabled him to form a hoplite army of maximum size and administrative efficiency.[124] As a *conditor* of Rome's military strength Servius merited a place in Ovid's celebration of June. Since, on generic grounds, Servius' state-of-the-art hoplite force had to be excluded, the poet, instead, represents the king as a peace-loving ruler devoted to the foundation of temples and cults, making use of a historical tradition that Servius was connected with the original archaic temple in the Forum Boarium. Consequently the king who, like Romulus, was famous for his military classification, is credited with the *pietas* of the Aeneadae, and this is underlined by miraculous flames which appear in the child Servius' hair.[125] Servius is, as a result, enmeshed in a generically suitable comparison with the priest-rulers Numa and Augustus.[126] Ovid signals Servius' true contribution to the Roman state by naming as his father Volcanus, who was both an ancient god of war associated with the Tubilustrum (*Fast.* 5.

[120] The Theban legend was a popular theme on Etruscan temples, sometimes linked to contemporary political ideology, as for instance the pediment relief, from Temple A at Pyrgi, of the Seven Against Thebes, illustrating divine condemnation of tyrannical hubris. The same temple has a statue of Hercules welcoming Ino/Mater Matuta from their Theban homeland. These may be seen in the Pyrgi Room at the Villa Giulia in Rome.

[121] Liv. 5. 19. 6. The temples were both rebuilt in 212 BC (Liv. 24. 47. 15–16, 25. 7. 5–6).

[122] Dumézil (1980) 1–87, 129–38, suggests that Camillus cultivated this goddess in her capacity as Dawn, the time of day when, according to Plutarch, three of Camillus' significant victories were won.

[123] See Weinstock (1971) 112–27.

[124] Liv. 1. 42. 4–43. 13, D.H. 4. 14–18. 3.

[125] *Fast.* 6. 635–6. In Virgil's *Aeneid* miraculous flames appear in the hair of Iulus (*Aen.* 2. 682), Aeneas (10. 270–2), Augustus (8. 680–6), and Lavinia (7. 71–7), singling them out as chosen to advance the destiny of Rome.

[126] It was Servius Tullius who founded the Roman system of urban *vici* each with its own compital cult, which Augustus later reformed.

725–6) and a fire god who manifests himself, prior to Servius' conception, *inter cineres obsceni forma virilis* (*Fast.* 6. 631).[127]

Ovid's claim that the twin temples to Mater Matuta and Fortuna were founded by Servius Tullius (578–34 BC) has been confirmed by recent archaeology which dates to the first half of the sixth century BC the first archaic temple on the site of the, realigned, republican temples to Fortuna and Mater Matuta.[128] The acroterial statues of Hercules and Minerva and the terracotta plaques with the chariot procession are thought to belong to a refurbishment in the late sixth century which may correspond to a change of ruler or dynasty, confirming either Servius' succession to the throne of Tarquinius Priscus or Ovid's story of the murder of Servius by his daughter Tullia and her husband, L. Tarquinius, in order to usurp his father-in-law's throne.[129] In connecting the temple with Servius Tullius, Ovid was drawing on a tradition still current in Augustan times. Since it is uncertain which goddess was the original dedicatee of the archaic temple, Ovid must have extrapolated from the later temples, perhaps those built in 212 BC, the dedications to Fortuna and Mater Matuta.

Ovid's celebration of the cults of Fortuna and Mater Matuta demonstrates how the poet's antiquarian interests enrich his compositional technique. The greatness and the novelty of Ovid's *Fasti* lay in the intellectual breadth of his study of Roman religion on the site of Rome. To sum up, Ovid's use of Bacchic imagery is an essential indication that he understood the cult of Mater Matuta to be a fertility cult. At the same time he understood that the cults of Mater Matuta and Fortuna were associated also with military success, the religious ceremonial of triumph and apotheosis in the Forum Boarium. This ties in closely with Ovid's month of June, in which it is *militiae labor*, rather than intellectual achievement, which points the way to the stars (see Introduction 4.5).

[127] Cf *Fast.* 5. 725–6. See too Capdeville (1995) 423 and Coarelli (1983) 161–78.

[128] *Fast.* 6. 479–80, 569.

[129] *Fast.* 6. 585–620. For Herakles' apotheosis in sixth-century Athenian political propaganda, represented in the iconography of chariot processions, see Boardman (1972).

Ovid took a pride in his consultation of antiquarian sources and alludes to this on several occasions.[130] His antiquarian allusions are an essential part of his literary genre. They merit being deciphered as part of the wide-ranging erudition which was characteristic of his Alexandrian heritage. Through the intellectual subtlety of his literary style, these allusions contribute to a narrative which should, in many instances, be interpreted symbolically rather than literally.[131]

4. Themes

Almost without exception the themes recurrent in *Fasti* 6 relate to 'Augustan' subjects, matters of contemporary interest or ideology which had become topical in Augustan poetry. There are some interesting thematic correspondences between Horace's six 'Roman Odes' and Ovid's *Fasti* 6, composed at least thirty years later. The two works represent, respectively, the opening and closing years of Augustus' Principate. In 29 BC, in the aftermath of Augustus' conquest of Egypt, deification of a living ruler came into sharp focus, and in two 'Roman Odes' Horace returns to the theme of the apotheosis of Hercules, Romulus, and Augustus.[132] The present need to expiate national guilt and *neglegentia deorum* was Horace's starting point for advocating a restoration of Roman temples,[133] and, in the same vein, of the virtues of a simple diet against the sin of *luxuria*,[134] reflecting the Princeps' personal values. Three references to Carrhae reminded Horace's readers that the Parthian capture of Roman standards remained unavenged and the temple of Mars Ultor as yet unbuilt,[135] while the symbolic motif of Gigantomachy,[136] elemental evil pitted

130 *Fast.* 1. 387, 2. 274.

131 A valuable article by John Scheid, which, incidentally, outlines the history of criticism of Ovid's historicity in matters of religion (1992: 118), concludes that Ovid's *Fasti* is 'a well-informed book' and that the poet 'is neither ignorant, wrong nor merely descriptive' but rather, 'clever and subtle'.

132 *Carm.* 3. 2. 21–2, 3. 3. 9–18.

133 *Carm.* 3. 6. 1–2: *delicta maiorum immeritus lues | Romane, donec templa refeceris.*

134 *Carm.* 3. 1. 18–19: *non Siculae dapes | dulcem elaborabunt saporem.* Cf. *Fast.* 6. 172: *nec petit adscitas luxuriosa dapes.*

135 *Carm.* 3. 2. 3–4, 3. 5. 3–6, 3. 6. 9–10.

136 *Carm.* 3. 4. 49–64. Cf. 3. 1. 7.

against the guardian gods of Rome, recalled the military threat only recently averted at Actium. Finally, in an extended speech of smouldering resentment towards the Roman descendants of Aeneas, Horace's Juno herself, the divine instigator of Roman war, promises reconciliation, but in the most grudging terms: *graves* | *iras et invisum nepotem* | ... *Marti redonabo.*[137] All these themes reappear in *Fasti* 6, but the passage of time, some thirty-five years after Actium, is evident in Ovid's shifts of emphasis.

It is Juno who undergoes the most essential transformation in *Fasti* 6, and this becomes clear in the proem, where, to bolster her right to the *titulus mensis*, she affirms, more than once,[138] her position as the matriarch of Rome's divine dynasty of war, and associates herself, affectionately now, with the *invisum nepotem* of Horace's ode,[139] making her final plea for the *titulus mensis* in dynastic terms: *at nostri Roma nepotis erat.* Losing none of her essential belligerence, for Juno had a long history as a Roman deity of war, the former persecutor of the Aeneadae now claims *posuisse fideliter iras* (*Fast.* 6. 41); she appears to concede the union of the dual lines of the Aeneadae and Romulus, her words reflecting the contemporary iconography of the statuary of the temple of Mars Ultor. Two new themes appear in *Fasti* 6 which are not present in Horace's Roman Odes.[140] Carna's resuscitation of Proca, heir to the throne of Alba Longa, belongs to a group of stories of 'endangered princelings' which echoed problems in Augustus' own line of succession, while the theme of divine fire and divine descent, diversely represented by Vesta and Volcanus, reflected the rising importance of the dynastic cult of Vesta after Augustus, as Pontifex Maximus, created a Vestal hearth in his Palatine house.

When Horace's Augustan themes reappear in the final book of Ovid's *Fasti*, they are coloured both by the spirit of the times and by the inherent humour and complex artistry of a genre where dynastic myth, Roman history, and religion are dexterously interwoven with

[137] *Carm.* 3. 3. 18–44.

[138] *Fast.* 6. 51–5, 63–4.

[139] *Carm.* 3. 3. 31.

[140] This theme is best represented in *Fasti* 2, where first Romulus and Remus, then a single male child of the Fabii, miraculously escape death to continue the family line.

Fig. 7 Juno of Lanuvium, Sala Rotunda, Museo Vaticano, Rome. Large marble statue of Juno Seispes Mater Regina of Lanuvium, first century AD, holding spear and shield. Juno's goatskin is carved in realistic detail, with long horns curving out behind the goddess' head and resting on her shoulders. A serpent passes under the hem of her robe to emerge, with bared fangs, between her two sandals (cf. Prop. 4. 8. 3–4). (Courtesy of Alinari, Inst. Neg.)

literary topoi. Ovid's Augustan themes reflect essential messages of Augustan iconography which had been reiterated all over Rome in the increasingly elaborate mythological and astrological symbolism of new dynastic monuments.[141] Another important aspect of the themes of *Fasti* 6 is their relationship to those present in *Fasti* 1. Striking thematic correspondences and contrasts achieve a series of overarching frames, which link the beginning and the end of the work. The themes of war and apotheosis in *Fasti* 6 contrast with the themes of peace and birth[142] in *Fasti* 1. Both books are linked by the moral theme of the virtues of simple food, while Carmentis' association with birth and abortion in *Fasti* 1 corresponds to the theme of endangered princelings in *Fasti* 6. Finally, Ovid's passage on animal sacrifice in Book 1 corresponds with substitution sacrifices of Carna and Volcanus in Book 6. All this will become clearer in an analysis of the salient themes in *Fasti* 6.

4.1. War: Juno and Iuventas

The month of June, in the middle of the fighting season, commemorates no fewer than seven military anniversaries and two major military threats in Roman history: the Gallic siege and the Second Punic War. The underlying theme of war in *Fasti* 6 is anticipated by a programmatic prologue centred on a contest for the *titulus mensis* between Iuventas, who champions the Roman *iuvenes*, Romans of military age who fight in Rome's armies, and Juno, whose most ancient dual role in Roman cult encompassed both war and fertility. The ancient idea that success in war achieved civic prosperity and fecundity was symbolized by the costume of goatskin, lance, and shield of Juno Seispes Mater Regina of Lanuvium. This was also the essence of the iconography of the Ara Pacis Augustae. At other sanctuaries her title, Juno Curitis, might evoke Juno of the spear (*Curitis*) or Juno, guardian of the city (*Quiritis*), but may also have marked her association with the Servian *curiae* where enrolment signalled eligibility for military service.[143] An image occasionally

[141] Examples of this are the Ara Pacis Augustae and the Aedes Concordiae, dedicated by Tiberius in AD 10. On this see Kellum (1990).

[142] In *Fasti* 1. 617–36 Carmentis is celebrated as a goddess associated with childbirth in a story where she counteracts an epidemic of self-induced abortion.

[143] See Liou-Gille (1998) 76–8. As Juno Sororia she had an altar beside Janus Curatius near the Tigellum Sororium. All three monuments seem to have represented in some way the passage of boys into *iuvenes* and full adult membership of Rome's military forces. Juno's association with Janus here marks a further link between the patronal deities of *Fasti* 1 and 6.

struck on Roman coins showed an armed Juno driving a chariot and wearing her goat's headdress.

In the contest for the *titulus mensis*, Juno and Iuventas present their credentials in a way which enables the reader to interpret them as two different representatives of Roman warfare. Juno's role as a warrior goddess is central to her claim. Beginning with her persecution of the Trojan Aeneadae, one of the powerful themes of Virgil's *Aeneid*, to which the Augustan poets made frequent allusion, she gives an impressive list of Rome's enemies which she has supported in the past, including, among her historic examples of military patronage, the city of Carthage. This has particular point for the month of June, which contains the anniversaries of two of the most significant battles of the Second Punic War: defeat at Lake Trasimene in 217 BC and victory at the River Metaurus in 207 BC. Juno's final argument is purely dynastic: she merits worship in Rome because this has the blessing of her son, Mars the war god, *tu pollens urbe nepotis eris* (54), and because Rome has been founded by her belligerent grandson, Romulus.[144] Juno's divine dynasty of war, Juno–Mars–Romulus, looks back to the archaic Italian Juno of Lanuvium.[145]

Taking a cue from her mother's citation of her illustrious divine connections, Iuventas promptly offers as counter-argument the *virtus* of the two most famous paradigms for Roman *iuvenes*: her own husband, Hercules, and Romulus, who first divided the Romans into fighting (*iuniores*) and non-fighting (*seniores*) classes. Ovid's poetic imagery of the rivalry of the two goddesses symbolizes the tensions between Juno, the instigator of war, and Iuventas, the patroness of the *iuvenes* who are the perpetrators of military engagement.

Juno's literary persona as a goddess of war in *Fasti* 6 provides a counterweight to Janus' pacific role in *Fasti* 1: *nil mihi cum bello* (253). Janus had emerged from relative obscurity to become a god of Peace in the reformed religion of Augustus, who had formulated his establishment of the Pax Augusta with the proud claim of having

[144] *Fast.* 2. 142.

[145] This dynasty has its beginnings in the garden of Flora (*Fast.* 5. 229–54), whom Ovid depicts selecting a flower to bring about Juno's parthenogenic conception. Promising Flora honour in Romulus' city, Mars uses almost the same words as he uses to his mother: '*tu quoque Romulea*' *dixit* '*in urbe locum*' (5. 260. Cf. 6. 54).

closed the doors of Janus' temple three times.[146] But Juno, too, had her place in the New Order. On the Ara Pacis Augustae, opposite Aeneas sacrificing on the left, stood Mars and Romulus, Juno's son and grandson, in the balancing right-hand panel. Aeneas' sacrifice represented Roman *pietas*, the ancestral gods brought from burning Troy, and sacrifice performed in peacetime. Mars and Romulus represented the martial *virtus* which made Pax Augusta possible. The *pietas* which Aeneas exemplified in cult practice, Romulus demonstrated in conquest. That Juno was also enmeshed in this ideological religious dichotomy is made clear by her line of argument in Ovid's proem to *Fasti* 6.

Juno and Janus had ancient links. Both were honoured on the Kalends of the month and, as deities of inception, each had a role in initiatory rites: Janus for *iuvenes*, as they passed from boyhood into full members of the citizen body, and Juno for girls, when they achieved the status of married women. It was in their capacity of civic deities of Rome's first thirty *curiae* that Juno and Janus each had an altar standing near the Tigellum Sororium, honouring respectively Juno Sororia and Janus Curatius.[147] In *Fasti* their respective patronage of January and June forms the outer frame of the first half of Ovid's calendar poem, so that the two deities appear to stand in diametric opposition as the instigators of Peace and War. In a work so intricately structured as Ovid's *Fasti* it may be assumed that Ovid intends Janus' association with Roman *iuvenes* in Book 1 to balance the arguments of Iuventas in Book 6.

The polarity of Augustan Peace and Augustan War, the contrasting themes of Virgil's Shield of Aeneas, belongs to the natural order of the Roman year, to January and June respectively. Janus' month is a celebration of civic order, and its closural passage for 30 January marks the celebration of the Ara Pacis Augustae, on which the procession of Roman priesthoods, the imperial family, and Roman citizens mirrors the procession of magistrates which Ovid describes

[146] *RG* 13. See Galinsky (1996) 106–21. On the importance of Janus as the poet's voice in his *Fasti* see Barchiesi (1991) and Green (2004a).

[147] The cult of the Tigellum Sororium, supposedly the beam under which Horatius had to pass after killing his sister, was celebrated on the Kalends of October and was associated with the cults of the *curiae*. See Fest. 380L, Liv. 1. 26. 13, D.H. 3. 22. 7, and Holland (1961) 77–91.

on 1 January (71–88). The god himself is the harbinger of lasting peace: *Iane, fac aeternos pacem pacisque ministros* (1. 287), who brings order out of chaos and stands, ever vigilant, as the divine guardian on the threshold of the Cosmos: *me penes est unum vasti custodia mundi* (119). As Peace and War are thematically contrasted in the proems of Book 1 and Book 6, so they provide, respectively, the closural focus for January, in Ovid's celebration of the Ara Pacis Augustae, and for June, in the sequence of myths of apotheosis which ends with the apotheoses of Quirinus and Hercules vindicating the valour of the Roman *iuvenes*, to symbolize the triumph of *virtus* and *pietas*, two cornerstones of Augustan ideology.

4.2. Food: Carna and Vesta

In Roman literature no theme supplied a more cogent literary illustration of the contrast between the simplicity of the Golden Age and modern Roman *luxuria* than the topic of food. A comparison of the *paupertas* of ancient Rome and the banquets of the present day was a theme popular with the Augustan poets,[148] and this was further encouraged by Augustus' personal aversion to gastronomic extravagance. In *Fasti* 1, Janus' observations on the former simplicity of New Year gifts (1. 185–228) correspond to the poet's reflections in Book 6 on the modern taste for *adscitae dapes*, brought from far-flung corners of the Roman empire (172–6). Ovid contrasts with this the fibre-rich casserole of pork, emmer, and beans consumed on the feast day of Carna (6. 169–71), the goddess who ensures the health of the *viscera* of Rome's fighting men.

This is not the only occasion in Book 6 on which food relates to the companion theme of war. In his extended passage on the Vestalia Ovid returns to the subject of bread in a military context with his aition of the floury (*candida*, 394) altar of Iuppiter Pistor. The topic of bread-baking was appropriate for this honoured Vesta, not only for her guardianship of the Roman hearth but also for her patronage of the bakers' donkey, which was a popular theme in the paintings decorating the *lararia* of Pompeian bakeries. When the guardian deities of Rome appeal to Jupiter to raise the Gallic siege, Vesta is

[148] Hor. *Carm.* 3. 1. 17–48.

Fig. 8 Lararium fresco from Pistrinum in Pompeii [Regio VII. xii. 11. See Boyce (1937) no. 316]. Vesta is enthroned, wearing a green robe, yellow chiton, violet mantle, and a white veil with golden crown. She holds a cornucopia and *patera*. Behind her throne stands the miller's donkey. On the altar before her are ears of corn and hanging fillets. Below two crested and bearded serpents, flanking the marble altar, may represent the baker's Genius and his wife's Juno. (Photograph courtesy of D.A.I., Rome, Inst. Neg. 1931. 2459.)

ordered to see to it that the Romans can disguise their state of famine by bombarding the Gauls with bread (*Fast.* 6. 377–88). The fictitious tale recalls Livy's use of the food shortage during the Gallic siege to illustrate the endurance and loyalty of Manlius' troops, who, on the point of starvation, nevertheless refrained from eating the sacred geese and showed their gratitude to Manlius by offering him donations from their scanty rations (Liv. 5. 48. 4–9). Stories concerned with bread-baking are juxtaposed with this story, which begins with Mars' appeal for Jupiter to help the Romans, and the parallel story of Mars' appeal to Jupiter in Book 2 for Romulus to be deified.[149] Ovid prefaces his story of Vesta and the millstone donkey with an allusion to Vacuna (*Fast.* 6. 307–10), the ancient hearth goddess who was honoured in days when bread was baked on terracotta tiles in the ashes of the fire. Similarly the apotheosis of Romulus is followed by the Fornacalia (2. 513–33), the festival of the goddess Fornax, who enables the tough emmer husks to be burnt off without scorching the grain inside. Ovid illustrates his story of the rustic hospitality which Carmentis extends to Ino (6. 531–2) with the detail that the goddess bakes yellow cakes. Such cakes, simply baked on the hearth, were the traditional sacrifice offered to Juno as an ancient fertility goddess.

4.3. Fire: Vesta and Volcanus

An ancient shrine to Volcanus was situated outside the walls of the earliest Palatine settlement. This was associated with the Lapis Niger,[150] a black paving-stone close to the Comitium in the Forum Romanum, not far from a subterranean shrine, which was believed to have originated from a crack in the earth known as the *mundus cereris*. Volcanus' feast day, 23 August, preceded the day when the *mundus cereris*, which was a vaulted pit supposedly giving access to the Underworld, was opened, possibly to allow the dead free passage to the world above on a fixed day, serving the same purpose as the feast of the *Lemuria* (*Fast.* 5. 419–92). Volcanus and Ceres were therefore calendrically linked, and formed, with Proserpina, an ancient Roman triad of deities that was clearly linked to the growth of

[149] See Commentary *ad loc.*
[150] See Coarelli (1988) 1. 161–99, Ross Holloway (1994) 81–8.

Fig. 9 Sarcophagus, Capitoline Museum, Rome. Volcanus as a young warrior god, carrying hammer and caduceus, faces Bacchus/Liber, holding thyrsus and vine-branch, across a circular altar. A bucranion, a common feature in Augustan art, lies at Liber's feet. Since the head of Volcanus resembles iconographically the head of a Julio-Claudian prince, this may commemorate the assumption of the *toga virilis* by a young prince on the occasion of the *Liberalia* on 17 March (cf. Var. *L* 6. 14). The presence of Bacchus/Liber suggests the new young adult's right to participate in adult drinking at symposia. (Photograph courtesy of D.A.I. Rome, Inst. Neg. 1934. 2095.)

the corn and the theme of fertility. Volcanus' association with war is apparent in the Tubilustrum and in the custom of burning enemy armour as a sacrifice to Volcanus.[151] Behind the ancient conjunction of fertility and war, represented in the iconography of Juno of Lanuvium, was the simple truth that successful conquest established prosperity, fecundity, and agrarian abundance. The same message was expressed in the figure of Ceres, who personified the Pax Augusta on the Ara Pacis Augustae.

Volcanus' earliest function was as a god of young warriors,[152] a connection recognized in Ovid's day. A relief showing Volcanus, identifiable by the hammer he holds, with the face of a Julio-Claudian prince, possibly Gaius, facing Liber, seems to commemorate the prince's coming of military age and his assumption of the *toga virilis.* On 7 June Ovid describes watching the *Ludi Piscatorii* in the Campus Martius which were celebrated, particularly, by the Tiber fishermen. According to Festus this was the occasion for pouring live fishes into the flames on Volcanus' altar in the Campus Martius, as a substitution sacrifice in which the fish represented human life.[153] The ritual of human sacrifice in Rome was associated with war. Commenting on the immuration of two Greeks and two Gauls in the Forum Boarium in 228 BC, Livy describes the practice as un-Roman.[154] Human sacrifices were performed again in 216 and 114 BC to avert national danger, either to re-establish the *pax deorum* after a military disaster (after Cannae in 216 BC) or, in response to portents, as *piacula* to avert further national danger which might be occasioned by civic pollution.[155]

[151] See *Fast.* 5. 725–6, Liv. 1. 37. 5.

[152] In a detailed study Capdeville (1995) associates Volcanus with a young male god subordinated to a mother goddess, in the same way as Hercules is represented in early Central Italian art as subordinated to Juno. Volcanus resembles Hercules as a paradigm of the Roman *iuvenes.* Cf. also Dumézil (1970) 320–1, Schilling (1993) 2. 161 n. 204.

[153] Similar is Numa's response to Jupiter's demand for human sacrifice by offering a fish (*Fast.* 3. 339–43).

[154] Liv. 22. 57. 2–6. Cf. Plut. *Mor.* 284A–C.

[155] See Eckstein (1982) 69–81, who discusses the possibility that human sacrifice was intended to expiate civic pollution caused by unchastity among the Vestal Virgins.

To placate the angry gods after the Roman defeat at Lake Trasimene a *lectisternium* was performed in 217 BC, when Volcanus occupied the same couch as Vesta. In addition to their association with fire, Vesta and Volcanus represented a dichotomy of female and male sexual forces: the association of fire with generation. In Vesta's innermost storehouse was kept the sacred phallus, the *fascinum.* Volcanus' fire was said to contain the seeds of generation, an idea implicit in the founder myths of Romulus and Caeculus of Praeneste, which Ovid uses in his account of the parentage of Servius Tullius (*Fast.* 6. 627), born from a phallus on the hearth and marked by destiny through the portent of flames playing in his hair. Whilst Volcanus' fire was believed to be potentially destructive[156] and Vesta's beneficent, both deities were regarded as guardian gods of Rome. In Horace's fourth Roman Ode, Volcanus takes his place with *matrona Juno* and Apollo in repelling the giants from Olympus. Vesta's close association with the survival of Rome gained importance under Augustus, whose establishment of a Vestal shrine in his house was an outward symbol of dynastic power.

4.4. *The survival of endangered princelings*

The prototype of this theme was the legend of Aeneas bringing his young son Iulus from burning Troy through dangers at sea and wars in Italy. This tale of the origins of the Gens Iulia was so widespread in Augustan Rome that it became the subject of parody on the walls of Pompeian houses. By the time that Ovid was writing his *Fasti*, however, the theme had topical poignancy through the premature deaths of Augustus' nephew Marcellus and, later, his two grandsons, Gaius and Lucius.[157] The Princeps' preoccupation with the younger members of his family was apparent in his active involvement with their adoptions and progression into civic life.

In *Fasti* 6 the heir to the throne of Alba Longa, Proca, is saved from death and restored to infant health by the Roman goddess Carna, whose special care is the *viscera* of Roman *iuvenes.* Like the wolf's

[156] Volcanus was also said to be the father of Cacus (Virg. *Aen.* 8. 198, Ovid *Fast.* 1. 546), the personification of primeval wickedness. Cf. Virg. *Aen.* 7. 77.

[157] The premature death of Augustus' nephew, Marcellus, had already found echoes in Virgil's *Aeneid* in the deaths of Pallas, Lausus, and Euryalus.

rescue of the abandoned Romulus and Remus in Book 2,[158] Carna's care of Proca belongs to the 'miraculous survival' stories, which enhanced the belief that the destiny of both Rome and the Julian dynasty was ordained by the gods and divinely protected. The theme is prominent in *Fasti* 2, a book especially concerned with Roman ancestors. It appears in the story of the 300 Fabii, annihilated to a man at the River Cremera by Etruscans of Veii, leaving just one male survivor to continue the family line: *puer impubes et adhuc non utilis armis* (*Fast.* 2. 239).[159]

A second example of a child survivor in *Fasti* 6 is Ino's son, Melicertes, destined to become the Roman god Portunus. He escapes infanticide when his mother Ino leaps with him from the cliffs near Corinth. They are transported miraculously to Italy by nymphs, but their landfall in the Lucus Stimulae exposes Melicertes to a second danger: *sparagmos* at the hands of Arcadian maenads. Rescued a second time by Hercules, Melicertes' destiny is foretold by Carmentis: he will be deified as Portunus, the protector of Roman ships, while his mother will become the kourotrophos goddess, Mater Matuta. On Italian soil both become beneficent deities.[160] In Ovid's aetiological narrative, like Romulus and Remus and the Fabian ancestor of the great Cunctator, the 'endangered princelings' are rescued from untimely death in order that they can protect the Roman people or ensure that there is no break in Rome's divine dynasty.

As *Fasti* 6 moves towards its conclusion, Ovid narrates, within a group of apotheoses and katasterisms, the resuscitation of two more young princes, Hippolytus (745–9) and Glaucus, child of Minos and Pasiphaë (750–5). Verbal and thematic similarities with the story of Carna's revival of Proca suggest the theme of the importance of the *iuvenes* in the survival and advancement of the Roman state. Through Carna's role as a goddess responsible for watching over the lives of Roman *iuvenes* the theme of endangered princes is closely interwoven both with the themes of apotheosis and homely food, beneficial to the *viscera* of fighting men, and also with the role of Iuventas, as patron goddess of the *iuvenes* in *Fasti* 6.

[158] *Fast.* 2. 405–20.
[159] See Harries (1991) 158–62.
[160] See Parker (1997).

4.5. *Apotheosis*

Ovid signals the approaching closure of Book 6 with a cluster of legendary apotheoses—Hippolytus, Aesculapius, Romulus, and Hercules. Besides the obvious closural force of the theme, apotheosis in Augustan poetry characteristically implied that Hercules and Romulus, who in Book 6 represented Iuventas' chosen *exempla* for Roman *iuvenes*, had achieved apotheosis as a reward for their virtues and service to Rome. In Augustan poetry this theme carried the essential corollary that Augustus too would merit this reward when the time was ripe.[161] In *Metamorphoses* 15 the poet describes the apotheosis of Aeneas and Romulus before his extended description of the apotheosis of Julius, to which is appended the prospective apotheosis of Augustus.[162]

The achievement of divinity through *virtus* or martial heroism is presented by Virgil as a worthy model for the dynasty when Apollo congratulates Iulus for his heroism on the battlefield with the words: '*macte nova virtute, puer: sic itur ad astra | dis genite et geniture deos*' (*Aen.* 9. 641–2).

These words to the eponymous ancestor of the Iulii have the authority of Augustus' patron deity who hints prophetically at the apotheoses of Caesar and Augustus. This Virgilian endorsement of apotheosis provides a convenient interface between the first and the sixth book of Ovid's *Fasti.* In Ovid's strikingly elevated passage celebrating the *felices animae*, who are privileged in their understanding of the movements of the constellations (*Fast.* 1. 295–310), the poet claims that they achieve their wisdom and their place among the stars by withdrawing entirely from public life and military glory (*militiae labor*, 302): *sic petitur caelum; non ut ferat Ossan Olympus* (307).[163] Ovid's claim that the power of intellectual achievement is superior to conquest by force, symbolized by Gigantomachy, mirrors

[161] See Hor. *Carm.* 3. 2. 21–4, 3. 3. 9–12. For further examples see Nisbet and Rudd (2003) 30–1, 41–2.

[162] Ovid's rendering of this theme apparently culminated in a Getic version, *P* 4. 10. 25–32.

[163] On this passage, with its striking Lucretian and Virgilian resonance, see Fantham (1992*b*) 39–56, Newlands (1995) 27–50, Barchiesi (1997*a*) 177–8, Gee (2000) 61–4, Kenney (2002) 54–6, Green (2004*a*) 135–7.

Fig. 10 Front panel of Belvedere Altar, Museo Vaticano, Rome, *c.*7 BC. After Augustus' reorganization of Roman *vici* and the administration of the cults of the Lares Compitales, the altars of the *vici* were decorated with symbols and scenes representing the Domus Augusta in a simplified Augustan ideology (cf. Fig. 3). This panel depicts the apotheosis of Divus Iulius, the heroic figure ascending in a quadriga towards a sky god in billowing robes, top right. Top left is Apollo, as sun god in his own quadriga, to whom the obelix of Augustus' Horologium Solare was dedicated at this time. This representation of the sun god and 'Caelus' has affinities with the cosmic iconography on the cuirass of the Prima Porta Augustus. The smaller togate figure behind the quadriga of Divus Iulius represents Augustus standing in front of a temple. The larger, and therefore divine, female figure is Venus Genetrix pointing out the apotheosis to two princes, Gaius and Lucius Caesar. (Photograph courtesy of D.A.I. Rome, Inst. Neg. 1973. 1289.)

the theme of the Great Altar at Pergamum, where the giants represent the forces of barbarism, specifically the Gauls, attacking the sanctuary of Apollo at Delphi. Horace (*Carm.* 3. 4. 57–63) has the giants fail in their attack when they are opposed by Apollo and Pallas (57–8), deities of intellectual enlightenment, but also by Volcanus and *matrona Juno*,[164] who are military guardian gods of Rome. In view of the many thematic contrasts and correspondences between *Fasti* 1 and *Fasti* 6, the reader might anticipate in the latter a contrasting celebration of *pietas* and military prowess.

In *Fasti* 6 Rome's guardian gods bring about the rout of the Alpine Gauls who are besieging the Capitol. As in Livy's account of the Gallic invasion, the conquest is not decided simply by force but by Roman *pietas.* When Rome's struggle against the Gallic invaders is mentioned earlier, in Ovid's passage on Juno Moneta (183–90), Roman *pietas* is exemplified, as in Livy, by the heroic contributions of M. Furius Camillus and M. Manlius. In contrast to *Fasti* 1, where immortality is achieved by a pacific study of the constellations, in *Fasti* 6 it is unquestionably *militiae labor* with its essential Roman concomitant, *pietas*, that points the way to the stars: apotheosis. Had Ovid lived to complete his revision of all six books, he might have matched the grandiloquence of his eulogy of *felices animae* in *Fasti* 1 with a passage of comparable power in celebration of the essentially Roman virtue of *pietas* and its reward of apotheosis,[165] which is Romulus' and Hercules' pathway to heaven in *Fasti* 6.

5. Ovid's narrative technique

The sequence of holy days in the Roman calendar and the programmatic content of the proems which introduce each month are not the only influences on the narrative sequence of Ovid's *Fasti.* The life

[164] The expression *matrona Juno* recalls Ovid's *matrona Tonantis* in the proem to *Fasti* 6.

[165] Herbert-Brown (2002) 101–28, in a perceptive analysis of this passage, interprets *felices animae* specifically as astrologers, gifted with wisdom to interpret the movements of the constellations (cf. Man. 1. 40–2), and relates this passage to Augustus' publication of his horoscope in AD 11 and his edict of the same year, which made it illegal to consult astrologers concerning the death of a third person (Dio 56. 25. 5).

story of Romulus and Remus appears to flow chronologically across Books 2–5. Ovid recounts their exposure, rescue, and primitive community at the *Lupercalia* in Book 2, their rape of the Sabine women at the *Matronalia* in Book 3, the death of Remus and Romulus' foundation of Rome at the *Parilia* in Book 4, and Romulus laying to rest the unquiet ghost of Remus at the *Lemuria* in Book 5. However, in the poetic discourse of the proem to March the poet selects, analeptically, as an example of Mars' unwarlike activities, the twins' conception, while Romulus' apotheosis appears, as a prolepsis, at the *Quirinalia* in *Fasti* 2, which privileges Rome's founders and ancestors.

The elegiac genre imposes an empathetic and anecdotal character on Ovid's narrative passages.[166] Whereas epic narration progresses at the pace of the action with its characters expressing themselves in extended speeches made cogent by imagery and rhetorical structure, elegiac narrative strives to achieve emotional impact by empathetic descriptions, apostrophizing the principal protagonist, reflecting sententiously on his/her fate or breaking up the narration with bursts of colloquial dialogue and descriptions of ritual, hymns, and spells. A telescopic approach enables the poet-narrator to focus on scenes of pathos, while compressing previous events into succinct paratactic summaries. A typical example is the preface to Ino's arrival in Italy, where there is a summary of the tragic sequence of events which befell Ino from the moment that she took in her sister's child, Bacchus, until she attempts to commit suicide by leaping into the sea with her remaining child, Melicertes: *arserat Semele... accipit Ino (Bacchum)... intumuit Iuno... agitur furiis Athamas... Learcheas mater tumulaverat umbras* (*Fast.* 6. 485–91).

Another aspect of Ovid's narrative technique is his authorial fiction. In *Fasti* he is a homodiegetic narrator; that is to say, he has adopted the persona of a divinely inspired *vates* engaged in antiquarian research on the Roman calendar. Although the poet uses a didactic tone to impart information, he is, by his own admission, often unsure of his facts: *ut stat (viator) et incertus qua sit sibi nescit*

[166] Essential basic reading is Genette (1980). See also A. Barchiesi, 'Narrative Technique and Narratology in the *Metamorphoses*', in Hardie (ed.) (2002) 180–99, Kenney (2002) 27–89, and Murgatroyd (2005) 1–26 *et passim*.

eundum.[167] He is obliged to consult divine informants in the hope that their specialist knowledge will correctly inform his exegesis of a particular festival, and he uses their personal involvement to influence the slant and colour of the narration.[168] For example, Minerva's explanation of the aetiology of customs and name of the Quinquatrus Minores is distinctive for its poetic turn of phrase.[169] At times the poet is wittily ambiguous about the extent of divine input. Whilst Vesta 'corrects his ignorance'[170] on theological matters, *quae nescieram* (255), presumably including the essential nature of the goddess herself which Ovid admits that he has misunderstood: *diu stultus... putavi* (295), the reader must assume that the stage, rather than Vesta herself, provided Ovid's source for his *multi fabula parva ioci* describing her brush with Priapus. Meanwhile Bacchus' inspiration[171] poetically infused Ovid's narrative with Bacchic imagery and biased loyalty so that the subject of the tale, the god's infanticide Aunt Ino, is represented as a dutiful parent unfairly victimized by Juno.[172]

Audience involvement is essential to Ovid's *Fasti* narrative, which is a personal exchange with literary Rome, the educated elite who would decode the literary allusions which he uses to fill out a sometimes elliptical narration. Rome's leading poet flatters his imperial dedicatee, Germanicus, when he invites him to 'guide the reins', *vates rege vatis habenas* (*Fast.* 1. 25). Ovid's assumption of audience participation is demonstrated by his story of Ino, where intertextual allusions to excesses of Bacchic madness are transferred from Ino's literary persona to Juno and the maenads whom she incites. The poet involves his audience each time he apostrophizes his characters, reflects on their actions, or adds a parenthetic aside. When Hercules asks Ino what she is doing in the Forum Boarium, Ovid slips in a parenthetic *cognorat enim* ('for he recognized her') before continuing Hercules' speech: *matertera Bacchi, | an numen*

[167] *Fast.* 5. 3.

[168] See Miller (1983), Newlands (1995) 51–86, Green (2004a) 69–70.

[169] *Fast.* 6. 657–710.

[170] *Fast.* 6. 255–6: *quae nescieram quorumque errore tenebar | cognita sunt.*

[171] *Fast.* 6. 483–4: *Bacche racemiferos hedera distincte capillos | si domus illa tua est, derige vatis opus.*

[172] *Fast.* 6. 485–547.

quod me, te quoque vexat? (523–54). That Hercules evidently knows that Ino's devotion to her nephew, Bacchus, has landed her in trouble with Juno is intended to amuse the audience with the literary conceit that mythological characters from the same city, Thebes, must know each other's business.

The *varietas* of Ovid's storytelling technique is well illustrated by the narrative passages in *Fasti* 6.[173] Ovid's carefully crafted story of Carna/Crane is a double narrative, telling first how Crane received her magical power, and secondly how she used it to save the heir of Alba Longa. It represents the theme of 'endangered princelings', showing how a link connecting the Alban dynasty with the descendants of Romulus was nearly snapped (Introduction 4.4). Traditional narrative techniques, familiar to many cultures and contexts, are allied to literary devices which aim to move the narrative forward briskly. Ovid begins with a variation of the traditional storyline: 'Long ago and far away lived a maiden wondrous fair.' Having engaged with his Roman readers by citing a familiar local landmark, the Lucus Elerni beside the Tiber estuary, as the site of Crane's birth, the poet explains that the reason for the nymph's rejection of suitors was her passion for hunting, thus signalling his denouement in advance by invoking a well-known literary tradition. The imminent end to Crane's virginal existence is implicit in the literary associations embedded in the poet's picture of her ranging over the open country (*rura sequi*) with spear and nets (*iaculisque feras agitare*, 109; *nodosasque cava tendere valle plagas*, 110) and her physical resemblance to Diana (*nec erat, Phoebe, pudenda tibi*, 112).[174] A lively scene demonstrates Crane's method of shedding unwanted lovers. Simulating modesty, she proposes a cave for a sexual assignation, adding, colloquially, '*si secreta magis ducis in antra, sequor*' (116). As soon as her would-be lover's back is turned to enter the cave, Crane disappears. Coming events are, once again, foreshadowed in the

[173] These are: *Fast.* 6. 105–68 (the double narrative of Carna's rape by Janus and his gift which enables her to resuscitate the infant prince, Proca); three stories concerning Vesta: 319–47 (Priapus' attempted rape); 351–92 (Vesta ends the Gallic siege); 437–54 (Metellus rescues the Palladium); two cult stories for 11 June: 485–547 (Mater Matuta) and 585–620 (Fortuna/Tullia's regicide); and two stories for the *Quinquatrus*: 657–92 (the pipers' walk-out to Tibur) and 695–710 (the invention of the flute).

[174] See notes in the Commentary *ad loc.*

next line: *viderat hanc Ianus, visaeque cupidine captus* (119). Gods generally gratify instantaneous passion without delay and two-faced Janus is equipped to observe Crane's disappearing tactics. To avoid checking the flow of his narrative by recounting what has already been anticipated, Ovid pretends to call out to warn Crane, with a few timely reflections on her naivety:

> stulta! videt Ianus quae post sua terga gerantur.
> nil agis, et latebras respicit ille tuas.
> Nil agis, en! dixi . . .
>
> (123–5)

The sentence ends briskly with a one-line rape, which Ovid rounds off with Janus' portentous presentation of the *ius cardinis*, the power to guard entries: *ius pro concubitu nostro tibi cardinis esto* (127).

The aetion of Carna's gift supplies the essential component for the second narrative: the story of her protection of the Alban heir, Proca. Ovid's story of the attack on the infant prince is embedded between an extended ecphrasis of the *striges* and a detailed description of Crane's substitution sacrifice, with its formulaic incantation: *pro parvo parva, cor pro corde, pro fibris fibras, hanc pro meliore.* The narrative has all the hallmarks of rapid and uncluttered Ovidian elegiac narrative. Ovid's speculation whether *striges* are birds or spellbound witches (*sive . . . seu*, 141) ends, abruptly and unexpectedly, with their arrival in Proca's chamber: *in thalamos venere Procae* (143). The pathos of a repulsive role-reversal, in which the *striges* suck blood from the prince's infant breast, is heightened by the poet-narrator's emotive vocabulary as the nurse runs in answer to Proca's whimpering: *puer infelix vagit . . . territa voce sui nutrix accurrit* (146–7). A rhetorical question, *quid faceret?* (149), is neatly answered by the nurse's appeal to Crane and her direct colloquial response: *pervenit ad Cranaen, et rem docet. illa 'timorem | pone: tuus sospes' dixit 'alumnus erit.'* (151–2).

For variety, the essence of Ovidian narrative, the poet may occasionally simulate the stylistic features of another genre. An example of this is Ovid's 'tragedy', to which we might give the name 'Tullia'[175]

[175] *Fast.* 6. 585–620. See Introduction 4 and also notes in the Commentary *ad loc.* for an examination of Ovid's debt to Livy.

which, in common with Livy's version, consists of a series of clearly demarcated 'scenes' (Tullia incites her husband to regicide, Tarquinius seizes the throne, Tullia violates her father's corpse, Fortuna brings divine retribution) and in Tullia's extended speech to her husband Tarquinius, with its focus on dynastic murder (*quid iuvat esse pares, te nostrae caede sororis | meque tui fratris*, 589–90) and blood-guilt (*patrio sanguine tingue manus*, 596). The poet-narrator makes no attempt to interpose his authorial persona until the very end, when Tullia enters her father's temple of Fortuna, and Ovid heralds the miracle of the speaking statue with the parenthetic comment: *mira quidem, sed tamen acta loquar* (612). It is perhaps the timing of Ovid's return to his familiar persona that gives the words of Servius' statue a few lines later its distinctly Augustan resonance: *ne natae videant ora nefanda meae* (616).

In contrast to his 'Tullia' tragedy, Ovid transforms into a colourful and dramatic elegiac narrative an episode which Livy recounts sparsely, simply to illustrate Appius Claudius' interference in religious matters: the walk-out of the Roman pipers to Tibur.[176] Here Ovid's narrative begins with a metapoetic couplet of introduction, in which Minerva puts down her lance, signifying that she is now ready to engage in elegiac poetry. In a parenthetic aside Ovid expresses the wish that he had the skill to reproduce her scholarly discourse, which underlines his attempt to emulate Minerva's conscious artistry and grandiloquence: *sic ego. sic posita Tritonia cuspide dixit | (possim utinam doctae verba referre deae)* (655–6).

Minerva's speech reflects her position as patroness of dramatists and musicians. She begins by evoking a Golden Age of flute-playing when musicians were held *in magno honore*, poetically framing with a pair of matching couplets the event which suddenly destroyed this happy time.[177] The first couplet is distinguished by the striking spondaic triple anaphora *cantabat*... *cantabat*... *cantabat*, describing the pipers' illustrious role in the most solemn occasions of Roman civic life, during sacrifice at the temples, at *Ludi*, and at funerals, while the second, in a matching triple anaphora, *quaeritur*...

[176] Livy cites as his reason for telling the story: *ad religionem visa esse pertinere* (Liv. 9. 30).

[177] *Fast.* 6. 659–660, 667–8.

quaeritur...quaeritur, laments their absence. Between these two couplets, enigmatic words enhance the mystery shrouding the misfortune that 'shattered the practice of a delightful art' (*quod subito gratae frangeret artis opus*, 662) and the pipers leave Rome for Tibur.

At this point Minerva's poetic style gives way to Ovidian narrative and a social comedy full of twists, distinguished by its brisk pace, terse but cogent descriptive phrases, quick-fire dialogue, and dramatic climax. The opening couplet shows how Ovid builds, within a single elegiac distich, a cogent description by his choice of vocabulary and significant word order: *servierat quidam, quanto libet ordine dignus, | Tibure, sed longo tempore liber erat* (669–70). Two essential words, the pluperfect *servierat* and the adjective *liber*, frame the couplet, in which three phrases complete the portrait of Ovid's main character: a former slave, who has become, over a period of many years, a respected and valued citizen of Tibur. Ovid's second distich continues the process of scene-setting. Each word extends the reader's knowledge, the pentameter bringing to reality what has been anticipated in the hexameter: *rure dapes parat ille suo, turbamque canoram | convocat; ad festas convenit illa dapes* (671–2). A frame is provided by the key word *dapes*, which is qualified by balancing references, first to the host, *parat ille*, and then to the guests, *convenit illa*. In central position, its importance to the narrative underscored by enjambement, is the freedman's invitation to the pipers, *turbamque canoram | convocat*. The evening party at the freedman's villa is in full swing, and the *tibicines* are already witless with strong wine when a messenger bursts in with the news: 'Your former master is approaching!' The freedman, fearing for his carefully earned reputation in the community, breaks up the party and unceremoniously hustles the drunken *tibicines* into a nearby farm cart, where they sleep as it rumbles all the way to the Roman forum. A single word—striking for its typically Ovidian double prefix—*praecomposito nuntius ore* (674), points to the prearranged plot between the Roman senate and the leaders of Tibur to bring the pipers back to Rome, which forms the substance of Livy's account.

There is no doubt that Ovid's versatile use of the elegiac distich contributes to the character of his narrative style. The internal unity of the elegiac couplet, where the pentameter summarizes and enlarges a statement made in the hexameter, had a natural closural force. Couplets incorporating the traditional components of elegiac narrative—dialogue, sentimental reflection, invocation, ecphrasis, and swift-flowing forward momentum—could be built up, singly or in numerically balancing groups, into a pleasing structure.[178] This may be illustrated by Ovid's account of Vesta's breaking of the Gallic siege, which opens with an elegiac adaptation of Virgil's Council of the Gods at the beginning of *Aeneid* 10. Ovid's sonorous opening hexameter with polysyllabic words, epic vocabulary, and significant juxtaposition summarizes, in appropriate past tenses, the current situation, while the pentameter plainly states its effect, the shortage of food: *cincta premebantur trucibus Capitolia Gallis: | fecerat obsidio iam diuturna famem* (351–2). A second rolling hexameter announces the Council of the Gods, the epic concomitant to heroic warfare, and Jupiter orders Mars to speak. Mars' ten-couplet speech has the same import as that of Virgil's Venus: Rome's present misfortune belies Jupiter's promise of *potentia rerum.* Five steps of Mars' arguments are marshalled in five consecutive pairs of distichs. The last pentameter of all recapitulates the situation: *monte suo clausos barbara turba premit* (374). The speech is rhetorically embellished, like Juno's in the proem, with anaphora (*vidimus*, 363, 365), alliteration (363, 371), and, in the final couplet, the flourish of a tricolon crescendo (373–4), distinguishing Mars' peroration.

For Ovid the lightness and fluency of the elegiac metre with its self-contained distich offered a flexible medium for constructing a varied narrative. Besides its obvious aptness for fast-moving comedy, interjections, colloquial dialogue, and parenthetic asides, which were natural to Ovid's persona as a purveyor of aetiological narrative, Ovid's elegiac verse could sustain entertaining imitations of grander genres, a short tragedy, an extended prayer form, and poignant scenes of pathos. If the elegiac distich did not encourage extended similes or metaphors, it was ideal for brief astronomical notices about the rising and setting constellations and observations on the passage of time. A short factual statement in the hexameter might be followed in the pentameter by parenthetic comment, reflection, or

[178] A useful article illustrating Ovid's use of this technique in his *Ars Amatoria* is Miller (1997).

expansion. Ovid's range is well illustrated by the variety of narrative passages in *Fasti* 6. Between proem and epilogue there are two 'double' narratives (Carna's two stories and Minerva's two aetia for the *Quinquatrus*) which frame two major central sections: on 9 June, the triple narrative for the *Vestalia* (Priapus and Vesta, the Gallic siege and Metellus' rescue of the Palladium) and his *Matralia* 'diptych' on 11 June where Ino becomes Mater Matuta and Fortuna brings retribution on Tullia.

6. Ovid's debt to Livy in *Fasti* 6

A number of important military anniversaries fell in the month of June, which marked the height of the Roman campaigning season. In addition to these, Ovid's forays into early Roman history in *Fasti* 6 include the deposition of Servius Tullius, the Gallic siege, and the exodus to Tibur in 320 BC of Rome's *tibicines*, whose strike action had been provoked by a harsh censorial edict. Although both Cicero's *de Republica* and Dionysius' *Antiquitates Romanae* offered positive analyses of Rome's archaic and regal period, it was Livy's histories, written barely thirty years earlier than Ovid's *Fasti*, which provided the elegist not only with a reference work for factual detail but also with a foil against which he could exploit interesting tensions and generic comparisons.

Ovid echoes Livy's moralizing slant and emphasis on Roman *pietas*, subscribing, for the most part, to Livy's tenet that Roman military success depended on scrupulous religious observance,[179] an idea especially prominent in Livy's first six books, which cover historical events represented in *Fasti* 6. To illustrate this he makes apposite allusions to some of Livy's strongly delineated characters: M. Furius Camillus, M. Manlius Capitolinus, Appius Claudius Caecus, and L. Caecilius Metellus, the Pontifex Maximus. In addition to the murder of Servius Tullius and the Gallic siege, Ovid focuses on two other significant crises during the rise of the Roman republic: Hannibal's invasion of Italy in the Second Punic War and, through his allusions to Appius Claudius Caecus, the period of the Battle of Sentinum in 295 BC, which determined Rome's hegemony over the

[179] See Levene (1993) 175–203.

tribes of Italy.[180] Ovid's tersely allusive borrowing from Livy's substantial narrative is aided by the affinity between his *Fasti* and Livy's account of Rome's military history, with its conspicuous religious and moral subtext: Roman success is dependent upon Roman *pietas*. An example of this may be seen in Ovid's comparison of M. Manlius Capitolinus and M. Furius Camillus. Livy's account of Manlius' repulsion of the Gallic invasion (390 BC)[181] immediately follows the triumphant capture of Veii by Camillus (396 BC).[182] The historian is consequently drawn to express a moral comparison of the steadfastly religious Camillus with Manlius, whose glory is obfuscated by his subsequent treasonous act of sedition. The reader's awareness of this comparison enhances his appreciation of Ovid's first allusion to the Gallic invasion which comes on 1 June, the *natalis* of the temple of Juno Moneta which is associated with both Camillus and Manlius. Ovid hails the vower of the temple as 'Camille' and, although this was in fact the son of M. Furius, the younger Camillus' act of *pietas* conjures up his more illustrious father. The poet goes on to recall that Manlius' house once stood where the temple now stands, but has been razed through *damnatio memoriae*. A single couplet conjures up Manlius' catastrophic fall from the heroic defender of the Capitolium to the convicted criminal hurled from the *Rupes Tarpeiae*: *quam bene, di magni, pugna cecidisset in illa, | defensor solii, Iuppiter alte, tui* (187–8). Ovid's pentameter, with its solemn opening spondees, evokes Livy's assessment of the religious contribution of both Manlius and Camillus, for as Manlius physically stood on the Capitoline crags, *defensor solii Iovis*, so Camillus, when he delivered his passionate speech in defence of Roman cult practised in Rome, was no less a defender of Jupiter's Capitoline temple.[183]

Ovid's multifaceted portrait of Roman *pietas* touched on the Augustan topos of temple building and rebuilding as a sign of national regeneration, which had been succinctly advocated by Horace in a poem which belongs to the period following Augustus' return

[180] The importance of the Battle of Sentinum is made clear by Livy (10. 21. 12), who points out that four races have united against Rome, before describing unnatural portents, the *devotio* of P. Decius and the demand for a dictator to meet the crisis.

[181] Liv. 5. 47. 1–8. [182] Liv. 5. 21–2. [183] Liv. 5. 51–4.

to Rome in 29 BC: *delicta maiorum immeritus lues,* | *Romane, donec templa refeceris.*[184]

Using the ruined temple of Juno Sospita as a starting point for praise of Augustus as *templorum positor, templorum sancte repostor,*[185] the elegist rephrases the historian: *templorum omnium conditorem ac restitutorem.*[186] In this connection it is the *natalis* of the temple of Mens Bona on 8 June, founded to protect future Roman generals from the improvidence of Flaminius, which signals the second national crisis that Ovid commemorates in the month of June: Hannibal's invasion of Italy. A profusion of *piacula* were performed by the Romans to avert the Carthaginian menace. Livy describes how after their first defeat at the River Trebia in 218 BC the Romans attempt to placate gods who had power and influence in the business of war: large victims for Juno of Lanuvium, a bronze statue for Juno Regina of the Aventine, a *supplicatio* for Algidian Fortuna, a *lectisternium* for Iuventas, and a *supplicatio* for Hercules Custos.[187] All these divinities have a significant role in *Fasti* 6. Juno and Iuventas vie for the *titulus mensis* in the proem, Fortuna, guardian deity of King Servius, avenges his murder, and the month closes with the *natalis* of a temple built with the booty of war dedicated to Hercules Musarum. The catastrophic defeat at Lake Trasimene is attributed by Livy to Flaminius' high-handed neglect of augury and religious observance. In a surge of renewed *pietas* the senate decrees a consultation of the Sibylline books, which results in the vowing of temples to Bona Mens and Venus Erycina.[188] Threatening portents before the Roman victory at the River Metaurus in 207 BC are averted by a solemn procession of Roman women to the Aventine temple of Juno Regina and the sacrifice of two white cows.[189] These two anniversaries of the battles of Lake Trasimene and the Metaurus, the low and high points of the Second Punic War, occur contiguously on 22–3 June, which enables the elegist, on the eve of 23 June, to reflect on the reversal in Roman fortunes with the laconic *postera lux melior* (769).

Two important themes of *Fasti* 6, War and Food, with their moral corollaries of *pietas* and *luxuria*, initiate a generic dialogue between

[184] Hor. *Carm.* 3. 6. 1–2.
[185] Ovid *Fast.* 2. 57–62.
[186] Liv. 4. 20. 7.
[187] Liv. 22. 1. 14–18, 21. 62. 8–9.
[188] Liv. 22. 10. 10.
[189] Liv. 27. 37. 11–15.

historian and poet. Livy's enumeration of the privations of the starving Romans besieged by the Gauls[190] is transformed by Ovid into a distinctly aetiological exegesis about the origins of the altar of Jupitor Pistor in which Vesta miraculously provides flour to make bread for the soldiers to hurl from the ramparts as a sign of superabundance. Here again, Ovid's version is enhanced by a number of literary devices. In a Council of the Gods—a theme imposing on account of its Ennian prototype—the tutelary deities of Rome (Mars, Venus, Vesta, and Quirinus) appeal for Jupiter's help in breaking the siege. This passage has affinities with Mars' appeal to Jupiter to immortalize his son Romulus (*Fast.* 2. 481–90), and together they form one of the many overarching 'frames' which define and accentuate the formal structure of the six books. Mars rebukes Jupiter for delaying Romulus' apotheosis (2. 483–90) and Jupiter willingly accedes to his request. Similarly, when Mars castigates Jupiter for permitting the Romans to be humiliated by the invading Gauls (6. 355–78), Jupiter takes immediate action to ensure a Roman victory.

Another 'frame' linking Book 2 with Book 6 is provided by Ovid's two tragedies of the House of Tarquin, both of which follow Livy's structure, moral direction, and political outcome, for both result in a change of regime in Rome. The aetiological cult story for the ancient veiled statue in the temple of Fortuna derives from Livy's 'Tragedy of the House of Servius Tullius',[191] just as his 'Tragedy of Lucretia'[192] provides the model for Ovid's narrative for the Regifugium on 24 February.[193] Both historian and poet present their drama in three scenes: the birth of a criminal plot, the outrage itself (Lucretia's rape and Servius' murder), and a ghastly sequel (Lucretia's suicide and Tullia's violation of her father's corpse). The historian is concerned to show the negative effects of personal lust and ambition in the Tarquin dynasty in contrast to the single-minded loyalty which the early Romans were expected to show to the Roman state.[194] The elegist retains this background, but, in keeping with his genre, focuses on the motives and emotions of the central female characters, Tullia and

[190] Liv. 5. 48. 1. [191] Liv. 1. 46–8. [192] Liv. 1. 58.

[193] Ovid *Fast.* 2. 721–852.

[194] Cf. A. Feldherr, 'Livy's Revolution: Representation and Civic Identity in Livy's Brutus Narrative', in T. Habinek and A. Schiesaro (eds.), *The Roman Cultural Revolution* (Cambridge, 1997), 136–57.

Lucretia. In presenting his Roman *exemplum* of seemly (Lucretia) and inappropriate (Tullia) womanly conduct, his register is entirely elegiac. Lucretia's rape is described with emotive apostrophe and elegiac language; the elegiac *placent* introduces a catalogue of Lucretia's charms, her panic is described with elegiac empathy (*quid faciat? pugnet?... clamet?... effugiat?*) and, raped, she becomes a *victa puella*, who blushes to relate the whole truth. Tullia, in contrast, presents a portrait of the destructive ruthlessness inherent in a tragic heroine, triumphantly vaunting royalty's power to commit crime: *regia res scelus est* (595). Having goaded her husband to regicide, she violates womanly *pietas* by urging her reluctant driver to crush the dead king's face under her chariot wheels: *an exspectas pretium pietatis amarum?* (607). Such impiety seals her fate and, since this is an aetiological cult story, her punishment is exacted in the temple founded by her father. Livy's Lucretia dies uttering the memorable epigram: *nec ulla deinde impudica Lucretiae exemplo vivet*,[195] which establishes her as an example of chastity for Roman womanhood. When Ovid reintroduces this idea in the context of the Vestal Virgins, he gives it a religious and dynamic twist: under Augustus no Vestal will live unchaste (458, *hoc duce nec viva defodietur humo*). To his elegiac Lucretia he ascribes a more poignant and personal reason for suicide: *veniam vos datis, ipsa nego* (2. 830).

Livy honours Servius Tullius with the title *conditor* because of his military census, his organisation of the centuriate assembly by wealth, and his creation of a hoplite army.[196] Although this ties in with the role of Iuventas as goddess of the Roman *iuvenes* in *Fasti* 6, Ovid sidesteps any generic impropriety by celebrating Servius not as a military innovator but as a temple-founder. It will be seen that he deals with the military achievement of Appius Claudius Caecus in a similar way.

The third republican military landmark mentioned in *Fasti* 6 is the Battle of Sentinum[197] in 295 BC, when the Romans defeated a large force of Samnites and Gauls, allied to Umbrians and Etruscans, effectively ending resistance to the Romans' bid for supremacy among the Italian tribes. Ovid alludes to this crisis on 3 June, the

195 Liv. 1. 58. 10. 196 Liv. 1. 42. 4.
197 Liv. 10. 21. 11–15, 22–30.

natalis of the Temple of Bellona which had been vowed by Appius Claudius Caecus in his campaign against the Etruscans in the previous year (201–2). Ovid sidelines the military issue in favour of an epigrammatic character sketch of the temple founder fifteen years after Sentinum, in which he pays tribute to the old consul's perspicacity in urging the senate not to make terms with Pyrrhus until he had withdrawn his forces from Italy (6. 203–4):[198] *multum animo vidit; lumine captus erat.*

The same metaphor for blindness, *luminibus captus*, is used by Livy in the context of Appius Claudius being punished by the gods for interfering with the organization of Roman religion.[199] One of Livy's illustrations of Appius' interference, namely the protest of the Roman *tibicines* in the form of a voluntary walk-out to Tibur, is colourfully adapted as a social comedy to supply an aition for the costume of the *tibicines*, masks and women's dress, and their custom of wandering through the city on the occasion of the Quinquatrus Minores (657–92, see Introduction 5). The poet retains the essential facts of the story, embroidering the historian's terse account to create an entertaining and dramatic narrative.

Significant by his absence, however, is Appius Claudius Caecus, the harsh censor, whose edict forbade the *tibicines* to participate in the sacrificial banquet held in the temple of Jupiter, which is, in Livy's account, the root cause of the strike.[200] Ovid refers simply to a terrible blow which has fallen on the pipers: *quod subito gratae frangeret artis opum* (662), which he claims was compounded (*adde quod*, 663) by a minor restriction on their professional activities by an unnamed aedile. Ovid's complete omission of the harsh censor, who is the principal reason for Livy telling the story in the first place, seems to go beyond a wish to create a different, elegiac version. The odd wording, *adde quod*, which presupposes a previous fact, has led critics to suggest a lacuna (see note to line 663). A possible explanation of this may perhaps be found a few lines later in line 666: *exilium quodam tempore Tibur erat.* There is a distinct whiff of post-exilic revision, which suggests that, perhaps after Tiberius' accession in AD 14, the exiled poet might have felt it prudent to excise, from

[198] Cf. Cic. *Sen.* 16, *Brut.* 61.

[199] Liv. 9. 29. 11.

[200] Liv. 9. 30. 10: *in aede vescendi ius.*

between lines 662 and 663, a couplet or more echoing Livy's condemnation of the new Princeps' illustrious Claudian ancestor.[201]

In Livy's Preface the historian permits himself the fanciful aetiological reflection that the Romans have, by military conquest, proved themselves to be the children of Mars.[202] It will be observed that the author of *Fasti* has slyly, perhaps in the interests of introducing some elegiac pathos, created a pair of situations[203] where first Romulus himself and then the Roman army require Mars' paternal intervention in order to achieve an outcome worthy of the race: apotheosis or victory. The descent of the Roman race from Venus and Mars, a dynastic theme central to the iconography of Augustus' temple of Mars Ultor, seems to have been ingeniously manipulated for literary effect in Ovid's proem to *Fasti* 6. In her contest for the *titulus mensis Iunii* Ovid's Juno intends to be part of Rome's divine dynasty and equal to the patronal deity of April, Venus Genetrix. Crucial to the argument of her proem speech is her emphasis on her illustrious family connections, and she cites her husband Jupiter (*est aliquid nupsisse Iovi*, 27), her father Saturn, her son Mars, and her grandson Romulus. In short, she adopts a new 'Augustan' matriarchal persona, attributing the immense popularity of her worship in Romulus' city to the personal intervention of her son Mars himself:

> ipse mihi Mavors, 'commendo moenia' dixit
> 'haec tibi: tu pollens urbe nepotis eris'.
> dicta fides sequitur: centum celebramur in aris.
> (53–4)

[201] Appius had his niche and *elogium* in the Forum Augusti (see Degrassi 3. 19, no. 12). He is conjured up by Cicero (*Cael.* 14. 33) as an apt model of *prisci mores.* Two Claudian ancestors prominently praised in Suetonius' brief summary of Tiberius' ancestry (Suet. *Tib.* 2) are Appius Claudius Caecus, for advising against peace with Pyrrhus (cf. *Fast.* 6. 203–4) and Ti. Claudius Nero, who defeated Hasdrubal at the Battle of the River Metaurus (cf. *Fast.* 6. 769–70), a day which Ovid selects as more auspicious than its antecedant for 'Caesar' to advance his standards.

[202] Liv. Preface 7: *ea belli gloria est populo Romano ut, cum suum conditorisque sui parentem Martem potissimum ferat, tam et hoc gentes humanae patiantur aequo animo quam imperium patiuntur.* (So great is Rome's military glory that, when the Romans claim descent from Mars for their founder and themselves, the nations of the world accept this with the same patience with which they endure Roman domination.)

[203] Ovid *Fast.* 2. 483–90, 6. 355–78.

In reinventing herself as the divine grandmother of the children of Mars she has, like the descendants of Divus Iulius, adroitly incorporated herself into the dynastic family represented in the temple of Mars Ultor. In Livy's Preface *Mars parens* was intended to be entirely allegorical. Ovid's aetiological elegy, with its distinctly dynastic undertones, has ingeniously extended the Roman ancestral line from Mars to include Juno, putting the patronal war goddess of *Fasti* 6 into a prominent role as a divine matriarch no less important than *Aeneadum genetrix* herself.

7. The text

Extant today are some 170 manuscripts of Ovid's *Fasti*, of which five represent a tradition of three 'branches'. These are:

A *Vaticanus Reginensis* 1709. The oldest, in Carolingian script dating from the tenth century, contains *Fast.* 1. 1–5. 24. It is generally considered to be the most reliable text and preferable to *U*.

U *Vaticanus Latinus* 3262, *Ursianus*. Eleventh century from Monte Cassino in Lombard script, this contains a complete version of the six books of Ovid's *Fasti* except for the omission of *Fast.* 2. 853–64. Although *U* is generally considered inferior to *A*, it is of particular importance to *Fasti* 6, which is entirely missing from *A*.

D *Monacensis* 8122, sometimes called *Mallerdorfensis*. Twelfth century, containing all six books of Ovid's *Fasti*, omitting *Fast.* 1. 1–70. Merkel (1841) and Peter (1874) regard this as descending from the same archetype as *A* and *U*.

Z (in *AWC*) describes the family *IGM*:

I (*Ilfeldense*) and *G* (*Gemblacensis*) are very similar to one another, which may partly reflect their geographical proximity (see *AWC Praefatio*, p. viii).

I *Ilfeldense.* Eleventh century, containing several fragments from *Fast.* 1 and 2 as well as *Fast.* 2. 568–3. 204 and *Fast.* 4. 317–814, has now been lost.

G *Bruxellensis* 5369–73, known also as *Gemblacensis.* An eleventh-century ms which contains *Fast.* 1. 505–6. 812.

M *Oxoniensis Bodleianus Auct* F. 4. 25, known also as *Mazarinianus.* Fifteenth-century northern Italian. *Fast.* 6. 33–294 are out of order and follow line 406; 31–2 and 271–6 are missing altogether. *M* belonged to the library of Cardinal Mazarin and was later annotated by Nicolaas Heinsius (1620–81), who collated readings from *G* and other mss including *E* (*Erfurtanus*) and *B* (now in the Bodleian Library, No. 8860).[204]

Heinsius' illuminating marginal annotations in *M* were later incorporated into Burman's Variorum edition (Amsterdam 1727). Among the subsequent editions and textual histories of Ovid's *Fasti*, R. Merkel's 1841 edition should be mentioned for its perceptive and reliable textual notes, while F. Peeters is the only critic to include a conjectural stemma in his detailed *Histoire du Texte* (1939). The history of the manuscript tradition of Ovid's *Fasti* incorporated in the introductions to the editions of Bömer (1957–8) and *AWC* (1978)[205] is supported by Wormell and Courtney's comprehensive list of the mss of Ovid's Fasti in *BICS* 24 (1977) and John Richmond, 'Manuscript Traditions and the Transmission of Ovid's Works', in B. W. Boyd (ed.), *Brill's Companion to Ovid* (Leiden, 2002), 443–77.

[204] On this see E. J. Kenney, *The Classical Text: Aspects of Editing in the Age of the Printed Book* (Berkeley, 1974) 59–73.

[205] This is reviewed by J. B. Hall in *Proceedings of the African Classical Association* 16 (1982) 68–75.

List of Alternative Readings

The text used is the fourth edition (1997) of the Teubner (1978) by Alton, Wormell, and Courtney (*AWC*). This list shows the readings preferred by *AWC*, Bömer, who tends to follow Merkel, and this commentary in instances where there is uncertainty.

Line number	***AWC***	**Bömer**	**Littlewood**
2	*leges*	*lege*	*lege*
105	*Alerni*	*Elerni*	*Elerni*
107 & 151	*Cranaen*	*Cranen*	*Cranaen*
229	*detonso*	*dentosa*	*detonso*
434	*seu fuit*	*seu pius*	*seu pius*
662	*gratae*	*Graiae*	*gratae*
648	*vindex*	*iudex*	*iudex*
690	*collegi*	*collegae*	*collegae*
711	*nox*	*lux*	*nox*
757	*at Clymenus Clotho*	*Lachesis Clymenus*	*at Clymenus Clotho*
757	*teneri*	*reneri*	*reneri*

Structural Outline of Ovid's Calendar for June

1–100	**PROEM.** Juno, Iuventas, and Concordia, three Roman goddesses with military interests, claim the *titulus mensis.*
101–95	**1 June** *CARNARIA.* 105–30: Crane is raped by Janus and given power over doorways. 131–68: Crane offers a substitution sacrifice for the life of Proca, the Alban prince. 169–82: The benefits of the simple food of former times, now eaten to honour Carna. 183–95: *Aedes Iunonis Monetae, Martis ad Portam Capenam, Tempestatis.*
196–8	**2 June.** Evening rising of Aquila; morning rising of Hyades.
199–208	**3 June.** *Aedes Bellonae, ad Circum Flaminium.*
209–12	**4 June.** *Aedes Herculis Custodis, ad Circum Flaminium.*
213–18	**5 June.** *natalis* of the Quirinal temple of Semo Sancus Dius Fidius.
219–34	**6 June.** The Flaminica Dialis advises on auspicious wedding dates.
235–6	**7 June.** Morning setting of Bootes. 237–40: Substitution sacrifice of fish to the war god, Volcanus, in the Campus Martius.
241–8	**8 June.** *Aedes Bonae Mentis* built after Battle of Lake Trasimene.
249–468	**9 June** *VESTALIA.* 249–304: Theology: Vesta's nature, temple and cult. 305–18: Offerings to the Hearth Goddess; Vesta and the millstone donkey. 319–48: Priapus attempts to rape Vesta. 349–94: Vesta's bread miracle in the Gallic siege. 395–416: Ovid learns why *matronae* go barefoot at the *Vestalia.* 417–60: Metellus rescues the Palladium from fire in Vesta's temple. 461–8: Two military anniversaries: Callaicus' victory and Crassus' defeat.
469–72	**10 June.** Evening rising of the Dolphin.
473–648	**11 June** *MATRALIA.* *natalis* of twin temples in the Forum Boarium of Mater Matuta and Fortuna. 473–550: (1). Ino the infanticide becomes the kourotrophos goddess, Mater Matuta. 551–62: why slaves are

excluded from the temple and the goddess invoked by aunts. 563–624: (2). Tragedy of Servius Tullius and Fortuna's vengeance on the parricide, Tullia. 625–37: Servius' divine father, Volcanus. 637–48: Marital concord: two monuments built by Augustus and Livia.

649–50 **13 June.** *natalis* of *Aedes Iovis Invicti.*

651–710 *QUINQUATRUS MINUSCULAE.* 651–92: Minerva describes walk-out of the *tibicines* to Tibur. 693–710: The origin of the flute and the flaying of Marsyas.

711–12 **14 June.** Morning rising of Thyone.

713–14 **15 June.** Vesta's 'impurities' are cast into the Tiber.

715–20 **17 June.** Evening Rising of Orion and the Dolphin.

721–4 **18 June.** Third military anniversary: Roman victory at Mount Algidus.

725–8 **19 June.** Sun passes from Gemini into the zodiacal sign of Cancer. Ovid begins his countdown to the end of the month. Festival of Aventine Minerva.

729–32 **20 June.** *natalis* of temple of Summanus.

733–62 **21 June.** With the evening rising of Ophiuchus, Ovid begins a sequence of katasterism and apotheosis: Aesculapius revives Hippolytus, Polyeidus revives Glaucus.

763–8 **22 June.** Fourth military anniversary: Flaminius' defeat at Trasimene.

769–70 **23 June.** Fifth and sixth military anniversaries: Roman victories at Cirta and the River Metaurus.

771–84 **24 June.** Festival of Fors Fortuna on the banks of the Tiber.

785–90 **25–6 June.** A reveller notices Orion's belt, but not the summer solstice.

791–2 **27 June.** *natalis* of the Lares Praestites on Via Sacra.

793–4 **28 June.** *natalis* of *Aedes Iovis Statoris* on Via Sacra.

795–6 **29 June.** *natalis* of temple of Quirinus, a reminder of his apotheosis.

797–812 **30 June.** *natalis* of *Aedes Herculis Musarum* evokes a panegyric of the temple founder's daughter, Augustus' cousin, Marcia. Ovid hints at the conjunction of constellations of Hercules and Lyra.

Commentary on Ovid: *Fasti* Book VI

THE PROEM, 1–100

[Lieberg (1969) 923–43, Blank-Sangmeister (1983) 332–49, Miller (1983) 156–92, Kötzle (1991) 149–61, Miller (1991) 35–43, Hinds (1992), Newlands (1995) 77–8, Loehr (1996) 300–59, Miller (2002) 174–81.]

1. *The proems in the structure of Ovid's* Fasti

A feature of Ovid's structural intention for his *Fasti* is a loose pairing of the programmatic proems of his six books. In each case the similarity which makes them a pair serves to present an internal contrast. The proemia to *Fasti* 1 and 2 are self-consciously programmatic; imperial invocation is accompanied by an elegiac assurance that *arae* (1. 13) or *sacra* (2. 7), not *arma*, will be the poet's theme, which is defined more specifically as calendrical aetiology (1. 1, 2. 7), astronomy (1. 2), and dynastic anniversaries (1. 9, 2. 15–16). In the revised Book 1 the religious rituals of the Roman civic year and its rural counterpart unfold, their harmony sustained by Concordia and Pax Augusta. A literary promise of 'higher themes' at the beginning of Book 2, *nunc primum velis, elegi, maioribus iter,* heralds the celebration of Augustus' most illustrious title, *pater patriae*, in a month which recalls Roman founders and ancestors at the *Lupercalia* (2. 359–452), *Quirinalia* (475–512), *Feralia* (533–70), and *Caristia* (617–38). March and April are dedicated respectively to the divine parents of the Roman race, Mars and Venus, founders of Rome's dual ancestral lines from Romulus and Aeneas, March favouring Mars' worship and April fertility cults under the patronage of Venus Genetrix. May and June begin with a trio of Muses (*Fasti* 5) or goddesses (*Fasti* 6) presenting three alternative claims for the *titulus mensis*: in each case the name of a goddess (Maia/Juno), a Roman age-group (*maiores/iuniores*), and a political concept (*Maiestas*) or personification (*Concordia*). The poet concludes both prologues with a graceful and poetically apposite refusal to favour any one claim against another, and it becomes clear that all three exert their influence and have a place in the content of each book.

2. *Literary and Augustan discourse in the proems*

Books 1 and 6 are linked by a set of interlaced and interlocking, ring-compositional frames, defining the beginning and ending of the first six months. These matching stories offset a thematic contrast of Peace in January and War in June. January makes a stately progress from the civic order of the new magistrates' entry into office on the first day of the month to the great dynastic monuments of Tiberius' Aedes Concordiae and Augustus' Ara Pacis. The month of Juno, Iuventas, and Concordia, on the other hand, midway through the fighting season, records Rome's early struggle for dominion in a series of military anniversaries. It could be suggested that June has a greater potential than March to initiate the generically incompatible topic of War and the *ira* which flares up between Juno and Iuventas in the proem is symbolic [see Introduction 3]. The two months, January and June, are distinguished by literary motifs emphasizing the beginning and end of the work. Ovid begins January by introducing Janus, a god of both temporal and cosmic significance, in a dialogue of unparalleled length (*Fast.* 1. 89–288). As June draws to an end, closure is signposted five times in the countdown of the days to the end of the month, positioned like markers through a cluster of myths of apotheosis—Hippolytus, Aesculapius, Quirinus, Hercules—which precede the finale and suggest comparison with the ending of *Metamorphoses* 15.

The literary discourse initiated in the structure of these two books is apparent in their content. At the beginning of *Fasti* 1 Ovid appears to signal his literary predecessors by alluding directly to their works: *tempora cum causis* (1. 1) points to the *Aetia* of Callimachus, *lapsaque... ortaque signa* (1. 20) to Aratus, while *sacra... dies*, artfully framing the distich 7–8, suggests Propertius 4. 1. 69: *sacra diesque canam*. Ovid's affinities and divergences with these models have been the subject of detailed discussion [see Miller (1982), Barchiesi (1997*a*) 51–2, Fantham (1998) 11–20, Miller (2002) 174–80, Newlands (2002) 202–3, Green (2004*a*) 27–30]. There appears to be in the divine epiphanies of the proems a further underlying Augustan discourse. Book 3 opens with Mars taking off his helmet, in the same spirit as Minerva puts down her spear (*Fast.* 6. 655), as a sign that in Ovid's elegiac poetry, he must discard the warlike character which Ovid invokes in the opening word, *bellice* (*Fast.* 3. 1). The import of Ovid's graceful homage to Venus in Book 4 is that she will now be *celeberrima* not as the patron goddess of his love poetry but as the divine ancestress of the Gens Iulia, and this is signalled in the opening word, *alma* (*Fast.* 4. 1). In the two outer books, *Fasti* 1 and 6, Ovid uses his divine epiphanies to make two stylized programmatic statements. When Janus first appears, he discovers Ovid musing with his tablets on his knees: *sumptis agitarem mente tabellis.* The allusion to Callimachus, surprised by Apollo (*Aet.* fr. 1. 21–2 Pf.), is sharpened by the fact that Janus has affinities with Augustus' patron god, Apollo (Macr. 1. 9. 6, 8. See Green (2004*a*) 125 n.). When Ovid encounters Juno at the beginning of *Fasti* 6, he is seeking inspiration in a lonely glade watered by a pure spring. In each scenario the poet's initial fear is allayed by the god, whom he is able to identify by distinguishing characteristics, which point to the type of poetry Ovid is engaged in. Two-faced Janus holds a rod and keys (1. 99), for he is the doorkeeper of the cosmos, who has the power to direct the poet in his study of the rolling year with its changing constellations. His overt pacifism (253: *nil mihi cum bello*) sounds like a literary negation of epic. [See Miller (1983) 164–74, Barchiesi (1991) 14–17, Hardie (1991) 60–4, Green (2004*a*) 70–1.]

In *Fasti* 6 Ovid recognizes Juno because she resembles her cult statue in the temple of Jupiter Optimus Maximus. Since she represents the most ancient Roman cult of the Capitoline Era, she is in a position to guide him in his study of *sacra... annalibus eruta priscis* (1. 7). She begins by promising him *ius numen videndi* as a practical expedient and warmly endorses his novel use of the elegiac metre for topics which she describes as *magna* (6. 21–4). In contrast to the pacific Janus the goddesses of this proem have much to do with war. Analysis of the poem confirms that what Juno describes as *magna* does indeed include *bella*, seemingly beyond the very borders of generic correctness. Ovid's Juno is drawn from ancient cult and Roman literature; she evokes both Juno of Lanuvium, the ancient Italian warrior goddess, and Virgil's malignant Juno who bursts open the doors of Janus' temple. Still flashing menacing sparks of her former belligerence, the self-confessed champion of Carthage demands the *titulus mensis* for a month which commemorates a major defeat as well as two victories in the Punic Wars. Even her claim to prefer Rome to the many cities which she has favoured in the past is double-edged, for this recalls the ferocity of her former hostility to Rome. The course of Juno's hatred for and final reconciliation with the Aeneadae ends somewhat equivocally in Virgil's *Aeneid.* In response to Jupiter's wishes Juno, finally, *mentem laetata retorsit* (*Aen.* 12. 841); she withdraws her opposition to Latium's new rulers provided that Aeneas and his followers abandon the Trojan name, language, and dress. Similarly Horace has Juno demand the extinction of Troy as the condition for giving her support to Rome (*Carm.* 3. 3. 18–68). However, Dido's curse has promised eternal hostility between Rome and Juno's city, Carthage (Virg. *Aen.* 4. 622–9), and Jupiter, in the Council of the Gods (*Aen.* 10. 11–15), assured the assembled deities that they will have a future opportunity to vent their rivalries: *adveniet iustum pugnae... tempus.* [See Feeney (1984) 339–62, E. L. Harrison, 'The Aeneid and Carthage' in A. Woodman and D. West (eds.), *Poetry and Politics in the Age of Augustus* (Cambridge, 1984) 95–116.] The infamous pride, jealousy, and vengeful character of Virgil's Juno are apparent in her carefully argued case. However, with a mischievous Ovidian twist, the poet reiterates, in the same *sedes*, the key word *nepotis*, to conjure up a new 'Augustan' Juno: a matriarch conscious of her dynastic importance, who quotes the words of her son Mars, '*tu pollens urbe nepotis eris*' (*Fast.* 6. 54), and concludes her speech with the apparently clinching argument: *at nostri Roma nepotis erat* (64).

1–20: *It is not certain why this month is so named. I will list the reasons, you take your choice. Mortals cannot look upon the gods, people say, but we poets are divinely inspired and, because I write about religion, it is fitting that I should see the immortals. I was pondering on the origin of June when I saw... no, not one of those goddesses who appeared to Hesiod nor one who appeared to Paris. But yet, she it was! The sister of her own husband. As recognition dawned, I turned pale, but she allayed my fear.*

1. ***hic quoque mensis habet dubias in nomine causas*:** Ovid's opening line links the month of June with May, which also (*quoque*) lacks an undisputed patronal divinity (cf. *Fast.* 5. 1: *quaeritis unde putem Maio data nomina mensi? | non satis est liquido cognita causa mihi*).

The poet embarks from the same point of departure and initially maintains a superficially parallel structure:

Book 5	**Book 6**
Uncertain origins of the month's title (1–2)	Uncertain origins of the month's title (1–2)
The poet is unsure where to search (3–6)	Divine inspiration of the *vates* (3–8)
He appeals to the Muses on Mount Helicon (7–8)	He visits a secluded grove (9–12)
The Muses appear, divided in their opinions (9)	Epiphany of Juno (13–19)

The descriptions of these two inspirational groves differ significantly. In the proem to *Fasti* 5 Ovid invokes the Muses and their traditional haunt with pretentious grandiloquence. In *Fasti* 6 he destabilizes the familiar literary *Dichterweihe* of Hesiod (*Theog.* 22–35) by including an allusion not to the *Theogony*, but to Hesiod's *Works and Days* (*praeceptor arandi*, 13, 14), and in his admission that he never set eyes on the Muses. His poetic direction is suggested by his encounter with Roman Juno beside a chattering stream in what proves to be a Roman grove, *antiqua religione sacer* (cf. *Fast.* 3. 264).

2. *quae placeat, positis omnibus ipse lege*: 'when all the causes have been laid before you, select (the one) which pleases you.' Ovid uses an abbreviated version of the idiom *ponere ad oculos* (*OLD* s.v. 11*c*) which he uses at *Rem.* 300. Despite the support of Merkel (1841) and *AWC* for the reading of *U*, *leges*, the imperative *lege*, the reading of *GM*, is convincing because of its sense, its colloquial ring, and Ovid's tendency to use imperatives in his proems (1. 3, 25, 2. 18, 3. 2, 7, 4. 1, 5. 7).

3. *facta canam, sed erunt qui me finxisse loquantur*: Ovid here resorts to the claim traditional in poetic prologues that he is a purveyor of Truth (cf. Hes. *Theog.* 27–8, Ovid *Ars* 1. 1, *vera canam*). In his *Fasti* Ovid, imitating Callimachus' didactic style, offers a range of 'proofs' which are speciously appropriate to his subject matter, Roman religion, to assure incredulous readers that the miraculous occurrences which he relates have actually taken place: the stage (*Fast.* 4. 326: *mira sed et scaena testificata loquar*), antiquity (4. 203–4: *pro magno teste vetustas | creditur; acceptam parce movere fidem*) or simply a miracle witnessed by the *vates* himself (3. 370: *credite dicenti, mira sed acta loquor.* Cf. 6. 612 and Call. fr. 442 Pf.).

4. *nullaque mortali numina visa putent*: 'and they think no gods have appeared to a mortal.' An erroneous point of view. Ovid's readers have already, in the previous five books, witnessed numerous conversations beween the poet and the gods.

5. *est deus in nobis: agitante calescimus illo*: 'there is a divine power within me and when it stirs, I am on fire with inspiration.' The theme of poetic inspiration, common in Hellenistic and Roman literature, is associated with Bacchus (Hor. *Carm.* 2. 19. 6, Prop. 3. 2. 9), with the poet's own skill (Ovid *Ars* 3. 549. Cf. *P* 3. 4. 93), while the 'heat' of poetic inspiration, Statius' *Pierius calor* (*Theb.* 1. 3), is humorously reversed to become, in Tomis, *solacia frigida* (*P* 4. 2. 45. Cf. Hor. *Carm.* 3. 25, where inspiration occurs in a frigid landscape). Similarly, in *Met.* 2. 641, Ovid's Ocyrhoë becomes incandescent with prophetic inspiration: *incaluit deo.* It might be suggested that the phrase *agitante calescimus*, with its sharp alliterative *t...t*, *c...c* combined with short vowels, conveys onomatopoeically the idea of whipping up creative energy.

6. *impetus hic sacrae semina mentis habet*: the poet's urge to create, *impetus hic*, originates from *sacrae semina mentis*, 'sparks of divine inspiration' (6). The word *semina* has a philosophical resonance. Ovid's description of poetic inspiration has affinities with Cicero's statement, in the context of the immortality of the soul, that a poet cannot compose *sine caelesti aliquo mentis instinctu* (*Tusc.* 1. 64), but also with the Stoic doctrine of fire in creation, a concept which is present in Virgil (*Aen.* 6. 730–1), where Anchises explains the return of souls to the *anima mundi*: *igneus est ollis vigor et caelestis origo | seminibus.* It is a characteristic feature of Ovid's elegiac verse to place a key word immediately before the main caesura in the pentameter for emphasis so that the reader is prepared for what follows. In this instance the word *sacrae* points forward to the following couplet in which Ovid claims that he has a right to see the gods because his subject is *sacra*.

7–8. *fas mihi praecipue voltus vidisse deorum | vel quia sum vates, vel quia sacra cano*: Ovid claims that he especially (*mihi praecipue*) is permitted to see the faces of the gods because he is *vates* and writes about Roman religion. The poet mentions that he cannot 'look upon the faces of the gods' when the god is grotesque, like Janus (*Fast.* 1. 147–8) or, like Vesta, invisible (6. 253–4). The Augustan poets used the term *vates* to refer to a poet of elevated themes which included religion and cosmology [see Newman (1967), Hardie (1986) 16–18]. The poetic activity of a *vates* was often described by the word *canere* [see Miller (1991) 9, Green (2004*a*) 28]. Ovid introduces this with a phrase that has religious connotations, *fas mihi*: 'it is divinely ordained that I should.' Concluding his dedication to Book 1, Ovid uses the word *vates* to describe both himself and his dedicatee, Germanicus, *vates rege vatis habenas*, beginning the hexameter in the formulaic language of Roman religion and concluding the pentameter with a prayer: *si licet et fas est*... | *auspice te felix totus ut annus eat* (*Fast.* 1. 25–6). Throughout his *Fasti* Ovid uses the word *vates* to refer to himself as a poet of the Roman calendar and religion: both Janus and Mars, at the beginning of their books, address Ovid as *vates operose dierum* (1. 101, 3. 177), as *vates* Ovid invokes the favour of Bacchus (*Bacche, fave vati*, 3. 714) and, more intimately, Venus (*et vatem et mensem scis, Venus, esse tuos*, 4. 14). [See Pasco-Pranger (2000) 275–91.]

9–10. *est nemus arboribus densum, secretus ab omni | voce locus, si non obstreperetur aquis*: the densely wooded grove, remote (*secretus*) from all sound save that of a murmuring stream, was a literary *locus* for poetic inspiration (cf. Call. *Aet.* I fr. 1. 27–8 Pf., *Hymn* 2. 112). The Roman poets adapted this to suit their purpose: Propertius (3. 1. 1–2) to express his allegiance to the Alexandrian poets: *Callimachi Manes et Coi sacra Philitae | in vestrum quaeso me sinite ire nemus* (cf. Hor. *Carm.* 1. 1. 29–32, 3. 4. 5–8); Lucretius to indicate his originality in using hexametric verse to expound the philosophy of Epicurus, who was reputedly hostile to verse: *avia Pieridum peragro loca nullius ante | trita solo. iuvat integros accedere fontis | atque haurire.* (1. 926–8, cf. Virg. *G* 3. 291 ff., 3. 40–1: *Dryadum silvas saltusque sequamur | intactos*, Prop. 3. 1. 18 and Hor. *Carm.* 3. 25. 12–14). The description of the waters which Roman poets drank from the stream indicated the type of verse they might be inspired to compose, for example, Ennius' *magni fontes* (Prop. 3. 3. 5), Propertius' *Philitea aqua* (3. 3. 52), and Ovid's own *exiguis haustibus* (*Fast.* 3. 274). Such descriptions might be highly allusive and symbolic. Virgil's well-known phrase *itur in antiquam silvam* (*Aen.* 6. 179) refers both to the context, Aeneas entering an ancient forest, and to the poet's own intertextual borrowing of material from the archaic (*antiquus*) Ennius. [This passage is fully discussed by Hinds (1998) 10–16. On sources of poetic inspiration see W. Kroll, *Studien zur Verständnis der römischen Literatur* (Stuttgart, 1924) 24–43, A. Kambylis, *Die Dichterweihe und ihre Symbolik* (Heidelberg, 1965), and Knox (1985) 107–19.]

11–12. *hic ego quaerebam, coepti quae mensis origo | esset*: as the word *origo*, signifying *aition*, suggests, Ovid's visit to a grove with inspirational waters to learn the origins of the month derives from Callimachus' Dream (*Aet.* 1 fr. 2. 1–5 Pf.), in which he tells how Hesiod receives his inspiration from the Muses on Mount Helicon. Ovid does not identify his grove, but the appearance of Juno might suggest to Roman readers the grove sacred to Juno below the Esquiline (Ovid *Fast.* 2. 432). In the parallel passage in Book 5 Ovid's periphrastic reference to the Muses' fount of inspiration is elaborated with an extravaganza of Greek polysyllabics to the point of geographical inaccuracy in order to, as Barchiesi puts it, out-Callimachus Callimachus: *dicite, quae fontes Aganippidos Hippocrenes | grata Medusaei signa tenetis equi!* (*Fast.* 5. 7–8). [See Barchiesi (1991). On the hydrography of Mount Helicon, see W. Clausen, *A Commentary on Virgil, Eclogues* (Oxford, 1994) 199–201.]

13–14. *ecce, deas vidi, non quas praeceptor arandi | viderat, Ascraeas cum sequeretur oves*: the combination of *ecce* and the polyptoton *vidi* . . . *viderat* heighten the drama of Juno's epiphany. The Muses (*deas*), and their meeting with Hesiod among his sheep in Boeotia (*Ascraeas oves*), initially described by Hesiod himself (*Theog.* 22–5), became part of the literary programme set out by Callimachus (*Aet.* 1 fr. 2. 1–2 Pf. and 4. fr. 112. 5–6 Pf.) and was taken up by Virgil (*Ecl.* 6. 70, *G.* 2. 176) and Propertius (2. 10. 25–6). [For a summary of divine epiphanies initiating literary inspiration, see Nisbet and Hubbard (1978) 315–6. The Alexandrian notion of a poetic lineage passing from Hesiod to Callimachus and its acceptance by the Augustan poets is fully discussed by Cameron (1995) 362–86, who includes a comprehensive bibliography. See also Ross (1975) 32–4, 119.]

13, 15. *non quas . . . nec quas*: having created an appropriate setting for a divine epiphany Ovid continues to build up, only to disappoint, our expectations by naming two famous groups of goddesses whom he did not see: the Muses and the trio of Paris' Judgement. As Miller (1991: 38) perceptively observes: 'unspoken aspects of both divine encounters cited leap to mind in the present context.' Although Hesiod's encounter with the Muses occurred in his *Theogony*, the *praeceptor arandi* (13) belonged to the *Works and Days*, which was of obvious relevance to Ovid as the poet of *tempora, dies*, and *Romani anni* (21). The Judgement of Paris is cited here partly because of the difficulty of the choice involved (*contulit*, 14), which Ovid passes over to his readers (*quae placeat, positis omnibus ipse lege*, 2). By finishing the pentameter with the studiedly casual correction *ex illis sed tamen una fuit* (16), which he then rephrases, *ex illis fuit una* (17), to put *una* in a more emphatic position, Ovid moves steadily towards his climax from the less impressive group (*deas*, 13) to a single goddess (*una*, 17) instantly identifiable by the subsequent epic periphrasis: *sui germana mariti.*

15–16. *nec quas Priamides in aquosae vallibus Idae | contulit*: 'nor those whom the son of Priam encountered on the slopes of well-watered Ida.' The numerous springs on Mount Ida (Hom. *Il.* 8. 47, 14. 157, 20. 59) are mentioned in Book 4 as a favourite haunt of the Magna Mater (4. 250). Ovid's description of the secluded grove and his terror at seeing the goddess has strong similarities with *Heroides* 16.53–68, where Paris describes to Helen his encounter with the three goddesses on Mount Ida. The ancient rivalry between Juno and Venus and their hostility/allegiance to Troy and the Aeneadae, which runs through Augustan literature, highlights the theme of the Trojan ancestry of the *Gens Iulia.* Allusions to the celebrated beauty contest and its sacred Trojan venue are frequently mentioned in an Augustan context. (cf. Hor. *Carm.* 3. 3. 18–19, *Ilion, Ilion | fatalis incestusque iudex*). Venus' victory is mentioned, in Ovid's proem to April in conjunction with her illustrious Julian descendants (4. 121–4), while the proem to Juno's month finds Juno again rehearsing her grievance *Idaeo iudice victa* (44). The reader's suspense is heightened by the pause after the enjambement of *contulit*. Following a dactylic first foot in the pentameter, this is a common feature of Ovidian elegiacs.

16. *ex illis sed tamen una fuit*: 'but yet she was one of those.' A colloquially worded sentence; *tamen* belongs to a range of prosaic adverbs, including *bene*, *male*, and *paene*, which Ovid frequently uses in elegiac verse. [Kenney (2002) 42–3 contrasts Ovid's 830 instances of this to Virgil's 64.]

18. *quae stat in arce Iovis*: anticipating his readers' scepticism concerning the identity of the gods whom he encounters, Ovid claims that he recognizes Juno from a cult statue which he has seen in the Capitoline temple of Jupiter Optimus Maximus. Coins from the reigns of Vespasian and Domitian depict this temple with the three cult statues of Jupiter, Juno, and Minerva (Steinby 3. 438).

19. *horrueram tacitoque animum pallore fatebar*: Ovid's pallor and speechlessness mirror his reaction to Janus (*Fast.* 1. 93–8. cf. 3. 331–2, Virg. *Aen.* 4. 279–80).

The Speeches of Juno and Iuventas

Juno's speech, '*De titulo mensis sui*', illustrates Ovid's skill in adapting conventional Roman rhetorical technique to the feminine arguments of the imperious goddess who outlines her credentials in a formal sequence of *exordium*, *narratio/argumentum*, and *peroratio*, using devices familiar from traditional Roman oratorical practice. Both she and her daughter, Iuventas, present their cases, *De titulo mensis sui*, in the style of a courtroom drama and, since Ovid is cast as the *iudex*, each goddess begins with a brief *captatio benevolentiae*. The disparity of their arguments reflects the character of the protagonists. Juno presents her credentials sequentially: she possesses superior qualifications of birth and marriage; she merits honour for having put Rome's interests before her own despite her ties with numerous other cities. Finally, her own son, Mars, who is father of the Founder, has personally granted her a place in Roman cult.

Juno's Speech

21–64: *'Have the courage, poet of the Roman year, to celebrate great matters in your elegiac verse. Your literary innovation has won you the right to behold the gods. June takes its name from Juno. It's no small thing to be Jupiter's wife and sister. I was the first daughter of Saturn, who came to this land first, which is why Rome is named Saturnia.* **33–40:** *As Jupiter's spouse, I share his temple. Will you grudge me the patronage of June, when that tart (Maia) gives her name to May? Am I to call no month my own when I am named Lucina from the very days that constitute a month?* **41–52:** *If this were so, I would regret relinquishing my anger, dutifully, against the Trojan race. I would regret that Sparta, Argos, my own Mycenae, ancient Samos have taken second place to— Latium! Not to mention King Tatius and my Junonicultists of Falerii. But I have no regrets. No race is dearer to me.* **53–64:** *Mars himself promised me power in my grandson's city. And so it was. Smoke rises from one hundred altars. Yet there is nothing that I value more highly than the honour of the month. Look at the calendars of Aricia, Laurentum, Lanuvium! They all have a month of Juno. Tibur and Praeneste too. And those towns were not founded by Romulus.'*

21–3. *'o vates Romani conditor anni | . . . ius tibi fecisti numen caeleste videndi'*: 'O poet who first expounded the Roman calendar . . . you yourself have won the right to behold the gods.' Rephrasing Ovid's opening claim (7–8) that, as *vates*, he has the right to see the gods, Juno's *exordium* begins with a traditional *captatio benevolentiae* and she compliments her '*iudex*' on winning for himself (*fecisti*) by his poetic endeavours the right to behold her. Whilst *conditor*, used in a literary sense, could simply mean 'poet of the Roman year' (*OLD* s.v. 3), here it more probably takes on a meaning closer to 'founder of a genre' (cf. Plin. *Nat.* praef. 26, 35. 199, Quint. *Inst.* 10. 1. 95, and *OLD* s.v. 2a). Ovid had used *conditor* to describe an earlier literary invention, his mock-didactic *Ars Amatoria* (*P* 2. 11. 2, *Naso, parum faustae conditor Artis*), which Miller (1991: 155, n. 114) rightly, I think, extends to cover the poet's invention of the *ars* which he expounds. The programmatic statement at the beginning of *Fasti* 2, *nunc primum velis, elegi, maioribus itis* (3), appears to claim that, in combining panegyric with imperial anniversaries, Ovid has widened the scope of his *Fasti* beyond that of Propertius' fourth book. Propertius, however, had already pointed the way by writing an extended encomium of Augustus' victory at Actium (4. 6. 11–67) which featured so much battle description that he concludes, almost apologetically *bella satis cecini* (4. 6. 68). He suggests that he is initiating a generic innovation of terrifying magnitude in attempting to celebrate Augustus' most sacred title, *pater patriae*, in elegiacs: *quid volui demens elegis imponere tantum | ponderis?* (125–6). In *Fasti* 6, in continuance of this poetic discourse, the poet cites Juno as his authority for the suitability of the elegiac metre (*exiguos modos*, 22, *numeris tuis*, 24) to describe religious festivals.

22. *'ause per exiguos magna referre modos'*: 'poet, who has dared to expound high themes in a humble metre.' Traditionally *audere* signified the courage of writers who attempted a new form or style. Catullus apostrophizes the historian Nepos, *cum ausus es unus Italorum* (Cat. 1. 5–6), Horace describes Lucilius' first venture into satire: *est Lucilius ausus | primus in hunc operis componere carmina morem* (Hor. *Serm.* 2. 1. 62), while Virgil uses *ausus* in his claim to place his *Georgics* in the tradition of Hesiod: *ingredior sanctos ausus recludere fontis | Ascraeumque cano Romana per oppida carmen* (*G* 2. 175–6; cf. Lucr. 1. 117–19, Ovid *Am.* 2. 1. 62). Horace, in his passage on matching matter to metre (*AP* 73–98), pairs *exiguos* with *elegos*: *quis tamen exiguos elegos emiserit auctor | grammatici certant* (77–8). The adjective *exiguus* seems to have had literary connotations of 'slender', 'light', 'inadequate for epic', an idea which Ovid may have intended to convey when he visits the grove of Egeria, *dea grata Camenis* (*Fast.* 3. 275) and drinks *exiguis haustibus* (274) from Egeria's stream, the irregular murmur of which (*incerto lapidosus murmure rivus*, 273) suggests the 'limping' quality of the elegiac couplet with its unequally matched hexameter and pentameter: *versibus impariter iunctis* (Hor. *AP* 75; cf. Ovid *Am.* 2. 17. 21). Since Ovid describes Egeria's grove *antiqua religione sacra* (*Fast.* 3. 264), devoting eight lines to its association with myth and legend, the inspiration he derives from the stream might be associated with his chosen material: the aetiology of sacred places and rituals. [See Pasco-Pranger (2000) 291–312, where Egeria and her association with King Numa have been examined in a literary context.] Ovid professes to feel it was daring or avant-garde to use the elegiac metre for religious aetiology, possibly because Augustus was omnipresent in Roman religion; this aspect of Ovid's poetic programme resurfaces on several occasions. Consequently, in the proem to *Fasti* 6 Juno's blessing and support for Ovid's use of the lowly elegiac metre (*exiguos modos*) for the Roman calendar is significant.

24. *'cum placuit numeris condere festa tuis'*: significantly Juno repeats the word *condere*, as she used *conditor* in line 21 to emphasize that Ovid is the first Roman poet to explain the festivals of the Roman calendar in verse, which she identifies as elegiac in the words *numeris tuis*, 'your own metre'. If Ovid follows Callimachus' example in using elegiacs for aetiological poetry, lines 21 and 24 underline the Roman poet's awareness of the difference between the wide-ranging Hellenic antiquarianism of Callimachus and the patriotic implications of a poem celebrating Roman religious festivals (*numeris condere festa tuis*) within the framework of the Julian calendar (*Romani conditor anni*).

25–6. *'ne tamen ignores . . . | Iunius a nostro nomine nomen habet'*: 'for the avoidance of doubt . . . June takes its name from mine.' Initially tactful, 'in case you should be unaware', Juno continues more assertively, 'and so you are not misled by a common misconception', and finishes with a blunt statement of fact: 'June derives its name from Juno.' I am indebted to John Miller for drawing my attention to the striking assonance which reiterates the second syllable of Juno, *no(stro) no(mine) no(men)*, at the centre of the pentameter as well as to the pattern *-isse Iovi, Iovis esse* in line 27.

27. *'est aliquid nupsisse Iovi, Iovis esse sororem'*: the centre of the hexameter is the focus for a striking sound pattern, *-isse Iovi, Iovis esse*, arranged chiastically which draws attention, through polyptoton, to Juno's dual relationship with Jupiter. The irony implicit in the understatement, *est aliquid*, is present in several examples of this idiom from Ovid's exile period, for example, *est aliquid magnis crimen abesse malis* (*Fast.* 1. 484. Cf. *P* 2. 7. 65, 2. 8. 9).

28. *'fratre magis, dubito, glorier anne viro'*: 'I'm not sure whether to preen myself more on account of my brother or my husband.' The key words *fratre* and *viro* frame the pentameter in the centre of which stand the two verbs *dubito* and *glorier*. By expanding Virgil's simple *et* *soror et coniunx* (*Aen.* 1. 47), Ovid humorously exploits Juno's double relationship with Jupiter here as on several occasions in his *Metamorphoses* (*Met.* 1. 620, 3. 266).

29. '*si genus aspicitur*': cf. *si torus in pretio est* (33). Maintaining her courtroom style, Juno proceeds to illustrate the two aspects of her pedigree, birth and marriage, in two pairs of balancing couplets.

30. '*Saturni sors ego prima fui*': *sors* is used uniquely here in the sense of offspring, as though there were some primordial sanction in Juno being 'allotted' first to her father, Saturn. The word calls to mind Saturn's better known *sors*, the oracle which tells of his overthrow by his son Jupiter which Erato mentions in connection with the noise made by the Curetes: *reddita Saturno sors haec erat* (*Fast.* 4. 197). As often, Ovid repeats, for rhetorical effect, the point he has made in the hexameter: *Saturnum prima parentem | feci* (29). The rhetorical force of the triple repetition, *Saturnum... Saturni... Saturnia*, highlights the ancient god whose archaic temple stood on the lower slopes of the Capitoline Hill where processions would pass on the way up to the temple of Iuppiter Optimus Maximus. Ovid, who tends to weave together cult stories from deities celebrated within a specific quarter of Rome, includes in the first quarter of *Fasti* 6 a group of cults centred on the ancient Capitol. As Saturn's daughter, Juno has a right to honour in the city in which the cult of Jupiter was predominant during the 'Capitoline Era'. Jupiter's expulsion of Saturn gives *Saturnia Roma* an edge which has affinities with Virgil's fondness for juxtaposing hostile nations (cf. *Karthago Romanis*, *Aen.* 10. 12, *Troias Achivis*, 10. 89). This emphasis on Rome's ancient titanic origins is balanced in Janus' speech in *Fasti* 1 where there is an almost matching triple allusion: *Saturnum receptum* (235) (*gens*) *Saturnia* (237), *Saturnia invidiosa* (265–6). The Roman poets derived the expression *gens Saturnia* from the expulsion of Saturn in the same way as Latium was said to derive from *latente deo* (Virg. *Aen.* 8. 357–8). Ovid later highlights the ancient origins of Vesta, who is associated with the elements of fire and earth, by describing her as *virgo Saturnia* (383), in whose care are the most sacred symbols of Rome.

32. '*haec illi a caelo*': Ovid elides the long *i* of *illi* with the long *a* before *caelo* (cf. Prop. 2. 14. 10, and see Platnauer 76).

33. ***'si torus in pretio est; dicor matrona Tonantis'***: the humorously incongruous juxtaposition of the domestic *matrona* with Iuppiter Tonans is repeated in *Metamorphosis* 2. 466 (cf. *matertera Bacchi*, *Fast.* 6. 523). Jupiter's association with thunder and weather is generally reflected in his epithets Pluvialis, Imbricitor, Serenator, and Fulgurator. Augustus' personal association with Iuppiter Tonans (*RG* 19, Suet. *Aug.* 29. 1) led him to found an exquisitely decorated marble temple overlooking the Forum Romanum (Ovid, *Fast.* 2. 69, Plin. *Nat.* 34. 79, 36. 50). The thunderbolts of Augustus' wrath and the implicit equation of Augustus and Iuppiter Tonans provide a leitmotiv in the exile poems (*Tr.* 1. 1. 72, 81–2, 1. 3. 11, 1. 9. 21, 4. 3. 1, 4. 8. 45, 5. 2. 53, 5. 3. 29–30, 5. 14. 27). [See Weinstock (1971) 300–5, Barchiesi (1997*a*) 25.] The poetic equation of Augustus with Jupiter was a feature of imperial panegyric (*Fast.* 3. 421), which implied the further equation of Livia with Juno, which appears in such lines as *sola toro magni digna reperta Iovis* (*Fast.* 1. 650), an idea rephrased in *P* 3. 1. 117. Such reminders of Juno's domestic powerbase, her feuds with the Aeneadae and her stepson Hercules, might suggest for some a humorous parallel with Livia's less-than-cordial relationship with her Julian stepfamily. [On Livia–Juno see K. Scott, 'Emperor Worship in Ovid', *TAPA* 61 (1930) 43–69, Barratt (2002) 208–14.]

34. ***'iunctaque Tarpeio sunt mea templa Iovi'***: the old name for the Capitoline Hill was Mons Tarpeius (Var. *L* 5. 41). The temple of Jupiter Optimus Maximus was built on the SW eminence above the cliffs overlooking the Tiber, known as *Rupes Tarpeiae* (cf. Prop. 4. 4. 29, *Tarpeia . . . ab arce*). Juno mentions three times her joint occupancy of Jupiter's temple (*Fast.* 6. 18, 34, 52), disregarding the third member of the Capitoline triad, Minerva, and stresses her own propinquity to Jupiter in pointedly domestic terms: *hic teneam cum Iove templa meo* (6. 52). In reality the Capitoline temple was known as *aedes Iovis Optimi Maximi.* Although the temple was not dedicated until the first year of the Roman Republic (Liv. 2. 8. 6–8), it had been vowed by Tarquinius Priscus and the building probably completed in the reign of the second Tarquin (Liv. 1. 55. 1), using Etruscan workmen from Veii, who had been commissioned to make a terracotta cult statue of Jupiter (Plin. *Nat.* 35. 157) and possibly one of

Juno to which Ovid alludes in line 18 [see J. R. Fears, 'The Cult of Jupiter and Roman Imperial Ideology', *ANRW* II. 17. 1 (1981) 7–139]. It is significant that Augustus initiated a new religious focus from the Capitoline gods to his own Palatine precinct, which had obvious affinities with the Athenian acropolis in its heroon (*casa Romuli*) and 'cave of Pan' (the Lupercal).

35. *'an potuit Maio paelex dare nomina mensi'*: Juno descends abruptly from the dignity of her Roman cult figure to Hera-like jealousy of Jupiter's mistress Maia, who, though a mere *paelex*, has claimed the *titulus mensis* for May (*Fast.* 5. 81–106).

37. *'cur igitur regina vocor princepsque dearum'*: Juno's official cult title in Rome and in other cult centres was *regina* (Cic. *Dom.* 144, *Ver.* 184). This title came with her from Veii to her new temple of Juno Regina on the Aventine. At her major cult centre at Lanuvium she was Juno Seispes Mater Regina.

39. *'an facient mensem luces, Lucinaque ab illis | dicar?'*: Juno's specious argument that days (*luces*) make up the month and Juno Lucina derives her name from this is no more than legal casuistry (cf. *Fast.* 3. 255, *tu nobis lucem, Lucina, dedisti.* Cf. *Fast.* 2. 449–50). Pliny offers the alternative suggestion (Plin. *Nat.* 16. 235) that Lucina derives from *lucus*, specifically a sacred grove below the Esquiline Hill. A connection with fertility and childbirth becomes apparent if we assume that Pliny's grove is the grove sacred to Juno described by Ovid (*monte sub Esquilio . . . | Iunonis magnae nomine lucus*, Ovid *Fast.* 2. 435–6). As a symbol of her power to promote fecundity, Juno of Lanuvium was traditionally depicted wearing the skin of a male goat with large horns while, according to Ovid, the goat sacrifice acceptable to Juno is *dux gregis cornu per tempora dura recurvo* (*Am.* 3. 13. 17).

41–7. *'tum me paeniteat . . . paeniteat . . . paeniteat'*: Juno's use of the present subjunctive in a conditional sense carries the weight of a threat. If Ovid were disinclined to grant her the *titulus mensis*, then she would perhaps reconsider her policy of appeasement. The triple anaphora gives rhetorical emphasis to Juno's claim that her reconciliation with Rome has obliged her to make major concessions: to renounce her previous position of righteous indignation (towards Troy) and to cede her personal loyalty and inclination (on behalf of Carthage, Sparta, Argos, Mycenae, and Samos).

41. '*causa duplex irae*': to add poetic weight to these six lines Ovid echoes closely the Virgilian Juno's reasons for persecuting the Trojans at the very beginning of the *Aeneid.* Her *causae irarum saevique dolores* (*Aen.* 1. 25) are recalled in the words of Ovid's Juno, who claims that her *causa irae* is twofold, that she is grieving (*dolebam*, *Fast.* 6. 43) both *rapto Ganymede* (43; cf. *Aen.* 1. 28, *rapti Ganymedis*) and *forma*... *Idaeo iudice victa* (44; cf. *Aen.* 1. 27, *spretaeque iniuria formae*). Virgil's Juno adds to these *et genus invisum* (*Aen.* 1. 28) which corresponds to Ovid's *in genus Electrae Dardaniaeque domus* (42; cf. *Fast.* 4. 31–5), a reference to the Trojans' ancestor Dardanus, child of Jupiter and—another *paelex*—Electra. Finally, in the same two passages, both Virgil and Ovid offer as proof of Juno's partiality for Carthage the fact that she keeps there her *currus et arma* (*Aen.* 1. 16–18, *Fast.* 6. 46). This may have taken the form of a statue of an armed Juno in her chariot [see R. G. Austin, *Commentary on Aeneid 1* (Oxford, 1971), line 17]. Through the ritual and formula of *evocatio*, a tutelary god of an enemy city, often common to both sides, could be persuaded to leave that city for Rome provided that he received in his new abode comparable honours such as a temple, a statue, and *Ludi Votivi.* The transportation of Juno's *currus et arma* to Rome corresponds to Macrobius' description of an *evocatio* from Carthage of a major goddess (Macr. 3. 9. 7–8). Juno's worship in Carthage was historical; Hannibal is recorded dedicating an altar to Juno Lacinia in 205 BC when the tide of the Punic Wars had turned in Rome's favour (Liv. 28. 46. 16). In *Fasti* 6 (763–70) anniversaries are commemorated of the Roman defeat at Lake Trasimene in 217 BC (22 June) and their victories at the River Metaurus in 207 BC and over Syphax at Cirta in 203 BC (23 June) which heighten the tensions implicit both in Juno's expression of her devotion to Carthage and Iuventas' support for the heroic struggle of the Roman *iuvenes.*

48–51. '*subposuisse*... *succubuisse*': continuing the structural balance begun by the triple anaphora *paeniteat*... *paeniteat*... *paeniteat*, at the beginning of this section of Juno's argument, these two perfect infinitives carry the same meaning and occupy the same place in consecutive pentameters.

49–50. '*adde senem Tatium Iunonicolasque Faliscos* | *quos ego Romanis succubuisse tuli*': the wording is interesting. Ovid, who is concerned with dramatic effects, reminds the reader by his choice of words that manipulation of fact is part of courtroom rhetoric. Juno claims that she has induced (*tuli*) old King Tatius to be subjugated to Rome. Here *tuli* should be taken in the more forceful sense of 'induced' (Stat. *Theb.* 4. 755; see *OLD* s.v. 2*b*) rather than simply 'allow' (*OLD* s.v. 21). Concordia, who later stresses the virtue of joining forces, phrases this more diplomatically, implying that Romulus and Tatius formed a mutually agreeable alliance: *binaque cum populis regna coisse suis* (94). Rome's conquest of Juno's Faliscan worshippers, in whose cult activities Ovid and his wife participate in *Amores* 3. 13, is recorded in *Fasti* 3. 843–4. The territory of the Faliscans lay some distance north of Rome between the lands of the Etruscans and the Sabines. Their tutelary goddess was Juno Curitis. Iconographically represented holding a spear, she was, like Juno of Lanuvium, a fertility goddess who promised victory in battle, which is attested by terracotta antefixes from her temple representing *sileni* and other Dionysiac motifs, which can be seen in the Villa Giulia, Rome. The chief sanctuary of Juno Curitis was an Etruscan-style temple with three *cellae* at Celle, which stood outside the city of Falerii (Ovid *Am.* 3. 13. 35). In 241 BC the Faliscans were conclusively defeated by Rome and their city destroyed. Ovid's reference to *Iunonicolas Faliscos* would be readily understood because their new settlement, Falerii Novi, was officially registered as *colonia Iunonia.*

51. ***'sed neque paeniteat nec gens mihi carior ulla est'***: Juno is now building up her speech to an emotional climax. A final *paeniteat* picks up the triple *paeniteat* (41–7). The goddess' claim that Rome is dearer to her than any other city recalls by verbal allusion Jupiter's prophecy at the end of the *Aeneid*: *nec gens ulla tuos aeque celebrabit honores* (12. 840).

52. ***'hic colar, hic teneam cum Iove templa meo'***: 'here let me be worshipped, here may I share a temple with my dear Jupiter.' The optative present subjunctive brings a note of pleading into Juno's allusions to divine domesticity in Jupiter's Capitoline temple, which is emphasized by Ovid elegantly rephrasing *mea templa Iovi* (34) in the same *sedes.*

53–4. ***'ipse mihi Mavors "commendo moenia" dixit | "haec tibi; tu pollens urbe nepotis eris."'***: Juno moves from her husband to her son, Mars, who, she claims, has promised his mother power in her grandson Romulus' city. In Book 5 Mars expresses similar appreciation to the humble Flora, who helped Juno to become pregnant in the first place: '*habeto* | *tu quoque Romulea,' dixit, 'in urbe locum*' (*Fast.* 5. 259–60). This mother–son relationship is underlined in Mars' month in a passage which explains why Roman *matronae* worship at Mars' shrine: *mater amat nuptis; matris me turba frequentat* (*Fast.* 3. 251). The third and sixth months, March and June, are linked by the relationship between their patronal deities; both deities are associated with war and with generation (Mars) or fertility (Juno). [See D. Porte, 'La Fleur d'Olène et la naissance de Mars', *Latomus* 92 (1983) 877. Kötzle (1991) 130, sees Juno's role as Mars' mother as a proof of her function of fertility goddess.]

58. '*suburbani dant mihi munus idem.*': Juno now unfolds her *peroratio* with solemn anaphora *inspice... inspice* (59–62). *munus idem* refers to the *titulus mensis* which she claims she already has in the calendars of Aricia, Laurentum, Lanuvium, Tibur, and Praeneste. Ovid's reference to Praeneste is probably a compliment to Verrius Flaccus, whose *Fasti Praenestini* Ovid follows closely in his *Fasti* and which was eventually carved in marble and posted up, with a statue of Verrius himself, in his home town of Praeneste. No Fasti survive from Laurentum and from the *Fasti Lanuvini* only seven days of *mensis Ianuarius* [Degrassi 236]. Further allusions to the contents of Roman and Latin calendars may be found in *Fast.* 1. 289, 657–8, 3. 87–98. [See Pasco-Pranger (2000) and Miller (2002) 172–3.]

63. '*Iunonale leges tempus!*': 'in their calendars you will read "month of Juno"!' Ovid refers to the marble slabs or wooden boards on which the civic calendars or *Fasti* were posted in public places. The poet has apparently coined the words *Iunonale* and *Iunonicolas* (49), as in *Met.* 4. 173 he coined *Iunonigena.*

63–4. '*nec Romulus illas* | *condidit, at nostri Roma nepotis erat*': the final stage of Juno's argument (53–64) begins and ends with Rome's founder, her grandson Romulus. Since, she argues, she is honoured in cities that Romulus did not found, her implicit conclusion is that she deserves to be honoured in Rome, which he did. *Roma nepotis* (64) is a rephrasing of *urbe nepotis* (54), making this last section, in which Juno describes the honour she receives from the other towns of Latium, a short ring composition beginning and ending with Rome.

Iuno, Iuventas, and Hercules: divine trinity of Roman war

It is worth considering more closely the tripartite relationship of Juno, Iuventas, and Hercules in the context of Roman warfare. The only occasion when the three deities were honoured together in Rome was in 218 BC, after the Roman defeat at the River Trebia, when Hannibal was ravaging Italy with his army: Juno was given a bronze statue for her temple on the Aventine and a *lectisternium* was held in Rome for Iuventas and Hercules (who was called, in connection with his monuments in the Forum Boarium, Invictus, Victor, and Triumphator, Liv. 21. 62. 9). Before the end of the subsequent quarter-of-a-century all three received a temple: Juno Sospita (dedicated 194 BC, Liv. 32. 30. 10), Iuventas (dedicated 191 BC, Liv. 36. 36. 5–6), and Hercules Musarum (dedicated 189 BC. See notes on 30 June). The June anniversaries of Roman battles with the Carthaginians, which Ovid records in *Fasti* 6, may be said to have a close association with the two goddesses of the proem. In terms of Roman religious cult the mother-and-daughter relationship of Juno and Iuventas is symbiotic. The ancient Juno of Lanuvium embodied the very spirit of war, as her iconography suggests. This provided the foil and the spur to *virtus* in Roman *iuvenes*, offering them the spectacle of the ultimate triumph of apotheosis. It was with the *iuvenes*, Romans of military age, that Iuventas was associated, as her name suggests. In a well-known passage (D.H. 4. 15. 5) Dionysius, quoting the *Annales* of L. Piso (fr. 14) traces this back to the archaic military classification of Servius Tullius, describing how annually men of military age were obliged to contribute a coin to the treasury of Iuventas in Rome. Because of their influence over Roman warfare Juno and Iuventas were singled out for particular honour in the dark years of the Second Punic War. It was during this period that Iuventas became Hellenized and identified with Hebe, daughter of Hera and wife of Herakles. In 217 BC, after the catastrophic Battle of Lake Trasimene, a *ver sacrum* was vowed in the event of a subsequent Roman victory. This directly concerned all Roman *iuvenes*, for all male children born during a 'consecrated spring' were obliged to go into voluntary exile on attaining adulthood. In 207 BC the consul M. Livius Salinator vowed a temple to Iuventas (Liv. 36. 36. 5–6), the goddess of the *iuvenes* or young warriors, if Rome were victorious in the Battle of the Metaurus. The battle, on 23 June, resulted in a spectacular Roman victory (Liv. 27. 49. 5–6) and the temple was duly built and dedicated. Burnt down in 16 BC, it was restored some three years later by Augustus (*RG* 19), an indication of his encouragement of *collegia iuvenum* in activities based upon military skills such as the *Lusus Troiae* and his promotion of his two grandsons, Gaius and Lucius. Augustus' restoration of the Aedes Iuventatis appears to be commemorated in an Ode of Horace (*Carm.* 4. 4), which was written, probably, in the same year. It celebrates the valour of Drusus, tempered by the paternal wisdom of Augustus (*Augusti paternus in pueros animus Nerones*, 27–8). [See M. Putnam, *Artifices of Eternity: Horace's Fourth Book of Odes* (Cornell 1986) 81–100.] The last third of Horace's poem consists of a bitter speech by Hannibal, lamenting his brother Hasdrubal's defeat at the Metaurus at the hands of Drusus' ancestor G. Claudius Nero, in which the Carthaginian leader refers to Rome as 'the race from the charred remains of Troy' (*gens quae cremato fortis ab Ilio*, 53). Juno's intimidating allusions to her former antipathy to Troy and her loyalty to Carthage in the proem to *Fasti* 6 appear to be part of the same literary discourse.

Iuventas' speech

65–89: *Juno finished speaking. I turned round to see the young wife of Hercules. 'I would not oppose my mother's wishes,' she said. 'I hope to win my case by being conciliatory. She is the queen of Capitoline Jupiter. I claim only the honour of the month. Why should this month not be named after the wife of Hercules? Through Hercules' mighty name this land is in my debt. Here he drove the cattle and here Cacus drenched the Aventine with his blood. In more recent times Romulus classified the Romans by age into two groups, warriors and councillors. He named June for the younger, the previous month for those of riper years.'*

65. *finierat Iuno, respeximus: Herculis uxor*: Ovid turned round and 'looked in the opposite direction', where he saw Iuventas who therefore stood facing her mother, which makes dramatic sense in what has thus far seemed like a courtroom drama. Like Juno *sui germana mariti* (17), Iuventas is introduced with a periphrastic allusion to her more illustrious husband. The word order is significant. By referring to Iuventas as *Herculis uxor*, Ovid succeeds in separating the two names, Juno and Hercules, only by Ovid, their *iudex*, subject of the verb, *respeximus*. This evokes Juno's hostility towards her stepson Hercules, which recurs later in the story of Ino (6. 521–4) and is only grudgingly resolved in the final lines of the poem (800). Hercules' marriage to Juno's daughter, Iuventas/Hebe, was a consequence of Juno's reconciliation with Hercules after his apotheosis. Hercules and Iuventas, as a divine couple, do not have a significant position in Roman cult or Roman poetry. There is, however, an allusion to them in Virgil's memorable line: *nec deus hunc mensa, dea nec dignata cubili est* (Virg. *Ecl.* 4. 63), which recalls the Homeric picture of the couple enjoying Olympian feasts and matrimonial felicity (Hom. *Od.* 11. 602–4) [see W. Clausen, *A Commentary on Virgil, Eclogues* (Oxford, 1994) 145].

66. ***in voltu signa vigoris erant*****:** 'In her face was evidence of youthful vigour.' This is an allusion to Iuventas as Youth.

67–8. ***'non ego, si toto mater me cedere caelo | iusserit, invita matre morabor' ait*****:** feigned courtesy is not uncommon among the goddesses of Virgil's *Aeneid*, as, for example, in the exchange between Juno and Venus concerning the liaison of Dido and Aeneas (*Aen.* 4. 93–113). Here, however, it is part of a domestic comedy in which Ovid seems to parody two female character types. In contrast to Juno's arrogant self-assurance the ostentatiously self-deprecatory Iuventas seems like a pale shadow of her illustrious husband. Like two social-climbing senators' wives, both try to score by making boastful claims about their husbands' position in Rome's divine hierarchy, until in the end Iuventas' oleaginous humility evaporates in a burst of anger when their interests conflict and the goddesses clash angrily in an undignified domestic flare-up.

69. ***'nunc quoque non luctor de nomine temporis'*****:** 'I'm not going to make a fuss about the name of a time-period.' Iuventas' speech begins, like Juno's, with a *captatio benevolentiae.* This highlights the contrasting personalities of the two goddesses, for whereas Juno builds up a picture of her own importance, Iuventas devotes two couplets to expressing the hope that her very humility will influence Ovid in her favour.

70–2. *'blandior et partes paene rogantis ago | remque mei iuris malim tenuisse precando | et faveas causae forsitan ipse meae'*: Iuventas' claim, *partes paene rogantis ago*, shows an interesting conflation of the language of the law-courts, where *partes* means one side in a lawsuit, and of the acting metaphor, *partes agere*: 'I take the role.' She continues to use legal terminology, preferring to 'win her case' (*rem mei iuris malim tenuisse*, 71) and Ovid's support (*faveas causae meae*, 72), by gentle persuasion (*blandior*, 70, *precando*, 71). The word *causa* here has the double significance of a case in the law-courts and of the *aition* in question, namely the origin of *mensis Iunius*.

71. *'malim tenuisse'*: the more acceptable usage here would be *malim tenere*, but Ovid, like the other elegiac poets, not infrequently substitutes the perfect for the present infinitive. [See Platnauer 109–11.]

73–4. *'aurea possedit socio Capitolia templo | mater et, ut debet, cum Iove summa tenet'*: 'Mother lives on the golden Capitol in the temple which they share. It is right and proper that she resides with Jupiter in the high places.' The splendour of the restored temples of Augustus' Rome, with their marble and gold decoration, made *aurea* an appropriate commonplace in Augustan poetry (Virg. *Aen.* 8. 347–8, *Capitolia . . . aurea*). Janus also mentions Rome's golden temples (*Fast.* 1. 223–4). [See Green (2004*a*) *ad loc.*]

75–6. *'at decus omne mihi contingit origine mensis: | unicus est de quo sollicitamur, honor'*: 'all my glory, on the other hand, comes from the origin of the month. Unique is the honour that I ask.' The key words *decus* and *honor* frame the couplet while *unicus*, central to Iuventas' argument, occupies a prominent position at the beginning of the pentameter. By asserting simply that she has no other source of glory, Iuventas effectively counters Juno's cumulative evidence of her high rank and many honours.

77. *'quid grave si titulum mensis, Romane, dedisti | Herculis uxori?'*: a line memorable for its combination of colloquial and oracular style. *Quid grave, si . . . ?* (what harm is there if . . . ?) belongs to the abbreviated language of comedy, where *quid* is not infrequently coupled with a single word, leaving the rest of the clause to be deduced from the context, and Cicero's letters (see Pl. *Bac.* 79, 732 and Cic. *Att.* 15. 12. 1 and 3. 17. 1). *Romane*, in contrast, is a form of address associated with solemn moments in Roman poetry, most famously Anchises' prophetic address to Romans yet unborn: *tu regere imperio populos, Romane, memento* (Virg. *Aen.* 6. 851), and Horace's portentous reflections on Roman guilt for the Civil Wars: *delicta maiorum inmeritus lues | Romane, donec templa refeceris* (Hor. *Carm.* 3. 6. 1). Ovid himself, like Virgil, places *Romane* as the penultimate word in the hexameter, when he uses this appellation to enhance the solemnity of two oracular utterances: *Mater abest, Matrem iubeo, Romane, requiras* (*Fast.* 4. 259, cf. *Met.* 15. 637). An initially flippant line concludes on a note of unexpected solemnity, heralding the resonant pentameter: *Herculis uxori posteritasque memor.* Like her mother, Iuventas offers her illustrious marriage as her first claim to the month (cf. *Fast.* 6. 27, *est aliquid nupsisse Iovi*).

78. '*posteritasque memor*': Iuventas feels that 'mindful posterity' should join Ovid in assigning the *titulus mensis* to Hercules' wife. An 'Alexandrian footnote' is suggested by the word *memor* at the end of the pentameter, which precedes two couplets succinctly recalling Hercules' conquest of Cacus, which had been related with greater detail and artistry by Virgil (*Aen.* 8. 190–279), Ovid (*Fast.* 1. 543–78), as well as by Livy (1. 7. 4) and Propertius (4. 9. 1–20). This story gained popularity in the Augustan period, where it symbolized the struggle between Good and Evil exemplified by the battle between Augustus and Antony at Actium. [See Hardie (1986) 110–18, Morgan (1998) 175–98.]

79–82. '*haec quoque terra . . . huc . . . hic*': mother and daughter both emphasize their arguments with familiar rhetorical devices. The bare bones of the story of Hercules and Cacus are neatly built into the framework of a tricolon focused on Rome, which mentions the debt of Rome (*haec terra*) to Hercules' wife, the hero's journey to Rome (*huc*), and his heroic deed on the site of Rome (*hic*). From Virgil's and his own earlier version of the story Ovid selects three familiar graphic details: *captas adpulit boves* (80), (*Cacus*) *male defensus flammis et dote paterna* (81), and *sanguine tinxit humum* (82). The over-succinct hendiadys 'ill defended by his flames and his father's heritage' (81) assumes the reader's familiarity with these two earlier descriptions of Hercules' conquest of the fire-breathing monster who is endowed with the flames of his father, Vulcan.

82. '*Cacus Aventinam sanguine tinxit humum*': the juxtaposition of the monster and the place of his defeat is repeated on a previous occasion: *Cacus Aventinae... silvae* (*Fast.* 1. 551). [A useful entry on 'significant juxtaposition' may be found in the appendix on word order in S. J. Harrison, *Commentary on Aeneid X* (Oxford, 1990) 288.]

83. '*ad propiora vocor*': Iuventas proposes to turn to matters chronologically closer to hand, suggesting that Romulus, Rome's founder, can perhaps provide an even more cogent example. Once again there is parallelism in the speeches of Juno and Iuventas: both begin with their illustrious husbands in their role as Roman gods and close with Rome's founder, Romulus. The Greek tradition set out in Hesiod (fr. 25. 26–33, Merkelbach and West), describing Hera's persecution of Herakles in his lifetime and her acceptance of him as her son-in-law after his apotheosis (cf. Ovid *Fast.* 6. 524, 800), has affinities with the heroic legend of Romulus, who is a victim of Juno's hostility during his lifetime on account of his mother, Ilia, being a priestess of Trojan Vesta: *invisum nepotem | Troica quem peperit sacerdos* (Hor. *Carm.* 3. 3. 31–2). He later becomes reconciled with Juno after her conciliatory transformation of his earthly wife, Hersilia, into Hora, goddess of youth. Ennius may be the source for parallels with Herakles/Hebe in his story of the apotheosis and marriage of Romulus [see Feeney (1984) 188–9]. Both Hercules and Romulus are represented in Augustan literature as heroic benefactors of the Roman race who are rewarded by apotheosis (Hor. *Carm.* 1. 12. 25–33, 3. 3. 9–12). According to Livy, Romulus gave active support (*suscepit*) for the cult of Hercules in Rome because he was himself *immortalitatis virtute partae... fautor* (Liv. 1. 7. 15).

83–4. '*populum digessit ab annis | Romulus in partes distribuitque duas*': 'Romulus classified his citizenry according to age and divided them into two groups.' Iuventas has already allotted three couplets to the *argumentum Herculis* (77–82), three balancing couplets now follow presenting the *argumentum Romuli* (83–8), the substance of which is the facile etymology which derives *mensis Maius* and *Iunius* from Romulus' division of the population into *maiores* and *iuniores* (cf. *Fast.* 5. 55–78). Ovid was no doubt aware that this act of Romulus was recorded by M. Fulvius Nobilior in the Fasti which were exhibited in the temple of Hercules Musarum, the dedication of which closes Book 6: *Fulvius Nobilior in fastis quos in aede Herculis Musarum posuit, Romulum dicit postquam populum in maiores iunioresque divisit, ut altera pars consilio, altera armis rem publicam tueretur, in honorem utriusque partis hunc Maium, sequentem Iunium mensem vocasse* (Macr. 1. 12. 16). [See Maltby 318 Iunius.]

85–6. *'haec dare consilium; pugnare paratior illa est | haec aetas bellum suadet, at illa gerit'*: characteristically the pentameter rephrases the content of the hexameter. Iuventas' argument that June is named for the *iuniores* or *iuvenes* allows her to formulate Romulus' military divison of the Roman people. Ovid himself later avoids mentioning Servius' greatest achievement, his centuriate assembly, because of its generic incompatibility, and presents the king instead as a *dux placidus* and temple-founder.

87. *'mensesque nota secrevit eadem'*: 'he distinguished the months in the same way.' The word *nota* is used here not in the literal sense of a distinguishing mark (cf. *Fast.* 3. 429, 6. 206), but metaphorically to indicate the character or criterion which distinguishes May, the month of the *maiores,* from June, the month of the *iuniores* (*OLD* s.v. 3, 4).

88. *'Iunius est iuvenum, qui fuit ante, senum'*: Iuventas concludes by stating her case plainly in the same way as Juno in line 26 (cf. *tertius a senibus, iuvenum de nomine quartum, Fast.* 1. 41). The age of the *iuvenes* was 17–45, of the *senes* 46–60 years.

89. *dixit, et in litem studio certaminis issent*: Ovid reverts to the courtroom language apparent in Juno's speech (21–64). *Litem ire,* meaning 'to go into court', is an example of Ovid's use of legal terminology which far outstrips that of any of the other Augustan poets. Ovid's legal metaphors are discussed by E. J. Kenney, 'Ovid and the Law', *YClS* (1969) 243–63, who suggests a connection with his personal experience in an official capacity as a *decemvir stlitibus iudicandis* (*Fast.* 4. 383–4) or among the *centumviri* (*Tr.* 2. 93–6) or *tresviri capitales* (*Tr.* 4. 10).

Concordia's speech and Ovid's conclusion

The political resonance of Concordia

[Levick (1976) 36, (1978) 227–8, J. R. Fears, 'The Cult of Virtues and Roman Imperial Ideology', *ANRW*, II. 17. 2: 886–91, Fantham (1985) 262, Kellum (1990) 276–8, Herbert-Brown (1994), Green (2004a) 290–3.]

When M. Furius Camillus vowed the first temple of Concordia in Rome in 397 BC (Ovid *Fast.* 1. 637–50, Plut. *Cam.* 42. 3) in the decade of the Veientine Wars and the Gallic invasion, he was advertising the political harmony achieved by admitting plebeian candidates to the consulate. If it were built at all, and there is some doubt, Camillus' temple was built on the lower slope of the Capitoline Hill overlooking the *comitium* in the Forum Romanum. A parallel may be drawn between the Roman cult of Concordia and the Greek cult of Homonoia, whose shrines appeared close to the *Bouleuterion*, in the cities of Magna Graecia, marking the change, at the same period, from aristocratic oligarchy to a wider democracy (cf. Liv. 6. 42. 9–14). [See Emmanuele Curti, 'From Concordia to the Quirinal', in Bispham and Smith (eds.) (2002) 77–91.] Cults of Concordia invariably indicated political disunity as is illustrated by the story how, following the murder of G. Gracchus, L. Opimius built the temple of Concordia which was immediately defaced by a nocturnal graffitist with the slogan, 'Discord built this temple of Concord!' (Plut. *G. Gracchus* 17. 6). The slogan *Concordia ordinum* became a rallying-cry for Cicero, who ordered the trial of the Catilinarian conspirators to be held in the Aedes Concordia, where the senate met on several occasions at times of civil discord (Cic. *Cat.* 3. 21. 20, *Phil.* 2. 19). The slogan reappeared after the murder of Caesar, particularly in the context of the second triumvirate and at the time of the reconciliations between Augustus and Antony in 40 and 35 BC [see Weinstock (1971) 266].

The temple of Concord was restored by Augustus after Actium. He set up statues to Janus Concordia, Pax, and Salus in 11 BC, which Ovid commemorates, significantly, in the centre of his work together with the Ara Pacis (*Fast.* 3. 881–2). Under the Principate, as it had before, Concordia was generally proclaimed by a reigning power or faction which felt itself under threat from opposition. Tiberius announced the restoration of Opimius' temple of Concordia in 7 BC in the wake of a successful war and his own triumph over the German tribes. There were close links between Pax Augusta and Concordia. When, however, the temple was finally dedicated by Tiberius in AD 10, it was intended to emphasize the restoration of harmony of the Domus Augusta after a period of dynastic discord over the succession. The dedication was significantly celebrated on 16 January, the anniversary of Octavian receiving both the title Augustus and the twin laurels beside the door of his Palatine house (Aug. *RG* 34. 2) to honour his establishment of the Pax Augusta in 27 BC.

The close ideological association of Pax Augusta and Concordia is clearly relevant to Concordia's appearance in Ovid's proem to *Fasti* 6. With the addition of the adjective *Augusta*, Pax and Concordia emphasized that their very existence depended on Augustus' victory at Actium and on his beneficent rule, maintaining harmony between all factions. Both Pax and Concordia might be described, as Concordia is in this couplet: *placidi numen opusque ducis* (92), 'the very spirit of the peace-loving leader'. Pax and Concordia contribute to the balance and tension in the Augustan dialogue between *Fasti* 1 and 6. Ovid's revised Book 1 concludes with Pax being welcomed to her own Ara Pacis Augustae on 30 January, the birthday of Livia, Tiberius' mother (*Fast.* 1. 711), while the Aedes Concordia Augustae was dedicated on 16 January, the anniversary of Octavian becoming Augustus (649–50). Again Ovid apostrophizes Concordia as the guiding spirit in Livia's Aedes Concordiae within her husband's Porticus Liviae (*Fast.* 6. 637), a passage set in contrast to the dynastic disharmony in the palace of Servius Tullius, as well as giving her a voice among what might be described as *numina belli,* Juno and Iuventas (6. 93–6).

89–96: *Iuventas finished speaking. A quarrel was brewing in which filial devotion would have been lost in anger. Then came Concordia, the very spirit of Augustus. She told how Tatius and brave Quirinus had united their peoples saying, 'June takes her name from Unity!'* **97–100:** *Pardon, goddesses, not by* *my arbitration shall the matter be decided! Consider yourselves equal as far as I'm concerned. Troy fell when Beauty came to judgement!*

90. *atque ira pietas dissimulata foret*: 'all trace of filial devotion would have been obliterated by her rage.' The primary meaning of *dissimulare* is 'to conceal', implying a conscious attempt to make something appear different from the way it really is (*OLD* s.v. 1). Although this clearly means that Iuventas' involuntary burst of temper obscures her dutiful affection for her mother, Ovid's choice of *dissimulare* and his artful juxtaposition, *ira pietas dissimulata*, creates the impression that Iuventas' *pietas* may be less than genuine. In this case, Iuventas' guilefully ingratiating promise (67–8) that she would obey her mother, even if it were Juno's desire to exclude her from the abode of the immortals, is entirely specious and masks a resolute ambition to win for herself the *titulus mensis*.

91–2. *venit Apollinea longas Concordia lauro | nexa comas*: the impact of this line is heightened by its distinctive alliteration and assonance and the balance of the pentasyllabic adjective, *Apollinea*, and its tetrasyllabic noun, *Concordia*. In dramatic terms this is the moment for pacific intervention. The laurel wreath associates Concordia directly with Augustus, the door of whose Palatine house was flanked by twin laurel trees in recognition of his patron Apollo's assistance at the Battle of Actium. As Concordia's thin disguise unequivocally suggests the Princeps, so the goddesses' rivalry must surely also suggest the notorious clashes of ambition among the female members of the Domus Augusta, which the Princeps attempted to resolve.

92. *placidi numen opusque ducis*: Concordia is described as 'the very spirit and creation of the peace-loving leader'. Although it was Tiberius who restored the temple of Concordia in AD 10, it is clear that, in this context, *dux placidus* refers to Augustus. The appellation *dux placidus* occurs on two other occasions in Book 6, referring to Numa (6. 259) and Servius Tullius (6. 582), all three being linked by their beneficent rule, pursuit of peace, and devotion to Roman cult and the foundation of temples.

93–5. *haec ubi narravit Tatium fortemque Quirinum | binaque cum populis regna coisse suis | et lare communi soceros generosque receptos*:

the battle between Romans and Sabines, following the famous 'rape', owes its frequency as a literary example to the *gener/socer* relationship of the opposing forces: *tum primum generis intulit arma socer* (*Fast.* 3. 202). The full story of the conflict is to be found, appropriately, in *Fasti* 3, where Ovid, for generic expediency, dwells less on the fighting than on the peace initiative of the Sabine wives, just as Concordia's use of the example in Book 6 focuses on the reconciliation and union of the warring races: *bina . . . regna coisse, lare communi . . . receptos.* On his Shield of Aeneas, as his third picture of early Rome, Virgil describes the two kings, Romulus and Tatius, standing before Jupiter's altar, holding out offerings before they make a treaty and kill a pig (*Aen.* 8. 639–41; cf. 12. 169–71). The iconographic image enriches Concordia's speech. In his celebration of the *natalis* of Juno Moneta (*Fast.* 6. 183–190) Ovid evokes a second image from the Shield of Aeneas (*Aen.* 8. 652–62), Manlius' defence of the Capitol during the Gallic Siege. Virgil uses these scenes as important steps in the legend of Rome's rise to supremacy [see David West, '*cernere erat*: The Shield of Aeneas' (1975–6), repr. in S. J. Harrison (ed.), *Oxford Readings in Vergil's Aeneid* (Oxford 1990) 295–304, and Harrison (1997) 70–6]. In Ovid's *Fasti* 6 they also mark *pugnata in ordine bella* (*Aen.* 8. 629), establishing a cogent literary contrast with Janus' claim, *nil mihi cum bello*, in *Fasti* 1. Servius notes that statues of the two kings represented in this scene stood in the Via Sacra, which took its name from their oath of confederation (Fest. 372L. Cf. D.H. 2. 46. 3). It is relevant to this passage that, in Livy's version of the unification of the two races, Hersilia, wife of Romulus, pleads for reconciliation on the grounds that *ita rem coalescere concordia posse* (Liv. 1. 11. 2).

96. *'his nomen iunctis Iunius' inquit 'habet'*: Concordia Augusta tries to solve the impasse by offering the facile but improbable solution that Iunius derives its meaning from *iungere.* Since coalition with Rome implied accepting Roman supremacy, it might be said that Concordia represents the consequence of successful war. Concordia Augusta was ideologically closely linked to Pax Augusta, which could only be achieved by Victoria Augusta, represented by Juno and Iuventas. Warring goddesses were a poetic cliché and a clash between goddesses associated with different aspects of war has added poetic value. Wittily underlining his point by having Concordia 'dress up' in

Augustus' Actian laurels, Ovid reminds his readers that Concordia Augusta also included harmonious relations between members of the imperial family [see Levick (1978) 227–8]. The well-testified existence of increasing dynastic tensions in the years AD 6–7, when Ovid might have been writing this book, suggests a complex reading. Augustus' simultaneous adoptions of his co-heirs, Tiberius and Agrippa Postumus, formalized on 26 June AD 4, will have met with a lack of enthusiasm from both sides of his family. Any sense of triumph felt by Tiberius at being, at last, officially designated Augustus' heir was blighted by this unflattering association with his young stepson, Postumus. Augustus' attempts to conciliate the Julian and Claudian factions of his family had included his arrangement of a marriage between Germanicus and Agrippina, his granddaughter, ensuring that his own great-grandchildren remained within the line of succession, for Tiberius had, as a condition to his own adoption, been forced to make his nephew, Germanicus, his son and co-heir with his natural son, Drusus. Without imputing any concealed identity to either Juno or Iuventas, it is sufficient to suggest that, faced with a clash of dynastic interests, the Princeps had a reputation for acting as a peacemaker.

98. ***res est arbitrio non dirimenda meo***: 'the case cannot be brought to a conclusion by my arbitration.' Returning to legal phraseology, Ovid declares his inability to choose between the contestants.

99. ***ite pares a me!***: 'Go, equal in my judgement!' Ovid refuses to choose between the goddesses' suggested etymologies in the same way as he evades making a choice between those of the Muses (*Fast.* 5. 108–10). The suggestion here that it would be dangerous to take sides is an instance where readers may interpret the text on different levels. In the context of war it is clear that Juno, Iuventas, and Concordia all have their part to play; each represents a different and essential constituent of Roman war. In terms of poetic discourse there are other lines of interpretation. In the proem to *Fasti* 6, a book which returns to the theme of War rather more than is generically proper, Juno, a powerful literary goddess of war, formally gives her seal of approval to Ovid's unusual mode of aetiological elegy. In this Juno's role is contrasted with the role in *Fasti* 1 of Janus, arbiter of Peace: *Iane, fac aeternos pacem pacisque ministros* (*Fast.* 1. 287). Like Juno and Venus in Virgil's *Aeneid*, Juno and Janus appear to have conflicting interests in Ovid's *Fasti*, for instance in the Tarpeia episode (1. 259–74). Since such divine conflict belongs to epic, Ovid 'reduces' this episode to an elegiac level by exploiting such feminine motifs as Juno's 'jealousy' (*Saturnia invidiosa*, 265–6), Tarpeia's love for Tatius, and her preoccupation less with *arma* than with *armilla*, golden armbands. [On this episode see Peter Keegan, '*Feminea lingua*', in Herbert-Brown (ed.) (2002) 131–4.] Ovid's use of the motif of the Judgement of Paris is, to some extent, initiated by the need to focus on Juno's wounded vanity in order to 'elegize' his unavoidable combination of Virgil's Juno and Juno Seispes Mater Regina of Lanuvium (see Introduction 5).

100. *plus laedunt quam iuvat una duae*: the threat posed by the two unsuccessful contestants on Mount Ida is similarly voiced in Ovid's hymnic aretalogy of Venus in Book 4: *caelestesque duas Troiano iudice vicit | ah! olim victas hoc meminisse deas.*

H KAL. IUN. N *CARNARIA*, 101–182

[G. Dumézil, 'Carna', *Latomus* 38 (1960) 87–100, H. Parry, 'Violence in a Pastoral Setting', *TAPA* 95 (1964) 268–82, Dumézil (1970), B. Otis, *Ovid as an Epic Poet* (Cambridge, 1970) 396–400, Roger Dunkle, 'The Hunter and the Hunted in the *Aeneid*', *Ramus* 2 (1972) 127–42, W. Fauth, 'Römische Religion im Spiegel der *Fasti* des Ovid', *ANRW* II. 16. 1 (1978) 104–86, Gregson Davis, *The Death of Procris: Amor and the Hunt in Ovid's Metamorphoses* (Rome, 1983) 25–100, Miller (1983) 164–74, Porte (1985) 230–2, Conte (1986) 115–19, Hardie (1991), C. M. McDonough, 'Carna, Proca and the *strix* on the Kalends of June', *TAPA* 127 (1997) 315–44, Green (2004*a*) 67–70, Habinek (2005) 251–4.]

1. *The cult of Carna*

Macrobius reports that a shrine to Carna was dedicated by L. Iunius Brutus on 1 June on the Caelian Hill in fulfilment of a vow made in the year in which the Tarquins were expelled. The origins and nature of the goddess Carna are meagrely attested. Nevertheless they show an interesting network of association with physical vigour, death, and the liminal area between, our only two ancient sources for Carna's cult being this passage, *Fasti* 6. 101–82, and Macrobius 1. 12. 31–3. Both Ovid and Macrobius indicate that the only ritual prescribed for the *Carnaria* is the consumption of a homely dish composed of beans, bacon, and spelt. Ovid's light-hearted comment that this fibrous food was good for the bowels (6. 181–2) seems to have had some connection with Macrobius' statement that Carna protected vital organs such as liver, heart, and viscera: *hanc deam vitalibus humanis praeesse credunt; ab ea denique petitur ut iecinora et corda quaeque sunt intrinsecus viscera salva conservet* (Macr. 1. 12. 31). Macrobius attributes Brutus' cult of Carna to his belief that Carna guided his heart to deceive Tarquinius Superbus with his feigned stupidity. The first day of June, a month associated with *iuniores*, young and vigorous warriors such as L. Iunius Brutus, *tribunus celerum*, was an appropriate day on which to pray for the vigour which Carna had the power to grant. They might also pray for her protection through the passage from full vigour to death, the lot of the Roman soldier which is implicit in the military disasters recorded in *Fasti* 6.

Carna's affinities with the Cult of the Dead, on account of the prominence of beans in her cult, has the uncompromising support of Bömer (1957–8: 343): 'Unbestritten ist dass Carna in Verbindung zum Totenkult stand.' Beans, the festal fare of the Carnaria, figure in the two rituals which Ovid describes in his accounts of Roman ancestor cult: at the *Lemuria* a *pater familias* offers black beans to unquiet shades, whilst at the *Feralia* beans are revolved in the mouth of the *anus ebria* in a magic rite to silence gossips. On the *Carnaria*, which was, according to Macrobius, known as the *Kalendae Fabariae*, Varro reports that a bean pottage is 'offered as a sacrifice' to the gods: *Kalendis Iuniis et publice et privatim fabatam pultem dis mactant* (Non. 539L). Further evidence for Carna's association with death may be adduced from a sepulchral inscription from Pannonia, dated some time before AD 31, which asks that roses be brought to his tomb during the *Carnaria* (*CIL* 3. 3893). Ovid specifically instructs Romans to bring flowers to family tombs at the *Parentalia* (*Fast.* 2. 539), following the example of Aeneas at his father's tomb in Sicily:

purpureos iacit flores (Virg. *Aen.* 5. 79. Cf. *Aen.* 6. 884: *purpureas spargam flores*). Red roses in the Pannonian inscription correspond to the reddish-purplish flowers mentioned by both Virgil and Ovid.

2. *Literary and Augustan discourse in the double cult story of Crane*

Crane's association with Janus forms a 'frame' linking *Fasti* 6 with *Fasti* 1. Janus' power to open and close doors has calendric significance and his doorkeeping appears to be extended to control the cosmos: *me penes est unum vasti custodia mundi* (Ovid *Fast.* 1. 119). As Janus opens the calendar year on 1 January, so he reappears on 1 June to give Crane the *ius cardinis* in a book which closes the first half of Ovid's *Fasti.* It is possible to see Carna's feast day in the month of June associated not only with the *iuniores*, whose *viscera* she guarded, but also with the two women's cults of 11 June. Crane's double story forms a structural link with the double celebration of the goddesses of the Matralia, 11 June, whose temples form a connected pair in the Forum Boarium and who also have a, more tenuous, association with war and conquest [see p. 151]. The second half of Crane's narrative, her rescue of Proca, links her to the first cult of 11 June, that of Mater Matuta, who received prayers for the protection of other women's children, possibly at times when they lacked the direct care of their own mother. McDonough ('Carna, Proca and the *strix*') cites the votive offerings of inner organs found at the temple of Mater Matuta at Satricum as a direct connection between the *kourotrophos*, Mater Matuta, and Crane who protects Proca when his royal parents are powerless to do so. Ovid's first Crane story, her rape by Janus, may be interpreted as a 'rite of passage' from virginity to womanhood. In this she is closely associated with the goddess of the second cult of 11 June, Fortuna, who presided over a woman's sexuality during the liminal state between bridal virginity and matronal fecundity. Ovid accompanies his story of Janus' rape of Crane with the traditional literary imagery of the myth of the conquest of the virgin huntress who spurns love. C. Sourvinou-Inwood sees this as analogous to the subjugation of a girl by marriage ['A Series of Erotic Pursuits: Images and Meanings', *JHS* 107 (1987) 131–53]. Another dimension is offered by P. Vidal-Naquet (1986: 106–28), who interprets the virgin hunter, and also the myth of Melanion, as a youth, an ephebe, on the threshold of the rite of passage into full manhood, membership of the state and its hoplite force, and marriage. Both of these interpretations are represented symbolically in Ovid's story of Crane receiving from Janus the guardianship of doorways, both literally and figuratively, liminal places. The evidence which Vidal-Naquet adduces to associate the myth of the virgin huntress with the *epheboi*, or in Roman terms the *iuvenes*, is obviously of considerable relevance to *Fasti* 6. Ovid's version of this myth is entirely Romanized, for the god who presided over the passage from boyhood to full citizenship through military enlistment was Janus Curatius (Introduction 4.1).

Finally, Ovid's aetiological exegesis permits an Augustan interpretation. The *strix* threatens the life force of the Alban princeling, who is a vital link in the dynasty leading from Aeneas to Augustus (Introduction 4.4). Ovid's theme of endangered princelings has affinities with the Augustan poets' practice of enhancing Rome's contemporary glories by allusions to seemingly insurmountable dangers which threatened the fledgling state, a theme represented in *Fasti* 6 by the Gallic invasion (*Fast.* 6. 351–92) and the Second Punic War (241–6, 765–8).

3. *Calendric notation in Ovid's* Fasti

[Rüpke (1995), 258–60. See also Merkel (1841) 32, Michels (1967) 22–54, Herbert-Brown (1994) 15–22.]

In his second Teubner edition (1850–2) Merkel was the first to divide the different calendar entries in Ovid's *Fasti* with headings indicating the date and its festival. In common with other modern editions of Ovid's *Fasti* [Bömer (1957–8), *AWC* (1978), and Fantham (1998)], I have prefaced each of Ovid's entries with its Roman calendric notation which indicates, first, the nundinal day (H), secondly the lunar date in relation to Kalends, Nones, or Ides (KAL.), and finally the day's religious status (N). The capital letters signifying *nundinae* and *Feriae Stativae* may require some explanation. The word *Nundinum* (originally a genitive plural referring to a twenty-four-day period containing three market days: *trinum nundinum*) signified the eight-day Roman week, each day of which was marked in the calendar by the letters A–H. During each calendric year market day (*nundinae*) fell on the same letter day in each succeeding eight-day cycle. The first *nundinae* of the year was determined by the appropriate magistrate counting nine days from the last market day in December, so that the Roman week, like our own, was unaffected by the end of the year and simply ran over. 1 January, however, was always designated by the letter A, with the result that each year *nundinae* usually fell on a day of a different letter. In 46 BC, when the Julian calendar first came into effect, *nundinae* fell on H, in the following year C, in 44 BC on F and in 43 BC on A, a day which Macrobius considered ill-omened (Macr. 1. 13. 17). Market days, however, seem to have suffered regular disruption. Macrobius (1. 13. 16) claims that they were not permitted on the *Kalends* of January or on any *Nones*, nor was it permitted to hold markets and *comitia* on the same day (Plin. *Nat.* 18. 13, Macr. 1. 16. 29). On such occasions market day was cancelled until the following week. Dio, however, makes it clear (60. 24. 7) that in 44 BC *nundinae* could be postponed to another day to avoid *Feriae*.

Feriae Stativae were the religious holidays which were marked in the Roman Fasti, as opposed to the *Feriae Conceptivae* or movable feasts, which could not, literally, be set in stone. Among the *Feriae Conceptivae* were the *Ambarvalia*, *Compitalia*, and *Feriae Sementivae.* Ovid illustrates the point when he describes how, as he scanned the Roman Fasti for *Feriae Sementivae*, his fruitless search was interrupted by a helpful Muse, logically pointing out, '*quid a fastis non stata sacra petis?*' (*Fast.* 1. 659–60). Both kinds of *Feriae*, however, affected the status of the day, which Ovid outlines briefly (*Fast.* 1. 45–60). On a day designated N (*nefastus*) religious observance dictated that it was permitted neither to go to court to transact legal business nor to hold a public assembly (Var. *L* 6. 30: *vocantur dies nefasti per quos dies nefas fari praetorem do dico addico, itaque non potest agi*). On a day marked *F* (*fastus*, Var. *L* 6. 29) the courts were open for civil law, and on a day marked C (*comitia*, Macr. 1. 16. 14) voting could take place in public assemblies. Other days were designated EN (*Fast.* 1. 50). Such *dies intercisi* Varro (*L.* 6. 31) defines as days when civic activities might take place in the middle part of the day, since early morning was the time allocated for sacrifice, and at the end of the day the entrails of the sacrificial animal were *porrecta* or offered on the altar fires prior to the sacrificial dinner which would have been attended by the appropriate priesthood or *sodales* associated with that cult. Both these parts of the day, being devoted to the gods, were of course *nefasti*. Since the term *endoterocisus* does not appear in any of the ancient sources to describe *dies intercisi*, but *endoitium* (meaning *initium* as opposed to *exitium*) does, a convincing calendric abbreviation, E(ndoitio, exitio)N(efas), is proposed by Rüpke (1995: 268–9). Lastly, forty-nine days in the Julian calendar are marked NP. The meaning of P has been differently interpreted by commentators, who agree on *nefasti* for N, since all the days so marked were clearly in some way *religiosus*. Again, I am inclined to accept Rüpke's suggestion of *Nefastus Piaculum*, on the grounds that, since all the days marked *NP* were *Feriae*, a religious rite (*piaculum*) would have to have been performed.

The Story of Carna and Janus

101–12: *The first day is yours, Carna, goddess of the hinge. An ancient tale tells how the nymph, Crane, received this power. You will be better informed by my poem. Crane was born in the Lucus Elerni, where still today the priests perform holy rites. Vainly pursued by suitors, she preferred to hunt with darts and nets. People even mistook her for Phoebus' sister.* **113–30:** *When some youth propositioned her, she used to say, 'Not out here. Lead the way into a secluded cave and I'll follow.' Then she would vanish. When Janus spotted her, smitten with passion, she repeated her usual ruse. Silly girl! Janus sees what is going on behind his back! He's got her in his arms under the rocks! Having satisfied his desires, Janus gave Crane power over doorways as recompense for her lost virginity!*

101. *Prima dies tibi, Carna, datur; dea cardinis haec est*: although Ovid uses the name Crane in his two cult stories, in this opening invocation he gives the goddess her traditional name, Carna. To suit his elegiac tale of Janus the door-god's rape of Crane, and his ensuing gift of the *ius cardinis* as *pretium virginitatis*, Ovid's literary version capitalizes on a specious connection: *dea cardinis haec est*. Outside this passage, however, Carna has no connection with *cardo-inis*.

The name of the goddess of the hinge was, according to Augustine (*CD* 4. 8, 6. 7), Cardea. Ovid often indicates a new section of his poem with striking sound effects such as we see in this opening couplet. The staccato alliteration of the hexameter with its combination of consonants *d*, *t*, and *c*, and short vowels, *i* and *a*, contrasts with the mellifluous assonance of the pentameter with its figures of repetition and chiasmus. In this way Ovid passes from the harsh Latin *Carna, dea cardinis* to the more euphonious Greek *nymphe Cranaen* (107) to create the right atmosphere for his mythological rape scene [see Porte (1985) 231].

102. *numine clausa aperit, claudit aperta suo*: 'through her powers she opens what is closed and closes what is opened.' A symmetrical pentameter in chiasmic form (abcCBA). Ovid often uses variations of this form in his pentameters. Here the symmetry is enhanced, as often, by assonance. Patterns and thematic links may be detected between major and minor passages in all the books of Ovid's *Fasti*. Here Ovid's focus on the verbs *aperire/claudere* anticipates the formal opening of Vesta's inner storeroom or *penus* for nine days on 7 June and its closing on 15 June. These are formally marked in the *Fasti Philocali* as *Vesta aperitur* and *Vesta cluditur* (Degrassi 249). As the *penus Vestae* is opened to reveal *sacra* associated with the fertility and prosperity of the Roman state, so Carna's powers of opening and closing doors are connected to her guardianship of Roman physical well-being.

103–4. *obscurior aevo | fama*: 'the story has become unclear through time.' The same sentiment is expressed by Virgil's Latinus, also in an aetiological exegesis (Virg. *Aen.* 7. 205): *fama est obscurior annis.*

105. *adiacet antiquus Tiberino lucus Elerni*: *AWC*'s *Alerni*, the reading of *U*, is here cautiously rejected in favour of the emendation *(H)elerni*, the reading of *GM*, which is the choice of Merkel (1841), Pighi, and Bömer. The grove lay near the Tiber estuary outside the city, where Ovid no doubt pictured Crane hunting (*Fast.* 2. 67: *qua petit aequoreas advena Thybris aquas*). By Augustus' day the sacred groves which Ovid mentions (2. 435–6, 3. 295, 6. 503) were sacred precincts with few, if any, trees, where religious ceremonies could be held. Further examples of urban *luci* were Lucus Semelae/Stimulae (*Fast.* 6. 503);

Lucus Furinae, thought to have been the sanctuary of an ancient chthonic deity (Cic. *ND* 3. 46), where G. Gracchus was murdered in 121 BC (Plut. *G. Gracchus* 17. 2); and Lucus Petelinus, chosen for the trial of M. Manlius Capitolinus in 384 BC (Liv. 6. 20. 11) so that the judgement was not influenced by the sight of the Tarpeian Rock where Manlius had famously driven the Gauls from the Capitol and from which, if found guilty, he himself would shortly be hurled [see T. P. Wiseman, 'Topography and Rhetoric: The Trial of Manlius', *Historia* 28 (1979) 32–50.]

106. ***pontifices illuc nunc quoque sacra ferunt*:** the rites performed in the Lucus Elerni by the *pontifices*, as representatives of Roman state religion, honoured Juno Seispes Mater Regina, the Roman goddess of war and fertility, to whom all Kalends were sacred, rather than the minor deity, Carna. In *Fasti* 2. 67 people are said to flock to a Lucus Elerni beside the Tiber on 1 February, the feast day of Juno Sospita, whose temple was situated not far from the river in the Forum Holitorum [see Rüpke (1995) 297].

107. ***inde sata est nymphe*:** two interpretations are possible. Either Crane has become, poetically, the daughter of Elernus, who is not otherwise known or, simply, she is a foundling child of the Lucus Elerni because she was born there. Ovid's story of Crane and Janus offers a good example of the poet's narrative technique. The poet first sketches the story so far: Crane's habitual evasion of unwanted suitors and her solitary hunting in the imperfect tense (*solebat*, 109 . . . *credebant*, 112 . . . *reddebat*, 114) are combined with other past tenses where grammatically appropriate (*dixisset*, 113, *iit*, 117). He then switches to the livelier historic present for an anecdote in which Crane sheds a would-be lover in the bushes (*resistit* . . . *latet*, 117–18).

107. ***Cranaen dixere priores*:** the name Crane, which does not appear in any other ancient text, seems to be an Ovidian invention. Although the more important mss offer differing disyllabic readings here and at line 151, both Merkel (1841) and Pighi have attempted to solve the metrical difficulty with, respectively, the trisyllabic *Cranaen* and *Cranien*. Of these two *Cranaen* is the choice of *AWC*. Dumézil suggests that the alternative manuscript reading, Glane, from *glanum*, associates Crane with the grain contained in the soup eaten on her day [see Dumézil (1975) 225–3].

108. ***nequiquam multis saepe petita procis*****:** like Daphne (Ovid, *Met.* 1. 474–9), Crane has many unwanted suitors but she cherishes her virginity, preferring the pleasures of the chase. Crane's pursuit and conquest by Janus corresponds in most of its details to the literary topos of the virgin huntress who becomes the quarry in an erotic hunt in an idyllic pastoral landscape, which has its roots in Euripides' tragedy of *Hippolytus.* Worship of the virgin goddess Artemis, who presided over hunting and virginity, is at the heart of the concept that those devoted to hunting animals scorn the pursuit of love. Flaunting disdain for love sends out a literary signal that the virgin huntress is destined to become the hunted, the prey of an amorous pursuer. Ovid explores this paradigm in a group of myths in the *Metamorphoses* in which Daphne, Syrinx, and Arethusa are variously 'hunted' by their suitors.

109. ***rura sequi*****:** *sequi* carries here the sense of 'ranging across' [*OLD* s.v. 9]. Cf. Virg. *Aen.* 2. 736–7: *avia cursu | dum sequor.*

109–10. ***iaculis feras agitare solebat | nodosas cava tendere valle plagas*****:** Crane's hunting gear, her spears and nets, which frame the couplet, foreshadow the weapons of Love—Cupid's darts and Janus' tricks—which will eventually ensnare her as their quarry. The chiasmic pattern of the pentameter, abcBA, diverges slightly from the classic 'Golden Line' in which nouns and adjectives are arranged in the same order, ABCab.

111–12. ***Phoebi tamen esse sororem | credebant, nec erat, Phoebe, pudenda tibi*****:** in ancient literature, from Euripides' *Hippolytus* to Ovid's Actaeon (*Met.* 3. 155–252), the harsh consequences of tenaciously preserved virginity are closely associated with the cult of Artemis. Ovid underlines Crane's distaste for her suitors and her devotion to hunting by mentioning, as a literary signal, her resemblance to the virgin goddess. For the same reason Daphne, a nymph of similar inclination, is described as *innuptae aemula Phoebes* (Ovid *Met.* 1. 476) and Syrinx *posset credi Latonia* (696). The same imagery is used to describe Dido when she first appears, not virgin but still loyal to her first husband, Sychaeus: *qualis in Eurotae ripis aut per iuga Cynthi | exercet Diana choros* (Virg. *Aen.* 1. 498–9). At the onset of her passion for Aeneas, Dido is compared to a wounded doe (*Aen.* 4. 69–72), while Aeneas himself is said to look like Apollo, the master archer, with his weapons ominously clanging on his shoulders, when he goes out to join her for the fateful hunt which will end in Dido's 'capture' (147–9).

113. *dixisset amantia verba*: the pluperfect subjunctive *dixisset* underscores the *froideur* of Crane, who will not even listen to *amantia verba* outside the privacy of a cave.

115. *'haec loca lucis habent nimis et cum luce pudoris'*: Crane makes a coy excuse: 'There's too much light out here and in broad daylight it's too embarrassing' (cf. Jupiter to Io: *'pete,' dixerat, 'umbras | altorum nemorum'* (*Met.* 1. 590–1). Rape in the countryside often takes place in a shady refuge from the light of the (all-seeing) sun and the heat of the day (cf. Ovid *Met.* 5. 614). To avoid the repetition of *nimis*, Ovid has replaced the more usual *nimis pudoris* with *cum luce pudoris*, making use of a colloquial idiom with *cum* [see Wills (1996) 264]. Twice Ovid breaks his narrative with a couplet of direct speech reflecting the voices of, first, Crane and then Janus. Crane uses colloquialisms and a feminine alliteration of soft liquid and aspirant sounds in the hexameter (*haec loca lucis habent nimis*, 115), while reiterated sibilants in the pentameter give the impression that she has dropped her voice to a whisper.

116. *'si secreta magis ducis in antra, sequor'*: linked to an adjective, *magis* can form a periphrastic comparison: 'a more remote cave'. This usage is found above all in Roman comedy, which suggests that it was probably colloquial and therefore suits the context of Crane's own words.

119. *viderat hanc Ianus visaeque cupidine captus*: the instantaneous nature of Janus' passion resembles Mars' on seeing the sleeping Ilia: *Mars videt hanc, visamque cupit, potiturque cupita* (*Fast.* 3. 21). The onset of Janus' passion is described with a judicious combination of pluperfects (*viderat... usus erat*, 119–20) and participial resumption, picking up the main verb from the previous clause as a participle in the subsequent sentence (*visae*, 119). The formula is apt for one-line rapes (cf. *Fast.* 4. 445, *Met.* 4. 316, etc.). [For a collection of examples of participial resumption see Wills (1996) 310–25.]

120. *ad duram verbis mollibus usus est*: the idiom *ad duram*, instead of the dative *durae*, is occasionally found in Roman poetry to indicate the recipient of praise, harsh words, or simply factual information (cf. *dulce rideat ad patrem*, Cat. 61. 212).

121. *remotius antrum*: the most famous example of passion in a cave following a hunt in Latin literature is, of course, Virgil's description of Dido and Aeneas (*Aen.* 4. 165–72). Earlier, however, Aristophanes uses a cave with its conventional literary associations in his comedy *Lysistrata*, where the women stage a conjugal strike. Like Crane, his Myrrhine objects to sex in the open and demands a more secluded spot (922–3), whereupon she meets (and disappoints) her husband, Kinesias, in the cave of Pan. The playwright prefaces this scene with a chorus telling the story of Melanion who rejects marriage and devotes himself to hunting (781–96). Caves appear several times in Roman elegy as a place for outdoor assignations (see Prop. 3. 13. 33–4, Ovid *Ars* 2. 621–3).

122. *destituitque ducem*: the resumption of Ovid's sequence of historic present (*iubet... sequitur*, 120–1) is again broken by an unexpected perfect, *destituit*. This alliterative phrase, conspicuous in the second half of the pentameter, marks a pivotal point in the story: overlooking Janus' power of double vision, Crane has made the foolish mistake of using her usual technique to discard her two-faced suitor, who watches her hide and follows her to her hiding place.

124–5. *nil agis, et latebras respicit ille tuas.* | *nil agis, en! dixi, nam te sub rupe latentem*: 'You'll achieve nothing. He can see your hiding place. Absolutely nothing! Look! I told you—(he's grabbed) you hiding there under the rocks!' The literal meaning of *respicere*, to look round or back at someone, has a piquancy in the case of Janus who has eyes at the back of his head. The poet now apostrophizes Crane in elegiac fashion, making the rape all the more vivid by describing it as though it were taking place before his eyes. For dramatic effect *nil agis* is repeated for emphasis at the beginning of the pentameter and the subsequent hexameter. Cf. *Fast.* 4. 240–1: *a pereant partes, quae nocuere mihi!* | *a pereant dicebat...* [For further examples see Wills (1996) 111–20.]

127. '*ius pro concubitu nostro tibi cardinis esto*': as god of the door Janus offers an apt gift. In contrast to Crane's colloquial speech (115–16), Janus' solemn spondees are enhanced by a pattern of assonance, including the archaic *esto*, so that he seems to intone his pompous pronouncement, emphasizing his key points by alliteration: *ius pro concubitu . . . cardinis*, 127, *pretium positae (virginitatis)*, 128.

129–30. *spinam qua tristes pellere posset | a foribus noxas—haec erat alba—dedit*: the whitethorn, *spina alba*, is traditionally credited with apotropaic powers. Among his examples for whitethorn being used in the ancient world to ward off evil, Frazer quotes Festus (283L), who records that one of the three boys who escorted a Roman bride to her new home carried a torch made of whitethorn [see Frazer (1929) 4 *ad loc.*].

Crane saves the Alban prince, Proca, from the *striges*

131–43: *There are rapacious birds which prey on children, when their nurses are absent, and violate their bodies. Known as* striges *because of their ghastly nocturnal shrieks, they entered Proca's chamber.* **143–54:** *Proca, five days old, was a succulent dainty, and they sucked dry his infant breast. Answering his cries, his nurse discovered that his cheeks had been lacerated. She appealed to Crane, who promised to cure him.* **155–68:** *Three times Crane touched the door with an arbutus twig, and sprinkled the entrance with water, setting outside the raw entrails of a pig. Then she recited her spell, poured a libation, and set out the sacrifice, forbidding those present to watch. In the small window she put Janus' twig. After this no bird touched the child's cradle and Proca was restored to health.*

131. *sunt avidae volucres*: Ovid's second story purports to show how Crane uses her whitethorn wand to divert harm from the doorway. In fact, it is a cult story illustrating her power, as the Roman goddess Carna, to protect human *viscera* in potential Roman *iuvenes.* His first words, *sunt avidae volucres*, introduce the *striges*, powerful female birds, which became in popular legend vampires or witches said to prey on small children (cf. Plaut. *Ps.* 819–21, Hor. *Ep.* 5. 39, Ovid *Am.* 1. 8. 1–20, Apul. *Apol.* 3. 21, Petr. *Sat.* 63, 134).

131–2. *non quae Phineia mensis | guttura fraudabant*: 'not those which deprived Phineus of his food'. Ovid's *avidae volucres* are not the Harpies, who stole Phineus' food in Apollonius' *Argonautica* (2. 178–499) and reappear in Virgil (*Aen.* 3. 210–18) as malevolent demons, repulsive hybrids with virgins' faces and clawed hands. The word *guttur*, used here to refer to Phineus' desire for food, conveys a sense of ravening hunger. It is used by Virgil to refer to both Cacus (*Aen.* 8. 261) and Cerberus (6. 421). More commonly *guttur* was used specifically to refer to a bird's crop (*OLD* s.v. 1*c*).

133–4. ***grande caput, stantes oculi, rostra apta rapinis; | canities pennis, unguibus hamus inest***: the Harpies' mythological form is absent from Ovid's more factual ornithological description of broad and massive heads, staring eyes, predatory beaks, grey plumage, and hooked claws. The five segments of this description may be aptly applied to most European owls of the *striges* variety, probably the birds of ill omen mentioned by Horace (*Ep.* 5. 20), Tibullus (1. 5. 52) and Propertius (4. 5. 17). *canities pinnis* is not intended to indicate greyness, but rather the owls' whitish underparts or mottled and barred plumage which are distinctive in twilight. Finally, Ovid's sound-play echoes sense in this vivid description.

135. ***puerosque petunt nutricis egentes***: children most at risk from *striges* are *nutricis egentes*; they lack the assiduous care of a nurse or kourotrophos in the place of their natural mother. A witch represents a negative, destructive, and therefore unnatural mother figure akin to the ancient archetype of a stepmother. The contrast of good and bad mother substitutes is a pervasive theme in *Fasti* 6. An important passage in the second half of the book celebrates the cult of Mater Matuta, formerly Ino, the devoted kourotrophos, who stands in direct contrast to Juno, the malevolent stepmother, who has caused the murder of the children of both Ino and Hercules (*Fast.* 6. 524) and who, in the final lines of the poem, offers, but only grudgingly, a reconciliatory hand to her stepson: *cui dedit invitas victa noverca manus* (800). In this passage Crane, a true kourotrophos, protects the infant prince Proca from the witch. When, in Horace's fifth *Epode*, a small boy is kidnapped to provide ingredients for a love potion by the witch Canidia and her three female companions, *petere*, a word often associated with violence and rape, is the word which the boy uses to threaten reciprocal vengeance on the witches after his death: *petam voltus umbra curvis unguibus* (Hor. *Ep.* 5. 93).

136–7. ***et vitiant cunis corpora rapta suis; | carpere dicuntur lactentia viscera rostris*****:** 'they violate bodies of children snatched from their cradles and are said to prey on the inner parts of suckling babes.' Petronius (*Sat.* 63) tells how the dead child is robbed of his heart and intestines by *striges*, who substitute a straw doll in its place. It is within Carna's power to heal and restore the damage which the vampires inflict on a child's *viscera*, which are described as *lactentia* (137) because the child is as yet unweaned.

138. ***et plenum poto sanguine guttur habent*****:** 'their crop is full of the blood which they have drunk.' Because the *striges* are vampires, they suck the child's blood. The chiastic structure of this pentameter is enhanced by assonance and alliteration.

139–40. ***sed nominis huius | causa, quod horrenda stridere nocte solent*****:** 'but the reason for this name is that they have a habit of shrieking, making night full of terror.' Ovid tells us that the *striges* owe their name to their habit of emitting high-pitched, sibilant shrieks (*stridere*) in the night. The gerundive adjective, *horrenda*, is proleptic; the night becomes terrifying because of the shriek of the *striges*. Petronius (*Sat.* 63) graphically compares their shrieking to that of a hunted hare: *subito stridere strigae coeperunt; putares canem leporem persequi.* [See S. G. Olifant, who suggests that the *strix* has more in common with a bat than an owl, 'The Story of the *strix*, Ancient', *TAPhA* 44 (1913) 133–49 and 'The Story of the *strix*, Isidorus and the Glossographers', *TAPhA* 45 (1914) 49–63. For a discussion of the etymology of the word *striges*, see Porte (1985) 245–6.]

142. ***neniaque in volucres Marsa figurat anus*****:** 'a Marsian spell fashions old crones into birds.' Ovid considers whether *striges* were born as birds, *sive igitur nascuntur aves*, 141, or were originally old women who were transformed into birds by a spell: *seu carmine fiunt*, 141 (cf. Fest. 414L). The Marsians, renowned for their magic skills, had a distinguished pedigree since they claimed descent from Circe and Odysseus (Plin. *Nat.* 7. 15). Marsian incantations (*nenia Marsa*) were reputedly powerful (cf. Virg. *Aen.* 7. 750, Hor. *Ep.* 5. 75–6, Ovid, *Ars* 2. 102). On this subject Habinek, (2005) 251, describes Carna as 'a virtual doublet' of Carmentis. He associates both goddesses, and Juno Monera, who shares Carna's feast day, with foundation, in particular the rituals of song and sacrifice [cf. Sabbatucci (1988) 182–92].

143. ***in thalamos venere Procae: Proca natus in illis | . . . quinque diebus***: Ovid moves his narrative forward by ending his extended description of the *striges* with a brief statement of their arrival in Proca's nursery, which is seamlessly followed by their attack on the baby. The poet often repeats names in polyptoton (cf. *Fast.* 6. 27: *Iovi, Iovis*). At five days old Proca's flesh is particularly appealing to the *striges*: *praeda recens avium* (144). Proca survived to become an Alban king, the father of Aemulius and Numitor (Liv. 1. 3. 10), who has his place in Ovid's extended Roman genealogy from Dardanus to Romulus (*Fast.* 4. 29–60. Cf. Liv. 1. 3. 6–10, D.H. 1. 71. 4–6, Ovid *Met.* 14. 609–21).

145. ***pectoraque exsorbent avidis infantia linguis***: 'with greedy tongues they suck the baby's breast dry.' No mere infanticides, these witches carry their reversal of the role of nurturing mother figure to the limit so that, instead of suckling the child in their care, they themselves drain (*exsorbent*) the contents of their victim's *pectora infantia.*

146. ***at puer infelix vagit opemque petit***: Grotesquely Ovid describes the child's discomfort in words that suggest the normal wailing of a small baby which needs to be fed.

147. ***territa voce sui nutrix accurrit alumni***: effective word order and sequence of events enhance Ovid's narrative. For maximum impact Ovid built up the fearsome appearance of the *striges*, describing their threat to children, before moving in to their attack on Proca. The baby's wailing, *infelix vagit*, 146, is now picked up by *voce sui . . . alumni*, while *territa*, the ominous opening word, introduces the next character in the drama, the *nutrix*, who occupies a central position just before the fourth-foot caesura.

148. ***et rigido sectas invenit ungue genas***: 'she found his cheeks ripped by the hard talons.' The force of this pentameter is heightened by its chiastic word order. What the nurse actually finds when she looks into the cradle is succinctly foreshadowed by the unpleasantly suggestive adjectives *rigido* and *sectas.*

149. ***quid faceret?***: her panic and indecision are prolonged by this typically elegiac apostrophe (cf. *Fast.* 3. 609: *heu fugiat? quid agat?*).

149–50. ***color oris erat qui frondibus olim | esse solet seris quas nova laesit hiems***: 'his face was the colour that leaves sometimes have which the onset of winter has damaged.' The child's deathly pallor is underlined by Ovid's imagery of dying leaves. The image of leaves seared by winter frost becomes a topos in Ovid's exile poetry, e.g. *Tr.* 3. 8. 29, where this line is only slightly altered (cf. *Tr.* 5. 13. 6. and *Ars* 3. 703). The *striges* have the power to drain their victim's colour by their touch. Petronius (*Sat.* 63) describes the pallor of a Cappadocian who has pierced a vampire with his sword: *corpus totum lividum... quasi flagellis caesus quia scilicet illum tetigerat mala manus.*

151. ***pervenit ad Cranaen***: see note on line 107.

151–2. ***'timorem | pone! tuus sospes,' dixit, 'alumnus erit.'***: Ovid places strategically crucial words at focal points throughout the couplet: *timorem* at the end of the hexameter, *pone* enjambed at the beginning of the pentameter, and *sospes*, at the pentameter break, picked up by *erit*, the closing word. Terse, laconic speech is favoured by helpful nymphs in *Fasti* (cf. Egeria (*Fast.* 3. 289–90): '*ne nimium terrere! Piabile fulmen | est.*').

153–4. ***venerat ad cunas; flebant materque paterque | 'sistite vos lacrimas, ipsa medebor,' ait***: this couplet well illustrates the impact of Ovid's versatile tense changes in paratactic narrative, where each verb contributes the force of its own tense to the progress of the tale: pluperfect (*venerat*), imperfect (*flebant*), imperative (*sistite*), future (*medebor*).

155–6. ***protinus arbutea postes ter in ordine tangit | fronde, ter arbutea limina fronde notat***: threefold repetition of ritual action, traditional in ancient magic, is emphasized by Ovid's twice repeated *arbutea fronde* and *ter*, as he enumerates the parts of the door which must be touched with arbutus to dispel evil (cf. *Fast.* 2. 573).

157. ***spargit aquis aditus (et aquae medicamen habebant)***: water was regularly used as a purificatory measure in magic and chthonic worship (cf. Virg. *Ecl.* 8. 64, *Aen.* 4. 635, 6. 229–30).

158. ***extaque de porca cruda bimenstre***: 'and the raw entrails from a two-month-old pig.' The pig's vital organs are raw (*cruda*) and they are exposed in the open air, so they are distinguished from the wholesome sacrifice of beans and emmer porridge offered to Carna and eaten inside by her worshippers [see McDonough, 'Carna, Proca and the *strix*', 332–3].

159–60. '*noctis aves, extis puerilibus . . . | parcite*': 'birds of the night, do not harm the child's vital organs!' Crane's emphasis on *viscera*, which is underlined in the wording *extis puerilibus* instead of *puero*, emphasizes the goddess Carna's function as guardian of the *viscera* of Roman *iuvenes*.

160–1. '*pro parvo victima parva cadit. | cor pro corde, precor, pro fibris sumite fibras*': Carna recites the formulae which accompanies her 'sacrifice of substitution' in which she replaces the human with an animal victim (cf. *Fast.* 3. 339–42). Greek and Roman magic ritual required the celebrant to say aloud what he was doing and to what purpose (cf. Theoc. *Id.* 2. 62, Virg. *Ecl.* 8. 72–84, Ovid *Fast.* 2. 581, 5. 437–8). Essential to this ritual is the repetition *pro parvo . . . parva*, *cor . . . pro corde*, *pro fibris . . . fibras*, which mirrors the concept of recompense and restitution. A very similar sacrifice of substitution is cited by Porte (1985: 272), from an inscription (*CIL* 8. 4468) where the repeated words are: *anima pro anima, vita pro vita, sanguis pro sanguine* [see Wills (1996) 192]. See headnote on *Ludi Piscatorii* (p. 75).

162. '*hanc animam vobis pro meliore damus.*': Crane's substitution of a pig for the life of Proca is similar to Numa's substitution of a fish in place of the human life which Jupiter demands: *postulat hic animam, cui Numa 'piscis', ait* (*Fast.* 3. 342).

163. *prosecta sub aethera ponit*: *prosecta* was the correct term for a portion of meat which had been removed from its carcass for sacrificial purposes (Var. *L* 5. 110). It could then be offered to the gods: *porrecta*.

164. *quique adsint sacris, respicere illa vetat*: 'she forbids those who are attending the rites to turn and look.' Participants in Greco-Roman magic or religious rituals are always forbidden to look back in rites involving ghosts or other supernatural beings, which may otherwise be seen taking possession of placatory offerings laid out for them (Ovid *Fast.* 5. 439. Cf. Theoc. *Id.* 24. 95, Virg. *Ecl.* 8. 102).

165. *virgaque Ianalis de spina subditur alba*: 'and Janus' wand of whitethorn is inserted.' The whitethorn twig which Janus gave to Crane (130) is placed on the windowsill so that it can now be used for the purpose for which it was intended: *qua tristes pellere posset | a foribus noxas* (129–30). This line is much corrupted in the mss. The conjecture *subditur*, adopted by *AWC*, replaces *ponitur* which is the reading favoured by Merkel (1841).

168. *et rediit puero, qui fuit ante color*: normal health returns to the child with his rosy colour. The connection between ruddy cheeks and healthy vigour is summed up by Dumézil (1970: 386), who associates the Pannonian's request for red roses at the *Carnaria* 'with the desire of the deceased in his love for life that each year, on the festival of the goddess who *vitalibus humanis praeest*, the flowers which most closely resemble the complexion of the living cheeks should be offered to his shade as a poetic recalling of his happy years of life'.

Ovid's third aition for the Carnaria: why people eat pork, beans, and emmer on Carna's feast day

The virtues of simple food

Structurally this passage forms another overarching frame with *Fasti* 1. 185–228, where Janus reminisces about Rome's former simplicity. Thematically the passage belongs to a group of stories in which the theme of food in *Fasti* 6 is diversely associated with military matters: here luxurious dining is contrasted adversely with the simple diet associated with the goddess who protects the *viscera* of Rome's fighting men (see Introduction 4. 2). The Proca story, illustrating Carna's protection of *viscera*, and Ovid's description of the nutritious and homely dish eaten on her feast day are separated by his unexpected digression on Roman gluttony (169–82), from a passage which celebrates the dedication of the temple of Juno Moneta. Because this temple was built on the site of the house of the Roman commander M. Manlius Capitolinus, Ovid is reminded of the Gallic siege of 390 BC in which Manlius played a heroic part which represents a period when the Romans were as yet unspoilt by *luxuria*. In Livy's account the Roman soldiers, faced with *summa inopia*, stoically refrained from eating the sacred geese (Liv. 5. 47. 4), threw bread down from the citadel to give an impression of plenty (5. 48. 4), and rewarded Manlius' heroism with gifts from their own meagre rations (5. 47. 7–8). The impact of the gluttony passage is thus accentuated by the two framing sequences, which celebrate respectively the frugality and abstinence of former times. This type of thematic link is important to the internal structure of the books of Ovid's *Fasti*; for another example, see note on lines 647–8. The Capitoline geese reappear in the passage on sacrifice in *Fasti* 1 where, in contrast to the Roman care for the sacred geese on the Capitol, the decadent Egyptian goddess Isis receives an offering of *foie gras* (1. 453–4).

169–82: *You ask why, on the first of the month, people eat fat pork casseroled with beans and emmer? Carna is an ancient goddess who thrives on traditional dishes. She dislikes foreign food. Once fish swam undisturbed, oysters were safe, and Latium had no idea of Ionian riches. The peacock was valued for its plumage. No exotic animals came to Rome. People used to appreciate the pig killed on festal days and the land produced only beans and emmer. Your bowels will remain healthy if you observe this diet on Carna's day.*

169–70. *pinguia cur illis gustentur larda kalendis | ... rogas?*: the custom of eating a particular dish on a god's feast day had its origins in archaic society, where a ritual banquet was held in a civic hall near the sanctuary with an equal distribution of sacrificial meat, music, and ceremonial drinking. Ritual dining spread to the Etruscan and Latin settlements of Central Italy during the seventh and sixth centuries. Religious festivals provided the occasion for sacrifices followed by civic banquets which continued to be held by the *sodalitates* of public priesthoods through the Roman Republican period. The theme of sacrificial banquets on religious festivals returns near the end of the book, in Ovid's story of the walk-out of the Roman *tibicines* at the *Quinquatrus* (6. 651–92), for Livy's version of the same story emphasizes that the pipers strike because they have been excluded from the *Epulum Iovis.* Varro's statement (Non. 539L) that on 1 June a sacrificial dish of beans is offered *publice et privatim* suggests that, mirroring the public sacrificial banquets, the cessation of civic business on public holidays gave families the opportunity to share a festive meal of beans and pork after Carna had received her own portion. [See A. Ratje, 'The Adoption of the Homeric Banquet in Central Italy in the Orientalising Period' and Nevio Zorzetti, 'The *Carmina Convivalia*', in Oswyn Murray (ed.), *Sympoticum: A Symposium on the Symposium* (Oxford, 1990) 280–8 and 289–309,

J. Scheid, 'La Spartizione a Roma', *StudStor* 25 (1984) 945–56, Dunbabin (2003), 50–1.]

171. *prisca dea est, aliturque cibis, quibus ante solebat*: Ovid's argument, that antique goddesses prefer simple rustic offerings, is advanced for Cybele (*Fasti* 4. 372) and Pales (4. 744) [see Porte (1985) 482]. Beans and pork, however, also represented traditional country fare. Jaded by city life, Horace longs for his country estate, books, idleness, wine—and a rustic cassoulet of beans and pork: *o noctes cenaeque deum!* (*Serm.* 2. 6. 65).

172. *adscitas... dapes*: unlike the homely Italian beans and pork favoured by Carna, a true *prisca dea* (171), 'adopted banquets' signified dinners where the produce was imported from other countries to satisfy the contemporary Roman taste for luxurious and exotic dishes. This contrast offers the poet the opportunity for a six-line digression, in which he evokes the simplicity and innocence of the Golden Age by describing several living creatures who then enjoyed primeval security: the fish swam *sine fraude* (173), the oyster lived *in conchis tuta* (174), the crane had escaped the attention of the gourmet (176), and the peacock was admired only for its plumage (197). Traditionally imported goods belonged to the negative signs of Roman progress. Ovid describes how simple meatless sacrifices were offered in archaic Rome in the days before sea trade brought foreign unguents to Roman altars (*Fast.* 1. 337–53).

173. *piscis adhuc illi populo sine fraude natabat*: 'and their fish still swam in safety.' The word *adhuc*, like *nondum*, was a conventional signpost to a description of life in the Golden Age accompanied by moral reflection on the virtues of the simple life (cf. Tib. 1. 3. 37, Ovid *Met.* 1. 94, *Fast.* 1. 339). The word *fraude* hints at the sort of meretricious gourmandise which made fish dishes both a currency and a criterion for *luxuria* in Rome. Wealthy Romans trawled the markets for the finest specimens or bred them in fishponds (*stagna*) at their villas; sauces were created which became a byword for extravagance (Hor. *Serm.* 2. 4. 37–9, 2. 8. 42–53, Juv. 4. 15–17, 5. 92–8 *et passim*). [Fish as a luxury is discussed by N. Hudson, 'Food in Roman Satire', in S. Braund (ed.), *Satire and Society in Ancient Rome* (Exeter, 1989) 69–87.]

174. ***ostreaque in conchis tuta fuere suis***: 'oysters were safe in their shells.' Nisbet and Hubbard (1970) point out that *tutus* used in this context, in Hor. *Carm.* 1. 17. 3 and 4. 4. 17, can mean not only safe but also 'protected' (from *tueor*). Oysters, like Ovid's other two examples, crane and peacock, were considered delicacies (see Hor. *Serm.* 2. 2. 21–30, 2. 4. 33, Juv. 1. 143, 4. 140–1, 13. 170, Petr. *Sat.* 70. 6), and had their place in the recipe book of Apicius, whose refined palate was a byword in gourmet society in the principate of Tiberius.

175. ***Ionia dives***: 'rich Ionia', the coastal region of Asia Minor, had a reputation for effeminacy among the more puritanical Romans. Plautus (*Stich.* 769) and Horace (*Carm.* 3. 6. 21) refer to loose dancing [see Nisbet and Rudd (2004) 106], Propertius (1. 6. 31) to unmanly songs.

176. ***nec quae Pygmaeo sanguine gaudet avis***: 'nor the bird which delights in the blood of the Pygmy.' This line is an almost verbatim translation of a line from Callimachus' *Aetia* (fr. 1. 14 Pf.). The literary fame of the crane derives entirely from the story to which Ovid alludes, the hostility between Pygmies and cranes (cf. Hom. *Il.* 3. 3, Mela 3. 81, Plin. *Nat.* 10. 58). Horace features the crane as a recherché dish at Nasidienus' dinner (*Serm.* 2. 8. 87), while Apicius offers six recipes for sauces to complement this delicacy.

177. ***et praeter pennas nihil in pavone placebat***: 'nor was there any delight in the peacock apart from its plumage.' The alliterative line makes the same point as Horace (*Serm.* 2. 2. 26–30). The peacock reappears in Roman literature as an example of luxurious dining after the orator Hortensius served his guests roast peacock to celebrate his election to the college of augurs (Cic. *Fam.* 9. 18. 3–4). Ovid opens his passage on the bird sacrifice with an observation on their comparative security during the Golden Age: *intactae fueratis aves* (*Fast.* 1. 441).

178. ***nec tellus captas miserat arte feras***: although *ante* is the reading found in *UGM*, supported by Merkel (1841), *AWC*'s *arte* is much more graphic: 'nor had the world exported to Rome wild creatures guilefully ensnared.' Apicius offered recipes for Italian wild boar and venison but not for African exotica, which were exhibited in the circus where their outlandish appearance could be appreciated.

179. ***sus erat in pretio***: 'a pig was highly valued.' The expression, which has a rural ring, is Urania's choice to describe the value of a face furrowed with wrinkles (*ruga senilis*) in ancient as opposed to modern Rome (*Fast.* 5. 58). Ovid uses the same expression in another passage in which the Iron Age introduces moral decline (*Fast.* 4. 405). This passage which began with praise of Ceres' gift of agriculture goes on to recommend that Ceres should receive as a sacrificial victim not ploughing-oxen but *ignavam . . . suem* (cf. *Fast.* 1. 349, *prima Ceres avidae gavisa est sanguine porcae*). The pig appears to have been Ceres' usual sacrifice, and the traditional autumnal slaughter of the family pig in rural Italy (*caesa sue festa colebant*) lies behind Cato's description of a sacrifice of pork, beans, and grain to Ceres at harvest time (Cato *Agr.* 134).

180. ***terra fabas tantum duraque farra dabat***: in this line Ovid summarizes the diet of ancient Romans: beans and emmer. Archaeological finds indicate that beans were eaten in Central Italy in the Bronze Age. They proved a hardy crop which became used widely in Rome (Hor. *Serm.* 2. 3. 182–3, Mart. 10. 14, 10. 48. 16, Plin. *Nat.* 18. 117), as they are in Italian cuisine today. The hardiest and outstandingly nutritious Italian cereal crop was emmer, which could be grown in wet or dry soil. Being stored in its husk, it needed no threshing and kept well in granaries. The husks had to be removed by burning, which meant that when it was baked into bread as flour, it was being baked for the second time: *passuraque farra bis ignem* (*Fast.* 1. 693). [See M. T. Spurr, *Arable Cultivation in Roman Italy, 200* BC–AD *100*, JRS Monograph No. 8. (1989) 12, 105–6.]

181–2. ***quae duo mixta simul sextis quicumque kalendis | ederit, huic laedi viscera posse negant***: 'whoever eats a mixture of these two on the sixth Kalends, his bowels, they say, cannot suffer harm.' The satirists' references to Roman gluttony are often accompanied by health warnings (Hor. *Serm.* 2. 2. 21–2, Pers. 3. 94–7, Juv. 1. 140–5). Conversely, Ovid concludes Carna's feast day by assuring his readers that her unsophisticated dish of beans and pork on the Kalends of June will have a beneficent effect on their bowels. By ring composition the poet is able to return to and emphasize Carna's guardianship of human *viscera*. As part of the network of poetic association, the theme of food, with its moral undertones, links two episodes on the Kalends of June: the feast of Carna and the *natalis* of the temple of Juno Moneta.

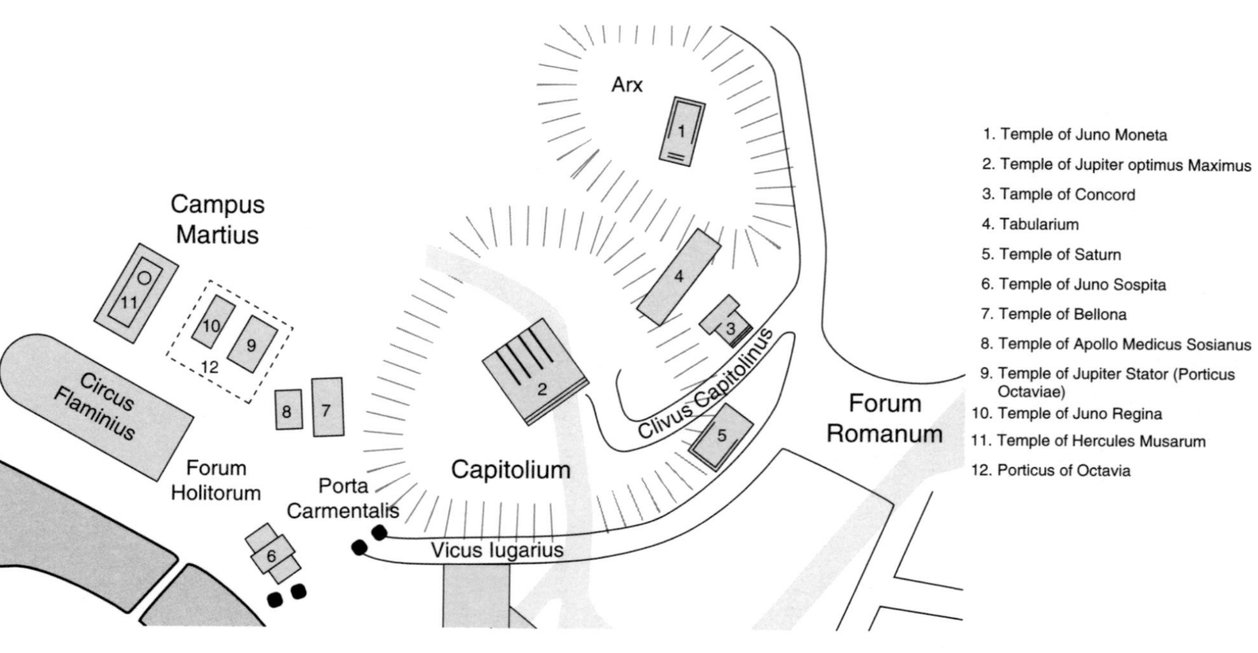

Plan 2. Capitolium: *Fast.* 6. 183–248, 351–94

JUNO MONETA, 183–190

[Dury-Moyaers and Renard (1978) 142–202, Radke (1965) 221–3, Palmer (1974) 29 ff. On Juno's geese see N. Horsfall, 'From History to Legend: Manlius and the Geese', *CJ* 76 (1980) 298–311, A. Ziolkowski, 'Between the Geese and the *Auguraculum:* The Origins of the Cult of Juno on the Arx', *CP* 88: 3 (1993) 206–19. For Juno Moneta as an oracular goddess see M. Guarducci, 'Un antichissimo responso dell'oraculo di Cuma', *Bullettino della Commissione Archeologica Comunale in Roma* 72 (1946–8) 129–41, N. Purcell, 'Atrium Libertatis', *PBSR* 61 (1993) 125–55, F. Coarelli, 'Moneta, le officine della zecca di Roma tra Repubblica e Impero', *AIIN* 38–41 (1994) 23–65, Meadows and Williams (2001) 27–49, Purcell (2003) 26–33.]

1. The Temple of Juno Moneta

The temple to Juno Moneta stood on the *arx*, a rocky eminence on the Capitoline Hill overlooking the Forum Romanum. Cicero's suggestion that the name Moneta derived from the verb *monere* (*Div.* 1. 45), because, during an earthquake, a voice from this temple had demanded the expiatory sacrifice of a pregnant sow, may be corroborated by the old Roman legend that Juno's sacred geese warned the Roman commander M. Manlius Capitolinus of the approach of the Gauls in 390 BC (Liv. 5. 47. 4, D.H. 13. 7–8, Plin. *Nat.* 10. 51. Cf. Virg. *Aen.* 8. 652–62, Prop. 3. 3. 12); the temple is depicted in a relief from Ostia with three perturbed geese outside flapping their wings. Since the circumstances of this story antedate the dedication of the temple of Juno Moneta in 344 BC (Liv. 7. 28. 4), the geese, if they existed at all, would have to have been cooped up in an earlier shrine to Juno Moneta, and there is some archaeological evidence for an earlier archaic temple on the same site, or in the nearby *auguraculum* [see Meadows and Williams (2001) 32, n. 32].

Moneta is the name used for Mnemosyne, mother of the Muses, by Livius Andronicus in his translation of the *Odyssey*, and Hyginus cites Jupiter and Moneta as parents of the Muses (*Fabula* 27. 1). The name Mnemosyne or Memory is well suited to the role of Juno

Moneta, who guarded an unimpeachable record of historical events for Roman posterity. In Moneta's temple were stored the *Libri Lintei*, the records of annually elected consuls, dating from 444 to 428 BC, which were inscribed on linen cloth (Liv. 4. 20. 8). From 273 BC the Roman silver mint and its workshops were attached to the temple of Juno Moneta (Liv. 6. 20. 13). Moneta's guardianship of Roman coinage was an encouragement for Roman moneyers to use coinage, a true record of events, as a means to glorify their families by commemorating heroic family legends.

A saddle of land, known as *inter duos lucos*, 'between two sacred precincts', lay between two sacred repositories of Republican Roman archives: the temple of Capitoline Jupiter, where treaties were stored and time was measured by nails hammered into the door posts, and that of Juno Moneta, where consular Fasti were kept and coinage minted. Extending up to this height and overlooking the Forum Romanum was a building on two or three levels. It has been suggested [Purcell, 'Atrium Libertatis'] that this housed, on the upper level, the Atrium Libertatis, the office of the censors, who were responsible for land registry, adjudicating claims for citizenship, as well as assessing the wealth and property of individual Romans. Below this were probably two more levels, with galleries overlooking the Forum, belonging to the *Tabularium* or archive office. This was connected by a covered staircase with the temple of Saturn, which housed the *Aerarium* or Treasury, and perhaps also physically linked to the temple of Juno Moneta [Coarelli, 'Moneta...']. All this constituted a civic complex responsible for finance and record-keeping of which Juno Moneta's temple was an integral part. Juno Mnemosyne, or her Latin equivalent Moneta, was an apt name for the guardian goddess of standards of measurement [see Meadows and Williams (2001)] and historical data, whose function was to ensure that records be neither falsified nor forgotten.

Essential to the Romans' concept of state religion was the conjunction of chronology with the monuments and topography of Rome. Purcell (2003: 26–33) aptly describes the archaic Capitoline temple of Jupiter Optimus Maximus, sited on the Roman acropolis, as 'a deliberately created focus for the identity of the Roman community'. The achievements of Republican Rome—Fasti, treaties, and coinage—were preserved on the Capitoline acropolis and the early

Republican Roman historians marked the Capitoline Era with the expression *post Capitolinam aedem dedicatam*. The measurement of Republican time inherent in the Capitoline cults of Jupiter Optimus Maximus and Juno Moneta had an Augustan equivalent in the Princeps' *Horologium* in the Campus Martius. Here the pointer of Augustus' giant sundial, the Egyptian obelisk, which he had dedicated to Sol/Apollo, bisected the Ara Pacis on the Princeps' birthday, the September equinox, plainly reiterating the Augustan ideological message that the Actian and Egyptian victories had brought the blessings of *Pax Augusta*.

Ovid uses the *natalis* of the Aedes Iunonis Monetae to focus both on the Gallic invasion in the early fourth century BC (185–90) and on the two generals who distinguished themselves in this conflict: M. Manlius Capitolinus and M. Furius Camillus. This section leads into a series of Republican temple foundations all associated with Roman wars: Bellona (3 June), Hercules Custos (4 June), and Bona Mens (8 June). By evoking the past importance of the ancient Republican temples on the Capitoline Hill, he also sharpens his focus on Augustus' new dynastic acropolis on the Palatine, where the temples of Apollo, Magna Mater, and Victory and the house of Augustus with its Vestal shrine celebrated the victory at Actium and the Trojan origins of the Aeneadae whose descendant now guarded the Vestal flame on which Rome's survival depended. Augustus emphasized religious continuity with a past more ancient than the archaic and Republican Capitoline sanctuaries. His Palatine acropolis had, in common with the acropolis of Athens, a founder's heroon in the *casa Romuli*, while the Lupercal cave below had a forerunner in the Athenian cave of Pan. This may owe its origins to a general Hellenizing influence in the mid-Republic, but it also, perhaps, reflects the close religious ties which developed between Athens and the cities of Rome, Pergamum, Ilion, and Samothrace in the second century BC. (See headnote on lines 417–24, p. 130.)

2. *Structural links in Ovid's celebration of Juno Moneta*

The poet of the *Fasti* achieves a graceful ring composition by paying tribute to Mnemosyne and her daughters on the first and last day of June respectively, for he honours Juno Moneta, guardian of the consular *Fasti,* on 1 June, and on 30 June Hercules Musarum, in whose temple M. Fulvius Nobilior had placed Fasti celebrating *natales* of temples founded by the Roman Republican nobility [see Rüpke (1995) 366]. The Muses, whose inspiration now guides the poet's celebration of the Roman religious calendar, are the guardians of Roman Fasti in two Roman temples.

183–90: *Even on the Capitoline Hill the temple of Juno, which you vowed, celebrates your achievements, Camillus. Here stood the house of Manlius who drove the Gallic warriors from Jupiter's Capitol. He would have died honourably defending Jupiter's throne. The title Traitor was his lasting claim to fame.*

183–4. ***arce quoque in summa Iunoni templa Monetae | ex voto memorant facta, Camille, tuo*****:** the *arx* defined the area enclosed within the early fortifications at the summit of the Capitoline Hill (Liv. 6. 20. 9) which included both the northern and the southern summits and the saddle which lay between. Although the word *arx* was often used loosely, as here, to refer to the Capitoline Hill where this temple stood, it could also be narrowed down to signify the slightly higher and more northerly rocky eminence where the house of M. Manlius Capitolinus was later replaced in 384 BC by the temple of Juno Moneta (Liv. 6. 20. 13). Linked to the phrase *arce in summa,* 'at the summit of the citadel', the word *quoque* implies that even in this high place there is a temple which celebrates the fame of M. Furius Camillus, the conqueror of Veii and a deeply religious patriot, whom Valerius Maximus (1. 8. 3) cites as the temple's founder. In fact, the temple of Juno Moneta was vowed by the son of Camillus, another Roman general, L. Furius Camillus, in 348 BC, in the course of a battle against the Aurunci. By simply using the *nomen,* Camillus, Ovid reminds his readers of his more illustrious father, M. Furius Camillus, whose character provides a contrast with his contemporary, M. Manlius Capitolinus, indicted for treason four years after his heroic repulsion of the invading Gauls from the *arx* and flung from the very rock from which he had repelled the invaders. The careers of these two leaders are similarly interwoven for the purpose of moral comparison in Livy's Book 6, in which M. Manlius is shown to be envious of M. Furius Camillus whose renown threatens to eclipse his own: *uni invideret eximio simul honoribus atque virtutibus M. Furio* (Liv. 6. 11. 3). Ovid's eight-line passage on the temple of Juno Moneta highlights two Roman leaders who play a significant part in Livy's description of the Roman conquests of the first half of the fourth century. [See, for the contrast between Camillus the *alter conditor* and Manlius who degenerates into a Catiline figure, E. Burck, *Vom Menschenbild in der römischen Literatur: Ausgewählte Schriften*, ed. E. Lefevre (Heidelberg, 1966); T. P. Wiseman, 'Topography and Rhetoric: The Trial of Manlius', *Historia* 28 (1979) 32–50; C. S. Kraus, *Livy, Ab Urbe Condita Book VI* (Cambridge, 1994), Jaeger (1997) 67–93.]

185. *ante domus Manli fuerat*: *ante* here has temporal significance. The house of the Manlii, built on the site of the future temple of Juno Moneta (Liv. 6. 20. 13), had given the family the cognomen Capitolinus.

186. *a Capitolino reppulit arma Iove*: 'he drove the Gallic forces from (the temple of) Capitoline Jupiter.' By giving Jupiter his full title in a stately pentameter Ovid reiterates the title of the temple which Manlius saves as well as the cognomen Capitolinus, which belongs to his family. According to Livy's account this cognomen had the potential danger of attributing to Manlius divine honour equal to that of Jupiter himself: *quem prope caelestem, cognomine certe Capitolino Iove parem fecerint* (Liv. 6. 17. 5). By alluding to the cults of both Jupiter and Juno in this passage Ovid emphasizes the sacredness of the Capitoline Hill at this period and the danger of Rome's most sacred precinct falling into enemy hands (cf. Hor. *Carm.* 3. 5. 12: *incolumi Iove et urbe Roma*, 3. 30. 7–9, Ovid *Fast.* 6. 349–94). This is further enhanced by his intentionally misleading apostrophe, *Camille* (see note on 183–4), since M. Furius was renowned for his *pietas* and his unshakeable conviction that Rome could never be replaced as a centre of Roman religion (cf. Liv. 5. 51–4). Ovid's juxtaposition of the Gallic attack and the Capitoline temples was an iconographic expression of early Rome's struggle against overwhelming odds and the triumph of Roman *pietas*, exemplified by M. Manlius and the two Camilli. In the same way Virgil juxtaposes Roman religion with the threat of the Gallic invasion of the 390s on the Shield of Aeneas, where he shows the dancing Salii and Luperci next to his image of

Manlius driving back the Gauls from the Capitol (*Aen.* 8. 652–6. Cf. Liv. 5. 41. 3–4) [see Harrison (1997) 70–6].

187. *quam bene, di magni, pugna cecidisset in illa*: 'How nobly would he have fallen in that battle!' This couplet has a strong moralizing tone reinforced by the invocations to *di magni* and *Iuppiter alte.* Following the opening couplet with its mention of Camillus, Ovid suggests that Manlius' defeat of the Gauls on the Capitol was his finest hour, when he was worthy of comparison with M. Furius Camillus, father of the temple founder.

188. *defensor solii, Iuppiter alte, tui*: Manlius might be said to be defending Jupiter's throne when he repelled the Gauls from the rocks near the temple of Jupiter Optimus Maximus.

189. *damnatus crimine regni*: 'condemned on a charge of treason.' The location of Manlius' family home beside the great centre of Capitoline worship evidently engendered uneasy feelings after Manlius was found guilty of treason and executed, for it was decreed that henceforward no Roman patrician might build a private house on the Capitol in the vicinity of Rome's most sacred religious complex (Liv. 6. 20. 14). The repetition of the words *crimine regni* at the end of the hexameter establishes a link between the razing of the traitor Manlius' house and Augustus' demolition of the excessively opulent town-house of Vedius Pollio on the Esquiline in order to build the Porticus Liviae: *haec aequata solo est nullo sub crimine regni | sed quia luxuria visa nocere sua* (6. 643–4). The reader is reminded, in line 647, *sic agitur censura*, that Augustus could assume the uncompromising moral principles of a stern Republican censor, and such moral reflection is underlined by the fact that the passage under discussion celebrates Juno Moneta, as though the message, already clear, required the emphasis of Mnemosyne or The Warner. These two examples of houses in high places being razed as a mark of retributive justice might suggest comparisons with Augustus' house, which stood on the Palatine, surrounded by the most sacred shrines of the Augustan Age: the resplendent temple of Apollo, whose assistance at Actium had inaugurated the Augustan era, the newly restored temple of Cybele, the *casa Romuli*, and, within Augustus' house, as Ovid frequently reminds his readers (*Fast.* 3. 415–28, 4. 949–54, 6. 456), the Vestal flame itself, sacred symbol of Roman power.

190. ***hunc illi titulum longa senecta dabat*****:** 'this title [Traitor] has been his for many a long year.' The idiom, *longa senecta*, clearly appealed to Ovid. It is found twice in *Fasti* 5 in this *sedes* in the pentameter: with its less common meaning, as here, in line 132, and its usual meaning, 'a long old age', in line 70.

MARS AD PORTAM CAPENAM, TEMPESTAS, 191–196

191–6: *The same day is sacred to Mars, whose temple is situated beside the paved road within sight of the Porta Capena. We conceded that you, too, merited a shrine, Tempestas, when our fleet was nearly wrecked off Corsica. If you are interested in constellations, today marks the rising of great Jupiter's eagle. The next day summons the Hyades.*

191. ***lux eadem Marti festa est*****:** before the temple of Mars Ultor was built, the most important shrine to Mars in Rome was this temple of Mars beside the Porta Capena, which was dedicated during the Gallic Wars on 1 June 388 BC, by T. Quinctius (Liv. 6. 5. 8).

191–2. ***quem prospicit extra | adpositum Tectae porta Capena Viae*****:** 'the Porta Capena looks out towards (the temple) beside the Paved Road.' The Via Appia was eventually paved as far as Capua by Appius Claudius Caecus in 312 BC and a paved road (*tecta via*) was extended up to the temple itself a few years later (295 BC, cf. Liv. 10. 23. 12). Ovid uses *quem* to refer to Mars himself (*Marti*, 191) instead of to his temple. The temple stood outside the pomerium beyond the Porta Capena, between the first and second milestones on the Via Appia, which ran all the way to southern Italy, providing a direct route for Roman armies to Brundisium, Sicily, and North Africa. The temple offered an assembly-point for the Roman army and from here an army set out to confront the Gauls who invaded Latium in 350–49 BC (Liv. 7. 23. 3, cf. D.H. 6. 13. 4). The military importance of this road is underlined by a number of other shrines, no longer extant, to Honos, Virtus, and Fortuna Redux built along this stretch of the Via Appia.

193–4. ***Tempestas*****:** the Roman cult of Tempestas corresponded to the Greek cult of the Winds. Nearer to the city walls and the Porta

Capena than the temple of Mars was the Aedes Tempestatis, which was dedicated by L. Cornelius Scipio (cos. 259 BC) after the Roman fleet had been caught in a storm off Corsica (*CIL* 6. 12897. Cf. *ILS* 3277, 3278, 3279: inscriptions from three marble altars from Antium dedicated respectively to The Winds, Neptune, and Calm Sea. The temple was built on the Via Appia, not far from the Tomb of the Scipios. In an inverse propempticon Horace promises a lamb to Tempestates if they will wreck the ship of Mevius (Hor. *Ep.* 10. 23–4. Cf. Virg. *Aen.* 5. 772).

195. *haec hominum monimenta patent: si quaeritis astra*: the diaeresis at the fourth-foot caesura accentuates Ovid's contrast of *hominum monimenta* with *astra.* This line has the same resonance as his encomium on the *felices animae* who devote their lives to understanding the movements of the constellations (*Fast.* 1. 295–310), scorning the transitory glory of *militiae labor* (302), which is represented by the two temples of Mars and Tempestas.

196. *tunc oritur magni praepes adunca Iovis*: in this book Ovid offers ten astronomical notices, as compared with *Fasti* 5 which has fourteen. These notices are all very brief: the risings of the Eagle (6. 196), the Hyades (197–8, 711–12), the setting of Bootes (235–6), the rising of the Dolphin (471–2, 720), Orion (719, 787–8), and Ophiuchus (735) and Ovid's customary notification that the sun is passing into another zodiacal sign, from Gemini to Cancer (726–7). Fox (2004: 124–6), who includes a subtle allusion to the conjunction of Hercules and Lyra in the night sky on 30 June (see note on line 812), estimates that Ovid's asterisms for June are 80 per cent accurate. Since Ovid takes care to vary his poetic descriptions of the constellations, it is probable that he uses *adunca* to describe the Eagle's curved talons since he has already mentioned its beak and tawny colour on 25 May: *grata Iovi fulvae rostra videbis avis* (*Fast.* 5. 732), an earlier rising than 1 June which more closely corresponds to Columella's 1 and 2 June (11. 2. 45) and Pliny's 3 June (*Nat.* 18. 255). [For a discussion of Ovid's divergencies from Pliny and correspondence with Columella see Ideler (1825) 137–69, who suggests that the similarities between Ovid and Columella point to a common source.] In augury *praepes* signified a bird of good omen. It is used of Jupiter's eagle by Ovid (*Met.* 4. 714).

A IIII NON. IUN. F, RISING OF THE HYADES, 197–198

197. ***postera lux Hyadas, Taurinae cornua frontis | evocat*:** 'tomorrow's dawn summons the horns of the bull's brow.' Ovid alludes poetically to the Hyades' position marking the horns of the constellation Taurus. The Hyades make five separate appearances in Ovid's *Fasti*, where they rise on 2, 14, 27 May and 2, 15 June. [See Ideler (1825) 153–5 and Fox (2004) 122, who suggests that *lux* frequently implies a dawn rather than an evening rising, which is suggested by *nox*.]

198. ***et multa terra madescit aqua*:** 'the earth is drenched with a mighty downpour.' Traditionally the Hyades heralded rain.

B III NON. IUN. C, BELLONA, 199–208

199–208: *The following day is said to be the anniversary of the temple of Bellona, vowed during an Etruscan war. Bellona always smiles on Latium. The blind Appius Claudius, who built the temple, saw much with his inner eye when he refused to make peace with Pyrrhus. From Bellona's temple a small patch of ground faces the Circus (Flaminius). There is a small column of no small fame. From here a spear used to be cast when Rome declared war against a king or people.*

199–200. ***Mane ubi bis fuerit*... | ...*bis uda seges*:** 'when morning comes for the second time and again the crops are damp with dew.' These two mornings are 2 and 3 June. Ovid favours morning dew in his range of periphrastic expressions for the arrival of each new day.

201. ***hac sacrata die Tusco Bellona duello | dicitur*:** the goddess Bellona had, like Juno Moneta, Mars at the Porta Capena, Tempestas, and Bona Mens, martial associations appropriate to Juno's month. She was depicted fully armed like Juno Sospita and was believed to represent battle-rage, the fury of a soldier engaged in battle. The Aedes Bellonae was vowed by Appius Claudius Caecus in 296 BC during a war against the Etruscans (*Tusco duello*) and Samnites, which ended in 295 BC with the Battle of Sentinum (Liv. 10. 19. 17). The archaic *duello* is used here, as it sometimes is by Horace, to signify a distant Republican battle (Hor. *Carm.* 3. 5. 38, 14. 18). Bellona herself was sometimes described as Duellona (Var. *L* 5. 73). The temple stood near the Circus Flaminius, the gathering-point for the Roman triumphal procession which would then progress past the temple of Bellona and, about 100 metres further on, the temple of Juno Sospita in the Forum Holitorum. Like other temples to deities of war, such as Mars and Volcanus, Bellona's temple was outside the pomerium in accordance with the precepts of Etruscan haruspicy (cf. Vitruvius 1. 7. 1). Here the senate could receive foreign envoys (Liv. 30. 21. 12) and adjudicate triumphs to victorious generals. The temple figures in the aftermath of battles mentioned later in *Fasti* 6: a triumph was here refused to M. Claudius Marcellus after his conquest of Syracuse (Liv. 26. 21. 1) but granted to C. Claudius Nero and M. Livius Salinator after their victory at the Metaurus (Liv. 26. 28. 9).

203–4. ***Appius est auctor, Pyrrho qui pace negata | multum animo vidit*****:** Ovid distinguishes the two generals by alliteration corresponding to the initial letters of their names. Pyrrhus' involvement with the cities of Southern Italy (280–275 BC) is the subject of Ennius' *Ann.* 6. Appius Claudius Caecus was consul in 296 BC, when he vowed the Aedes Bellonae. When he opposed peace with Pyrrhus some fifteen years later he was blind and infirm (Plut. *Pyrrh.* 18–19, Liv. *Per.* 8, Val. Max. 8. 13. 5). His career is outlined as follows: 'Appius Claudius Caecus, son of Gaius, censor, twice consul, dictator, thrice interrex, thrice praetor, twice curule aedile, quaestor, thrice military tribune. He captured several towns from the Samnites, routed an army of Etruscans and Sabines, prevented peace being made with Pyrrhus, paved the Via Appia in his censorship, conveyed water into the city, and built a temple to Bellona' (*ILS* 54).

204. ***lumine captus erat*****:** the same idiom for blindness is used by Livy (9. 29. 11. cf. *OLD* s.v. 21*a*), who hints that Appius Claudius Caecus lost his sight when he committed the sacrilege of replacing with public slaves the Potitii, who were the hereditary priests of Hercules' cult at the Ara Maxima during his censorship in 312 BC.

205. *prospicit a templo summum brevis area Circum*: 'from the temple a small field faces the Circus (Flaminius).' Ovid describes a small patch of land (*brevis area*) with its symbolic column of war (*columna bellica*) which was used for the ritual of *indictio belli* mentioned by Livy (1. 32. 13). When Rome's immediate neighbours had been subdued so that it was no longer possible to fling a spear from Roman soil into enemy territory, the Romans abandoned the ancient, long-winded *ius fetialis*, which Livy describes at length (1. 32. 6–14). Before declaring war on Pyrrhus a small field was purchased into which a spear could be cast, which represented the territory of the foreign power against which Rome had declared war: *solet hasta manu, belli praenuntia, mitti* (207). Favouring the revival of ancient practices, in 32 BC Octavian performed the old fetial ritual at the temple of Bellona to give greater solemnity, and a public statement of the *Romanitas* represented by his forces. Most significantly this action proclaimed that he was declaring war on the foreign armies of Cleopatra rather than pursuing a civil war against Antony (Dio 50. 4. 4–5). [See Ogilvie (1965) 127–36, *BNP* 2. 7–8, 131.]

206. *non parvae parva columna notae*: 'a small column of no small importance.' Ovid's description is enhanced by the polyptoton: *parvae parva*. Polyptoton, the repetition of words, often juxtaposed and in different cases, is a characteristic of Ovid's style which encourages the reader to pause to reflect on an unexpected contrast or parallel (cf. *Met.* 1. 720, 3. 390, 13.495). [See Wills (1996) 228.]

C PR. NON. IUN. C, HERCULIS MAGNUS CUSTOS, 209–212

209–12: *The other end of the Circus (Flaminius) is protected by Hercules, as the sibyl ordained. The temple's anniversary falls on the day before the Nones. If you want to know who was responsible for the building work, it was Sulla.*

209. *altera pars Circi Custode sub Hercule tuta est*: since the identification of the temple of Bellona (220 BC) by Coarelli (1983) near the eastern end of the Circus Flaminius, *altera pars Circi* must mean further to the west. This part of the Circus, says Ovid, is safe (*tuta*) because it is under the protection of Hercules the Guardian. Shrines to Hercules were traditionally built near gymnasia, amphitheatres, and circuses and the temple may originally have been an integral part of Flaminius' complex, which Sulla restored more than a century later. The Circus Flaminius was not equipped with the usual facilities for a race-track (central division, starting-gates, seating) because it was the assembly-point for the triumphal procession, a purpose reflected in the dedications of the peripheral temples, many of which are dedicated to divinities associated with war: Bellona, Castor and Pollux, Hercules Custos, Mars, Jupiter Stator, Juno Regina, and Volcanus. During the Second Punic War a *supplicatio* to Hercules and *lectisternium* for Hercules and Iuventas took place here in 218 BC (Liv. 21. 62. 9) and a temple to Iuventas, vowed by M. Livius Salinator before the Battle of the Metaurus (Liv. 36. 36. 5–6), was added later.

210. ***quod deus Euboico carmine munus habet***: 'the god owes his temple to Sibylline prophecy.' The word *munus* is often used for a temple, signifying an offering to a god (*OLD* s.v. 3). Ovid indicates that the temple was founded in response to a prophecy in the Sibylline books, which were consulted after Flaminius' debacle at the Battle of Lake Trasimene in 217 BC. The poetic allusion, *Euboico carmine*, to the settlers from Euboea who came to Cumae (cf. Virg. *Aen.* 6. 2) provides a link with Sulla, whose name was sometimes thought to be a shortened form of Sibylla (Macr. 1. 17. 27). In 79 BC Sulla retired to Cumae, the scene of his military successes in Campania during the Social War.

212. ***si titulum quaeris, Sulla probavit opus***: 'if you wish to know the donor of the temple, Sulla approved the work.' The word *titulus* summed up the distinction of being the founder or restorer of a temple, whose name would be inscribed in the Fasti which listed *natales* and *tituli* of temple founders, an example of which is M. Fulvius Nobilior's Fasti in the Aedes Herculis Musarum. By saying that Sulla 'gave his official approval to the work', Ovid suggests that this temple already existed and was restored by Sulla sometime before 78 BC, the year in which games in honour of Hercules may have been commemorated on Roman coinage. [See T. P. Wiseman, 'The Games of Hercules', in Bispham and Smith (eds.) (2000) 108–14.] Sulla's particular regard for Hercules was demonstrated by his vow to give the god a tithe of his entire estate (Plut. *Sull.* 35. 1), so it would not have seemed inappropriate for him to restore the temple honouring Hercules Custos who had shielded him from dangers that threatened him during the campaigns of the Social War.

D NON. IUN. N, SEMO SANCUS DIUS FILIUS, 213–218

213–18: *I was wondering whether I should attribute the Nones to Sancus Fidius or to you, Father Semo. Then Sancus told me, 'To whomsoever you give it, I shall have the honour. I have three names. That was Cures' wish.' So it was this god whom the ancient Sabines honoured with a temple which they built on the Quirinal Hill.*

213–14. *quaerebam, nonas Sanco Fidione referrem* | *an tibi, Semo pater*: Ovid shortens the long *o* in *Semo* for metrical convenience (cf. *Fast.* 2. 527. See Platnauer 51). Ovid suggests three alternatives: Sancus, Fidius, or Semo, names derived from the god's customary appellation, Semo Sancius Dius Fidius, in which the Roman name, Dius Fidius, is prefaced by its Sabine equivalent, Semo Sancius (*CIL* 6. 567: *Semoni Sanco Deo Fidio*, 6. 568: *Sanco sancto Semoni Deo Fidio*. Cf. D.H. 2. 49. 1). Dius Fidius represents Jupiter in his capacity as the recipient of binding oaths, and a statue of Semo Sancus Dius Fidius stood on the Tiber island, the location of a shrine to another god of oaths, Jupiter Jurarius. Semo Sancius seems to have been his Sabine counterpart. His Umbrian form appears in the Iguvine Tablets as Fisos Sansios. Varro (*L* 3. 660) quotes a source which identifies Dius Fidius as the son of Jupiter, known as Sancus to the Sabines and Hercules to the Greeks. Propertius was obviously aware of this when he used the Sabine appellation to address Hercules at the end of his elegy on the aetiology of the Ara Maxima: *Sance, pater, salve, cui iam favet aspera Juno.* | *Sance, velis libro dexter inesse meo* (Prop. 4. 9. 71–2, cf. Fest. 254.13L). Sancus' temple, which had its *natalis* on 5 June, was dedicated on the Quirinal in 466 BC by Sp. Postumius.

215. ***'cuicumque ex istis dederis, ego munus habebo'***: 'to whomsoever you give it, I will have the honour.' The character and origins of Ovid's divine informants tends to be apparent in their speech. Sancus' blunt response and choppy sentences seem designed to reflect the antique rusticity of this Sabine deity [see Miller (1983) 156–92].

217. ***hunc igitur veteres donarunt aede Sabini | inque Quirinali constituere iugo***: Ovid attributes to the Sabines the foundation of an ancient temple to Semo Sancus Dius Fidius which stood on the Quirinal. It was believed to have been founded under the Tarquins and dedicated in 466 BC by Sp. Postumus Albus Regillensis (D.H. 9. 60. 8). Not far from the temple was the Porta Sanqualis, which may have taken its name from Sancus. Pliny (*Nat.* 8. 194) reports that the temple contained a statue of Gaia Caecilia, believed to be either Tanaquil herself or her daughter, and votive offerings which were thought to represent Tanaquil's spindle and distaff.

E VIII EID. IUN. N, 219–234

[Schilling (1954) 43–4, 164, Boëls (1973) 77–100.]

Ovid asks the Flaminica Dialis to recommend an auspicious date for his daughter's wedding

219–34: *When the time came to give my beloved daughter in marriage, I was trying to choose a suitable date for the wedding. The period after the Ides of June was auspicious. The Flaminica Dialis said, 'Until the sweepings from Vesta's temple are carried down the Tiber, I may neither comb my hair nor cut my nails nor sleep with my husband, though he be Jupiter's priest. Don't rush the wedding. Better your daughter marries when Vesta's flames shine on a clean floor.'*

219–20. ***est mihi sitque, precor, nostris diuturnior annis, | filia***: Ovid's enjambement of *filia* emphasizes the affection he feels for his only daughter from three marriages, Perilla, who was living with her husband in Libya at the time of Ovid's banishment

(Ovid *Tr.* 1. 3. 19–20, 4. 10. 75). The poet's prayer that she may outlive him, *nostris diuturnior annis*, suggests a theme often expressed by ancient poets: a parent's regret for the premature death of offspring (Hor. *Carm.* 3. 9. 15–16).

220. *filia, qua felix sospite semper ero*: the ties of affection which bind Ovid (*felix semper*) and his daughter (*filia sospite*) are emphasized by the interlocking alliteration of *f* and *s.*

221–2. *tempora taedis* | *apta*: 'a proper time for marriage.' Ovid uses the same expression when he dismisses the three days of the *Lemuria*, a time when offerings are brought to the family dead and, like the nine *Dies Parentales* in February, wholly unsuitable for weddings (*Fast.* 2. 557–62, 5. 485–6). The juxtaposition of marriage and death was considered as inauspicious as that of marriage and war; consequently Ovid advises brides to avoid the month of Mars: *arma movent pugnas, pugna est aliena maritis* (*Fast.* 3.395). Although the poet appears to make the facile suggestion that battles are ill-omened for married couples, in fact he is touching on religious strictures arising from the belief that marriage had a negative effect on campaigning, while sexual abstinence and virginity were conducive to military success (see *Vestalia*, headnote 1. p. 80). It was the Vestals who prayed for the success of the Roman armies (Cic. *Font.* 48).

223. *tum mihi post sacras monstratus Iunius idus* | *utilis est nuptis*: Ovid is advised to give his daughter in marriage only *post sacras Ides*, 13 June. Kalends, Nones, and Ides, together with the day that followed each of these, were all regarded as *nefasti* and unsuitable for legal or civic business or religious ceremonies. Since the sweepings from Vesta's temple could therefore not be ritually removed and the temple closed until 15 June, Ovid's Roman readers would understand that the earliest possible date for his daughter's wedding would be 16 June (cf. Fest. 296L).

224. *utilis et nuptis, utilis esse viris*: in addition to its internal rhyme, the pentameter has a distinctively symmetrical word pattern accentuated by the alliteration of *s* and *t* and the repeated *i* and *u.*

226. *coniunx sancta Dialis*: to advise him on a suitable date for his daughter's marriage Ovid consults the highest authority. The wife of the Flamen Dialis, the Flaminica Dialis, ensured the fertility and prosperity of Rome (cf. *Fast.* 2. 27, 3. 397). She was the very symbol of Roman marriage, and this was reflected in her costume which included the *flammeum*, the bridal veil representing impregnating fire, a twig from a pomegranate tree in her hair to promote fertility, and on her feet shoes made from a sacrificial animal like the leather thongs of the Luperci. At times of the year which were considered inauspicious for girls to marry, Ovid notes that the Flaminica assumed the garb of mourning (*Fast.* 3. 397–8).

227–8. '*donec ab Iliaca placidus purgamina Vesta | detulerit flavis in mare Thybris aquis*': allusions to Vesta's Trojan origins became canonical in Virgil, who describes her inner sanctuary: *Pergameumque Larem et canae penetralia Vestae* (*Aen.* 5. 744. Cf. 2. 293–6, Ovid *Fast.* 3. 141–2, 417–18). The River Tiber was not characteristically *placidus*. A catalogue of Tiber flooding from Roman times to the building of the Tiber embankment in the twentieth century may be found in Nisbet and Hubbard (1970) 18–19, 24. The silt caught in Tiber's swirling eddies encouraged wide use of the word *flavus*, on which Bömer quotes Heinze's comment: 'ein poetischer Euphemismus für *limosus* oder *turbidus*.' The euphemism became a cliché in the Augustan poets (Virg. *Aen.* 7. 31, Hor. *Carm.* 1. 2. 13, 1. 8. 8, 2. 3. 18, Ovid *Met.* 14. 448, *Tr.* 5. 1. 31). However, the poets' love for the Tiber encouraged the pathetic fallacy to encroach on realism, so it was poetically fitting that the sweepings from Vesta's temple should be carried peacefully (*placidus*), almost respectfully, downstream. Similarly, in *Fasti* 1. 241 it is seemly for Janus, author of civic peace and order, to describe his neighbourhood river as *placidissima . . . harenosi Thybridis unda*. Conversely, Aeneas' future tribulations are mirrored in Virgil's vision: *Thybrim multo spumantem sanguine* (*Aen.* 6. 87). In reality, like any major European river, the Tiber is, and was, as changeful as Proteus.

227. *purgamina*: on the last day, 15 June, the sweepings from the Vestals' ritual cleaning of the temple (*purgamina*, 227) were cast into the Tiber. The *Fasti Furii Filocali* (Degrassi 249) notes on 7 June *Vesta aperitur* and on 15 June *Vesta cluditur*, while the *Fasti Venusii, Tusculani*, and *Maffeiani* (Degrassi 58, 103, 477) add to 15 June the letters *q. s. d. f.*, which Varro (*L* 6. 32) explains as *quando stercus delatum, fas*. The *purgamina* were carried to the Tiber along a narrow alley leading past the Clivus Capitolinus and through a gateway known as the Porta Stercoraria (Fest. 466. 32L). Once the 'impurities' had been ritually cast into the Tiber, the day became open for legal business. The intervening period, from the time that the doors of the *penus Vestae* were opened on 7 June until they closed on 15 June, was regarded as *religiosus* because the *penus* or storehouse within the Aedes Vestae was opened for nine days. During this time Roman *matronae* were permitted to enter to view the sacred contents (Fest. 296L): *penus vocatur locus intimus in aede Vestae tegetibus saeptus, qui certis diebus circa Vestalia aperitur*). The visit of the *matronae* seems to have been a religious duty performed to promote national prosperity and possibly also personal fecundity. So what in the *penus* was exposed to the matrons' view? In addition to the sacred *fascinus*, a model of a phallus, and the Palladium, the Vestals looked after water and *mola salsa*, salted meal, for sacrifices and also the ashes from the October horse and those of the calf foetus sacrificed at the *Fordicidia* in April (*exta bovis gravidae*, *Fast.* 4. 671). These ashes, however, were mingled by the Vestals and ceremonially scattered on the *Parilia*, 21 April, to promote the fertility of the land on a day regarded as the birthday of Rome, and so they were no longer inside the *penus* to be venerated in June. Allusions in Virgil to the most holy *sacra*, which may have included the *fascinus* with the Palladium, suggest that these remained unseen by all but the Vestals in an inner recess of the *penus* (Virg. *Aen.* 5. 744–5). We are left with *mola salsa* and holy water. Since Vesta's own festival on 9 June corresponded with the purification of her shrine and a period of sexual abstinence observed by the *Flaminica Dialis*, it seems probable that the visit of the matrons may have focused on the goddess' purity as the source of Rome's prosperity, their ritual being limited to praying as they watched water from the sacred spring being poured and *mola salsa* sprinkled on the altar fires. [On the possibility of an inner *penus* which was not opened at this time, see Radke (1981) 358–60.]

229–30. '*non mihi detonso crinem depectere buxo,* | *non ungues ferro subsecuisse licet*': 'I may not comb my hair with the smooth boxwood nor cut my nails.' Since the hair of the Flamen Dialis was cut with a bronze knife, *ferro* may be specific, but it is more probable that the Flaminica was forbidden to cut her nails at all on *dies religiosi*. Even on days which were not *religiosi*, the Flaminica must bury her nail-clippings or hair under a fruitful tree (Gell. 10. 15. 15). The word *depectere* carries here the implication of thorough combing which might lead to hair being unintentionally pulled out. During this period of ritual purification there must be no stray hairs or nail-clippings which might be used harmfully in magic rites. Boëls (94) suggests that a woman's hair, like her feet, had magical powers associated with fecundity and for this reason she did not comb her hair during the period when marriage was inadvisable in March (*Fast.* 3. 393–8). The Flaminica in her official capacity wore her hair long so that it could, for certain ritual occasions, be piled on top of her head in a *tutulus* (Fest. 484–5L, Var. *L* 7. 44). At times inauspicious for marriage, when she was obliged to wear mourning, her long hair was loosed, uncombed, about her shoulders (see note to line 266). *AWC* retains the reading *detonso*, which refers to the boxwood comb (the neuter noun *buxum*) as 'stripped' or 'smooth'. Heinsius' conjecture *dentosa*, the reading preferred by Bömer, puts the emphasis on the danger of hairs falling from the teeth of the comb, here in its feminine form, *buxus*. Pighi (1973: 66) offers the ingenious explanation that although the Flaminica's long hair could not be cut, the teeth of the comb could and were symbolically stripped off the comb on *dies religiosi* as a sign that she was not permitted to comb her hair.

231. '*non tetigisse virum, quamvis Iovis ille sacerdos*': a distinctive pattern of alliteration, *s* and *v*, combined with repeated *i*, is concentrated in the centre of the line: *-isse virum, quamvis Iovis ille.* The Flaminica preserved ritual chastity while the temple of Vesta was being purified in order that the priestly couple should exemplify the religious injunction against marriages at this period. By using the concessive *quamvis*, Ovid humorously implies that sexual activity with the high priest of Jupiter might somehow be less improper. This has, instead, the effect of reminding his readers of Jupiter's reputation for promiscuity.

232. '*quamvis perpetua sit mihi lege datus*': 'although he has been bound to me legally in perpetuity.' The Flamen Dialis and the Flaminica could only be married by the rite of *confarreatio*, which was, until death, indissoluble: *matrimonium flaminis nisi morte dirimi ius non est* (Gell. 10. 15. 23). Their union was considered essential to the well-being and fertility of the state. On the death of his wife the Flamen was obliged to resign from his priesthood.

234. '*ignea cum pura Vesta nitebit humo*': 'when Vesta's fire will sparkle on a spotless floor.' The floor has been newly swept and the flames from Vesta's hearth are reflected on the polished marble. Ovid conjures up the same imagery when Vesta manifests herself in his own home with a purple light reflected on the floor: *laetaque purpurea luce refulsit humus*, 252.

F VII EID. IUN. N, *LUDI PISCATORII*, 235–240

[G. Dumézil, 'Les Pisciculi des Volcanalia', *REL* 36 (1958) 121–30.]

The substitution sacrifice of live fish to Volcanus

At the Ludi Piscatorii, held in the Campus Martius on 4 June, a substitution sacrifice of live fishes was poured into the altar flames. Festus claims, first, that the fish are a substitution for a human sacrifice, and secondly, that the sacrifice may have been performed on the archaic altar which stood within the Area Volcani at the western end of the Forum Romanum: *piscatori ludi vocantur qui quotannis mense Iunio trans Tiberim fieri solent a praetore urbano pro piscatoribus Tiberinis, quorum quaestus non in macellum pervenit sed fere in aream Volcani quod id genus pisciculorum vivorum datur ei deo pro animis humanis* (Fest. 274L, cf. Var. *L* 6. 20). This suggests that the sacrifice was made to Vulcan rather than to Tiber, in whose honour the Ludi were celebrated by the Tiber fishermen (Ovid, *Fast.* 6. 239–40). Similarly Ovid tells how, to expiate lightning, Numa offers Jupiter a fish in place of a human life: *postulat hic animam, cui Numa 'piscis' ait* (*Fast.* 3. 342. And cf. Carna's substitution sacrifice, *Fast.* 6. 160–1). In a military context a significant substitution sacrifice might take the form of *devotio*, where a senior general would sacrifice himself in place of Rome and her legions, as exemplified by P. Decius Mus (Liv. 8. 9. 5–12. Cf. Macr. 3. 9. 9–15). [The substitution sacrifice of *devotio* is discussed by Oakley (1997) 477–86 and H. S. Versnel, 'Self-sacrifice, Compensation and the Anonymous Gods', in *Le Sacrifice dans L'antiquité*, Fondation Hardt Entretiens 27 (1981) 143–63.]

235–40: *After the Nones the third moon expels Lycaon and the Bear no longer fears what is behind her. I remember seeing games in the Campus Martius which honour the gliding Tiber. It is a holiday for the folk who haul in dripping nets and bait bronze hooks with tiny morsels.*

235. ***tertia post Nonas removere Lycaona Phoebe | fertur*****:** Callisto was the Great Bear or Ursa, and her son, by Jupiter, was Arctophylax, the Bear Warder, also known as Bootes. After Callisto had been transformed into a bear, Arctophylax, who did not recognize his mother, hunted her with a spear before both were transformed into constellations (*Fast.* 2. 183–92). Once the constellation of Arctophylax has set, the Bear ceases to 'fear (her son's approach) behind her' (*a tergo non habet Ursa metum*). Strictly speaking, Arctophylax should be Lycaonides after Lycaon, who was Callisto's father [see Ideler (1825) 140–3]. On the setting of Bootes on 7 June, Ovid is in agreement with both Pliny (*Nat.* 18. 255) and Columella (11. 2. 45).

237–8. ***tunc ego me memini ludos . . . | aspicere*****:** Ovid claims that he saw the Ludi Piscatorii in progress in the Campus Martius (*in gramine Campi*, 237). Personal involvement as a starting-point for a description of a festival or local custom was a device used by Callimachus (*Aet.* fr. 178–9 Pf. line 10. Cf. Ovid *Amores* 3.13.1–2, *Fasti* 6. 395–8).

238. ***memini ludos . . . | . . . dici, lubrice Thybri, tuos*****:** Ovid remembers being told that the patron deity of the games was Tiber himself. Festus suggests that the patron was Volcanus and that the games were held on the other side of the Tiber (Fest. 274L). According to Merkel (1841: 103), this information derives from Verrius Flaccus.

239–40. ***qui lina madentia ducunt | quique tegunt parvis aera recurva cibis*****:** the games are enlivened by Ovid's terse but vivid description of the Tiber fishermen who 'haul in their wet nets and fill bronze hooks with small bait'. Although *lina* can refer to fishing-lines, and might be thought to do so here in the same sentence as fish-hooks, the more picturesque image of fishermen hauling in their nets can be supported quite well: *ducere* can be used for hauling in fishing nets (*OLD* s.v. 21) and *lina* is used by Ovid to describe nets for hunting animals: *lina madent... cruore ferarum* (*Met.* 3. 148).

F VI EID. IUN. N, *BONA MENS*, 241–248

[Champeaux (1987) 2. 18–22, Schilling (1954) 233 ff.]

The cult of Good Sense

After defeating the Romans at the River Trebia in 218 BC, Hannibal moved south during the following spring. Circumventing C. Flaminius and his army at Arezzo (Arretium), under the cover of a morning mist he took up a position in the hills which rim the north-east shore of Lake Trasimene. Flaminius did not observe the proper religious formalities before advancing southwards (*neglegentia caerimoniarum auspiciorumque*, Liv. 22. 9. 7), nor did he take the trouble to reconnoitre adequately before entering the valley, with the result that his army was ambushed and almost annihilated. When the news reached Rome and the extent of the disaster had been assessed, the Sibylline books were consulted. After their defeat at the Trebia, the Romans had made offerings to Juno, Iuventas, Hercules, and Fortuna, deities associated with military success; all these deities received a temple in the first twelve years of the second century BC. A temple was vowed to *Bona Mens*, Good Sense and Prudence, which had been so conspicuously lacking in C. Flaminius, and it was decided that a second temple should be built to Venus Erucina (cf. *Fast.* 4. 865–76), who could watch over Roman interests in Sicily from her shrine at Eryx, which was situated between Rome and Carthage and the scene of fighting during the First Punic War. This second temple was vowed by the highest authority in Rome, the dictator Q. Fabius Maximus Cunctator, and the temple of Bona Mens by T. Otacilius Crassus (Liv. 22. 10. 10), who was related to Fabius by marriage (Liv. 24. 8. 11). Together, as *duoviri aedibus dedicandis*, they built the two temples on the Capitol as a pair separated only by a drainage channel (Liv. 23. 31. 9. Cf. Hor. *Carm.* 1. 2. 33). The Augustan poets associated the fertility cult of Venus Erucina with Trojans who were said to have settled at Eryx in Sicily. Venus of Eryx's Sicilian sanctuary was eventually taken by M. Claudius Marcellus in 212 BC, when he captured Syracuse (cf. Virg. *Aen.* 5. 759–60, Ovid *Fast.* 4. 872–6).

241–8: *Good Sense has a shrine vowed through fear during the Punic Wars. War had broken out afresh and after the consul's death all feared the Moorish forces. Fear banished Hope until the senate vowed a shrine to Sense, and Hope sprang up anew. The temple's anniversary falls six days before the Ides.*

241. *Mens quoque numen habet*: 'Good Sense too possesses divine power.' Propertius invokes Mens as the divine power which has released him from his blind passion for Cynthia (Prop. 3. 24. 19). Ovid, in his Triumph of Amor (*Am.* 1. 2. 31–2), mockingly depicts the virtues, Pudor and Bona Mens, in shackles, as prisoners in Love's triumphal parade. Much of Ovid's comedy here derives from his transference to the context of *militia amoris* of Bona Mens, an abstract deity whose temple and military association go back to the darkest days in the Second Punic War.

241–2. *delubra videmus* | *vota metu belli*: Bona Mens had been chosen to receive a temple as a direct result of the incautious Flaminius' defeat. The Romans were well aware that they would continue to need the guidance of Bona Mens, so long as Hannibal and his army remained in Italy where they could rely on the support of Italian tribes hostile to Rome. *metu belli* clearly refers to the Romans' fear of future battles.

243. *perfide Poene*... | *Poene, rebellaras*: as a race, the Carthaginians had a reputation for perfidy, and Ovid makes another reference to the perfidious Carthaginian in *Fasti* 3. 148. Ovid's second apostrophe perhaps refers directly to their leader, Hannibal, who can hardly be said to 'rebel' against Rome, which was a hostile power; *rebellaras* must mean 'had initiated a new outbreak of war', since the Battle of Lake Trasimene was the first offensive of a new fighting year, winter having intervened after the Battle of the River Trebia.

243. ***leto consulis***: the consul, C. Flaminius, was killed early in the Battle of Lake Trasimene. His colleague, Gn. Servilius Geminus, had sent a detachment of 4,000 cavalry to support him but they were annihilated in the plain below Assisi (Asisium) as Hannibal's army marched south through Umbria towards Spoleto (Spoletium) (Liv. 22. 8. 1).

245–6. ***spem metus expulerat: cum Menti vota senatus | suscipit et melior protinus illa venit***: the Romans attempted to restore *pax deorum* first by consulting the Sibylline books and then by religious ritual. Livy gives a detailed account of the vowing of the two temples, the *supplicatio*, the three-day lectisternium displaying all twelve Olympian gods, the *Ludi*, and the sacrifice of no fewer than 300 victims (Liv. 22. 9. 7.–22. 10. 10). These measures received much public support. It would be tempting to suggest Ovidian word-play: that, after the senate had vowed a temple to *Mens*, Good Sense (*Bona Mens*) became Better Sense: *melior protinus illa venit.* The Ovidian distich, however, is usually a self-contained unit, and the word *illa* may refer further back to another feminine abstract noun mentioned before *Mens*: *Spes* at the beginning of the hexameter: 'and forthwith she (Hope) was revived.'

247. ***aspicit instantes mediis sex lucibus Idus***: the ever-present calendric requirement of time notification is accomplished with an elegant chiasmic pattern, ABCDcb, in which the 'pressing Ides' (*instantes Idus*) literally press in on the six days in between, *mediis lucibus*, nicely framing the key word, the number six.

G V EID. IUN. N, *VESTALIA*, 249–460

[Guarducci (1964), Hildebrecht Hommel, 'Vesta und die frührömische Religion', *ANRW* 1. 2. (1972) 402–21, Radke (1981) 343–72, Beard (1980) 2–27, Fraschetti (1988), Williams (1991), Korten (1992), Herbert-Brown (1994) 65–80, 125–7, Beard (1995) 166–77, Newlands (1995) 123–40, Steinby, 5. 125–8, 128–9, Fantham (1998) on *Fasti* 4. 949–54, Staples (1998), Gee (2000) 92–125, Parker (2004) 563–601.]

1. *Vesta's temple and the origin of her cult*

The Aedes Vestae, a circular tholos temple at the eastern end of the Forum Romanum, is thought to have its earliest origins in the regal period. The present structure is now dated to the period after the temple fire in 241 BC. The east-facing door of the temple was barely a dozen steps from the entry to the Atrium Vestae, the living quarters of the Vestal Virgins. In the centre of the shrine was a rectangular shaft which may have been a repository for ashes or for other sacred rubbish, and the innermost storehouse or *penus*. During the Gallic invasion of 390 BC the *sacra* were transported to Caere by waggon, including the Palladium and the *fascinum* or sacred phallus, as well as other sacred objects, possibly the terracotta pot containing the Megaloi Theoi (Liv. 5. 40. 7–10).

The cult of Vesta in Rome was thought to date back to the early regal period (D.H. 2. 65, Plut. *Rom.* 22. 1, *Numa* 11. 1) when the Vestal flame was originally associated with the hearth fire of the king, while the Vestal Virgins represented the royal women (cf. Ovid, *Tr.* 3. 1. 29–30). The uncertainty whether they represented fecund wife or virginal daughters derives from the ambiguity of their virginal duties of tending the flame and temple and, on the other hand, their matronal costume and role in rites to promote fertility of the land in such festivals as the *Fordicidia* and the *Parilia.* The cult of Vesta was central to Rome's state religion and Vesta's official title was *Vesta publica populi Romani Quiritium.* The efficacy of Vesta's cult depended on the immaculate chastity of its ministrants, the Vestal Virgins, whose function it was to offer prayers and sacrifice for the Roman state (Hor. *Carm.* 1. 2. 26–8). The enduring belief in an association between sexual abstinence and military success is well illustrated by Pliny's story, appositely quoted by Parker (2004: 574), of a Vestal, condemned to immuration for unchastity, who pointed out that Domitian's record of military successes proved that her chastity was inviolate (Plin. *Epist.* 4. 11. 7). At the same time the Vestal hearth and flame symbolized a generative fire which was thought to maintain the prosperity of the Roman state. The generative power of fire is illustrated by the story of the birth of Servius Tullius (*Fast.* 6. 625–36). The connection of generative power with the cult of Vesta was implied by the *fascinum* or sacred phallus which was kept within Vesta's *penus* or storehouse with the Trojan Penates and the Palladium. The sexual ambiguities in Vesta's cult may point to the liminal or interstitial status of the Vestals believed to have the power to mediate between the human and the divine. The only authority between the Vestals and the Roman state was the Pontifex Maximus. It was the responsibility of the Pontifex Maximus to select new Vestal Virgins, over whom he had *patria potestas*. Under the Republic the office of Pontifex Maximus gave its incumbent seniority and authority over other Roman priests, including the *flamines* and the Vestals, although he was not permitted to enter the Vestal shrine.

2. *Vesta under Augustus: a dynastic cult*

Vesta gained new importance in Augustus' restructured Roman religion. When Augustus became Pontifex Maximus in 12 BC, he circumvented the requirement of an official residence near the Aedes Vestae by establishing a new shrine to Vesta within his Palatine house. This sent out a dynastic message that the Palatine was now the principal focus of Augustus' state religion and also that the sacred hearth of the Roman people was once more within the house of the ruler: *stet domus! Aeternos tres habet una deos* (*Fast.* 4. 954. Cf. *Met.* 15. 864–5). Any suggestion that Vesta and Apollo had become Augustus' household gods is obviously hyperbolic, for Apollo's temple stood adjacent to Augustus' house [cf. Gradel (2002) 116, n. 18]. The complex of buildings associated with the worship of Vesta included the Aedes Vestae, the Atrium Vestae, where the Vestal Virgins lived, and the Regia, which was the official residence of the Pontifex Maximus, although it seems probable that the Pontifex Maximus lived elsewhere, since the Regia may have been a consecrated building (Fest. 347L), which may have contained a shrine to Vesta (Var. *L* 6. 22). He was, as a man, prohibited from entering the Vestal shrine, as Ovid's Metellus was well aware when he says: *vir intrabo non adeunda viro* (*Fast.* 6. 450). A radical change occurred, therefore, when Augustus created a Vestal shrine in his Palatine house within six weeks of becoming Pontifex Maximus. The importance of this event is evident from the fact that 28 April, the *natalis* of Vesta's shrine in Augustus' house, was designated NP in the Roman calendar, as was 6 March, the anniversary of Augustus' election to Pontifex Maximus in 12 BC. Augustus' tenure of this priestly office emphasized his dynastic link with the Aeneadae, and this is made clear in Ovid's *Fasti*: *ortus ab Aenea ... sacerdos* (3. 425. Cf. *Met.* 15. 864–5). Augustus' kinship (*cognatio*) with Vesta, to which Ovid alludes in this passage, represented the ancient and symbolic relationship between members of a royal house and their ancestral gods [see Bömer (1987), 525]. Herbert-Brown suggests that Ovid retrojects this dynastic relationship on to Caesar who held the office of Pontifex Maximus from 63 BC until his death. When Ovid's Vesta rescues the body of Caesar on the Ides of March, she exclaims: *meus fuit ille sacerdos* (*Fast.* 3. 699). On the occasion of the vowing of the temple of Mars Ultor, Augustus' great oath of vengeance on the murderers of his adoptive father begins: *pater... Vestaeque sacerdos* (*Fast.* 5. 573), an indication that the Roman hearth and state had been violated by the murder of Vesta's priest [see Herbert-Brown (1994) 70–3].

Demonstrating a scrupulous observance and respect for Roman sacral law, Augustus did not attempt to seek election to Pontifex Maximus until after the death of Lepidus, who had held the office after the death of Caesar (see Introduction 2). During this intervening period, however, he was able to initiate religious reforms as a member of almost every other Roman priesthood. From AD 14, when Tiberius succeeded Augustus, the priesthood was designed to pass from father to son within the Domus Augusta. It was evidently regarded as a cornerstone in Roman dynastic religion.

3. Vesta and the Penates

It was an essential part of the cult of Vesta that her temple sheltered both the sacred flame and the Penates which had been brought from Troy. The significance of Virgil's frequent references to Vesta in conjunction with the Penates (*Aen.* 2. 508–14, 5. 744, 9. 257) is reinforced by Macrobius' statement (Macr. 3. 4. 11) that sacrifices were made to Vesta with the Penates. This was a ritual which Augustus encouraged all Roman magistrates to perform at Lavinium because it was a place closely associated with the Trojan ancestors of the Gens Iulia. An inscription discovered near Lavinium honouring 'Lare Aineia D' indicates that in Lavinium Aeneas enjoyed the cult status of a deified hero-founder, which in Rome was accorded to

Hercules, Romulus-Quirinus, and Divus Iulius. The sanctity which Virgil invests in the Trojan Penates is a clear indication of their importance in Augustus' reconstruction of Roman religion, while Aeneas' destiny as Rome's founder is underlined by repeated references to his awareness that he is bound to his divine burden (*Aen.* 1. 67–8, 378, 3. 11–12, 148–9, 5. 632) from the moment when he is first told by Hector: *sacra suos tibi commendat Troia penates* (2. 293). Virgil's vision of Augustus at the Battle of Actium, depicted on the Shield of Aeneas, carries the clear ideological message that Augustus defends Rome from her enemies in concert with the Trojan Penates: *Augustus agens Italos in proelio Caesar cum . . . penatibus et magnis dis* (8. 678–9). The expression *magnis dis* is applied by Weinstock, in his analysis of a further inscription on a bronze tablet from Lavinium, to the Dioscuri as the Roman Penates and to the Great Gods of Samothrace. An integral part of Augustus' dynastic recasting of Roman religion was Vesta's close association with the Trojan Penates and Lar Aeneas as a divine hero-founder-ancestor of the Roman people which was apparent in the cult at Lavinium and Augustus' insistence that it was here that Roman magistrates performed their official act of loyalty to the Roman state. [see S. Weinstock, 'Two archaic Inscriptions from Latium', *JRS* 50 (1960) 112–18, Sabbatucci (1988) 202–6].

Vesta enlightens Ovid concerning the origins of her cult

249–56: *Look kindly on me, Vesta! I was deep in prayer when I sensed your holy presence as the flagstones glowed purple. Men may not look on you, goddess, and without instruction, I was enlightened.* **257–64:** *In Rome's fortieth year the guardian goddess of the flame received a temple, built by the peace-loving Sabine king. The roof was thatched, the walls wattle and daub. This patch of land, now the Vestal complex, was once the palace of bearded Numa.*

249. ***Vesta, fave*:** Ovid opens his *Vestalia* with a traditional hymnic invocation which he repeats elsewhere in the *Fasti*, the variant *ades* sometimes replacing *fave* (*Fast.* 4. 1. *Alma, fave.* Cf. 3. 2, 5. 663). Such invocations normally continue with a reference to the parentage or to a particular characteristic of the god addressed. Since, as Ovid claims, Vesta has no physical form, the poet here avoids mentioning humanizing physical detail. There are other vestiges of the conventional hymnic form to be found here: the triple anaphora addressed to the goddess: *tibi* (249) . . . *ad tua* . . . *sacra* (250) . . . *te, dea* (254), the word *laetus*, applied here to the ground instead of to a worshipper made joyful by the divine presence, and finally, the tentative *si licet* clause to pardon the poet's presumption in approaching such holy matters: *ad tua si nobis sacra venire licet* (250).

249. *nunc operata resolvimus ora*: the expression *ora resolvere* heralds a solemn utterance which may sometimes be prophetic (as Proteus in Virg. *G.* 4. 452. Cf. Ovid, *Fast.* 1. 255). That Ovid's pronouncement will be concerned with sacred matters is encapsulated in the verbal adjective *operata* (*OLD* s.v. 2).

250. *ad tua si nobis sacra venire licet*: hymnic invocations often invite the deity to grace the rites with his presence (Hor. *Carm.* 1. 2. 30 *venias*, 3. 18. 3 *incedas*, Ovid, *Fast.* 3. 2 *ades*). Since this is impossible in Vesta's case, for Ovid maintains that she has no human form (253–4), *venire* here applies to the poet.

251. *in prece totus eram*: the idiom recurs in comedy and Cicero's letters (cf. Hor. *Serm.* 1. 9. 2, *nescio quid meditans nugarum totus in illis*). Here Ovid's absorption in prayer is rewarded not by an epiphany but by the sense of Vesta's divine presence: *caelestia numina sensi* (251).

252. *laetaque purpurea luce refulsit humus*: 'the ground glowed, radiant with rosy light.' The anticipation of the hexameter (*caelestia numina sensi*, 251) is fulfilled in a pentamenter in which the poet, praying in his home, since men were barred from entering Vesta's shrine, sees the ground bathed in purple radiance; the royal colour is perhaps symbolic of Vesta's relationship to the Julian dynasty. Janus' epiphany is similarly anticipated by refulgence in Ovid's house: *lucidior* . . . *domus* (*Fast.* 1. 94). The serenity accompanying Vesta's presence contrasts, however, with the horror inspired by Janus' double face. Mynors (1990: 230) notes that the adjective *laetus* recurs in the *Georgics* in the context of Nature with the meaning 'fruitful' (eighteen times) or 'rejoicing' (eleven times). Less frequently applied to inanimate objects, *laetus* can imply a state of radiance and spiritual harmony emanating from a divine source, for instance, *locos laetos*, the domain of the blessed shades (Virg. *Aen.* 6. 638, cf. Hor. *Carm.* 1. 10. 17). In a literal sense the dull stone floor acquires luminescent warmth and life. Figuratively the ground rejoices because it is blessed by the presence of the guardian goddess of the Julian house.

253. *non equidem vidi*: for a similar humorous adaptation of the epic formula *vidi egomet*, 'I saw with my own eyes' (Virg. *Aen.* 3. 623) see Horace (*Serm.* 1. 8. 23), where Priapus spots a witch in his garden.

253. *valeant mendacia vatum*: 'so much for the lies of the poets!' *valeant* serves as 'a formula of scornful dismissal' (*OLD* s.v. 3*d.* Cf. *Fast.* 6. 701, *valeas mea tibia!*). With comic sophistry Ovid assures his readers that he will not claim to have seen Vesta herself because he does not lie in the manner of other poets. This 'proof' of his veracity is intended to enhance the vatic integrity of the chronicler of the Roman year. Ovid concludes a poem devoted to this theme: *exit in immensum fecunda licentia vatum* (*Am.* 3. 12. 41). It was not uncommon in Greek and Roman poets to find aspects of the poet's 'persona' coexisting with 'autobiographical' details not all of which were historically accurate [see E. L. Bowie, 'Lies, Fiction and Slander in Early Greek Poetry', in Christopher Gill and T. P. Wiseman (eds.), *Lies and Fiction in the Ancient World* (Exeter, 1993), 31–7]. Ovid's vision of purpurescent flagstones is reported as 'poetic reality' no less than his visit to the Flaminica Dialis to ascertain the most auspicious wedding date for his daughter. In ancient times the 'lies of the poets' was a pertinent topic. Hesiod's Muses distinguish between historical truth and 'fiction which resembles reality' and claim to be purveyors of both (*Theog.* 26–8), while Aristotle considered, from a moral standpoint, that literature should be less concerned with historicity than a plausible representation of human character. As Feeney puts it: '(Ancient critics) were much more concerned about the moral worth and philosophical value of making fictional statements than about . . . the nature of their reality, whereas the mainstream of modern criticism has the reverse priority.' [See D. C. Feeney, 'Towards an Account of the Ancient World's Concepts of Fictive Belief', in ibid. 230–44. Cf. W. Rösler, 'Die Entdeckung der Fictionalität', *Poetica* 12 (1980) 283–319.]

254. ***nec fueras aspicienda viro***: 'nor should you have been seen by a man.' Only the Vestal Virgins and on specified occasions Roman *matronae* were permitted to enter Vesta's shrine. On occasion, in his *Fasti*, Ovid expresses a religious prohibition with a negative, a gerundive, and the word *vir*, implying here a man of heroic stature, a Promethean type of hero who is willing to violate a religious taboo for the good of his people. Before the Pontifex Maximus Metellus breaks into Vesta's shrine to rescue the Palladium from fire, he announces: *vir intrabo non adeunda viro* (*Fast.* 6. 450). The insistently reiterated *vir... viro* underlines his determination to break a religious taboo. In a third example, where Numa engages in a duel of wit and words with Jupiter to save a Roman life, he wins the god's respect and compliance because he is 'a (heroic) man not to be sidetracked from confrontation with a god': *o vir colloquio non abigende deum* (*Fast.* 3. 344).

255–6. ***sed quae nescieram quorumque errore tenebar***: 'but my ignorance and error (were corrected).' Juno prefaces her demand for the *titulus mensis* with a similar hexameter, alluding to the pitfalls of ignorance and error (*Fast.* 6. 25): *ne tamen ignores vulgique errore traharis.* The close similarity between the two lines and their position at the head of each passage concerning these two major Augustan goddesses highlights the contrast between the immanent authority of Vesta's flame and Juno's imperious demands.

257. ***dena quater memorant habuisse Parilia Romam***: words such as *memini* and *memoro* traditionally introduce a 'poetic memory' or 'Alexandrian footnote' alluding to the same theme treated by an earlier poet [see Conte (1986) 40–100, Miller (1992) 11–31, Hinds (1998) 1–20]. The *Parilia,* much celebrated in Roman poetry, was believed to have had its origins in a spring fertility festival honouring the rural divinity, Pales, which became, in Romulus' day, the Feast of the Foundation of Rome. (Var. *R.* 2. 1. 19. Cf. Prop. 4. 4. 73, *urbe festus erat—dixere Parilia patres*). The notion that an event so momentous was incorporated into a shepherds' festival gave colour and ideological weight to the 'then–now' topos recurrent in the Augustan poets (cf. Virg. *Aen.* 8. 306–65, Prop. 4. 1, 4. 9–14, 9. 1–10, Tib. 2. 5. 33–4, Ovid *Fast.* 1. 243, 515–19, 4. 721–862, 6. 401–14). The *Parilia* endowed the Foundation with a Golden Age purity which Augustus attempted to commemorate in his city of marble by carefully preserving the cave of the Lupercal and the thatched *casa Romuli* [see Beard (1987) 1–15, Miles (1995) 137–78]. If we retrace the poetic memory suggested by the word *memorant*, it will be seen that Propertius and Ovid use the *Parilia*, with its Augustan ideological message, as the backdrop for two inauspicious early Roman legends: Propertius sets Tarpeia's betrayal of Rome on the *Parilia* (Prop. 4. 4), while Ovid's aition for the festival is dominated by the murder of Remus (*Fast.* 4. 807–62). Both Propertius (4. 1. 19–22) and Ovid mention the *Parilia* in the same context as the *Vestalia.* The connection in Roman religious thought requires some explanation. The Vestal Virgins burnt on their altar a calf foetus and blood from the 'tail' of the victorious horse in the October race (*vituli favilla*, *sanguis equi*, *Fast.* 4. 733). The two sets of ashes were mingled and kept together in Vesta's *penus*, awaiting Rome's birthday on the *Parilia.* The horse was an animal used in war and sacred to Mars. Dumézil argues that '*cauda*' in this context refers not to the horse's tail but to its penis, suggesting that the expiatory ashes (*februa tosta*) used for purification at the *Parilia* represented the conjunction of fecundity/Venus and male generation/Mars [see Dumézil (1975) 181–7].

258. *flammae custos aede recepta dea est*: as Roman hearth goddess, the Roman equivalent of the Greek Hestia, Vesta was believed to be the guardian of the flame brought by Aeneas from Troy (Prop. 4. 4. 69: *Vesta Iliacae felix tutela favillae.* Cf. Virg. *Aen.* 2. 296, 567, 5. 744, 9. 259).

259. *regis opus placidi*: if we accept Cicero's and Livy's claim that Romulus ruled for thirty-seven years (Cic. *Rep.* 2. 17, Liv. 1. 21. 6) forty annual celebrations of the *Parilia* (*dena quater*, 252) puts the foundation of Vesta's temple three years into Numa's reign. In describing Numa as *placidus*, a word signifying beneficent and peace-loving, Ovid aligns the Sabine king with Augustus and Servius Tullius who share this appellation in Book 6 (lines 92 and 582). The adjective has, I believe, an ideological significance here, for all three leaders appear in Book 6 as ktistic promoters of Roman cult; Servius and Numa found the temples of Fortuna and Vesta while Concordia, bedecked with Augustus' Actian laurels, is described as *placidi numen opusque ducis* (6. 92). Through Numa's and Augustus' guardianship of Vesta's sacred flame and Servius Tullius' miraculous conception on the hearth (631–4) all three leaders are associated with the symbolic fire of Roman destiny. The divine flames which flicker in Servius' hair (635–6) mirror the portentous flames described by Virgil which play about the heads of Ascanius (*Aen.* 2. 682–3), Aeneas (10. 270–1), and Augustus (8. 680–1).

259–60. *quo non metuentius ullum | numinis ingenium terra Sabina tulit*: 'no more god-fearing soul than he did the Sabine land bring forth.' This corresponds to the iconographic picture which Virgil offers of Numa, *ramis insignis olivae sacra ferens*, in Anchises' pageant of Roman hero ancestors (*Aen.* 6. 808–12). Numa's moral integrity is associated with his Sabine origins, a motif which is reiterated in Book 6 with the appearance of the antique and morally decent Sabine deities Semo Sancus and Vacuna (cf. Livy 1. 18. 4: *disciplina tetrica ac tristi veterum Sabinorum quo genere nullum quondam incorruptius fuit*). As Rome's first priest-king and reformer of Romulus' primitive Roman calendar, Numa has an important role in Ovid's *Fasti* where a network of symbolism and allusion marks him as the heir of Aeneas and the precursor of Augustus. [See Littlewood (2002) 175–97.]

261–2. *quae nunc aere vides... textus erat*: Ovid describes the original temple of Vesta as having a thatched roof (*stipula tecta,* 261) and walls made from wattle and daub, like the oval Iron Age huts found on the site of Rome (see note on lines 265–6). Coins from the mid-first century BC show the later temple with a low pitched roof, which, like the grillework over the windows, Pliny describes as being bronze or copper (Plin. *Nat.* 34. 13). The 'then–now' contrast is enhanced by the mood change from present indicative to imperfect subjunctive in the polyptoton *vides–videres.*

263–4. *hic locus exiguus, qui sustinet atria Vestae | tunc erat intonsi regia magna Numae*: Ovid implies that the Atrium Vestae, which was the largest building in a complex supporting the cult of Vesta, now occupies the same space as Numa's palace (Plut. *Num.* 14. 1, Ovid *Tr.* 3. 1. 30). Ancient sources do not distinguish between a *regia* in which Numa lived and the *regia* in which he fulfilled religious functions, which later became the official house of the Pontifex Maximus [see headnote 2, p. 81]. Archaeological excavations have revealed a sixth-century house near the Vestal complex and beside the Sacra Via, identified as *regia* because it contained a bucchero cup from the late sixth century marked with the graffito *REX*. It contained three rooms, one containing a circular hearth, and a large pentagonal courtyard, equipped with an altar and a water supply, where sacrifices could be made. It was decorated with terracotta antefixes and decorated lateral plaques [see Ross Holloway (1994) 61–5]. Ovid's allusion to Vesta's hearth in Numa's palace may suggest not only the perpetual fire which was believed to have burned in royal palaces of remote antiquity, but also the sacred flame which burned on the public hearth in Greek cities which would establish a long line of tradition and respectability for Augustus' annexation of Vesta in his Palatine home in 12 BC.

Vesta is compared to Terra

265–72: *The temple's shape is unchanged. Vesta resembles the Earth. Both possess an unsleeping fire. Earth and the hearth symbolically represent their central location. The Earth resembles a ball, suspended and unsupported in space. Its rotary motion keeps it poised, for it is a perfect sphere.* **273–6:** *It is central in the universe because it is uniformly convex.*

265–6. *forma tamen templi, quae nunc manet, ante fuisse | dicitur*: the circular form of Vesta's temple can be seen on coins from 55 BC and AD 22 and 73. Modern archaeologists share Ovid's view that the Atrium Vestae resembled the oval huts, represented by burial urns of this period, which were common to early Italic settlements. [See G. Boni, *Il Sacrario di Vesta, notizie degli scavi* (Rome, 1900), 159–91 and Ross Holloway (1994) 61–2. Frazer (1929) 4. 186 n. 3 supplies a useful bibliography.]

266. *et formae causa probanda subest*: 'The reason for the shape is entirely plausible.' Untroubled by the obvious difference between a circular temple and a sphere, Ovid now introduces a rational, 'scientific' explanation for the shape of Vesta's temple.

267. *Vesta eadem est et terra—subest vigil ignis utrique*: (cf. *Fast.* 6. 460: *Tellus Vestaeque numen idem.*) 'Vesta is the same as the Earth—both contain an unsleeping fire.' Ovid compares the fire in the centre of the house to geothermal heat. The identification of Vesta with Terra derives from Verrius Flaccus, recorded by Festus (320L): *rotundam aedem Vestae Numa Pompilius rex Romanorum consecrasse videtur, quod eandem esse terram, qua vita hominum sustentaretur, crediderit; eamque pilae formam esse, ut sui simili templo dea coleretur.* The clarity of Ovid's scientific exegesis is well illustrated by the distich (267–8) which is divided into three terse steps in his argument, each segment slightly longer than the one before: a tricolon crescendo. Didactic writing characteristically reinforces its precepts by repetition, which can take the forms of assonance and alliteration. Within each of Ovid's first two clauses in the hexameter there is a repetition of the sound patterns of the key words, *Vesta* and *ignis*: VESTa *eadem* EST *et terra*... IGNIS. A chiasmic effect is then achieved in the pentameter by the sound pattern of the word SIGNI*ficant* followed by *terra*.

268. *significantque sedem terra focusque suam*: both Earth and the hearth 'represent their own (*suam*) place in the universe'. The words *significant sedem* require further clarification: how does the earth 'symbolize its own position (in the universe)'? Ovid seems to imply that the *sedes* of both Earth and the hearth, being central, is symbolic of their importance in the universe and the house respectively.

269–70. *terra pilae similis nullo fulcimine nixa | aere subiecto tam grave pendet onus*: Ovid expands his proposition with devices commonly used in didactic poetry and scientific exegesis. After making a clear statement of his theme: *Vesta eadem est et terra*... | *significant sedem terra focusque suam* (267–8), he amplifies this, *terra pilae similis* (269–70), extends his explanation of how the earth remains poised in mid-air (271–6) with an *exemplum*, Archimedes' astronomical sphere (277–8), which he then continues to use as a point of comparison in his final summation (279–80). The clarity of the plain scientific language of this exegesis is embellished with simile, alliteration, metrical *varietas*, and enjambement. The poet's exegesis opens with a simile in which the Earth, like a ball, hangs suspended in space, wholly unsupported (*nullo fulcimine nixa*, 269), with air below it (*aere subiecto*, 270). It is the Earth's rotary motion (*volubilitas*, 272) which holds it in perfect equipoise (*libratum*, 272), and this is achieved only because the Earth is perfectly round with no projections (*angulus omnis abest*, 273). The word *volubilitas*, which indicates the effortless, perpetual movement of the orb in space, is used by Cicero in a description in which he, too, makes the point that this rotary motion would be impossible if the Earth were not perfectly round: *mundi volubilitas quae nisi in globosa forma esse non posset* (*ND.* 2. 49). Germanicus, in his translation of Aratus, also uses the word *libratus* (271) to describe the Earth held balanced in space on its axis: *axis et inmotus semper vestigia servat | libratasque tenet terras et cardine firmo | orbem agit* (*Phaen.* 19–21). The concept of the Earth rotating at the heart of a geocentric universe, maintained in equipoise by centripetal force, was an essential tenet of Stoic theology (Cic. *ND* 2. 115–16. Cf. Plato *Phaed.* 109*a*, Lucr. 5. 449–51, Virg. *Ecl.* 4. 50). Ovid alludes to this concept in Janus' description of the cosmos emerging out of chaos (*Fast.* 1. 109–10). For rhetorical emphasis there is a striking repetition of sounds apparent in the hexameter, *volubilitas libratum*, which corresponds to alliteration in the pentameter, *premat partes, angulus abest.*

273–6. *cumque sit in media rerum . . . mundus haberet onus*: an essential part of didactic exegesis is the amplification of a statement in different words. In these four lines Ovid rephrases his argument that the Earth is absolutely central in the universe (*mundus*). If it were not convex (i.e. perfectly round), Earth could not be held in the centre of the universe: *nec medium terram mundus haberet onus* (276). The phrase *angulus omnis abest* (272), which is used by Ovid on an earlier occasion to describe the shape of Numa's *ancile* (*Fast.* 3. 378), then introduces the corollary, that the absolute geocentricity of the Earth in the universe is not obviated by any projection (*angulus*) or concavity which would affect the central pull of gravity towards the centre of the Earth: *nec medium terram mundus haberet onus* (276). We should not doubt the authenticity of lines 271–6, which are omitted in some mss as a consequence of an homoeoteleuton (. . . *et onus* in lines 270 and 276). Whilst Ovid's train of thought runs smoothly from Earth suspended, like a ball, in mid-air (269–70) to a pertinent example provided by the sphere of Archimedes (277–8), there are sound arguments for retaining lines 271–6. *ipsa volubilitas* in line 271 explains, with succinct relevance, why the Earth remains poised in space. As his last word Ovid repeats the graphic word *onus*, with which he began his exegesis concerning Earth's equipoise in line 270, perhaps because he wished to underline the physical phenomenon of the Earth's solid mass (*onus*) being poised in air. Emphasis is achieved by the enjambement of *stat globus* (278) and *terra* (280), which contribute an almost Lucretian tone to this structural artistry.

Archimedes' astronomical sphere provides an *exemplum*

277–82: *Archimedes' globe hangs poised in the air: a miniature model of the vast heavens. The earth is poised in the centre of the universe as a consequence of its spherical shape. The shape of Vesta's temple is the same. A rotunda protects it from the rain.*

277–8. *arte Syracosia suspensus in aere clauso* | *stat globus*: 'The globe fashioned by Syracusian art hangs poised with air enclosed within.' The spherical form of the *orbis* (271) and its geocentricity within the *mundus* (276) leads smoothly into Ovid's *exemplum*: the Earth as it is seen in the astronomical sphere of Archimedes of Syracuse (237–12 BC) which was brought to Rome by M. Claudius Marcellus after his conquest of Syracuse (Cic. *ND* 2. 88, *Tusc.* 1. 63, Ovid, *Fast.* 4. 873–4). Cicero (*Rep.* 1. 21–2) distinguishes two model globes: a solid one which was kept in the temple of Honos et Virtus and another which was made of movable parts which showed the movements of the major constellations. A similar sphere, Cicero claims (*ND.* 2. 88), had been constructed by the Stoic Posidonius. Because Ovid describes the globe *in aere clauso*, this cannot be the solid globe and therefore must have been the one which showed the movements of the constellations.

278. *inmensi parva figura poli*: 'a miniature likeness of the vast heavens.' The juxtaposed adjectives emphasize the insignificant size of Archimedes' model in comparison with the immensity of the heavens which it represents.

279. *et quantum a summis, tantum secessit ab imis* | *terra; quod ut fiat forma rotunda facit*: for the third time Ovid restates in different words that the earth's centrality in the universe is achieved by perfect sphericity. Any sense of monotony is dispelled by the distinctive *varietas* of Ovid's metre in this couplet, where a ponderous succession of spondees in the hexameter gives way to a sequence of dactylics and alliteration in the pentameter: *fiat forma . . . facit.*

281. ***par facies templi***: 'the appearance of the temple is comparable.' By comparing the round temple with the spherical Earth, Ovid repeats a cosmological comparison which he has already adumbrated in line 267: *Vesta eadem est et terra.* The image or imitation of the cosmos represented in Homer's Shield of Achilles, with its depiction of human life at the centre, became a subject of allegory among the Greek philosophers. Familiar to Ovid's readers was Virgil's adaptation of this in his Shield of Aeneas (*Aen.* 8. 626–731) where Augustus' victory at Actium and his protection of Roman gods embodied the essential tenets of Augustan ideology. [see Hardie (1986) 340–76]. It is possible to extend the allegory to Vesta's circular temple: in the centre is the Vestal flame, the heart of the Roman state, and the *penus* with the Palladium and the Roman Penates, brought from Troy by Aeneas, ancestor of the reigning dynasty. Around these move Vesta's virgin priestesses performing sacred rituals with water and *mola salsa*, upholding the survival of the state and under the protection of Augustus, the Pontifex Maximus, who keeps another shrine of Vesta in his own house. [Williams (1991) 196: 'If Vesta is the earth (267), then Augustus is its military master and if the earth lies at the centre of the Universe (269–76), then by implication Virgil's Roman hearth is the focal point of the Universe.' Cf. Weinstock (1971) 42–50.]

282. ***a pluvio vindicat imbre tholus***: 'the dome protects it from rain showers.' The word 'tholus' signified a round temple with a domed roof or rotunda; it first occurs in Latin in Vitruvius when he discusses the architectural features of round temples (Vitr. 4. 8). Vitruvius specifies that the height of the rotunda should measure exactly half the diameter of the temple (4. 8. 3) and the curved steps of a monopteral temple, such as the Aedes Vestae, one-third of its diameter (4. 8. 2).

Why Vesta prefers virgin priestesses

283–94: *You ask why the goddess is served by virgin priestesses. Juno and Ceres were born to Ops and fathered by Saturn. The third child was Vesta. The other two married and had children. But Vesta shunned men and, being* *a virgin, she delights in a virgin priestess.* **291–4:** *Vesta is living fire from which nothing can be born, and so she is, correctly speaking, a virgin and loves virgin companions.*

285–6. *ex Ope Iunonem memorant Cereremque creatas* | . . . *tertia Vesta fuit*: Ovid again uses the word *memorant* because this is a direct quotation from Hesiod (*Theog.* 453–4). To explain why Vesta has virgin priestesses, Ovid claims that she alone of the children of Ops remained *impatiens viri*, 288. It was not unusual for Greek or Roman philosophical writers to use Hesiod's mythology to illustrate a scientific point as though the myth provided an allegorical interpretation of a scientific truth. As *vates* of the Roman calendar, Ovid uses this combination of Stoic astronomy, cosmic ideology, and Hesiodic myth to enhance his exegesis of the cult of Vesta, which she merits as an important figure in the Augustan pantheon. [Cf. T. H. Habinek, 'Science and Tradition in *Aeneid* 6', *HSCPh* 92 (1989) 223–55.]

289. *quid mirum virgo si virgine laeta ministra* | . . . *manus*: Ovid's facile aetiological explanation that the virgin goddess delights in virgin priestesses corresponds to his suggestion in his *Lupercalia* passage that the naked Faunus prefers his priests to be naked too: *ipse deus nudus nudos iubet ire ministros* (*Fast.* 2. 287). The idea has affinities with a requirement of Roman sacrifice that sacrificial victims should correspond in colour, sex, and age, to their divine honorand. In emphasizing by repetition a key word in a cult—*virgo, nudus, gravida, priscus*—the poet uses a range of rhetorical devices, enhancing his couplets with chiasmus, asyndeton, and anaphora [see Porte (1985) 482–7]. Here the words *virgo, virgine,* separated by *si*, occupy the centre of the line framed by the adjectives, *mirum* and *laeta.*

291–4. *nec tu aliud Vestam quam vivam intellege flammam* | . . . *capit*: 'Do not imagine that Vesta is anything more than a living flame.' Opening with the didactic formula *nec tu . . . intellege* (cf. Virg. *G* 2. 241–2, 3. 163, 4. 45, 62, 106), Ovid goes on to claim that nothing can be born from flame: *nataque de flamma corpora nulla* (292) because fire neither gives nor receives seed: *quae semina nulla remittit nec capit* (293–4). Cf Isid. *Orig.* 8. 11. 67: *et ideo virginem putant, quia* *ignis inviolabile sit elementum nihilque nasci potest ex eo.* This runs counter to Varro (*L* 5. 61: *mas ignis quod ibi semen*), which supports a group of Roman myths involving impregnation from a phallus on the hearth, including the conception of Servius Tullius, which is described by Ovid (*Fast.* 6. 631–4), of the mythical Caeculus, founder of Praeneste (Virg. *Aen.* 7. 678–81), and of Romulus (Plut. *Rom.* 2. 4–5).

Why Vesta lacks an image: the etymology of the goddess' name

295–8: *For a long time I believed that there were statues of Vesta. Later I discovered that in her temple was only a flame. Vesta has no image and nor does fire. 299–304: The Earth remains in space through its own force (of gravity). Vesta derives her name from this. The hearth is named from its heat. Once Vesta's hearth was near the entrance of the house, the vestibule. For this reason Vesta is invoked at the beginning of prayers.*

295–6. *esse diu stultus Vestae simulacra putavit* | . . . *tholo*: Ovid's ignorance lasted a long time (*diu*) because men were not permitted to enter Vesta's shrine to see for themselves. There seems, however, to have been no religious prohibition against making an image of Vesta; several coins show a statue dressed in the garb of a Vestal Virgin, on the roof of the tholus temple, which may have represented Vesta herself or a Vestal Virgin. Varro talks about Rome's twelve principal deities being represented in gilded statues in the Forum Romanum (Var. *R* 1. 1. 14), which may correspond to Ennius' list of twelve which includes Vesta (fr. 37 (62), Vahlen, *Ennianae Poesis Reliquiae* (Leipzig, 1903) 11). Two literary allusions to *simulacra Vestae* may be cited which would have lost their rhetorical impact if statues of Vesta were known to be banned: Cicero describes a statue of Vesta which has been spattered with the blood of the Pontifex Maximus (*Pontificis Maximi sanguine simulacrum Vestae respersum*, Cic. *de Orat.* 3. 2. 10), while Ovid describes Vesta's statue (*Vestae simulacra, Fast.* 3. 45–6) overcome with embarrassment at the sight of her Vestal, Silvia, going into labour with Romulus and Remus. According to the *Fasti Caeretani* (Degrassi 66) Augustus established and dedicated a *signum Vestae* in his new shrine to Vesta in his Palatine house. Recent scholarly opinion is divided over whether this represented Vesta herself and was therefore a radical departure from normal cult practice in the Aedes Vestae [see M. Guarducci (1971) 94] or whether Augustus had simply installed in his house a replica of the Vestal flame and the Palladium [Herbert-Brown (1994) 74–9, who cites *Fast.* 3. 421–2: *ignibus aeternis aeterni numina praesunt* | *Caesaris: imperii pignora iuncta vides*]. It was not unusual for Roman writers, alluding to a statue in the temple of Vesta, to mean by this the Palladium, which was a statue of Minerva (see Liv. 5. 52. 7, Cic. *Phil.* 11. 10. 24).

297. ***ignis inextinctus templo celatur in illo*****:** on 1 March, formerly the first day of the year, the Vestal flame was relit (Ovid, *Fast.* 3. 143). The Vestal who allowed the flame to die at any other time was whipped by the Pontifex Maximus (Fest. 94.1–5L).

298. ***effigiem nullam Vesta nec ignis habet*****:** by using *putavi* (295) and *didici* (296) Ovid has avoided saying directly that there is no statue of Vesta. Now he argues that it is impossible to represent either fire or Vesta in figural form.

299–300. ***stat vi terra sua, vi stando Vesta vocatur*** | ***causaque par Grai nominis esse potest*****:** 'The earth is kept stationary by its own force; Vesta takes her name from her stability; the same is true of her Greek name.' The etymology that Vesta is derived from *vi stando* corresponds to the Greek derivation of Hestia from *hestanai* (Fest. 320L). This line returns to the concept of geocentricity which Ovid outlines in lines 267–76. *vi stando* need not imply that the earth was 'absolutely stationary', as Frazer suggests [Frazer (1929) 4. 203]. It is more likely that Ovid, following Aratus, simply means that the Earth, revolving on its axis, was held in the centre of the universe by gravity. A loose approximation of Ovid's pun might be achieved by changing Vesta's name: 'the Earth is held in place by its own gravitational force; Gravitas (i.e. Vesta) takes her name from gravity.'

303. ***hinc quoque vestibulum dici reor, inde precando*** | ***praefamur Vestam*****:** ancient authors (Gell. 16. 5. 6–12, Macr. 6. 8. 19–20) derive *vestibulum* from the word *ve-stabulato*, in which the prefix *ve-*accentuates *stabulato*, giving the sense here of 'standing for a long time', the lot of Roman callers who were kept waiting in the *vestibulum*, the narrow passage leading to the street in Roman townhouses [see Maltby 641]. It is noted by *OLD* (s.v. 1*d*), following Gellius (16. 5. 5) and Macrobius (6. 8. 18), that the prefix *ve-* may denote either 'excess or deficiency in the word to which it is attached'. The reference to a hearth fire being situated at the front of the house in the previous line (*in primis aedibus*, 302) might be related to a suggestion of Nonius Marcellus (75L) that there was an altar to Vesta in the *vestibulum*, which should be taken in the looser sense of 'entrance' or 'front'. In its metaphorical sense *vestibulum* means the beginning or opening part of a speech (*OLD* s.v. 1*d*) and this would give line 303 a possible translation: 'for this reason I think the opening of a speech is so called because we open prayers with an address to Vesta' (cf. Cic. *Orat.* 50: *vestibula nimirum honesta aditusque ad causam faciet (orator) illustris*). [And see Merkel (1841) 183.]

304. ***praefamur Vestam, quae loca prima tenet***: 'we mention Vesta at the beginning of our prayers, because she occupies first place.' Ovid's claim that Vesta is mentioned first in Roman prayers (*praefamur*) is either a reference to her location in the front of a Roman house (302) or because she occupies the most important place (*loca prima*) in Roman religion. This does not mean necessarily that Vesta was mentioned first in the list of gods invoked, but simply that Romans began important prayers with an address that included Vesta: *Di patrii Indigetes et Romule, Vestaque mater* (Virg. *G* 1. 498. Cf. Cic. *Dom.* 57. 144, Ovid *Fast.* 4. 828). Juvenal reverses the order, *Ianus Vestaque* (Juv. 6. 386), suggesting that if Janus was traditionally invoked first, Vesta came last [see Holland (1961) 283]. It is part of the structure of Ovid's Roman calendar that Janus has a dominant role in Book 1 while Vesta occupies the most prominent passage of Book 6 [cf. Gee (2000) 120, who sees further correspondences in Ovid's use of this complementary pair of deities]. Bömer (1958: *ad loc.*) suggests, less probably, that Ovid's statement derives from the fact that Hestia, Vesta's Greek equivalent, regularly prefaced Greek prayers in a domestic context (cf. Ar. *Av.* 864, *V* 846).

The ancient rites of Vacuna, the hearth goddess

305–10: *Once it was customary to sit facing the hearth on long benches, believing that the gods were present at the table. Now when the rites of Vacuna* *are performed (the participants) stand and sit facing Vacuna's hearth. A trace of this old custom has survived to our day.*

305–6. *ante focos olim scamnis considere longis | mos erat et mensae credere adesse deos*: Ovid may be alluding to a sacrificial banquet held by a *sodalitas*, when he describes the participants seated on 'long' benches, to accommodate many *sodales*, at a meal where the gods were believed to be present. Ovid's word order supports this interpretation. The poet points to a religious context by framing the couplet with the two key religious words *deos* and (*ante*) *focos*. On each side of the central *mos erat* two balancing phrases, *olim scamnis considere longis* and *mensae credere adesse (deos)*, build up the picture of a ritual sacrificial banquet. On the significance of sitting on stools at a public banquet see Dunbabin (2003) 80–3. The theme of religious banqueting recurs, by implication, towards the end of *Fasti* 6 in Ovid's story of the walk-out of the *tibicines*, who have been excluded from the *Epulum Iovis*. The ritual of sitting to eat at long benches, instead of reclining on couches, in a room which incorporated the domestic hearth and the sanctuary of the household gods, might be thought to evoke the frugal simplicity of Rome's past (Columella 11. 1. 9: *consuescat rusticos circa larem domini focumque familiarem semper epulare... Sitque frugalitatis exemplum nec nisi sacris diebus accubans cenet*). However, Ovid's choice of the adjective *longus* suggests that the benches were designed to accommodate a large number of *sodales* at a sacrificial banquet. If Ovid had wanted to describe here a rural household sitting at the table in the presence of the family's Lares, he would probably have chosen an adjective emphasizing their rusticity, such as *rudis* or *acernus*.

307. *nunc quoque*: *mos erat* (then) is picked up by *nunc quoque* (now), a traditional formula which Ovid uses to signal an aition (see *Fast.* 1. 388, 4. 494, 504, 5. 428, 6. 533).

308. *ante Vacunales stantque sedentque focos*: 'they stand and sit facing Vacuna's altar.' A possible interpretation of *Vacunales* here would be the *sodales* of Vacuna, who stand and sit before her altar. However, the parallel position of *Vacunales* and *focos* at the end of each section of the pentameter suggests that the two words should be taken together. Vacuna was said to have a sanctuary near Horace's

Sabine villa (*Epist.* 1. 10. 49), and there is some epigraphic evidence that Vacuna was a goddess worshipped in Sabine territory, possibly associated with Victory (Plin. *Nat.* 3. 109, Var. fr. 1 Cardauns). The Sabines' reputation for simplicity and integrity made their deities a byword for homeliness, which corresponds to Ovid's description of the rites of Vacuna. Varro (*L.* 5. 74) includes the fire deities Vesta and Volcanus in his list of Sabine deities but does not mention Vacuna. [See Radke (1981) 305, Evans (1939) 90.]

310. ***fert missos Vestae pura patella cibos*****:** a simple offering of grain is given to Vesta, as goddess of the hearth, where bread was baked on the *patella*, a flat dish with a raised central boss used for food offerings (Fest. 293L), which appears in funerary art, in particular held by the reclining figures on Etruscan sarcophagi. Bömer comments (*ad loc.*) that *mittere* is the verb used for offerings to the dead (see *Fast.* 5. 437. Cf. Lucr. 3. 52, Virg. *G* 4. 545, 553). The similarly shaped *patera* was used for libations.

Vesta and the baker's donkey

311–18: *Look, bread hangs in garlands from the donkeys' necks and garlands adorn the rough millstones! In former times the farmers used their ovens for roasting emmer. Even the Goddess Oven had rites. Bread was baked under the ashes. For this reason the baker honours the hearth, the hearth goddess, and the little donkey who turns the millstone.*

311. ***ecce, coronatis panis dependet asellis*****:** the line recalls Prop. 4. 1. 21: *Vesta coronatis pauper gaudebat asellis*, in a context emphasizing the antiquity of the custom of garlanding donkeys at the *Vestalia.* The custom of garlanding farm animals as an indication of their freedom from daily toil is found in Tibullus' description of the *Ambarvalia,* where garlanded oxen stand before well-filled mangers (Tib. 2. 1. 7–8. Cf. Ovid *Fast.* 1. 663). Donkeys were honoured with a garland of loaves because they performed a task essential to breadmaking, turning the millstones (*scabra mola*, 312) which ground the flour for bread. The millstones in turn were honoured with floral garlands (*florida serta,* 312). Ovid introduces the custom of garlanding the donkeys with loaves in order to highlight, in his exegesis of Vesta's cult, Vesta's association with Roman bakeries, and evoke an image of Vesta as she was often depicted on the *lararia* of Pompeian bakeries between the two Lares. She tends to wear white, yellow, or violet clothing and carries a cornucopia to signify the abundance which it is hoped she will provide. On the occasions where there is an altar in the picture, it is sprinkled with grain or ears of corn. The donkey stands behind Vesta, signifying the part played by the animal in the milling of flour for bread. [See Boyce (1937), nos. 185, 236, 240, 247, 313, 316, 318, 419, 420.]

313. ***sola prius furnis torrebant farra coloni***: 'Farmers used to roast only emmer in their ovens.' The full meaning and implication of this couplet is revealed in *Fasti* 2. 513–33, the *Fornacalia*, where Ovid describes how the early Romans, whose long wars had limited their farming skills, roasted grains of emmer in primitive ovens (*flammis torrenda dederunt*, 521). This rough-and-ready method of removing the husks scorched the grain (*pro farre favillas*, 523) and fired their cottages (*ignes corripuere casas*, 524). The *Fornacalia* was a festival involving religious banqueting with dining rights which were limited to the membership of the individual *curiae*.

314. ***et Fornacali sunt sua sacra deae***: 'even the Oven Goddess has her own particular offerings.' Rites to the goddess Fornax appear to have been accompanied by a formulaic prayer (*legitimis verbis*, *Fast.* 2. 527).

315. ***subpositum cineri panem focus ipse parabat***: 'the hearth itself baked the bread which had been set under the ashes.' Ovid describes with graphic detail a method of bread-making widespread in primitive societies. Small loaves are set on a cracked tile (*tegula quassa*, 315) under the ash, resting on the warm ground (*tepido solo*, 314) to bake in the surrounding heat. This is the method used by Carmentis when she bakes cakes for Ino in Evander's Rome (*Fast.* 6. 531–2).

317. ***inde focum servat pistor dominamque focorum***: the bakers worship Vesta, mistress of the hearth, as a consequence (*inde*) of her hearth being used for early bread-making. Ovid has progressed from Vesta the hearth goddess (301–4) to her Sabine counterpart, Vacuna (307–10), to Fornax, the Oven Goddess (313–6), and now, closing the ring composition, he has returned to Vesta herself, the bakers' goddess (317–18).

318. ***et quae pumiceas versat asella molas***: 'and the little donkey who turns the rough millstones.' The millstones were traditionally made of rough stones to facilitate grinding. Since lava would have been too friable for this purpose, Ovid must be using the word *pumicea* metaphorically to imply rough stone. A more effective grinding medium would be the flintstones used in the *Moretum*: *tunsa Ceres silicum rapido decurrit ab ictu* (27). Ovid mentions the (female) donkey, *asella*, with an affectionate diminutive (*asinus* + *ella*) as he does on twelve other occasions, including a very similar pentameter ending: *scabras frangat asella molas* (*Med.* 58). Axelson (1945: 44–5) concludes that *asellus* is a poetic form of *asinus.*

Vesta's encounter with Priapus at Cybele's party

[F. Bömer 'Kybele in Rom', *MDAI[R]* 71 (1964) 130–51, Guarducci (1964) 158–69, Parry (1964) 268–82, Littlewood (1981) 381–95, Fantham (1983) 201–9, Wiseman (1984) 117–28, Fraschetti (1988), Williams (1991) 183–204, Miller (1991) 82–90, Richlin (1992) 158–79, Newlands (1995) 124–45, Barchiesi (1997*a*) 238–56, Fantham (1998) 125–64, Wiseman (1998) 23–4, 48–51, 72–4, Barrett (2002) 193–214, Peter E. Knox, 'Representing the Great Mother to Augustus', in Herbert-Brown (ed.) (2002) 129–74, P. Murgatroyd, 'The Rape Attempts on Lotis and Vesta', *CQ* 52 (2002) 622–4, Frazel (2003) 61–97, Erskine (2001) 203–24, Green (2004)179–203, Murgatroyd (2005) 81–95].

1. The origins and importance of the cult of Cybele in Rome

Livy (29. 11. 5–6) and Ovid (*Fast.* 4. 275–64) tell how, in response to a Sibylline oracle confirmed by Delphic Apollo, Cybele was brought to Rome in 204 BC and honoured with a temple on the Palatine. The transfer of the Magna Mater to Rome should be considered in the light of Roman politics in 205 BC: on the one hand, the last battle of the Second Punic War and the prospect of continuing the struggle with Carthage beyond Italy (Liv. 29. 10. 7) and on the other, the conclusion of the Macedonian War and Rome's increasing rapprochement with the Attalid rulers of Pergamum (Liv. 29. 11. 1–8,

12. 8–16). While Hannibal remained on Roman soil particular attention was paid to an oracle which stated unequivocally that a foreign enemy could be expelled from Italy by bringing to Rome the Idaean Mother. At the same time, Cybele's official title Mater Deum Magna Idaea underlines her connection with Mount Ida in the Troad, and Rome and Pergamum shared a cultural interest in the Trojan ancestry of their founders; this Trojan kinship bound the two allied states together with Ilion. The island of Samothrace was included in these cultic ties through the idea that Rome's Penates were the same as the Great Gods of Samothrace. The embassy sent to request that the Magna Mater be escorted to Rome demonstrated religious solidarity with Attalus of Pergamum, who had supported Rome against Macedon and undersigned the treaty on the Roman side with Ilion and Athens (Liv. 29. 12. 14). Attalus seems to have gone to some trouble to facilitate the transfer to Rome of the cult object, a meteoric stone, which was believed to represent Cybele (Liv. 29. 11. 6–7, Var. *L* 6. 13). On arrival in Rome, the stone was lodged temporarily in the nearby Aedes Victoriae during the building of Cybele's Palatine temple, which was hoped to be a propitious omen of the outcome of the war against Hannibal.

2. Cybele's role in the Augustan pantheon

It is clear that Rome's network of political alliances in Asia Minor helped to promote the concept of Rome's Trojan ancestry before Augustus purposefully incorporated Cybele into a religion which focused on the dynasty of the Aeneadae. Cybele's new importance in Roman cult reconstructed by Augustus became apparent in her prominent role as protectress of Aeneas and his Trojans in the course of Virgil's *Aeneid* long before Augustus rebuilt her temple on the Palatine in AD 4. The goddess who shared the Palatine with Apollo, Vesta, and Augustus makes her iconographic appearance in a simile in which she is the prototype of Dea Roma, mother city and capital of a vast empire: *qualis Berecyntia mater... centum complexa nepotes.* It is in this guise that she appears on the Gemma Augustea, crowning Augustus with laurels.

Cybele, like Vesta, appears in comparisons with Livia, whom Ovid described as 'a Vesta among chaste Roman matrons' (*P* 4. 13. 29), worthy alone, like Juno, to share Jupiter's bed (*Fast.* 1. 650.) A sardonyx which depicts Livia wearing Cybele's turreted crown and holding a bust of Augustus honours Livia's service to Rome as 'Mother of the Nation'. Statues representing Livia as Juno, Ceres, or Cybele originated not in Augustus' Rome but in the Greek East where members of the imperial family were easily assimilated into the role of gods. As Ceres Augusta, Livia guaranteed plenty. As Juno, she was regarded as a goddess propitious to marriage, before whose statue marriages might be contracted. As Cybele, she was a civic goddess. This does not represent an identification of Livia with Juno, Ceres, or Vesta, so much as a point of reference. The qualities which might be most appropriately associated with an Empress-Mother—majesty, abundance, chastity, the very embodiment of *mater patriae*—could be symbolically represented as Juno, Ceres, Vesta, or Cybele. Consequently the impropriety of Priapus' intrusion at a party given by Cybele and attended by Vesta lies not in any direct affront to Livia herself but to the august virtues represented by these divine protectresses of the Julian dynasty.

3. *Is there a case for retaining both Priapus stories,* Fast. *1. 391–440 and 6. 319–46?*

It has been much debated whether any artistic merit might have convinced Ovid to retain, in his final version, the story of Vesta and Priapus in *Fasti* 6, when there is an almost identical story of Lotis and Priapus in *Fasti* 1. Given time for revision, Ovid might have been tempted to excise altogether the Vesta–Priapus story where 'the seduction scene contrives to be both sober and tasteless' [Fantham (1983) 209, in favour of the carefully crafted longer version in Book 1, which appears to be the product of post-exilic revision]. Williams (1991: 196–200), on the other hand, uses the argument of contrasting details for retaining both versions, pointing out that, in *Fasti* 6, the host is not the komiastic Dionysos but chaste Cybele, that Silenus, whose donkey saves Vesta with a timely bray, was not even invited, and finally that, whilst Priapus' disgusting behaviour simply amuses Lotis and her fellow nymphs, he narrowly escapes being lynched by Cybele's outraged guests: *per infestas effugit manus*, 337. This is further expanded by Newlands (1995: 124–45), who describes as 'negative mirroring' (p. 125) the repetition in Book 6 of characters, themes and situations found in *Fasti* 1, including motifs which recur in the two stories of Priapus' attempted rapes. Another important strand of Newlands' perceptive exegesis is her consciousness of a social divide which separates Augustus' official Vesta, chaste goddess of the Palatine and of the Trojan Penates of the Julian dynasty and, on the other hand, *Vesta publica populi Romani Quiritium*, whose image, with her companion donkey, traditionally adorned the *lararia* of Pompeian bakers.

Now while the *Vestalia* is clearly the most important passage in *Fasti* 6, only four lines (455–8) are expended on Augustus' Vestal shrine on the Palatine, because the *natalis*, 28 April, belongs to *Fasti* 4 (949–54), where it is duly celebrated. The ancestral goddess of the Gens Iulia whom the Princeps took to his Palatine house was also both the patron goddess of the Roman bakers and the goddess of the Aedes Vestae in the Forum who protected Rome's *imperii pignora*. Since Augustus, who cultivated the Roman plebs as one of his power bases, encouraged popular religious cult, which is evident from his reorganization of the *vici* and their cults of the Lares Compitales (see Introduction 2.2), Ovid's celebration of the people's Vesta on 9 June appears to be entirely orthodox. Further, to a poet in the Callimachean mould and a Roman antiquarian—and Ovid was both—Vesta's popular connections offered colourful literary possibilities quite apart from her dynastic connection, which is fulsomely acknowledged at the end of *Fasti* 4. Between two serious passages on aspects of Vesta's cult, Ovid's philosophical-scientific exegesis of Vesta's physical nature and Metellus' violation of her shrine to rescue the Palladium, Ovid sets two entertaining 'literary' narratives, both of which affirm the popular image of Vesta as the patron goddess of Pompeian bakers, first by her rescue from Priapus by the donkey, her companion in the bakers' *lararia*, and secondly by her miraculous bread-making which saves Rome at the time of the Gallic siege.

Ovid applies the word *iocus* to those episodes which have affinities with mime or satyr drama and contain figures—Priapus, Faunus, Pan, Silenus, nymphs and satyrs—belonging to the Dionysian komos. The comedy of these Roman *ioci* is, almost without exception, phallic and relates directly to the fertility/fecundity for which the Roman gods are being invoked and honoured by *Ludi* on their festal day. Among these are the licentious tales of Anna Perenna impersonating Minerva at a marriage to Mars (*Fast.* 3. 695), Priapus' foiled rape of Lotis (1.390–440), Faunus' assault on Hercules dressed as Omphale (2. 302–56), and Priapus' attempt to rape Vesta (6. 319–48). All four have been classed as possible mimes or satyr plays [see Barchiesi (1997*a*) 238–56, Wiseman (1998) 23–4, 48–51, 72–4 and (2002) 283–7]. The last three contain specific references to Bacchus: Priapus sees Lotis at a Bacchic festival, Faunus assaults Hercules/Omphale in Bacchus' grove the night before sacred rites are performed to the god, and the uninvited donkey at Cybele's picnic is sacred to Bacchus.

Ovid's story of Lotis and Priapus in *Fasti* 1 is a literary version of a classic satyr drama intended to add colour to his discussion of Roman sacrifice, sacrifice and Ludi Scaenici being integral parts of religious celebration. The story of Vesta and Priapus, on the other hand, arose from Ovid's desire for a narrative which would combine Vesta and the donkey depicted with her in the bakers' *lararium*, a cult drama for the Bakers' Guild. The only possible justification for recounting a second time the story of the donkey braying to foil Priapus would seem to be the literary challenge of combining two antithetical deities, Vesta and Priapus, respectively the personifications of Chastity and Lust, in a drama, the sequence of which would already be anticipated by the reader. It is my view that Ovid's subtle alterations, which transform the Vesta story, justify the inclusion of both stories, particularly as they contribute another balancing contrast or 'frame' to Ovid's two peripheral books. The different sections of Ovid's *Vestalia* are linked by interlocking themes. The theme of bread-making links this passage to Vesta's rescue by the braying donkey (319–48) and to the allusion to the goddess Fornax (313–16), while the theme of *devotio*, hinted at in Ovid's mention of the Lacus Curtius (403), is inherent in Metellus' rescue of the Palladium.

319–26: *The tale of Priapus' discomfiture will make you laugh. Cybele invited the gods with some nymphs and satyrs. Silenus was there, although no one asked him. To cut a long story short, the party went on all night.* **327–36:** *Some of the guests strolled, others relaxed. Some played games, others dozed. Some danced. Vesta fell asleep just where she was. The garden god was darting here and there on the look out for a conquest. He spotted Vesta, apparently unaware* *of who she was.* **337–46:** *A wicked thought crossed his mind and he crept up stealthily. By chance old Silenus' donkey gave an untimely bray just when Priapus was beginning his assault. Vesta jumped up and they all came running, but Priapus escaped attempts to seize him.* **345–6:** *It is the custom of the people of Lampsacus to sacrifice the donkey to the garden god.*

319–20. ***praeterea referamne tuum, rubicunde Priape, | dedecus?*** the indiscretions and discomfiture of Priapus was a popular theme among Roman poets who apostrophized him as *rubicunde* or *ruber* on account his outsize crimson genitalia. Essentially the embodiment of a fertility cult, which had spread from Lampsacus on the Hellespont to Greece and then to Rome, ithyphallic Priapus, in his usual guise as the weatherbeaten *custos hortarum*, had a quaint directness which appealed to Hellenistic and Roman poets (see Virg. *Ecl.* 7. 34. Cf. *G* 4. 111, *Copa* 23, Hor. *Serm.* 1. 8).

320. ***est multi fabula parva ioci*:** a similar formula introduces Faunus' attempt to rape Omphale (*Fast.* 2. 304: *antiqui fabula plena ioci*). Ovid's use of the word *iocus* to describe a story linking the notoriously lewd Priapus with two chaste Augustan goddesses, Vesta and Cybele, merits investigation. Although Holleman's wide-ranging examples of anti-Augustan parody [Holleman (1975) 260–8] in Faunus' attempted rape of Omphale is not convincing, Ovid's Roman readers might well have found some topical mythological echoes of Augustus' notorious Lex Iulia de adulteriis coercendis in the discomfiture of the flamboyant would-be rapist. If there is, as Barchiesi (1997*a*: 247–8), suggests, a genre problem in Ovid's combination of material from satyr drama with allusions to Augustus' new cult of Vesta, a simple solution might be that Ovid regarded the appearance of characters familiar from mimes as being as equally evocative of Roman festivals as his vignettes of Romans drinking, dancing, and coupling to excess. The more illustrious the celebrand, the greater the potential for literary revelry. There was no clearer signal for this than the introduction of mythological figures from the Dionysiac komos. Religious festivals provided an excuse for laxer morals—and looser tongues.

321. ***turrigera frontem Cybele redimita corona*:** to add weight to her persona, Ovid introduces Cybele with her iconographic turreted headgear (cf. Virg. *Aen.* 6. 784–7, 10. 253, Ovid *Fast.* 4. 224). The crenellated crown is worn by Dea Roma on the Gemma Augustea where it signified the goddess' protection of the city. It has the same significance on the head of the civic goddess Venus Pompeiana, who appears with Vesta in one of the Pompeian bakers' *lararia.*

322. ***convocat aeternos ad sua festa deos***: elevated language continues through the pentameter with the solemn *convocat* and the identification of Cybele's party guests as *aeternos deos*, in a line verbally and rhythmically reminiscent of Ovid's panegyrical pronouncement concerning Augustus' establishment of a Palatine shrine to Vesta: *stet domus! aeternos tres habet una deos* (*Fast.* 4. 954).

323. ***convocat et satyros et, rustica numina, nymphas***: the anaphoric repetition of *convocat* invites the expectation of more illustrious guests than the nymphs and satyrs who traditionally attend alfresco revels in honour of Bacchus (cf. *Fast.* 1. 397–8, *Met.* 1. 192–5, Virg. *G* 2. 493–4). The difference between the revel in *Fasti* 1, where the entire komos appears to accompany Bacchus himself, including Pan, Silenus, and Priapus, and Cybele's gracious invitation to nymphs and satyrs to join a gathering of *aeternos deos* is subtle but clear. This line mirrors in part *Met.* 1. 192, which belongs to a passage where Ovid imagines the gods observing social divisions equivalent to those in Rome. Here Cybele's rustic guests, the divine *plebs*, favour exactly the same activities as those enjoyed by Ovid's Roman *plebs* at the Feast of Anna Perenna, who imbibe copiously, loll around on the grass, doze, or dance (*Fast.* 3. 523–42, cf. 6. 328–30). Roman Vesta has not been invited to join a komos, she has come along, with other respectable goddesses, to a rural party hosted by another Roman goddess, Cybele, in their mutual Trojan homeland.

324. ***Silenus, quamvis nemo vocarat, adest***: Silenus is unwelcome at Cybele's party because of his notorious *nequitia* and *inextincta libido* (*Fast.* 1. 413–14). Ovid's detail of Silenus' gatecrashing provides the happenstance which leads to the donkey being on hand to utter the untimely bray (*intempestivo . . . sono*) which saved Vesta's virtue. This enables the poet to focus on the familiar image of working cooperation between Vesta and the donkey from the walls of the bakers' *lararia*: Vesta seated with the donkey behind her chair, which allegorized the processes of grinding corn and baking bread. At the same

time Ovid wittily hints at the incongruous collaboration of the chaste goddess with the ass on which drunken Silenus rollicks through the komos.

325. *nec licet et longum est epulas narrare deorum*: Ovid backs up the excuse, 'it takes too long', *longum est*, with a religious taboo, *nec licet*, which, he says, prohibits him from recounting the banquets of the gods, although he goes on to add two more couplets describing the different ways in which the guests amuse themselves. By contrast, in *Fasti* 1 the only activities mentioned are drinking and erotic pursuits, when Pan, Priapus, and Silenus begin to eye the nymphs suggestively.

327. *in opacae vallibus Idae*: Mount Ida was a favourite haunt of Cybele and her worshippers (*Fast.* 4. 249–50: *amoenam fontibus Iden | semper... Mater amavit.* Cf. Virg. *Aen.* 10. 252). For her party on Mount Ida the goddess has selected a typical *locus amoenus*: a mountain valley shaded by trees (*opacae*) with a gently murmuring stream (*lene sonantis aquae*, 340). Like the mountain grove of Bacchus with its *garrulus rivus* (*Fast.* 2. 313–16) where Faunus is thwarted in his attempt to rape Omphale, and the rural cave where Janus rapes Crane, this is a classic *locus amoenus* suited to both rape and satyr drama (Vitr. 5. 6. 9). [See Parry (1964) 275–82.]

330. *viridem celeri ter pede pulsat humum*: Cybele's guests join in the three-beat dance known as the *tripudium*, a dance associated with religious holidays. It is danced by Cybele's followers in Catullus (63.26) and also by a farm labourer at a country festival (Hor. *Carm.* 3. 18. 15–16. Cf. Lucr. 5. 1402: *terram pede pellere*). It has been suggested that the dance, *tripudium*, is the Latin equivalent of the Etruscan word *triumpe*, deriving from the Greek *thriambos*, which not only occurs in the shout at Roman triumphs, *io triumpe*, but is also embedded in the *Carmen Fratrum Arvalium*, probably as a stage direction indicating at this point the performance of a *tripudium.* Etruscan music and musical instruments were adopted by the Romans, and so the existence of the Etruscan word *triumpe* alongside the Latin *tripudium* may be taken as further evidence of a double Etruscan–Latin culture in regal and early Republican Rome [see Bonfante-Warren (1970)].

331. *Vesta iacet placidamque capit secura quietem*: asleep in the midst of the nymphs, Vesta is a vulnerable target for Priapus, who seems at first to have no particular quarry: *nymphas deasque | captat et errantes fertque refertque pedes* (333–4). Here again there is a striking contrast with the Lotis story in *Fasti* 1, where Priapus pursues Lotis in the conventional manner of an elegiac lover with sighs and signals until he is snubbed by the disdainful nymph (420: *inrisum... despicit illa*). The peaceful innocence of Vesta's sleep contains an unexpected Virgilian allusion which enhances the contrast between her carefree and innocent slumber and Priapus' feverish sexual arousal. The reference is signalled by the words *placidam... quietam*, which occupy the same positions in the line and rhythmic value as Virgil's *placidum... soporem* (*Aen.* 4. 522). Here all nature sleeps except for Dido (*at... infelix... Phoenissa*, 529), who restlessly casts about in her mind her few remaining options, just as Priapus (*at ruber hortarum custos*, 333) runs back and forth trying to choose which nymph to rape. As the untroubled sleep of birds and animals highlights the wakeful Dido's regret (Virg. *Aen.* 4. 551) that she is unable to live an uncomplicated life *more ferae*, so Priapus' restless animal pursuit of casual sex contrasts with the chaste Vesta who, *secura*, enjoys *placidam quietem.*

332. *sicut erat, positum caespite fulta caput*: in the parallel story of Priapus' attempt on Lotis in Book 1 Lotis also falls asleep *sicut erat*, and the cause is explained in the next two words: *lusu fessa.* The words *sicut erat* imply a casual spontaneity infinitely more suited to the people's Vesta than to Augustus' *cognata dea.* Vesta's casual pose, with her head pillowed on the grass, makes her indistinguishable from the other partygoers and therefore fair game for Priapus.

334. *errantes fertque refertque pedes*: Priapus darts back and forth trying to choose his victim. His erratic progress recalls Faunus intent upon raping Omphale: *huc illuc temerarius errat* (*Fast.* 2. 335).

335–6: *aspicit et Vestam: dubium nymphamne putarit | an scierit Vestam; scisse sed ipse negat*: suspense is heightened by delaying the impending rape first by Priapus' indecision as he selects a victim, then by the poet's procrastination as he debates whether Priapus really knew that his victim was Vesta. This couplet is patterned with sound-play, alliteration, and assonance, which mirror the contrasting moods of Vesta and Priapus. The three opening words of the hexameter, *aspicit et Vesta*, combine repeated sharp consonants, *p...c...t* with short *i* and *e*, to convey the feverish searching of Priapus, which contrasts with the soporific assonance of *dubium nymphamne*, evoking the peacefully sleeping Vesta. The first half of the pentameter reinforces the sharp sounds suggestive of the impatient demigod and the line ends with an onomatopoeic hiss of defiance: *scisse sed ipse negat.*

337–8. ***spem capit obscenam*****:** Priapus' surreptitious advance on the sleeping goddess mirrors Faunus' attempt on Omphale which also begins *spem capit* (*Fast.* 2. 334). Here Priapus' *spem* is disgusting (*obscenam*, 337) because it is focused on Vesta, the very embodiment of chastity. Williams (1991: 204 n. 63) points out that the word *obscenus* also has the connotation of ill-omened.

338. ***et fert suspensos corde micante gradus*****:** similarly in *Fasti* 1. 426 Priapus advances *suspenso digitis...gradu.* Ovid uses a normal idiom, *corde micante*, to describe Priapus' thudding heartbeat (cf. *Fast.* 3. 36: *corque timore micat*). This, too, may be traced back to Faunus' attempt on Omphale by a more circuitous route. In a memorable scene where Virgil advises against lying in the grass at the time when a snake sloughs its skin, the poet uses *micare* to describe the snake's flickering tongue: *linguis micat ore trisulcis* (Virg. *G* 3. 439). At the moment when Faunus is about to pounce on Omphale, his fingers encounter Hercules' lionskin and he recoils abruptly, 'like a wayfarer who has disturbed a snake' (*Fast.* 2. 341–2). The reappearance of *micare* in line 338 at the very moment when Priapus is poised to strike is surely intended to conjure up the graphic image of a more literal 'snake in the grass'.

341. ***ibat ut inciperet longi deus Hellesponti* | *intempestivo cum rudit ille sono*****:** 'and he was just going to begin, the god of the long— Hellespont...' The climax of the story is wittily accentuated by a distich of artful word-order, which is enhanced by two, centrally placed, evocative spondaic polysyllables. The discomfiture of the would-be rapist and laughter at his phallic exposure is a stylized image drawn from satyr drama, which is a regular feature of Ovid's *ioci* (cf. *Fast.* 1. 437, 2. 345–6). Having devoted a distich to the question whether Priapus knew that Vesta was his victim (335–6), Ovid now uses his word-order to hint broadly at the phallic detail which he suppresses (cf. *Fast.* 1. 391: *caeditur et rigido custodi ruris* *asellus*). It is clear from the word-order that *longus* here is suggestive, and the poet prolongs the anticipation by putting the noun right at the end of the hexameter and slowing the tempo with the spondaic *Hellesponti.* This is then followed by *intempestivo* which fills the first half of the pentameter and mimics the long drawn out bray of the donkey. It also postpones the action, *rudit ille*, and the noise, *sono*, which wakes Vesta, is kept to the very end (cf. *Fast.* 1. 434: *intempestivos edidit ore sonos*). The purport of this succinct distich is spread over two couplets in the Lotis version, including graphic details which might seem unseemly associated with Vesta (*Fast.* 1. 431–6).

344. ***per infestas effugit ille manus***: Priapus barely escapes rough justice at the hands of Vesta's companions, who are not amused. His earlier attempt on Lotis, a sleeping nymph, is greeted with general merriment (*Fast.* 1. 437–8: *deus* . . . | *omnibus ad lunae lumina risus erat*), which was the more usual reaction to phallic discomfiture and part of the customary apotropaic laughter induced by the denouement of any satyr drama (cf. *Fast.* 2. 355–6, 3. 693–6).

345–6. ***Lampsacos . . . | 'apta' canens 'flammis indicis exta damus'***: 'Lampsacus sacrifices this animal, chanting, "We give to the flames as a fitting sacrifice these entrails of the spying donkey."' These words of the pentameter represent the formulaic expression of the Lampsacenes, who apparently did sacrifice donkeys to Priapus, uttered as they flung the ass's entrails onto the altar fires. Housman discards *asini* of the mss in favour of *canens*, on the grounds that Ovid always uses the word *asellus* for 'donkey' [A. E. Housman, *CQ* 24 (1930) 11–13]. The Lotis story ends in exactly the same way (*Fast.* 1. 439–40).

Vesta's gratitude is commemorated by the donkeys' garlands and their day of rest on her feast day

347. ***quem tu, diva, memor de pane monilibus ornas***: (cf. *Fast.* 6. 311) the poet now attributes the garlands of loaves which adorn the donkeys on the *Vestalia* as a sign of Vesta's gratitude for her timely rescue. The word *memor* may point to other instances of garlanded donkeys in Roman literature (Prop. 4. 1. 21, Ovid *Fast.* 6. 311).

348. ***cessat opus; vacuae conticuere molae*:** in Vesta's honour millers' donkeys have a holiday on 9 June and the millstones fall silent. This couplet (347–8) serves as a bridge, linking the mythological tale of Vesta and Priapus with Ovid's aition for the cult of Iuppiter Pistor. As he concludes the Vesta/Priapus story, Ovid returns to the point where he began in lines 311–12 with donkeys garlanded with loaves and the silent millstones, wreathed in holiday flowers.

Vesta saves the Capitol from the Gauls

[Ogilvie (1965) 734–43, Hardie (1986) 120–43, Levene (1993) 195–203, Miles (1995) 79–88, Harrison (1997), Jaeger (1997) 57–74, Erskine (2001).]

The Gallic siege in Augustan literature

The enormity of the Gallic siege of the Capitol and the threat to Rome's gods and city was represented by Virgil as comparable to the threat of the Egyptian hordes led by Antony and Cleopatra at Actium, both episodes prominent on the shield of Aeneas (*Aen.* 8. 655–62, 671–700). The Gauls' occupation of Rome in 390 BC and their siege of the Capitol was regarded by the Romans as a violation of sacred space comparable to the Galatians' attack on Delphi in 279 BC, which was depicted on the doors of Augustus' Palatine temple of Apollo (Prop. 2. 31. 12–14). The triumph of Rome's guardian gods over the forces of barbarism is the theme of Ovid's cult aition for the altar of Jupiter Pistor. For Ovid and Horace, as for Virgil and Livy, the eternity of Roman power coexisted, symbiotically, with the practice of Roman religion on the site of Rome. Mars' heavy irony, when he accuses Capitoline Jupiter of allowing the desecration of Rome's holiest shrines, is the elegiac counterpart of Horace's image of the Pontifex Maximus ascending the Capitolium in the company of a Vestal Virgin: *dum Capitolium | scandet cum tacita virgine pontifex* (Hor. *Carm.* 3. 30. 8–9; cf. Liv. 5. 52).

349–54: *I shall unveil the significance of the altar of Jupiter Pistor on the Capitol. Its cost was small, its reputation great. The Capitoline Hill was* *besieged by savage Gauls. The long siege had caused starvation. Jupiter summoned the gods before his throne and ordered Mars to speak first.* **355–60:** *'So you are entirely unaware of the sad state of affairs?' Mars began. 'You need me to put my grief into words? If you insist, I will summarize the cause of our shame. Rome is being crushed by an Alpine foe. Is this the city to which you promised world dominion?* **361–9:** *Rome had subjugated her neighbours and her prospects were flourishing. Now she is driven from her very hearth. We have seen military heroes slaughtered in their homes, Vesta's holy symbols taken from their temple. Do you imagine that (the Romans) still believe in the gods? If they stopped to consider that your temple is in ruins, they would know that worship and offerings achieve nothing.* **370–4:** *If only they could settle the issue on the battlefield! But the barbarians have them cooped up in their citadel, starving and terrified.'*

375–82: *Then Venus, Quirinus, and Vesta spoke up on behalf of Latium. Jupiter replied, 'These walls concern us all. The Gauls will be vanquished! Now, Vesta, convince them that Rome has a superabundance of the corn she lacks. Do not desert your post. Let flour be ground and dough be kneaded and baked.'*

383–6: *Jupiter gave his orders and Vesta nodded approval. It was midnight. Toil had wearied the generals and they slept. Jupiter roused them with a message in oracular speech.* **387–94:** *'Get up! Cast from your citadel into the enemy ranks the thing you least wish to surrender!' They woke and, confused by the riddle, wondered what it was that they must surrender reluctantly. Bread seemed to fit, so they threw loaves which clanged on shields and helmets. All hope was lost of starving Rome into submission. After the enemy had been repulsed, an altar was erected to Jupiter the Pounder.*

349. *nomine quam pretio celebratior*: 'more famous for its name than for its value'. In line 394 Ovid asserts that the altar was *candida*, which conjures up a picture of marble.

349. *arce Tonantis*: 'on the citadel of the Thunderer' suggests that the altar to Iuppiter Pistor was to be found within the Capitoline precinct where the Aedes of Iuppiter Tonans was dedicated in 22 BC. Varro derives the title Pistor from the verb *pinsere*, meaning 'to grind': *nec pistoris nomen erat, nisi eius qui ruri far pinsebat, nominati ita eo quod pinsunt* (*GRF* 204). The sense of pounding in the word *pinsere* makes it possible that the title Iuppiter Pistor might also be connected to Iuppiter Tonans, the Thunderer, whose temple stood nearby on the Capitolium.

350. ***dicam Pistoris quid velit ara Iovis*****:** the altar to Iuppiter Pistor is attested only in this passage and Lactantius (*Inst.* 1. 20. 33), who may have used Ovid as his source. Whilst it has been argued that Iuppiter Pistor was a corruption of some more probable title such as Iuppiter Tutor or Soter [see Porte (1985) 366–8], there seems to be no valid reason to discount Ovid's association of Jupiter with the process of milling flour for bread. The association of Iuppiter Pistor with the milling of flour on 9 June, the first day of the *Vestalia*, may have originated from the Vestal Virgins' responsibility for grinding a type of antique grain into flour for the *mola salsa*, a mixture of flour and salt, which was offered on Vesta's altar during her festival. It was therefore fitting that on this day donkeys and the millstones which they turned were honoured for their part in grinding grain into flour. This made them associates of Vesta's priestesses who also ground grain.

351. ***cincta premebantur trucibus Capitolia Gallis | fecerat obsidio iam diuturna famem*****:** in this couplet, which opens a new narrative, Ovid heightens the drama by sound patterns and evocative word-order: *Capitolia* is surrounded by *trucibus Gallis*, *iam* by *obsidio diuturna*, which is itself framed by *fecerat famem.* A succession of staccato consonants, *c*, *t*, *p*, *b*, suggests a hail of enemy weapons in the hexameter, while *obsidio iam diuturna*, across the centre of the pentameter, echoes onomatopoeically the long siege.

353. ***Iuppiter ad solium superis regale vocatis*****:** a Council of the Gods, to decide the outcome of human conflict, was a traditional epic motif (cf. Enn. *Ann.* fr. 51–5 Sk., Virg. *Aen.* 10. 1–117, Ovid, *Met.* 1. 175–252). Ovid signals this by such epic phrases as *protinus ille refert* (354), which introduces Mars' speech, which ends as grandly as it began with the epic periphrasis *virgo Saturnia* and the enjambement of *adnuit* (cf. *Fast.* 4. 221, 5.359, 6. 549). Ovid's Council is conducted with the formality of a meeting of the senate: the members are summoned (*superis vocatis*, 353), Jupiter orders Mars to open the debate (*incipe!*, 354), Mars sets out the bare facts (*referam breviter*, 357), supporting contributions are made (*multa locuta est*, 375),

Jupiter proposes a motion (*'publica,' respondit, 'cura est'*, 377), which is seconded by Vesta (*adnuit*, 384).

355. *scilicet ignotum est*: 'I suppose you are unaware...' Ovid uses *scilicet* to convey caustic irony (*OLD* s.v. 4*a*), as he does a few lines later (366, *putant aliquos scilicet esse deos!*). Mars' mode of expression here is cited by Heinze (1960: 68), as an example of epic diction being introduced by Ovid in elegiac verse (see note on line 366).

355. *quae sit fortuna malorum*: this phrase derives epic solemnity from Virgil's frequent use of *fortuna* in this *sedes* to signify misfortune (see *Aen.* 4. 434, 5. 710, 6. 615, 12. 677 *et passim*).

356. *et dolor hic animi voce querentis eget*: '(and I suppose that) the grief in my heart has to be put into words.' Similarly Venus, more in sorrow than in anger, *tristior et lacrimis oculos suffusa nitentes*, reproaches Jupiter for the hardships suffered by Aeneas (Virg. *Aen.* 1. 228–53).

357–8. *si tamen, ut referam breviter...| exigis*: 'If, however, you insist that I give you a brief summary.' Mars retains his senatorial style. The misfortunes (*mala*, 375) suffered by Rome are cause for humiliation (*pudori*, 357) not only to themselves but to Mars, their progenitor, as well as Jupiter who has promised them *potentia rerum* (359). Mars' speech contains three instances of rhetorically cogent enjambement where a key word runs into the next line followed by a pause: *exigis* (358), *Iuppiter* (360), and *sede* (366). The same stylistic device is found in Venus' speech to Jupiter (Virg. *Aen.* 1. 229–53), where the run-on words are *pollicitus*: (you) promised! 237, *insequitur*: (misfortune) pursues, 241, and *Troia*, 249.

358. *Alpino Roma sub hoste iacet*: in his summary of the events leading up to the Gallic invasion of Rome in 390 BC Livy also uses the comparatively unusual term *Alpini* (Liv. 5. 33. 11). It is more probable, however, that Brennus' band of Cisalpine Gauls belonged to one of the Celtic tribes from the Po valley (Liv. 5. 35. 4). Having threatened Clusium, they defeated the Romans at the River Allia, besieged the Capitol, and exacted a large sum of gold from the Romans before continuing on their way south (Livy 5. 38–48).

359. *haec est, cui fuerat promissa potentia rerum*: Ovid's Mars follows the same argument as Virgil's Venus, whose lament for the sufferings of Aeneas' Trojans is accompanied by her reproach that Jupiter had promised the Romans world dominion: *fore ductores... | ... qui terras omnis dicione tenerent, | pollicitus* (Virg. *Aen.* 1. 235–7. Cf. 10. 31–5). The words *potentia rerum* in this *sedes* recall Mars' earlier request to Jupiter to fulfil his promise of apotheosis for Romulus, where he argues that Rome is now sufficiently powerful to survive without him: *habet Romana potentia vires* (*Fast.* 2. 483). Mars' confidence that Jupiter must redeem his promise in the earlier passage balances his angry taunts here which reinforce his insistence on the need for divine intervention. These two passages are linked by the theme of baking bread. The *Quirinalia* (*Fast.* 2. 475–511) coincided with the *Fornacalia*, a celebration of Fornax, the goddess of the bread oven. Similarly the *Vestalia* (*Fast.* 6. 249–468) associates Vesta with the millstone donkey (311–18, 347–8) and the baking of bread to raise the Gallic siege (349–94).

361. ***suburbanos Etruscaque contudit arma***: 'and already Rome had crushed her neighbours and the armed might of Etruria.' We may assume that *suburbani* refers loosely to hostile tribes across Latium and Campania. Rome had formed an alliance with the Latin League after the decisive Battle of Lake Regillus in 493 BC and her campaigns against the Hernici, Sabines, Aequi, and Volsci had petered out by the end of the fifth century. *Etrusca arma* must refer exclusively to the three Veientine Wars which culminated in Camillus' capture of Veii in 396 BC.

362. ***spes erat in cursu***: 'their hopes were rising high.' The unstoppable progress implied by the idiom *in cursu* (*OLD* s.v. 8*b*) can be graphically illustrated by Ovid's use of it in other contexts; for example, to describe the speech in full flow of a garrulous bawd (*Am.* 1. 8. 109) or the unquenchable torrent of Hecuba's grief (*Met.* 13. 508). Virgil's Venus also alludes to the disappointment of Roman hopes (*speravimus ista, Aen.* 10. 42).

362. ***nunc lare pulsa suo est***: 'now she is driven from her home.' In the following lines, symmetrically introduced by the anaphora *vidimus* (363) ... *vidimus* (365), Ovid relates the events recorded in Livy (5. 40–1), although he reverses the order of Livy's two stories: the Vestals escaping to Caere with their sacra and the old *triumphatores* confronting the Gauls in their *atria.* After their defeat by Brennus'

Gauls at the Battle of the Allia in 390 BC, half the Roman army (some 20,000 men) fled to nearby, and recently defeated, Veii instead of returning to defend Rome (Liv. 5. 38. 5). Those capable of defending the *arx* took up a defensive position there, having abandoned the rest of the city: *lare pulsa suo est.*

363. *vidimus ornatos aerata per atria picta | veste triumphales occubuisse senes*: during the general exodus into the countryside, the old patrician senators arrayed themselves in their triumphal regalia (*picta veste triumphales*, 364) and seated themselves in their *atria.* The Gauls marvelled at their pose of silent, almost godlike, majesty (*se ferebant simillimos dis*, Liv. 5. 41. 8.), until M. Papirius indignantly rapped with his ivory staff a Gaul who curiously fingered his beard. The spell broken, massacre ensued. Ovid uses the expression *aerata per atria* to add epic grandeur to the nobility of the old Roman generals. In reality, the only bronze in early Republican *atria* is likely to have been bronze fittings attached to the doors or furniture.

363–5. *vidimus Iliacae transferri pignora Vestae*: after burying any sacred objects which they could safely leave behind, the Vestal Virgins took the rest of the sacred objects (*Iliacae pignora Vestae*), which may have included the Palladium and the *fascinum*, from their temple in the Forum and made their way to Caere, an Etruscan city friendly to Rome. Plutarch's account (Plut. *Cam.* 37) discloses that they had already buried under the temple of Quirinus two terracotta pots, one containing the ancient Samothracian gods of Dardanus (cf. D.H. 2. 66. 5) and another, traditionally empty, now filled with other *sacra*, which Plutarch does not identify but which might include the *mola salsa* and sacred vessels. It is probable that as they fled the city they were carrying more than a single cult statue, for a plebeian, Lucius Albinus, made his wife and children descend from their family cart to make room so that he could give them a lift to Caere (Liv. 5. 40. 7–10). Recent excavations show that Caere had two substantial sixth-century temples in addition to the temple to Juno, which suggests that Caere, like its port, Pyrgi, to which it was linked by a Sacred Way, was famous for its rich sanctuaries. It was an appropriate place for Vesta's *sacra* to find refuge. Livy throws some light on Rome's close ties with Caere in the fourth century, for he tells how M. Fabius, brother of the consul of 310 BC, had been educated there in the house of family friends, where he became fluent in Etruscan and conversant with Etruscan literature. The historian alludes to sources which indicate that it was not unusual for Roman boys to be educated in Latin and Etruscan, just as, in his own day, they were educated in Latin and Greek (Liv. 9. 36. 2–3). Evidently the Roman aristocracy of the fourth century enjoyed a higher level of culture through contact with friendly Etruscan cities, which owed their own cultural refinements to their long-standing contacts with Greece and Ionia. Rome's friendship with Caere is commemorated by Virgil (*Aen.* 8. 454–519), where Evander sends Aeneas to Caere as the foreign leader promised to the Caeretans by an oracle to replace the deposed Mezentius. Diodorus (14. 117. 7) claims that when the Gauls returned from their employment with Dionysius of Syracuse, during which they may have participated in the sack of Pyrgi in 384 BC, they were intercepted and defeated in the Trausian Plain by the Caeretans. Strabo (5. 2. 3) adds to this story that they recovered and returned to Rome the gold ransom which the Romans had been forced to pay to Brennus (cf. Liv. 5. 49. 1–7. See note on line 358).

366. *putant aliquos scilicet esse deos!*: 'and I suppose they imagine that the gods exist!' The spirit of this remark echoes the speech of Virgil's Iarbas to Jupiter Ammon, where he accuses his god, whom his people have dutifully worshipped, of turning a blind eye to injustice (*Aen.* 4. 218: *famemque fovemus inanem*). Conversely Virgil emphasizes that Dido is alien and un-Roman by making her express, with the same rhetorical irony, complete disbelief in Jupiter's involvement with Aeneas' destiny (*Aen.* 4. 379–80: *scilicet is superis labor est, ea cura quietos | sollicitat)*. The essence of the thought behind Mars' use of rhetorical *indignatio* requires fuller explanation. The Augustan writers frequently attributed national misfortune to *neglegentia deorum* (Hor. *Carm.* 1. 2. 29–30, 3. 6, Ovid *Fast.* 2. 547–55). The fullest statement of this belief is delivered by Livy's M. Furius Camillus, *diligentissimus religionum cultor* (Liv. 5. 50. 1), in the long speech which concludes Book 5, where this is a central leitmotiv (5. 51. 4–5: *omnem neglegentiam divini cultus exemptam hominibus putem, tamen tam evidens numen hac tempestate rebus adfuit Romanis... invenietis* *omnia prospera evenisse sequentibus deos, adversa spernentibus*). In this patriotic context Camillus singles out Jupiter, Vesta, Mars, and Quirinus (Liv. 5. 52. 6–7) as Rome's guardian deities, and he attributes to *neglegentia deorum* the reverses caused by the Gallic invasion (51. 6). Subsequently he implies that the Vestals' flight to Caere with the *sacra* of Vesta marked a resumption of *pietas* which was eventually rewarded by their ability to expel the Gauls (51. 9–10). Ovid uses this material in his Council of the Gods in *Fasti* 6 but gives it a different slant, for while the Romans' *pietas* appears unimpeachable, Jupiter is accused by Mars, supported by Vesta, Venus, and Quirinus, of *neglegentia rerum humanarum*, which may cause his worshippers to question whether their care of the temples and offerings of incense were entirely pointless. [On Livy's association of Roman *pietas* with military vicissitudes, see Levene (1993) 175–203.]

367–70. *at si respicerent qua vos habitatis in arce* | . . . *data sollicita tura perire manu*: *respicere* here clearly has the sense of considering a situation and regulating one's conduct accordingly (*OLD* s.v. 7*a*). Mars argues that if the Romans stopped to think about Jupiter's apparent indifference to the Gauls' sacrilegious attacks on the Capitoline sanctuaries (*tot domos vestras . . . premi*, 368), they would realize that the practice of religion was pointless (*nil opus in cura scirent superesse deorum*, 369) and withhold further offerings (*data tura perire*, 370). Ovidian gods, like their Roman worshippers, perceived religion as a contractual obligation. The comedy lies in Mars, who has a personal interest in Rome, sanctimoniously castigating Jupiter for neglecting the gods' side of this bargain: if the Romans are to continue to build temples and offer sacrifices, Jupiter's Capitoline temple must remain undamaged (387–8) and the offerings graciously accepted (369–70). Playing with the same idea of the gods' contractual obligations in *Fasti* 5, Ovid has Flora claim *turba que caelestes ambitiosa sumus* (5. 298), using the conventional expression *ture dato* (302) to describe offerings tempting enough to induce Jupiter to put away his thunderbolt.

371. *utinam pugnae pateat locus!*: 'if only there were space to fight!' It is part of the humour inherent in Ovid's elegiac recasting of epic characters that they concern themselves with practical realities. The war god expresses his frustration that the Romans, cooped up in the *arx*, cannot extricate themselves from their predicament by defeating the Gauls on the battlefield (see note on line 377).

375–6. *tunc Venus . . . Quirinus | Vestaque pro Latio multa locuta suo est*: this group of deities, bound to Rome with family ties, support Mars with lengthy pleas *pro Latio suo*. The fusion of the Roman descendants of Venus and Mars is set out in Ovid's genealogy (*Fast.* 4. 23–60). This mirrors the iconography of the temple of Mars Ultor, where Mars and Venus are grouped with Romulus on the pediment and with Divus Iulius, representing the Aeneadae, in the *cella*. Vesta, guardian of the sacred flame and Palladium, represents the living power of Roma, who is personified on the pediment, since Vesta herself has no tangible human form (*Fast.* 6. 295–6). Venus, Mars, Vesta, and Quirinus form the nucleus of Rome's guardian deities invoked by Ovid *Met.* 15. 861–70 and Vell. 2. 131.

375. *lituo pulcher trabeaque Quirinus*: *pulcher* is the adjective chosen by Ennius (*Ann.* fr. 75 Sk.) to describe Romulus when he reappears as Quirinus after his apotheosis. The ivory staff (*lituus*) and short purple tunic (*trabea*) were thought to be the traditional distinctive accoutrements of Rome's kings, associated above all with Quirinus (*trabeati cura Quirini*, Ovid *Fast.* 1. 37. Cf. 2. 503, Juv. 8. 259). Latinus appears in this costume (Virg. *Aen.* 7. 187). Historically, these belonged to Etruscan royal dress which was continued in the costume of the *triumphator* [see Bonfante-Warren (1970) 49–66].

377. *'publica,' respondit, 'cura est pro moenibus istis'*: 'We share a joint responsibility for those walls.' With partisan support from Venus, Vesta, and Romulus, Mars' sarcasm, like the scorn Virgil's Iarbas heaps on Jupiter Ammon (Virg. *Aen.* 4. 217–18), has reduced Jupiter to immediate compliance. He summons what shreds of dignity remain to him to announce his decision. Although the word *publicus* can simply mean 'for us all' (*OLD* s.v. 5), Jupiter's official response to the unanimous petition of the Guardian Gods of Rome intentionally suggests civic terminology. This elegiac 'realism' contrasts wittily with the oracular ambiguity of the pronouncement of Virgil's Jupiter in similar circumstances: *'fata viam invenient'*, *Aen.* 10. 113.

379. *'tu modo, quae desunt fruges, superesse putentur | effice'*: the colloquial *tu modo* often introduces didactic precepts (cf. Virg.

G 3.73, *Aen.* 4. 50). Because she is the goddess of the hearth, the place where primitive people traditionally baked their bread, Vesta is asked to be responsible for the miracle of creating the false impression that the Romans have plenty of food (*superesse putentur,* | *effice*).

381–2. ***'cava machina frangat* | *mollitamque manu duret in igne focus'***: 'let the hollow mill-stone crush (the grain) and let the hearth fire harden (the bread) softened by kneading.' The millstone with its hollow centre is to crush the whole grains (*quodcumque est solidae Cereris*, 381) to flour. *mollitam* from *mollire*, 'to soften', rather *molitum*, from *molere*, 'to grind', must be the correct reading here because the grinding process has already been described (*frangat*) and the next stage is kneading or 'softening' the dough before it is 'hardened' (*duret*, 382) in the baking process. The metrical quantities of *molitam* with its opening two short syllables, provide the clinching argument for the reading *mollitam*, which is upheld by Bömer and *AWC.*

383. ***fratris virgo Saturnia iussis* | *adnuit***: 'the virgin daughter of Saturn sealed with her approval her brother's command.' It is entirely proper that Vesta should give the casting vote of approval in an aetiological narrative which celebrates Vesta's association with the Roman bakers. Ovid gives added weight to her consent by using an epic-style periphrasis which reminds his readers that, as *virgo Saturnia,* Vesta is sister to both Jupiter and Juno.

385. ***iam ducibus somnum dederat labor***: 'toil had brought sleep to the generals.' This line now introduces the traditional literary pattern of a dream where a god appears to the sleeper, urging him to action which will further the drama (cf. Hom. *Od.* 6. 25–40, Virg. *Aen.* 2. 270–95, 3. 147–71, 4. 351–3, 555–70, 7. 81–106).

385–6. ***increpat illos* | *Iuppiter et sacro quid velit ore docet***: the ambiguity of Jupiter's oracular utterance is anticipated in the expression *sacro . . . ore.* The verb *increpat* signifies both a divine rebuke and an exhortation to action (see note on line 812).

387. ***'surgite!'***: the purpose of a divine visitation is to inspire prompt action from the sleeper. If he does not wake terrified by the apparition, like Ovid's Numa (*Fast.* 4. 667), he must, like the Roman generals here, be ordered to rise immediately (cf. Virg. *Aen.* 4. 569).

388. '*mittite quam minime mittere voltis opem*': 'surrender the resource which you least desire to give.' A striking alliteration of *m* and *t* combined with a repeated short *i* accentuates the opacity of Jupiter's oracular utterance.

389. *somnus abit, quaeruntque, novis ambagibus acti*: 'Sleep departed and, perplexed by the new riddle, they try to work out . . .' By placing *somnus abit* in this *sedes*, at the beginning of the line followed by *quaeruntque* and a second caesura, Ovid creates the impression of a sleeper waking and pausing to muse on a prophetic dream which may, as here, change the course of Roman history (cf. *Fast.* 3. 27–8, *Met.* 7. 643, 15. 653) or promise erotic fulfilment (*Met.* 9. 472). In *Fasti* 4. 661–8, Numa is visited in his sleep by Faunus, whose specifications for a sacrifice are incomprehensible to the king without Egeria's help (*ambages caecaque iussa*, 668).

390. *tradere quam nolint et iubeantur opem*: '(wondering) which resource they did not wish but had to surrender.' Whilst Ovid retains the essential framework of the previous pentameter (*mittite quam minime mittere voltis opem*, 388), the emphasis in the relative clause is now on the command which must be obeyed (and therefore must be first understood).

391–2. *esse Ceres visa est; iaciunt Cerealia dona | iacta super galeas scutaque longa sonant*: a typically Ovidian distich where a tricolon crescendo announces the solution of the riddle, the hurling of the bread, and the sound of loaves raining down on Gallic helmets and shields.

393–4. *hoste repulso | candida Pistori ponitur ara Iovi*: to conclude the passage harmoniously the pentameter forms a Golden Line, abCAB. Ovid's altar to Jupiter Pistor may have been built of white (*candida*) marble which conjures up a luminescent sheen. However, here there is a temptation to interpret Ovid's *candida* as floury so that it resembles the bakers who bring offerings to Jupiter Pistor, associated, in this context, with grinding flour rather than with thunder (see note on line 350). Ovid has diverged here from the historians' account (Liv. 5. 48. 8–9, D.S. 14. 116, Val. Max. 7.4.3, Plut. *Cam.* 22. 9), where Brennus' Gauls agree to lift the siege and depart on the payment of 1,000 pounds-weight of gold, which would hardly constitute a victory *hoste repulso*. He does not even consider, either here or in the earlier passage on Juno Moneta (183–90), the tradition that the Capitol was actually captured by the Gauls. [On this see N. J. Horsfall, 'From History to Legend: M. Manlius and the Geese', *CJ* 76 (1980–1) 298–311, T. J. Cornell, 'The Annals of Quintus Ennius', *JRS* 76 (1986) 247–8, Levene (1993) 198 n. 60.]

On the Via Nova Ovid meets a barefoot Roman *matrona* making her way down to the Forum

[Holland (1961), Boëls (1973), Richardson 406, Ross Holloway (1994).]

1. *The significance of bare feet at the* Vestalia

On the *Vestalia* Ovid sees the barefoot *matrona* walking down the Via Nova towards the Forum, which suggests that she is on her way to pay her annual visit to Vesta's temple. An old lady of the quarter tells the poet that the custom recalls a time when the Velabrum was entirely waterlogged and Vesta's precinct a bed of reeds. The origin of the custom, however, may be an ancient religious belief that this close contact with Terra would promote or maintain the woman's fecundity [Boëls (1973) 97]. The *Vestalia* is an appropriate time to do this, for, as Ovid points out: *Vesta eadem est et Terra* (*Fast.* 6. 267). The story demonstrates the cult of Vesta's close connection with the fecundity of the Roman *matronae.* It is another instance where the poet overlays antiquarian information with literary topoi such as his picture of the flooded Velabrum, and transforms a dry piece of information into a lively anecdotal narrative.

2. *Flooding in the Velabrum valley in early Rome and as a topos in the Augustan poets*

The Velabrum valley slopes down from the Forum Romanum towards the Forum Boarium and the Tiber between the Capitoline and the Palatine hills. It was bordered by two thoroughfares originally constructed on gravel banks, the Vicus Tuscus at the base of the Palatine, and the Vicus Iugarius at the base of the Capitoline Hill.

The whole valley was subject to flooding from the Tiber and, according to Varro (*L* 5. 43–4, 6. 24), the Velabrum was the place from which boatmen were to be seen plying their boats between the Aventine, the Palatine, and the Forum Romanum. Building began along the slope of the Via Sacra from the end of the seventh century when a fill had raised the level above that of the low-lying Forum. Similarly, as a protection against floods, in the mid-Republic a huge fill was required to raise the twin temples of Mater Matuta and Fortuna in the Forum Boarium 6 metres from its original archaic level [see Ross Holloway (1994) 80, 88]. Ovid dates Vesta's sanctuary, situated where the Via Sacra begins to rise, to a point in Numa's reign forty years after the Foundation (*Fast.* 6. 257–60. Cf. Solinus 1. 21–3). Work was begun on a drainage system in the Forum, of which the Cloaca Maxima was a part, during the reigns of the Tarquins (Liv. 1. 38. 6. Cf. D.H. 2. 50. 1–2), and the main channel was still, in the second century BC, an open ditch which ran across the Forum through the Velabrum and the Forum Boarium to empty in the Tiber (Plaut. *Curc.* 470–75). [On Janus' connection with the waterways in the Velabrum and the sluice gates, see Holland (1961).]

The Augustan poets regularly described the waters of the Velabrum valley, and this became part of the *tum–nunc* theme in Augustan elegy, which recalled a time before urban buildings had replaced the woods, lakes, and cliffs of the original site (see Tib. 2. 5. 33–8, Prop. 4. 2. 7–8, Ovid *Fast.* 2. 391). Both Tibullus and Propertius use their allusions to the waterlogged Velabrum to pun on the etymology of its name. Tibullus, who uses the word *vecta* (Tib. 2. 5. 36), to be carried in a boat which is rowed (*pulsa per vada linter aqua*, 34), appears to favour Varro's etymology from *vehere*: (cf. Var. *L* 5. 44). Propertius, on the other hand, makes it clear that he thinks that Velabrum derives from *velum*: *nauta per urbanas velificabat aquas* (Prop. 4. 9. 6). The subject of flooding in the Forum naturally introduces the topic of the Lacus Curtius, but Ovid makes no comment on the *devotio* of Mettus Curtius, which would provide a thematic link with the subsequent story of Metellus the Pontifex Maximus, who devotes himself when he enters Vesta's sanctuary.

395–416: *On Vesta's feast day I happened to be returning along the Nova Via when I saw a woman coming down barefoot. Noticing my amazement, an old*

19. Regia
20. Temple of Vesta
21. Atrium Vestae
22. Temple of Jupiter Stator (Sacra Via)
23. Comitium
24. Lapis Niger
24. Statue of Marsyas.

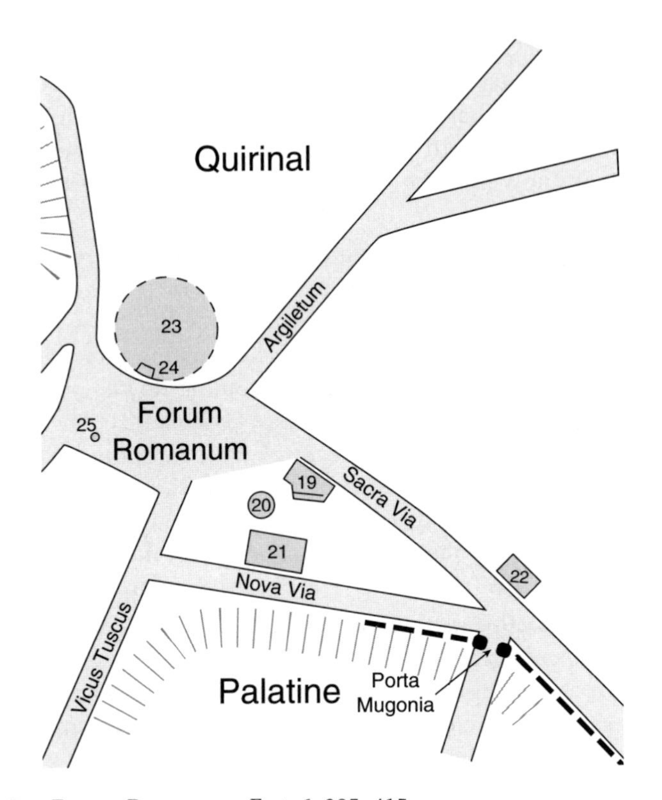

Plan 3. Forum Romanum: *Fast.* 6. 295–415

lady of the quarter invited me to sit beside her. 'Once marshes took the place of markets here', she said. 'When the floods came, the canal was awash with fast-flowing water. **403–8:** *That Lake Curtius is now dry land, but once it was a pool. Where the processions pass along the Velabrum on their way to the Circus,* *there used to be bulrushes. Often a returning party-goer would go singing along the waterways and harangue the boatmen with his tipsy talk.* **409–16:** *The changeful god (Vertumnus) had not yet been named for turning back the river. Vesta's sacred precinct was a reed-bed—you could not cross the swampy ground in shoes. Now the ground is dry, but still the custom lingers on.' She'd told the reason and I wished her well.*

393. *forte revertebar festis Vestalibus*: the feast day of Vesta provides a link between this passage and the aition of Iuppiter Pistor. In contrast with his elegiac adaptation of the epic Council of the Gods, which offered an appropriate backdrop for the Gallic siege, Ovid now adopts an anecdotal style reminiscent of Horace's *Sermones*, replete with small details characteristic of a natural raconteur, to sketch a personal encounter with two Roman women, the *matrona* with a taste for antiquity and the *anus*, who likes engaging passers by in conversation.

396. *illa | quae Nova Romano nunc Via iuncta Foro est*: Ovid describes the exact spot, as well as the date, of the encounter. He was returning (*revertebar*, 393) home along the Via Nova, one of the most ancient streets in Rome, which, as he explains, joins the Forum Romanum, when he saw the *matrona* 'coming down' (*vidi descendere*, 387) towards him (*huc*, 387). Since Ovid claims that his house stood near to the Capitol (*Tr.* 1. 3. 29–30), he should have been walking towards the Forum Romanum. In which case the poet must have turned to observe the *matrona.* Schilling (1995) explains her descent by suggesting that she was coming down the steps which led from Vesta's temple (see Plan 3: The Forum Romanum.)

398. *obstipui tacitus sustinuique gradum*: 'I stopped dumbstruck in my tracks.' Ovid's reaction (*obstipui*) suggests that it was unconventional, not to say unseemly, for a Roman *matrona* to approach the historic centre of the capital barefoot. His silence (*tacitus*) might imply that normally he would have uttered some word of greeting.

399. *sensit anus vicina loci iussumque sedere*: the poet's undisguised amazement catches the attention of an old lady (*sensit anus*) who lives nearby (*vicina loci.* Cf. Pl. *Rud.* 849, *senex vicinus Veneris*). She invites him to sit down, which suggests that she herself is already seated outside her house, as elderly Italians often are, to see what is going on in the street.

400. *adloquitur, quatiens voce tremente caput*: Ovid elsewhere emphasizes old age by the trembling of limbs or voice (see *Fast.* 3. 670, 5. 511; cf. *Met.* 8. 660, 10. 414, 14. 143, 15. 212). The quavering voice of the *anus* is suggested perhaps by a distinctive pattern of alliteration in the words *adloquitur quatiens.*

401. '*hoc ubi nunc fora sunt, udae tenuere paludes*': 'waterlogged marshland once encroached over what now are civic centres.' *AWC* retain *hoc*, which is the reading of mss *UGM.* The more obvious reading, *hic*, appears as an emendation in a group of *codices vulgares.* Pervasive damp is emphasized by the assonance of two words of kindred meaning, *udae... paludes* [cf. Ahl (1985), 316–17].

402. '*amne redundatis fossa madebat aquis*': 'when there was flooding, the channel was awash with running water.' The Tiber's propensity to flood continued into modern times (see note on lines 227–8). The word *fossa* implies a man-made channel, which may be both uncovered and covered over (*OLD* s.v. 1*a*). Ovid refers to a channel dug under the Tarquin dynasty, which was, during the Republic, an open ditch but had become part of the underground Roman sewers by Augustan times.

403. '*Curtius ille lacus siccas qui sustinet aras*': in Ovid's day the Lacus Curtius was an entirely dry natural depression in the Forum Romanum, which had been paved over so that people could toss coins to ensure the emperor's good health (Suet. *Aug.* 57. 1). It was thought to mark access to the Underworld, like the *mundus Cerealis.*

404. '*nunc solida est tellus: sed lacus ante fuit*': Varro (*L* 5. 148–50) offers three alternative explanations for the origin of the Lacus Curtius. His second version is the story related by Livy (1. 12. 8–10), describing how a young Sabine, Mettius Curtius, leading an attack to rescue the captured Sabine women, plunged his horse into a bog, which became known as Lacus Curtius. In view of Iuventas' claim that June is the month of the *iuniores*, Rome's young warriors, Ovid is probably thinking of Varro's first version: the story of Mettius Curtius' *devotio* in 362 BC (cf. Liv. 7. 6. 1–6), which is the not-unfamiliar story of a young warrior who sacrifices his own life as a *piaculum* to the gods, whose demand for sacrifice is manifested by a bottomless chasm which opens up in the Forum. When the sacrifice required is interpreted as being 'the greatest strength of the Roman people', Curtius instantly interprets this as the valour of Roman warriors (*arma virtusque*, Liv. 7. 6. 3). He pronounces the formula of *devotio* before riding fully armed into the chasm, which instantly closes over him, indicating the gods' acceptance of the sacrifice. [See Oakley (1997) 1. 96–102.]

405. '*qua Velabra solent in Circum ducere pompas*': 'where the Velabrum leads the processions to the Circus Maximus.' During the *Ludi Circenses* processions including statues of the gods progressed from the Capitoline Hill along the Vicus Tuscus to the Circus Maximus (Cic. *Ver.* 2. 1. 154).

406. '*nil praeter salices cassaque canna fuit*': 'there was nothing but osiers and hollow reeds.' This onomatopoeic alliteration *salices cassaque canna* evokes the rustle of dry reeds in the wind. Since *cassa canna* is nominative singular, *praeter* cannot be taken as a preposition with accusative. This is, instead, a comparatively rare example of *praeter* used as a disjunctive conjunction (OLD s.v. 9) instead of the more common *praeter quam* (OLD s.v. 3).

407. '*saepe suburbanas rediens conviva per undas | cantat et ad nautas ebria verba iacit*': Ovid rephrases a Tibullan image of a rustic returning from a festival (1. 10. 51: *rusticus e lucoque vehit male sobrius ipse*). A variation of this line, describing a star-gazing inebriate, may be found at line 785.

409. '*conveniens diversis ... figuris | nomen*': 'a name matching his diverse shapes.' Vertumnus' power to change his shape is colourfully described by Ovid in his tale of his courtship of Pomona (*Met.* 14. 623–771. Cf. Prop. 4. 2. 19–40, Tib. 3. 8. 13). Vertumnus' statue stood on the Vicus Tuscus outside the Forum Romanum near to the temple of Castor (Cic. *Ver.* 2. 1. 154, Var. *L* 5. 46, Liv. 44. 16. 10, Prop. 4. 2. 7–10). Varro describes Vertumnus as *deus Etruriae princeps (L* 5. 46), and this quarter of Rome was thought to derive its name from a colony of Etruscans who were allowed to settle there after they had given the Romans military assistance either during Romulus' wars with the Sabines (Prop. 4. 2. 49–52) or during the late regal period (Liv. 2. 14. 9). Vertumnus' cult may have been introduced much later in Rome, possibly around 264 BC, the year in which M. Fulvius Flaccus, whose statue stood in Vertumnus' Aventine temple, was awarded a triumph for his victory over the Etruscan Volsinii.

410. '*nomen ab averso ceperat amne deus*': 'the god (Vertumnus) had taken his name from the river turning back.' In a poem where Vertumnus comments on his view over the busy Forum Romanum, Propertius attributes the derivation of his name to the flooding river Tiber retreating within its banks (4. 2. 10: *Vertumnus verso dicor ab amne deus*).

411. '*hic quoque lucus erat iuncis et harundine densus | et pede velato non adeunda palus*': 'Here, too, there was a sacred precinct, set about with bulrushes and reeds, and a swamp which was unsuitable for crossing in shoes.' Merkel (1841) and *AWC* prefer the reading *lucus*, which Bömer identifies as a grove beside the Atrium Vestae, mentioned by Cicero (*Div.* 1. 101). Since this was situated roughly where the Via Sacra begins to rise, it would have been on slightly higher ground than the depression of the Forum Romanum, but may still have been damp enough to be described as *iuncis et harundine densus. U*, however, offers *lacus*, and it could be argued in favour of this reading that, following *hic quoque*, the distich describing two areas of wetland is framed by *lacus* and *palus*, while the following hexameter describes the retreat of the waters: *stagna recesserunt et aquas sua ripa coercet* (413), and finally in the pentameter the marshland becomes dry land: *siccaque nunc tellus* (414).

412, 414. '*et pede velato non adeunda palus | ... mos tamen ille manet*': by ending the old woman's narration with the comment that long ago this marshy area could not be crossed wearing shoes, Ovid returns to the *matrona* whose bare feet sparked his interest in the first place.

415–16. '*valeas, anus optime!' dixi | 'quod superest aevi, molle sit omne, tui*': although this *hospita anus* has given only a story, the warmth in Ovid's valedictory words evokes such literary prototypes as Theseus' farewell to the dead Hecale (Call. *Hec.* fr. 263 Pf).

Ovid describes how the Palladium came to Rome

[Cole (1984) 87–100, Gruen (1990), 5–34, Barchiesi (1998) 130–40, M. Sage, 'Roman Visitors to Ilium in the Roman Imperial and Late Antique Period: The Symbolic Function of a Landscape', *Studia Troica* 10 (2000) 211–32, Dieter Hertel, *Die Mauern von Troia.*

Mythos und Geschichte im antiken Ilion (Munich, 2003), Erskine (2001) 219–53, C. B. Rose, 'The Temple of Athena at Ilion', *Studia Troica* 13 (2003), Williams (1994) 42–5.]

Roman ties with the Trojan motherland

Political and religious ties between Rome, Ilion, Samothrace, and Pergamum had been developing since the First Macedonian War. In 203 BC Rome demonstrated both her kinship and Trojan ancestry by establishing in Rome the cult of Magna Deum Mater Idaea when Attalus of Pergamum himself negotiated with the Romans the transfer of the cult object representing Cybele to Rome. Concepts of temple architecture and decoration which were shared by Ilion, Pergamum, and Samothrace were absorbed and later copied in Rome. The new temple to Pallas Athene in Ilion, constructed in the third century (*c.* 240–30 BC), was a prominent civic monument, which was honoured by the rulers of Pergamum and a focus for sacrifices by visiting Roman generals (Liv. 37. 9. 7, 37. 37. 1–3). The temple contained a cult statue of Athene Ilias, wearing a polos (headdress) and chiton, holding both spear and distaff in the manner of the Palladium statue (see Apollod. 3. 12. 3), and this appeared on local coinage during Augustan times. When the temple had been damaged by C. Flavius Fimbria, who had attacked Ilion in 85 BC at the time of the Mithridatic Wars (Appian 12. 53), the people of Ilion had appealed to Sulla (Plut. *Sull.* 34. 4. And see Erskine (2001) 243–5). Augustus undertook to pay for the restoration of Trojan sanctuaries which included work on the temple of Athene which bore his name on its architrave. It is possible that the sanctuary of Cybele was also repaired at the time of Augustus' restorations. Her worship, popular in Ilion, Pergamum, and Samothrace, had gained stature in Rome after Virgil's portrait of her as an ancestral Trojan goddess. Cybele's temple in Rome, with those of Victoria and Apollo, formed part of the Palatine religious complex which surrounded the house of Augustus with its shrine to Vesta.

417–24: *I learned other details in my boyhood, but that is no reason to leave them out. At the time when the walls of Troy had been built by Ilus (who still*

Fig. 11 Marble Palladium statue from the *Theft of the Palladium* group in the Cave of Tiberius, Museo di Sperlonga, Italy. Early first century AD, h. 0.82 m. Archaic-style Palladium contrasting with the naturalistic style of the hand of Diomedes. The archaizing style was often used to suggest antiquity in cult statues during the Augustan period [see Zanker (1988) 239–63]. (Photograph courtesy of D.I.A. Rome, Inst. Neg. 1965. 104.)

possessed the wealth of Asia), a statue of Minerva is believed to have fallen from heaven. I was eager to see this; and I did see both the temple and the place where it fell. Pallas still has a temple, the Palladium is in Rome. **425–32:** *Apollo prophesied that the city would be safe so long as the goddess' statue was* *safeguarded. Ilus kept the statue in the citadel and passed its safekeeping to his heir, Laomedon. Under Priam it was inadequately guarded. This pleased Pallas, whose beauty had been rejected by Paris' judgement.* **433–6:** *They say Diomedes or devious Ulysses or the good Aeneas took it away. Who knows? It is Roman (now) and all-seeing Vesta guards it.*

417–18. ***cetera . . . | . . . praetereunda mihi*****:** by *cetera* Ovid means the story of the Trojan War and the capture of the Palladium which he studied in his boyhood (*didici puerilibus annis*). The gerundive *praetereunda*, which Ovid often puts, for metrical reasons, in this *sedes* as the penultimate word of the pentameter (*Fast.* 3. 344, 4. 470, 496, 5. 374), is balanced in the hexameter by another pentasyllabic: *puerilibus.*

419. ***moenia Dardanides nuper nova fecerat Ilus | (Ilus adhuc Asiae dives habebat opes)*****:** Ovid's depiction of the building of Troy offers the poet the opportunity of recalling simultaneously its ruin by means of Virgilian allusions. The words *moenia Dardanidum* begin an emotional line where Aeneas describes the Trojans pulling the horse inside the walls on Troy's last day (Virg. *Aen.* 2. 242). In contrast Ovid uses the same words to observe that Ilus' walls were new (*nova*, 419), when Troy controlled all the wealth of Asia. The emotional force of this allusion is intensified by epanalepsis of the name of the first king of Troy, Ilus, as the last word of the hexameter and at the beginning of the pentameter. When Virgil uses the epanalepsis, *Ilo, | Ilo*, his Ilus is a Rutulian pursued by Pallas (*Aen.* 10. 400–1). Earlier, however, Virgil uses the name Ilus for not the first but the last scion of the Trojan dynasty, Iulus or Ascanius (*Aen.* 1. 268). Quintilian (*Inst.* 9. 3. 44) describes this form of repetition as a device frequently used by the poets, quoting Virg. *Ecl.* 10. 72–3. [For more examples, see Wills (1996) 394–6.]

421. ***signum caeleste*****:** the statue is 'heavenly' because it is said to have fallen from the skies. For the same reason Ovid uses the same word to describe the *ancile* (*caelestia Martis arma*, *Fast.* 3. 259–60). Both shield and statue are given to Rome by the gods as *imperii pignora certa, Fast.* 3. 354.

422. ***urbis in Iliacae desiluisse iuga*****:** Platnauer (102) notes the tmesis caused by postponing *iuga* to the end of the line.

423. ***cura videre fuit; vidi templumque locumque*****:** the wording, *cura videret fuit*, of this parenthetic aside to his reader throws light on Roman enthusiasm for literary tourism. We know from *P* 2. 10. 21–42 that Ovid travelled to Asia and on to Sicily with a fellow poet, Pomponius Macer, who was writing a poem on the Trojan War. It had become fashionable for literary tourists to visit Rome's mother city, particularly after Augustus' restoration of buildings in the city of Ilion which may have begun shortly after his visit to Asia Minor in 20 BC. It seems that Ovid and Macer indulged in some literary sight-seeing in the Troad, as well as in Sicily.

424. ***hoc superest illi, Pallada Roma tenet*****:** *hoc* refers to Pallas' *templum* in Troy. By metonymy Pallas here signifies the Palladium (*OLD* s.v. 1*b*).

425. ***consulitur Smintheus lucoque obscurus opaco*****:** Ovid uses the epithet Smintheus on one other occasion only (*Met.* 12. 585), again in the context of the Trojan Wars. G. Kirk [*The Iliad: A Commentary, Vol. I, Books 1–4* (Cambridge, 1985) 57, n. on line 39] suggests that Smintheus may derive from Sminthe, a city in the Troad. There was, however, an Ionic temple to Apollo Smintheus in Ilion, constructed *c.*150 BC, containing a cult statue of the god. Since Apollo's words are unambiguous *non mentito ore* (427–8), *obscurus* must mean that the god himself was invisible (*OLD* s.v. 3) in the darkness of the grove, *luco opaco*, an appropriate place for divine revelation.

427. ***'aetheriam servate deam, servabitis urbem'*****:** 'Safeguard the heavenly goddess (and) you will safeguard your city.' Apollo's oracle confers the authority of antiquity on the Roman dictum that Rome's survival as an imperial power depended on the safeguarding of Vesta's *sacra*, which included the ancient cult statue of Pallas, the Palladium. By including in his *Vestalia* passage this oracle and the Vestals' flight to Caere to preserve *Iliacae... pignora Vestae* (365) at all costs, Ovid suggests legendary and historical precedents for Augustus' guardianship of Vesta's flame and statue in his Palatine house (*Fast.* 4. 949–54).

427–31. ***'servate... servabitis... servat... servata parum'*****:** to emphasize that the Palladium was guarded assiduously from its descent from heaven until Priam's reign, Ovid indicates the passage of time, first with a quadruple polyptoton, using variant forms of the verb *servare*, and secondly, by allusion to the three Trojan kings whose reigns span the history of Troy from its origins to its fall: Ilus, the founder Laomedon, whose treachery incurs divine retribution, and finally Priam, in whose reign the city falls to the Greeks because the statue is *servata parum.*

428. ***'imperium secum transferet illa loci'***: 'she will transfer dominion with her.' The key words, *imperium loci*, frame this crucial pentameter. The Palladium carried with it from Troy to Rome a guarantee of power for whomsoever kept the talisman statue in their city. Dionysius claims that Aeneas brought not only the Palladium to Rome but also the Great Gods of Samothrace which Dardanus had taken to Troy at the time of that city's foundation (D.H. 1. 69. 3–4, Macr. 3. 4. 7). As the original home of the Roman Penates, Samothrace was, like Troy, an ancestral homeland of the Romans and regarded as particularly sacred (Liv. 45. 5. 3). The numbers of Roman initiates into the Samothracian mysteries, which increased steadily from the end of the Macedonian Wars, may have included Ovid himself, when he visited Samothrace on his way to Tomis (*Tr.* 1. 10. 19–22) and, ten years later, Germanicus in AD 18 (Tac. *Ann.* 2. 54).

430. ***curaque ad heredem Laomedonta redit***: 'and its care passed to his heir, Laomedon.' Ovid favours this *sedes* in the pentameter for the pentasyllabic oblique cases of Laomedon (cf. *Ars* 3. 6. 54, *Her.* 16. 58. 206).

432. ***ex quo iudicio forma revicta sua est***: 'her beauty was vanquished by his judgement.' The fall of Troy was traditionally ascribed to distant mythological injustices. Ovid passes over the unscrupulous dealings of Laomedon in favour of the generically more suitable story of Priam's son, Paris', rejection of Pallas' beauty (*forma revicta*) on the occasion of his judgement (*iudicio*). Ovid alludes to Minerva's chagrin in the context of the fall of Troy and the recurrence of the theme of Paris' judgement in the context of Juno's potential vindictiveness towards Rome (*Fast.* 6. 44, 100).

433–4. ***seu gener Adrasti, seu furtis aptus Ulixes | seu pius Aeneas***: Ovid lists the three heroes who are said to have removed the Palladium from Troy: Diomedes, grandson of Adrastus, Ulysses, who abducted it in order to bring about the defeat of the Trojans (Virg. *Aen.* 2. 162–79), and Aeneas, who later rescued and brought it to

Rome as a constituent part of the Penates of the royal house. Adrastus' *gener* was in fact Tydeus, but the word may also be used loosely for subsequent descendants, as it is here for Diomedes. Their disparate motives towards Troy are indicated by Ovid's descriptions: *furtis aptus Ulixes* and *pius Aeneas.* The adjective *pius* distinguishes Aeneas' rescue of the Palladium from burning Troy from its theft by the two Greeks whose aim was to bring about Troy's downfall. Because of this I prefer the mss reading *pius* in line 434 to Courtney's conjecture *fuit*, although the latter reads more easily.

435–6. ***res est Romana: tuetur* | *Vesta***: 'the thing is Roman and Vesta looks after it.' The view that the Palladium was a sacred Roman cult object on which the destiny of Rome depended is found in Cicero and Livy (Cic. *Scaur.* 23. 48, *Phil.* 11. 10. 24, Liv. 5. 52. 7, 26. 27. 14). Here it forms an essential strand in the Vesta narrative.

The Palladium is rescued from Vesta's burning temple by L. Caecilius Metellus, Pontifex Maximus

[Herbert-Brown (1994) 63–73, Newlands (1995) 133–6. The destructive and protective potential of talismanic statues is discussed by C. Faraone, *Talismans and Trojan Horses* (Oxford, 1992) 15 n. 9 and 136–9, and Noel Robertson, 'Athene and Early Greek Society: Palladium Shrines and Promontory Shrines', in Matthew Dillon (ed.), *Religion in the Ancient World: New Themes and Approaches* (Amsterdam, 1996).]

The authority of the Pontifex Maximus in Republican times

The Pontifex Maximus had authority over the *flamines* and the Vestal Virgins (Liv. 1. 20. 3–7). However, he was not authorized to enter the Vestal sanctuary (*Fast.* 6. 254, 289–90). A Republican Pontifex Maximus was Vesta's priest only through his responsibility to ensure that the rituals essential to Vesta's cult were correctly performed. The Pontifex Maximus only became the 'priest of Vesta' after 28 April 12 BC, when Augustus transferred a shrine of Vesta to his Palatine house which he himself would tend: *quos sancta fovet ille manu, bene vivitis, ignes* (*Fast.* 3. 427). Herbert-Brown is right, I believe, when she says that Ovid has retrojected the role of personal priest of Vesta on to Julius Caesar 'to legitimate and camouflage' the dynastic implications of the office after it was accepted by Augustus. On the Ides of March Ovid's Vesta describes the murdered Caesar, who was Pontifex Maximus: *meus fuit ille sacerdos* (*Fast.* 3. 699). In poetic terms Ovid presents Metellus as an iconographic rescuer of Vesta's *sacra* from the threat of fire, following in the steps of Aeneas who rescued the Penates from burning Troy and L. Albinus who transported the Vestals and their *sacra* to Caere in 360 BC. These are forerunners of Augustus, who was to rescue Roman temples and rituals from their neglect during the Civil Wars and, in particular, shelter a new cult of Vesta in his Palatine home. Varro uses the imagery of rescuing Vesta's *sacra* from engulfing flames to describe his own 'rescue' of Roman religious rites from neglect by writing his *Antiquitates Romanae* [Cardauns (1976) 2*a*].

437–42: *Imagine the senate's alarm when Vesta was ablaze and her flame was engulfed in her temple! The holy fire burned amid the flames of arson—pure mingled with profane. The Vestals were helpless with terror when Metellus swept into their midst.* **443–7:** *'Hurry!' he roared, 'Wailing won't help! Get those "symbols of destiny" out with your own fair hands. Don't stand there dithering.'* **447–54:** *He saw them hesitate. Purifying himself, he prayed 'Absolve me. I enter, a man, where no man should go. If this be sacrilege, let me pay with my life so long as Rome be saved!' He burst in. Saved by her priest, the goddess approved his deed.*

437. *heu quantum*: this epic phraseology, used by Virgil to introduce Roman calamities (*Aen.* 6. 828, 8. 537), suggests the dire consequences of losing the Vestal flame in one of Rome's not-infrequent temple fires. The same ponderous expression introduces Ovid's reflection on Aemulius' attempted murder of Ilia's infant twins (*Fast.* 2. 408).

437–8. *quo tempore Vesta | arsit*: Cicero retells this story to wind up his defence of Scaurus (Cic. *Scaur.* 23. 48), the great-great-grandson of L. Caecilius Metellus, who was Pontifex Maximus 243–221 BC. Metellus had a distinguished career, being consul twice (251, 247 BC), dictator (224 BC), and *triumphator* (250 BC). His rescue of the Palladium, which happened in 241 BC during the

First Punic War (D.H. 2. 66), cost him his sight (Plin. *Nat.* 7. 139–41). A later fire in the Aedes Vestae had a more direct connection with the Carthaginian threat. In 210 BC, after the disasters at Trasimene and Cannae and before the Roman victory at the Metaurus in 207 BC, the temple caught fire as a result of arson caused by Rome's enemies, Capuans in the pay of Hannibal, who aimed either to engulf the Vestal flame or steal the Palladium and thereby ensure a Carthaginian victory (Liv. 26. 27. 14). Newlands (1995: 137–8) sees a suggestion of eroticism in the notion that Vesta's flame was 'on fire' (*Vesta arsit*), and suggests that sexual innuendo is inherent in the vocabulary throughout this passage: in the Vestals falling to their knees (442), Metellus' emphasis on his virility as he penetrates (*intrabo*, 449, and *inrupit*, 453) the sanctuary, and finally in Vesta's smug satisfaction with her *munus*: *factum rapta dea probavit* (453) [see J. N. Adams, *The Latin Sexual Vocabulary* (Baltimore, 1982)]. Without making any case for 'anti-Augustanism', it could be suggested that Ovid deliberately uses sexual vocabulary here to heighten the enormity of a man 'violating' the sanctuary of the chaste goddess who tolerates only immaculate virgin ministrants. This interpretation is borne out by the poet's continuing sequence of thought in lines 455–60, a short epilogue to the Vesta passage: the goddess has now been restored to a Trojan hearth. Under Augustus no unchaste Vestal will ever again violate the living Earth, which is the same element as Vesta herself. In short, the efficacy of the cult of Vesta, which depends on absolute purity and which promises Roman prosperity, is now guaranteed under Augustus' beneficent rule.

439–40. *flagrabant sancti sceleratis ignibus ignes* | *mixtaque erat flammae flamma profana piae*: 'Holy flames are ablaze with the flames of arson, and sacred fire is mingled with profane.' A characteristically Ovidian couplet, in which verbal artistry conveys the anomaly of a sacred flame being engulfed by an act of arson, suggested by *sceleratis* (439). Beside each instance of noun polyptoton (*ignibus ignes* ... *flammae flamma*) Ovid juxtaposes contrasting alliterative adjectives: *sancti sceleratis* ... *profana piae*. In each group the 'holy' flame surrounds, and symbolically engulfs, the 'profane' flame. [Wills (1991) 191–221, illustrates the use of polyptoton symbolically in contexts of battle, rivalry, and eroticism]. It is characteristic of Ovid's narrative style that he uses the imperfect and pluperfect tense, *flagrabant* (439) ... *erat* (440) ... *flebant* (441) ... *abstulerat* (442), to set the scene before continuing the dramatic sequence of events in the historic present (see Introduction 5).

441. *attonitae flebant demisso crine ministrae*: dumbfounded by the dreadful portent, the Vestal Virgins weep and loose their hair. Intimately concerned with the rites which ensure the survival and continuance of the Roman state, these priestesses play a significant role in Ovid's *Fasti.* On 1 March, the beginning of the old Roman year, they are responsible for relighting the Vestal flame (*Fast.* 3. 143) and decking their temple and the Regia with fresh laurels (137–41). On 15 April the chief Vestal performs the rite of the *Fordicidia* (4. 637–40) and sprinkles the ash at the *Parilia* to ensure the fertility of the land through the period of summer growth. Finally, on 14 May a Vestal casts into the Tiber the straw dolls, *stramineos Quirites* (5. 631).

443–7. *magna 'succurrite' voce | 'non est auxilium flere' Metellus ait* | ... *'dubitatis?'*: the vigour of Ovid's narration is enhanced by the disjointed bursts of Metellus' harangue, in which his brusque and authoritative commands, *succurrite* (443) ... *pignora virgineis fatalia tollite palmis* (445), give way to *me miserum* (447) as he recognizes that the Vestals are paralysed with terror and, as he cannot force them to rescue the Palladium, that he himself must break the religious taboo which forbade men to enter Vesta's sanctuary. The Palladium was concealed partly because of its potent magic and partly to avoid theft.

449. *haurit aquas*: 'he scoops up water.' A ritual of purification before he raises his palms in prayer. In Ovid's version of the story Metellus rescues the Palladium. In a passage in which he discusses the content of the Aedes Vestae, Dionysius (2. 65. 2–67. 1) suggests that Metellus might have rescued either the Palladion or Dardanus' ancient Samothracian gods, the 'Megaloi Theoi', which were, according to tradition, contained in a small terracotta pot (see note on lines 363–5). The cult of the Samothracian gods, which were identified with the Trojan Penates, derived from Ilion's association with Samothrace during the Hellenistic period. Epigraphic evidence suggests that the Samothracian gods were still worshipped in Ilion in the

Augustan period. [See Cole (1984), C. B. Rose, 'The 1997 Post-Bronze Age Excavations at Troia', *Studia Troica* 8 (1998) 87–90.]

449–50. *'ignoscite,' dixit,* | *'sacra.'*: the plural imperative is explained by *sacra*, which he addresses instead of Vesta herself. Metellus' speech conveys both *pietas* and heroism. As Pontifex Maximus, he takes upon himself the full responsibility as Rome's intermediary with the gods. This is underlined by verbal similarities with Ovid's story of Numa confronting Jupiter (*Fast.* 3. 329–66). Like Numa, Metellus observes scrupulously the correct formalities in addressing the gods. Even though he must lose no time in entering the burning temple, he prays first with hands upraised (*tollensque manus*, 449).

450. *'vir intrabo non adeunda viro'*: 'A man, I will enter where no man may go.' In asking pardon for breaking the taboo, Metellus uses words directly reminiscent of the Numa episode. His description of himself 'penetrating the impenetrable' recalls Jupiter's approving description of Numa as a man not to be diverted from converse with a god, *o vir colloquio non abigende deum* (*Fast.* 3. 344). Both sentences begin with *vir*, which suggests the heroism of surpassing human limitation, and continue with a negative gerundive suggesting the superhuman effort, in both cases, of breaking religious taboos for the good of the Roman people. While it is the shrine of Vesta which is *non adeunda* for Metellus, Numa himself is not to be deterred, *non abigende*, from face-to-face confrontation with Jupiter. In another example of the polyptoton *vir... viro*, Ovid imposes an epic and Virgilian shade of meaning by juxtaposing *vir* with *arma* (*Fast.* 5. 394: *'vir' que ait 'his armis, armaque digna viro.'*)

451–2. *'si scelus est, in me commissi poena redundet:* | *sit capitis damno Roma soluta mei'*: 'If I am guilty, let punishment fall on me. Let Rome be ransomed with my life!' Ovid rephrases the idea contained in the hexameter again in the pentameter: Metellus volunteers to pay with his life the guilt incurred by the sacrilege which he is about to commit by entering the sanctuary. In this he belongs, like Mettius Curtius, to the ranks of Romans who sacrifice themselves, in the act of *devotio*, by taking the guilt of the Roman people on their own head. The concept of a scapegoat is a form of substitution sacrifice such as Carna's substitution of a pig for Proca (notes on lines 160–2). [The myth that Metellus became blind as a result of violating the religious taboo and entering Vesta's shrine is discussed by A. Brelich, 'Il mito nella storia di Cecilia Metello', *Studi e Materiali di Storia della Religioni* 15 (1939) 30–41.]

453. *dixit et inrupit*: *factum dea rapta probavit*: the drama is accentuated by the sense pause at the third-foot caesura, the moment when Metellus might have anticipated divine retribution.

454. *pontificisque sui munere tuta fuit*: 'the goddess was saved by the sacrifice of her priest.' Anachronistically (see headnote 2, p. 82 and Introduction 2), Metellus is described as Vesta's priest. There may be a double-entendre in the word *munus*, which has the significance of a religious offering or sacrifice, but can also mean a sexual favour [see Newlands (1995) 138 n. 47].

Epilogue to the *Vestalia*: Augustus safeguards the Vestal flame and the Virgins' chastity

[A. Fraschetti, 'Le sepoltura delle Vestali e la città', in *Du châtiment dans la cité*, Collection de l'École Française de Rome 79 (Rome, 1984), Parker (2004). The probable form and contents of Augustus' shrine, based on evidence in the *Fasti Praenestini*, have been fully discussed by M. Guarducci (1964) 158–69, Fraschetti (1988) 941–65, Herbert-Brown (1994) 74–81, Fantham (1998) 275–6.]

Augustus' personal involvement with the cult of Vesta

The *Vestalia* could not pass without an allusion to the Vestal shrine and flame dedicated in Augustus' Palatine house. Ovid links Vesta, the Palladium, and the Pontifex Maximus here on the *Vestalia*, 9 June, as he does on 6 March, the anniversary of Augustus becoming Pontifex Maximus, priest of Vesta (*Fast.* 3. 417–26). In Augustus' dynastic religion he assumed, as Pontifex Maximus and Vesta's priest, responsibility for Vesta's sacred cult objects, the flame, and the cult statue, which represented his inheritance from his Trojan ancestor, Aeneas. The importance of Augustus' close association with Vesta's cult accounts for Ovid's frequent allusions to this in his *Fasti* (1. 527–8, 3. 29, 423–6, 4. 949–54, 6. 227–8, 455–6). When Augustus created a hearth of Vesta in his Palatine home, he would not have removed from the Aedes Vestae any of the *sacra* which were open to view when the *matronae* visited the Forum temple during the *Vestalia*. So what was in Vesta's new Palatine shrine? It is inconceivable that the flame was not an essential component. Ovid repeatedly refers to a Vestal flame (*Fast.* 6. 421, 428), and this mirrors the obvious dynastic importance of reinstalling Vesta's hearth or a replica of this in the ruler's home. It is artistically appropriate that a section which began with the Trojan origins of the Palladium (419–22) should conclude with the statement that Vesta's flame now burns *Iliacis focis* (456), on the hearth of Aeneas' descendant, Augustus. In his restoration of the entry for 28 April in the *Fasti Praenestini*, Degrassi (66) reconstructs: '*Feriae ex s c quod eo die [signum] et [ara] Vestae in domu Imp. Caesaris Augusti pontificis maximi dedicatast.*' It is unlikely that *signum* could mean a cult statue of Vesta, who was reputed to have none (cf. *Fast.* 6. 291–8). Perhaps it was a model of the Palladium, a statue which had a specific iconic form and of which there were known to be copies. *ara* has been interpreted as *aedis*, perhaps a small tholus temple like the one in the Forum.

455–60: *Auspiciously now the Vestal fire burns on a Trojan hearth. Under Augustus no priestess will be found guilty and immured. So perish the unchaste—buried in what they have defiled. For Vesta and Earth are the same element.e*

455. *nunc bene lucetis sacrae sub Caesare flammae* | *ignis in Iliacis nunc erit estque focis*: the pentameter echoes *Fast.* 3. 418.

457. *nullaque dicetur vittas temerasse sacerdos* | *hoc duce*: 'no priestess will be said to have desecrated her habit under Augustus.' This line recalls the words of Livy's Lucretia, who promises that her suicide will encourage other Roman girls to terminate an unchaste life (Liv. 1. 58. 10: *nec ulla deinde impudica Lucretiae exemplo vivet*). The woollen headbands, *vittae*, which constituted the traditional headdress of a Vestal Virgin, were symbolic of her office. At the end of the symbolic funeral procession which carried an errant Vestal to her immuration, her *vittae* were forcibly torn from her head to signify that she met her death no longer a priestess of Vesta (D.H. 8. 89. 4–5).

The *vittae* identify Juvenal's deflowered priestess (Juv. 4. 9–10: *vittata iacebat | sanguine adhuc viva terram subitura sacerdos*). An unchaste Vestal violated the *pax deorum*, which could only be restored by her being sacrificed for the good of the community. The dark hint of human sacrifice is lightened by the innuendo that no Vestal will be found unchaste under Augustus (*hoc duce*, 458), a humorous allusion, perhaps, to the 'success' of Augustus' notorious Leges Iuliae de maritandis ordinibus (18 BC) and *de adulteriis* (17 BC), which Martial would later describe as 'legalized adultery' (6. 7.) [See L. F. Raditsa, 'Augustus' Legislation Concerning Marriage, Procreation, Love Affairs and Adultery', *ANRW* 2. 13 (1980), 278–339, K. Galinsky, 'Augustus' Legislation on Morals and Marriage', *Philologus* 125 (1981) 126–44.]

458. *nec viva defodietur humo*: 'nor will she be buried in the living earth.' This points to the next distich in which Ovid is concerned less with the violation of the Vestal Virgin than with the violation of the goddess Vesta herself. For when an unchaste Vestal is buried *viva humo*, she violates *Tellus Vestaque numen idem*. Immuration in an underground tomb near the Porta Collina was the punishment suffered by the Vestals for sexual misconduct (D.H. 2. 67. 4, 8. 89. 4–5, Plut. *Numa* 10. 8). The last time that a Vestal Virgin was convicted and ritually immured was in 216 BC, directly after the military disaster at Cannae, and this was followed by the inhumation of two Gauls and two Greeks in the Forum Boarium (Liv. 22. 57. 6). Vesta's cult, on which the state was thought to depend, here intersects the darkest days of Hannibal's invasion of Italy and the rare expedient of human sacrifice in Rome. All three elements—Vesta's cult, the Second Punic War, and sacrifice—belong to the thematic structure of *Fasti* 6.

459–60. *quia quam violavit in illam | conditur, est Tellus Vestaque numen idem*: the enjambement of *conditur* and its prominent position at the beginning of the pentameter strikes a solemn note. The topic of Vestal immuration enables Ovid to say that the Vestal Virgin will be buried in 'that which she has violated' (*quam violavit in illam*, 459), thus achieving a ring composition by concluding the *Vestalia* passage with the very first concept which he formulated about Vesta at the beginning: *Vesta eadem est et terra* (267).

Military anniversaries: the victory of D. Iunius Brutus Callaicus and the defeat of M. Crassus at Carrhae

[Weinstock (1971) 128–32, Gruen (1985) 63–7, Bowersock (1990) 380–94, J. W. Rich, 'Augustus' Parthian Honours, the Temple of Mars Ultor and the Arch in the Forum Romanum', *PBSR* 66 (1998) 71–128.]

461–8: *On this day Brutus won the title Callaicus from his Spanish conquest. To be sure, joy is sometimes tinged with sorrow lest festal days bring unalloyed delight. At the Euphrates Crassus lost eagles, son, and army. Death came to him last. But Vesta said, 'Why gloat, Parthian? You will return the standards and the death of Crassus will be avenged.'*

461–2. *tum sibi Callaico Brutus cognomen ab hoste*: Ovid rounds off his cluster of aetiological stories for 9 June with an allusion to the *triumphator* D. Iunius Brutus, descendant of the subject of Accius' poem 'Brutus', whose victory against the Callici won him his cognomen in 136 BC (Vell. 2. 5. 1). Since Accius' first play is dated 140 BC (Cic. *Brut.* 229), his 'Brutus' was probably not part of the entertainment put on by D. Iunius Brutus Callaicus when, as praetor in 141 BC he organized the *Ludi Apollinares.* Accius' play may have been written for the dedication of the temple to Mars which Callaicus built with his Spanish booty, and which was decorated with appropriate verses composed by Accius (Cic. *Arch.* 11. 26).

463–4. *scilicet interdum miscentur tristia laetis | ne populum toto pectore festa iuvent*: the most conspicuous example in Ovid's *Fasti* of the sentiment that 'sadness sometimes mingles with joy, and festivals do not bring unalloyed pleasure' must surely be the Ides of March, the festival of Anna Perenna, where, after the final *iocus* of this cycle of merry tales and witty Virgilian inversion, Ovid adds: *praeteriturus eram gladios in principe fixos* (*Fast.* 3. 697), which leads into a finale on the subject of Augustus' filial vengeance. It is precisely this image of Augustus the Avenger which concludes Ovid's *Vestalia* passage: *quique necem Crassi vindicet, ultor erit* (468).

465. *Crassus ad Euphraten*: by juxtaposition Ovid contrasts Callaicus' victory with M. Crassus' disastrous defeat by the Parthians at

Carrhae in 53 BC, with the loss of Roman standards (cf. *Fast.* 5. 579–86). The contrast, triumph–defeat, achieved by mentioning both on the same day, enables the poet to return to the theme of Augustus' vengeance (*ultor erit*, 468), which he associates with the goddess Vesta on the festival of Mars Ultor on 12 May: *rite deo templumque datum nomenque bis ulto* (*Fast.* 5. 595). In this passage he alludes to two acts of vengeance as though they have become part of Augustan ideology. The first of these was Augustus' recovery in 20 BC of the standards captured from Crassus at Carrhae (*RG* 29. 2, Suet. *Aug.* 21. 3), which were then placed, symbolically, in the temple of Mars Ultor. The humiliation of captured standards rankled, as frequent allusions to the Parthian War suggest (Virg. *G* 3. 31, Hor. *Carm.* 1. 2. 51, 2. 13. 18, 3. 5. 3–4, Prop. 2. 10. 13–14, 3. 4. 6, 3. 12. 3, Ovid. *Fast.* 5. 579–94). Augustus had inherited the task of avenging Crassus from Caesar, who had twice been deprived of the opportunity to attack the Parthians: in 50 BC by the outbreak of civil war and in 44 BC by his own death (Dio 43. 51. 1). The temple was dedicated, symbolically again, in 2 BC on the eve of Gaius' expedition against the Parthians, although military revenge for the insult of the captured standards was to remain incomplete and Gaius was prematurely killed by a Parthian arrow. The triumphant iconography representing Parthians surrendering standards on the cuirass of Augustus' Prima Porta statue represents a vengeance which was never fully accomplished [see Gruen (1985) 63–7]. Augustus' second act of vengeance is no less ambiguous. In his *Fasti* Ovid represents Augustus' defeat of the forces of Brutus and Cassius at Philippi as a religious act of vengeance for their sacrilege in murdering the Pontifex Maximus, Vesta's priest: (5. 573: *si mihi bellandi pater est Vestaeque sacerdos* | *auctor*). In fact, the victory at Philippi was no cause for celebration, as it was a Civil War engagement, and it was thirty years later before the Pontifex Maximus was regarded as Vesta's priest (see Introduction 2).

467–8. *'Parthe, quid exsultas?' dixit dea 'signa remittes,* | *quique necem Crassi vindicet ultor erit.'*: as in Book 5, the poet addresses the Parthians directly (*Fast.* 5. 593). Appropriately, in Ovid's *Vestalia*, Vesta has the last word, as she does in Book 3, when she urges Ovid not to omit to mention the assassination of her priest: *ne dubita meminisse! meus fuit ille sacerdos* (*Fast.* 3. 699). The close association of Vesta's cult with the Pontifex Maximus, which had limited significance in Republican times, was essential to Augustus' dynastic concept of Roman religion.

A IIII EID. IUN. N, RISING OF THE DOLPHIN, 469–472

469–72: *When the flowers are taken off the donkeys and the millstones grind the corn, the sailor on his ship observes, 'The Dolphin rises with the coming of night.'*

471–2. *navita puppe sedens 'Delphina videbimus' inquit | 'umida cum pulso nox erit orta die.'*: a Greek accusative of *Delphin* replaces the more usual Latin *Delphinus*, found in Var. *R* 2. 5. 13, Plin. *Nat.* 18. 234 [see Green (2004a) 211]. Both Columella (11. 2. 45) and Pliny (*Nat.* 18. 576) agree with Ovid in taking 10 June as the correct time for the rising of the Dolphin, which is still to be seen on 18 June (*Fast.* 6. 720). The Dolphin rises again on 9 Jan. (*Fast.* 1. 457–8) and sets on 3 February (2. 79–80). A sailor on watch on deck would be most likely to observe the rising of the constellation. [See Ideler (1825) 148.]

B III EID. IUN. N, *MATRALIA*, 473–648

[Halberstadt (1934), Radke (1965) 208, Bonfante-Warren (1970), Bayet (1971) 241–70, J. Boardman, 'Herakles, Peisistratus and Sons', *Revue Archéologique* 1 (1972) 57–72, Castagnoli (1979) 145–52, Dumézil (1980), Salvadori (1982), Champeaux (1982) 1. 199–207, 243–4, Yves Bomati, 'Les Légendes dionysiaques en Étrurie', *REL* 61 (1983) 87–107, Coarelli (1988) 205–442, Bettini (1991) 77–99, Boëls-Janssen (1993) 341–72, Mertens-Horn (1996) 143–8, Ross Holloway (1994) 68–80, 142–56, Herbert-Brown (1994) 145–56, (2000) 171–202, Parker (1997) 37–72, Wiseman (1998) 35–51, Smith (2000) 136–46, Littlewood (2002) 191–211, Newlands (2002) 188–201.]

Fig. 12 Etruscan stone statue often described as Mater Matuta, third quarter of fifth century BC, h. 90 cm., Museo Archeologico, Florence. An archaic cinerary statue, discovered in 1846 in a chamber tomb, necropolis of La Pedata, Chianciano. The detachable head enabled the ashes of the deceased to be placed in the chest cavity. Although this indicates that the statue represents an aristocratic Etruscan woman, the iconography perfectly represents the beauty and dignity of the kourotrophos goddess, Mater Matuta, as she was worshipped in the cult centres of Satricum, Pyrgi, and the Forum Boarium. The winged sphinxes which form the arms of her throne suggest divinity, but might also represent the demons of death often found in Etruscan burials in the Chiusi area. (Photograph courtesy of Hirmer Verlag, Munich, Inst. Neg. 764.1522.)

1. *The cult of Mater Matuta*

On 11 June Roman *matronae*, who must be *univirae*, gathered to worship Mater Matuta. From its orgins this was, essentially, the cult of a fertility goddess, whose association with Dawn symbolized the birth and growth of plants and animals. This connection is apparent in Mater Matuta's earliest appearance in Latin literature, where Lucretius mentions Matuta, goddess of the rising sun, at the beginning of an account of the growth of plants and continues with the growth of man (Lucr. 5. 656, 740). Mater Matuta was also identified with Ilythuia or Lucina, goddess of childbirth; in statuary she was represented seated with a swaddled baby on her knee, showing that as a kourotrophos goddess, she watched over not only birth but also the growth of small children.

It is clear from archaeological evidence that the original temple precinct had affinities with two other archaic sanctuaries dedicated to Mater Matuta, in Etruscan Pyrgi and Latin Satricum (Liv. 6. 33. 5). In Pyrgi the two archaic temples were respectively associated with Leucothea (Temple A) with whom Mater Matuta was often identified (Cic. *Tusc.* 1. 28, *ND* 3. 48, Hyg. *Fab.* 2 and 223) as a kourotrophos deity, and (Temple B) with Hera/Uni/Astarte, goddesses associated with fertility and sexuality, but also with Ilythuia/Lucina, goddess of birth, and Thesan/Eos, goddess of Dawn. Similar votive offerings, including statuettes of women nursing children and female anatomical parts, uterus and breasts, have been found in the precincts of all three temples. Sacrificial remains from Satricum and the Forum Boarium feature female, sometimes gravid animals, indicating the cult of a goddess associated with fertility and nurture. This is supported by the terracotta decoration at all these sanctuaries which features Dionysiac figures and motifs. The implication of fertility in the title *Matuta* is evident in Juno Matuta (Liv. 34.53.3) and Pales Matuta (Schol. Verg. *G* 3. 1), who was believed to care for the ripening corn. The cults in the two temples at Pyrgi appear to represent different phases in the life of women. Ovid's account indicates that the two Republican temples in the Forum Boarium, dedicated to Fortuna and Mater Matuta, formed a similar complex dedicated to the cycle of women's cult. Fortuna presided over a woman's passage from virginity to fecundity in the early weeks of marriage, while Mater Matuta, a kourotrophos goddess, was responsible for the care of children entrusted to women who were not their natural mothers.

2. Hercules and the iconography of civic violence

It has been demonstrated that goddesses who represent in women's cult individual fertility and civic prosperity were often worshipped in conjunction with Hercules, whose cult represented struggle, victory, and triumph/apotheosis [Smith (2000) 144]. This is particularly true of the temple complex in the Forum Boarium, where several temples to the unvanquished Hercules clustered in a place where the triumphal procession would pass. Hercules' association with the Porta Trigemina is underlined by the proximity of this gateway to his shrines in the Forum Boarium [see Steinby 338, Richardson 310]. In Ovid's account of Mater Matuta this is reflected by Ino's meeting with Hercules and the clear implication that the struggles of these two figures from Greek legend foreshadow their apotheoses. The cult of Hercules was characteristically found beside harbours and commercial emporia all over the Mediterranean world. All three centres, Pyrgi, Satricum, and the Forum Boarium, were important commercial centres, inviting dedications, votive offerings, and cult participation from traders from Greece and the Orient. Pyrgi was the port of Etruscan Caere, Satricum was a river port some 10 km from the Campanian coast, while the Forum Boarium fronted onto the wharves of the River Tiber. In addition to her functions in women's cult, Leucothea, with her son Palaemon, themselves rescued from the sea, were believed to offer protection to mariners. Hercules had cultic links with both Portunus and Janus in the Forum Boarium [Bayet (1926) 275–8].

J. N. Bremmer's entry in *OCD* notes that the festivals of Ino-Leucothea contained elements associated with 'the dissolution of social order'. Hercules, too, had similar associations. The recurrent theme of a chariot procession on terracotta plaquess depicting Herakles, Athene, and other gods, may have had a more specific significance associated directly with the political movements characteristically associated with the sixth century when aristocratic oligarchies were being overturned by leaders with popular backing.

This theme on Attic Black Figure vases has been convincingly associated with the seizure of power in Athens by Peisistratus [see Boardman (1972)]. The Roman monarchy was not hereditary. During the archaic period it was not unusual for men of ambition and ability to migrate from one city state to another, and a foreigner, such as Sabine Numa or Titus Tatius or the Greek-Etruscan Tarquin dynasty, could aspire to rule in Rome (Liv. 4. 3. 10–17). A facet of the ideology of archaic tyrants was their claim to have attained power with divine support, which is evident in the gold tablets from Temple B at Pyrgi, where the Etruscan Thefarie Velianas honours Uni/Astarte (Juno) for bringing him to power. Another illustration of this may have been the tradition of Servius' relationship with the goddess Fortuna. The statue of Herakles with Athene found near the archaic temple in the Forum Boarium may be a direct reference to the accession of Servius Tullius, whose democratic tendencies may be suggested by his dedication of Fortuna's temple (Liv. 10. 46. 14) and by votive deposits on other archaic sites in Rome, including statuettes wearing the pileus, or cap of liberty.

3. *The twin temples in the Forum Boarium*

Excavations beneath the church of Sant' Omobono in the Forum Boarium in Rome have brought to light remains of one of the earliest (600–575 BC) archaic temples to be discovered in Latium. It is now thought to have been a temple dedicated to Mater Matuta which, at a much later period, was paired with an adjacent temple to Fortuna. Whilst this vitiates Ovid's claim that *both* temples were dedicated on 11 June by Servius Tullius (*Fast.* 6. 479–80, *Matutae sacra parentis | sceptiferas Servi templa dedisse manus*), it shows that Servius' foundation of an archaic temple to Mater Matuta was still a tradition current in Ovid's day (Liv. 5. 19. 6). Later in the sixth century, perhaps within the reign of Servius (578–534 BC), the first temple was seriously damaged by Tiber floods and redecorated with an entirely new style of iconography, currently on display at the Museo Montemartini in Rome. At the apex of the pediment now stood an acroterial terracotta statue of Hercules accompanied by Minerva, thought to represent the moment of apotheosis when the hero is presented to the gods on Olympus. Along the tympanum ran

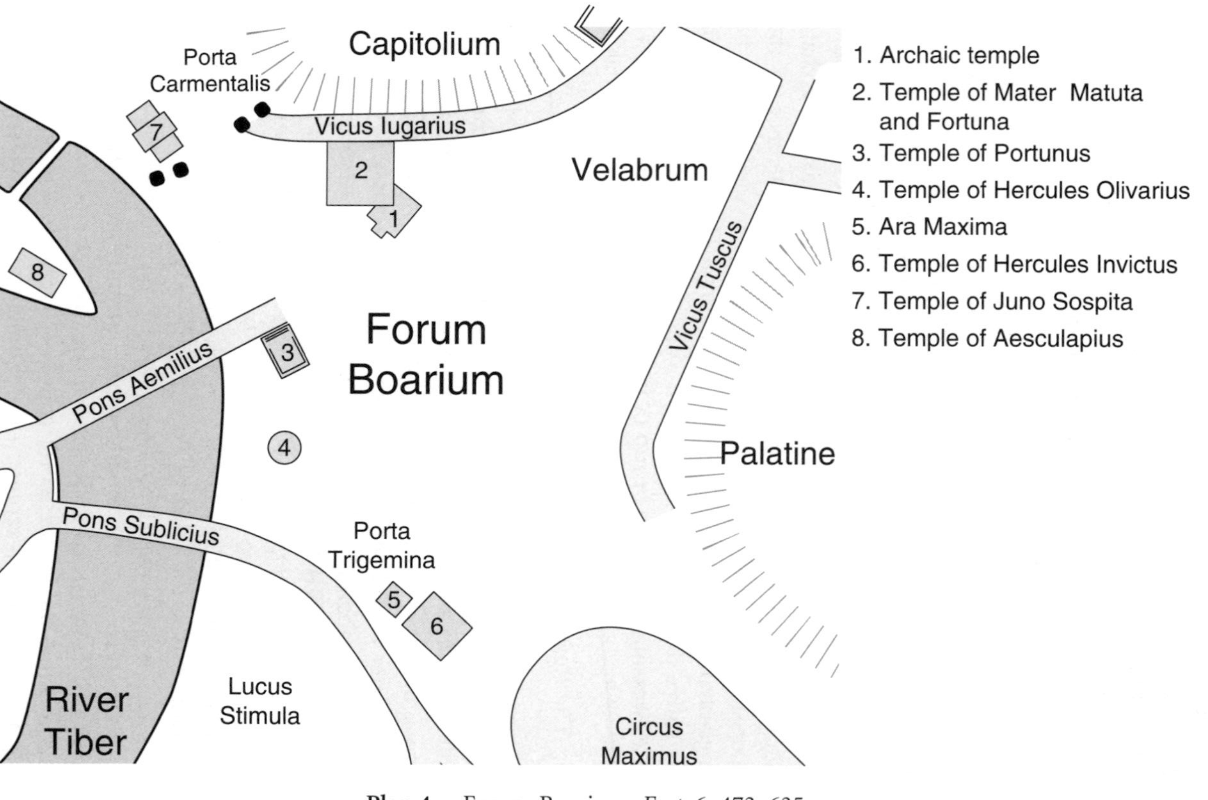

Plan 4. Forum Boarium: *Fast.* 6. 473–635

lateral plaques depicting a chariot procession including winged horses and, at intervals, a warrior accompanied by a female figure which may be a goddess: the iconography of apotheosis (see Introduction 3). All this suggests that the honorands of the temples in the Forum Boarium were goddesses associated with the dichotomy of military success and fertility. During the Republican period twin temples, to Fortuna and Mater Matuta respectively, were built on top of a fill which raised the level 6 metres above the original archaic temple, probably as a measure to protect the temple from the Tiber floods. The paired temples, now rotated on a different alignment, were reconstructed three times. It is uncertain whether Camillus' vow to dedicate a temple to Mater Matuta before Veii (Liv. 5. 19. 6, 23. 7) was ever realized. Reconstruction, possibly for the third time, took place after a fire in 213 BC (Liv. 24. 47. 15–16, 25. 7. 6).

4. *Ovid's literary account of the Theban goddess*

It is impossible to know how much of this tradition Ovid derived from his 'ancient chronicles' (*Fast.* 1. 7, *annalibus priscis*). The poet claims that the original pair of temples were dedicated on the same day by Servius Tullius, and his account of the two goddesses, Mater Matuta and Fortuna, feature motherhood and abuse of marriage, violence and apotheosis, which are all elements of cults associated with fertility and warrior goddesses. However, the poet's concern was to transform primitive cult material into sophisticated literary aetiology, enhanced by imagery which suggested widespread sanctuary art as well as allusion to literary cycles. In Ovid's story of Mater Matuta he taps into a nexus of myths associated with Ino, *Thebanae deae*, who was the daughter of Cadmus, king of Thebes (Call. fr. 91 Pf., Cic. *Tusc.* 1. 28, *ND* 3. 48, Apollod. 3. 4. 3). [See also T. Gantz, *Early Greek Myth: A Guide to Literary and Artistic Sources* (Baltimore and London, 1993) 176–180.] Her reputation as a kourotrophos goddess derives from her rescue of her sister Semele's son, Dionysus, from the anger of Hera. Ino's association with other people's children was otherwise less successful. The dark history of Theban bacchants began when Ino joined her sisters Agave and Autonoë in the murder and *sparagmos* of her nephew, Pentheus (Eurip. *Bacch.* 1129–36, *Med.* 1284). As the second wife of King Athamas, she deceived her husband, by means of burnt seeds (*semina tosta*, 556) and a false oracle, into agreeing to avert a famine by sacrificing his children from his first marriage; their death was averted only by the ram with the golden fleece, which transported Phrixus to Colchis (*Fast.* 3. 851–6). Because of Ino's protection of Bacchus, the children of Ino and Athamas fell victim to Juno's wrath, which drove their parents to madness and infanticide, a story which Ovid colours with the imagery of Bacchic possession [see Herschkowitz (1998) 8–36]. Three times responsible for the deaths of young members of her family, Ino's name was a byword for danger to children. The menage of Ino and Athamas was the subject of plays by all three major Greek tragedians. It is to these archetypal infanticides of Greek tragedy that Ovid alludes when he urges modern Inos and Medeas to stay away from the Roman family celebration of the *Caristia* (*Fast.* 2. 627–8). Destructive figures from Greek mythology tend to acquire a more beneficent character when they reappear as Roman gods in Latium, as Parker (1997) observes. Ovid's retelling of Ino's story in *Fasti* 6 transfers the destructive madness associated with Bacchic possession to the maenads of the Lucus Stimulae under the malevolent influence of Juno, and transforms Ino, bacchant and infanticide, into a model of Roman maternal solicitude and a kourotrophos goddess. While Ovid's account of Ino in Italy is unique, his allusions to Ino's Theban literary heritage embellishes and wittily destabilizes his story of Mater Matuta's arrival in Rome.

Like their temples, the paired cult stories of Mater Matuta and Fortuna take the form of a diptych: two parallel, but contrasting, passages in which virtue is rewarded and retribution meted out and the two goddesses are seen to triumph in their particular spheres of influence: childcare and marriage. Having resolved the discord in both passages, Ovid appends a coda which celebrates Livia's Aedes Concordiae in Augustus' Porticus Liviae, a tribute to the marital harmony of Rome's first couple.

Mater Matuta, 473–568

Bacchus is invited to describe the cult of his aunt, Ino

473–84: *At dawn respectable women offer yellow cakes to the Theban goddess. There is a busy quarter by the Tiber bridges where Servius founded a temple on* *this day. Bacchus, this concerns your family! Tell who the goddess is, why she bans serving women from her temple, and why she loves cakes.*

473. *iam, Phryx, a nupta quereris*: one of Ovid's more effective calendric notations. In the first half of the hexameter spondees accentuate Trojan (*Phryx*) Tithonus' conventional complaint (*quereris*) as his wife (*nupta*) rises from the marital bed (cf. *Fast.* 1. 461, 3. 403–4, 4. 943, 6. 729). As Dawn, however, she is also Mater Matuta, who has good reason to be up betimes on her own feast day. Two exotic adjectives, *Phryx* and *Eois* (474), present a combination of vowel sounds which evoke Eastern cult and herald the epiphany of Bacchus, who will be Ovid's informant for the story of his aunt Ino's adventures on Roman soil.

475. *ite, bonae matres, vestrum Matralia festum*: Ovid summons *matronae univirae*, who alone had the right to celebrate the *Matralia.*

476. *flavaque Thebanae reddite liba deae*: *liba* was the word given to cakes baked for sacrifice. As in any other sacrificial meal, the worshippers ate the rest after the goddess had had her portion. Varro (*L* 5. 106) notes that these yellow cakes were baked in a terracotta pot.

477–8. *pontibus et magno iuncta est celeberrima Circo | area*: the area near the Pons Fabricius and Pons Sublicius, north of the Circus Maximus, is described as *celeberrima*, 'thronged with people' (*OLD* s.v. 1). Ovid also applies *celeberrima* to the feast days of Bacchus (*Fast.* 3. 713), which is 'widely celebrated' and to Venus herself (4.13), who is 'greatly honoured'.

478. *quae posito de bove nomen habet*: a bronze statue of an ox was thought to have given the Forum Boarium its name (Plin. *Nat.* 34. 10, Tac. *Ann.* 12. 24), although Propertius derives the name from Hercules driving the cattle of Geryon to the Forum Boarium (Prop. 4. 9. 19–20). There is no evidence to suggest that it was ever a cattle market, which would have been incommodious, to say the least, among a group of sanctuaries close to a busy harbour (cf. *Fast.* 1. 582: *ubi pars urbis de bove nomen habet*).

479–80. *hac ibi luce ferunt Matutae sacra ... | ... Servi templa dedisse manus*: Servius Tullius dedicated the temple of Mater Matuta on 11 June. Ovid refers to the original archaic temple, believing that the precinct was shared by Fortuna's temple which the king dedicated on the same day: *lux eadem, Fortuna, tua est, auctorque locusque* (569).

481. ***quare famulas a limine templi* | *arceat*:** it was a customary part of the ritual of the *Matralia* for the *matronae* to bring into the temple a female slave whom they then drove out. Dumézil suggests that the slave represents Dawn which must be expelled before her nephew, the Sun, child of Night, can come to ripen the grain at this time of the summer solstice [see Halberstadt (1934) 15, Dumézil, *Déesses latines et myths védiques* (Brussels, 1956) 25, and (1980) 184–205].

483–4. ***Bacche, racemiferos hedera distincte capillos* | *... dirige vatis opus*:** 'Bacchus, distinguished by ivy in hair adorned with bunches of grapes.' Ovid frequently uses adjectives ending in *-fer*, which he sometimes coins (cf. *corymbiferi Bacchi*, *Fast.* 1. 393). The poet's choice of Bacchus as his informant is significant. The reason given is Bacchus' relationship to his aunt, *si domus illa tua est* (484), but the phrase recalls not only Ino's devotion to her nephew, Bacchus, but the Theban sisters' murder of Ino's other nephew, Pentheus. This heralds a series of intertextual allusions to Ino's Theban past through the medium of Bacchic possession, which provides much of the literary imagery of this passage. Ovid introduces Dionysiac colour in his story of Ino partly to enhance a story about Pentheus' aunt and Semele's sister but also, because Mater Matuta's cult was situated in a quarter of Rome which had ancient associations with the cult of Bacchus, to evoke the familiar imagery of fertility cult—maenads, *sileni*, Hercules, Juno—found in sanctuary art across Central Italy (see Introduction 3).

Ovid summarizes Ino's tragic history before her arrival in the Lucus Stimula

485–502: *Semele was dead. Juno, furious that Ino had taken in her child, drove her husband mad and he killed their son, Learchus. After performing funeral rites, Ino fled with her baby, Melicertes. Clutching the child, she leapt over the cliffs at the Isthmus and was carried by the nymphs through the sea to the Tiber mouth.*

485–90. *arserat obsequio Semele Iovis: accipit Ino | te, puer, . . . | . . . intumuit Iuno . . . | . . . agitur furiis Athamas*: Ovid's elegiac narrative technique is well illustrated in the following three couplets. The poet had already recorded these events with an epic focus on the destructiveness of Bacchic possession which traditionally pervades epic portraits of heroines in the grip of ungovernable passions (*Met.* 4. 416–562). The contrasting elegiac version in *Fasti* 6 dwells on the pathos of Ino's dignified suffering. Four verbs define four stages in Ino's domestic tragedy: *arserat Semele*, *accipit Ino | te,* puer, *intumuit Iuno*, *agitur furiis Athamas*, each sparking an emotive comment from the poet, in the pentameter, in the form of apostrophe or parenthesis. Dramatically the pluperfect *arserat* relegates Semele's story to a remoter past than Ino's devoted care, underlined by alliteration, *summa sedula . . . ope* (486), for her nephew Bacchus, whom the poet brings to the foreground with the apostrophe *te, puer* (486), 'when you were a boy'. Juno's incandescent rage, graphically described in *intumuit Iuno*, is quite disproportionate to Ino's 'crime', *quod . . . natum educet*, which is further elaborated in a typical elegiac aside, *at sanguis ille sororis* (488). The third couplet, following the same pattern, is completed with an apostrophe where word order enhances elegiac pathos: *tuque cadis patria, parve Learche, manu* (489). The murdered child, Learchus, is surrounded by the (paternal) hands that destroyed him. The past summarized, the reader is prepared for the next stage in Ino's story.

491–3. *maesta Learcheas mater tumulaverat umbras | et dederat miseris omnia iusta rogis | haec quoque funestos ut erat laniata capillos*: for emphasis *Learcheas umbras* echoes *Learchus* in the previous line. The two pluperfects, *tumulaverat* and *dederat*, enable Ovid to avoid a temporal clause and continue the immediate narrative, paratactically, with historic presents, *prosilit et . . . rapit*, in line 494. The erection of the burial mound, performance of proper rites, and the mother's hair rent in mourning (*funestos . . . laniata capillos*, 493) mirror the sombre sequence of events at Remus' funeral (*Fast.* 5. 451–4).

494. *cunis te, Melicerta, rapit*: Ovid creates a mood of elegiac pathos in addressing Ino's two small children directly (cf. *tuque cadis patria, parve Learche, manu*, 490). In each sentence the vulnerability of the children is heightened by an abrupt removal of symbols of childhood security: Melicertes is torn from his cradle (*cunis*) to be flung into the waves, while Learchus has died *patria manu.*

495–6. ***est spatio contracta brevi, freta bina repellit.* | *unaque pulsatur terra duabus aquis***: 'Reduced to a narrow isthmus, the land repels the sea on both sides, and one land is pounded by the onslaught of two seas.' Ovid introduces the typical ecphrasis formula: *est* followed by a geographical term picked up later by an expression such as *huc venit* (cf. *Fast.* 4. 338–9). The power of the sea at this desolate isthmus, pounded by waves on both sides, is emphasized by reiteration, *freta bina repellit*, *pulsatur duabus aquis.* This must refer to the Isthmus of Corinth, where there was a heroon of Palaemon sited between Megara and Corinth in honour of Palaemon/Melicertes. According to Pausanius (1. 44. 7), the Isthmian Games were founded by Sisyphus of Corinth in honour of the young Palaemon. The importance of Corinthian trade in the Hellenization of Central Italy is a fragment of the archaic background, which underpins Ovid's myth of Ino and Palaemon in the Forum Boarium [see Alan Blakeway, '"Damaratus", a Study in Some Aspects of the Earliest Hellenisation of Latium and Etruria', *JRS* 25 (1935) 129–49]. The Roman Ludi Magni were believed to have been founded in conjunction with the Isthmian Games in Greece by Tarquinius Priscus, the son of Damaratus of Corinth, who had emigrated to Etruria and married into the Etruscan aristocracy before becoming king in Rome (Cic. *Rep.* 2. 19–20, Liv. 1. 34. 2, 2. 36. 1, D.H. 3. 46).

497. ***insanis natum complexa lacertis***: Ovid's word order ensures that Ino literally embraces her son in her 'insane arms'. To apply *insanus* to parts of the body belonging to the person in the grip of insanity was not unusual (*OLD* s.v. 2*c*).

498. ***et secum celso mittit in alta iugo***: 'and from the highest cliff she took her child with her into the depths.' *natum*, in the previous line, is the object of both *complexa* and *mittit*, which Ovid uses transitively with *secum* instead of the more common reflexive *se mittere*, 'to plunge or cast oneself' (cf. Virg. *Aen.* 9. 644–5, *ab alto* | *aethere se mittit*, and 10. 633–4, *caelo se protinus alto* | *misit*). The vertical extent of Ino's leap is emphasized by the words *celso* and *alta.*

499–500. *excipit inlaesos Panope centumque sorores* | *et placido lapsu per sua regna ferunt*: the adjectives *placido* and *inlaesos* contribute to the impression of Ino's fall being gently cushioned in the arms of the Nereids. The fairytale quality of *Panope centumque sorores* recalls Virgil's description of Aristaeus who also, at a nadir in his fortunes, visits his mother Cyrene and her 'hundred' nereid sisters: *domum mirans genetricis et umida regna* (Virg. *G* 4. 363. Cf. Prop. 3. 7. 67). The desolate place of Ino's suicide attempt contrasts sharply with the encompassing waters of the gentle feminine world under the sea in which she now finds herself. Like Aristaeus, Ino has symbolically returned to the security of the womb from which she will be reborn, the stain of infanticide eradicated, to become a Roman kourotrophos goddess [cf. M. J. Putnam, *Vergil's Poem of the Earth* (Princeton, 1997) 278–82]. In Ino's cult in Greece her leap into the sea was a rite of passage which was associated with the initiation of *epheboi* in the cult of Leucothea.

501. *nondum Leucothea, nondum puer ille Palaemon*: the anaphora, *nondum* ... *nondum*, emphasizes that Ino and Melicertes have not yet received divine status and their new names, which Ovid gives in their Greek form: *Leucothea Grais, Matuta vocabere nostris* (545). They must undergo further sufferings in Latium before Carmentis' prophecy can be fulfilled. At Etruscan Pyrgi Ino was called by her Greek name, Leucothea; in Rome and Satricum she was Mater Matuta.

502. *verticibus densi Thybridis ora tenent*: 'they reached the Tiber estuary with its choppy waters.' In Latin literature swirling eddies (*vertices*) are found, as Pighi observes (*ad loc.*), in rivers, sea, or air. Virgil uses the same expression when he describes Aeneas entering the mouth of the Tiber. The strong current, as the Tiber reaches the sea, creates the impression of a mighty river (*Tiberinus* ... *verticibus rapidi et multa flavus harena*, Virg. *Aen.* 7. 31).

Ino is assaulted by maenads and rescued by Hercules

503–24: *At the Grove of Stimula Ino encountered a group of maenads who told her that she had reached Evander's kingdom. On the pretext that Ino was spying on their rites, Juno goaded them to snatch Melicertes from his mother. Ino's*

Fig. 13 Etruscan painted terracotta head of Ino, Pyrgi Room, Villa Giulia, Rome. Mid-fourth century BC from the front pediment of Temple A, Pyrgi, dedicated to Leucothea/Ilithyia. This statue is believed to be part of a group including a youthful Hercules welcoming Ino from their Theban homeland. The Theban legend was popular at this period in Central Italy. The rear pediment, showing the duel between Tydeus and Melanippus, with Athene, withholding immortality in disgust, is thought to represent an ideological condemnation of tyranny and praise of divine justice. (Photograph courtesy of D.A.I. Rome, Inst. Neg. 1973. 1258.)

shrieks for help were heard by Hercules, driving his cattle from Spain, who hurried to the rescue. At the sight of Hercules the maenads fled. Recognizing Ino, Hercules asked whether she was the victim of his own persecutor, the goddess Juno.

503. *lucus erat: dubium Semelae Stimulaene vocetur*: Ovid's alternative name, the Grove of Semele, evokes a chain of Dionysiac associations. Scene of the notorious Bacchanalian rites of 186 BC (Liv. 39. 12. 4), the Grove of Stimula/Semele lay between the Tiber and the Aventine (*CIL* 6. 9897). It was not far from the Aventine temple of Ceres, Liber, and Libera, built in the fifth century BC in time of famine on instruction from the Sibylline books [see Wiseman (1998) 35–48, Richardson 236, Steinby 4. 378]. Whilst this divine triad represented the Roman counterparts of the Eleusinian agricultural deities, Demeter, Iacchus, and Kore/Persephone, these names adumbrated another triad associated with the Dionysiac mysteries: Dionysos, Semele, and Ariadne. The imagery associated with this triad could be found at sanctuaries associated with fertility, including those of Mater Matuta at Satricum and in the Forum Boarium (see Introduction 3). By contrast, when Aeneas on his arrival in Italy first notices this grove along the Tiber shore, his impression is of waterfowl and songbirds (Virg. *Aen.* 7. 29–34).

504. *maenadas Ausonias incoluisse ferunt*: 'they say Italian maenads used to live here.' The word *ferunt* humorously suggests that there was a historical precedent for maenads and the cult of Bacchus in this grove from the days of Evander's settlement. Ino's arrival in Italy has affinities with the arrival of the exiled Evander (*Fast.* 1. 505) and of Aeneas (Virg. *Aen.* 7 and 8). The women Ino meets in the grove introduce themselves as Arcadian subjects of Evander, which signals a comparison with the arrival of Evander and Carmentis (*Fast.* 1. 505–6), creating another 'frame' linking Books 1 and 6. In both passages a Greek exile, Evander or Ino, is rescued from imminent danger by Hercules and a new cult is founded on the site of Rome. Each episode is concluded with hospitality offered to a new arrival, respectively Hercules and Ino, whose apotheosis is foretold by Evander's mother, the prophetess Carmentis (*Fast.* 1. 583–4, 6. 541–9). [See Salvadori (1982).] The exotic *maenadas Ausonias* offers a deliberate contrast with *Arcadas*, the epitome of rustic innocence. Mention of the Arcadians, their king, Evander (506), and

Ino's subsequent encounter with Evander's mother, Carmentis (529–48), and the hero Hercules (519–26), suggests comparison with the arrival of Virgil's Aeneas in Italy. Both Ino and Aeneas have fled their homeland and endured perilous journeys. Both are victims of Juno's anger. Ovid makes a point of alluding, like Virgil, to strong eddies in the Tiber estuary and the Tiberside grove, so it would seem that both are fated to come ashore at the same place. Both, too, experience a potentially damaging brush with maenads: Aeneas' prospective bride is swept off in a bacchanal led by her mother, Amata (*Aen.* 7. 85–405). Both receive hospitality from the family of Evander: Aeneas meets Evander at a time when the Arcadians are celebrating Hercules' conquest of Cacus (*Aen.* 8. 268–72), Ino is rescued by Hercules himself and is taken in by Evander's mother Carmentis (*Fast.* 6. 529–32). In *Aeneid* 8 Hercules has already achieved the apotheosis prophesied by Carmentis, and Aeneas and Evander honour him in a religious rite. In *Fasti* 6 Ovid reminds us that Juno's persecution of both Ino and Hercules will end with their apotheosis by making an anachronistic allusion to Hercules as Oetaeus (519). As Parker suggests (1999, *ad loc*), Ovid's Virgilian borrowing strengthens Ino's credentials as a Roman goddess. Quite simply, too, Ovid's Roman readers found elegiac adaptations of Virgil's epic entertaining, as is evident from Ovid's more extended narrative of Anna's odyssey in the steps of Aeneas and her ill-starred reception in Aeneas' new home (*Fast.* 3. 523–646).

507–8. *dissimulata deam Latias Saturnia Bacchas | instimulat fictis insidiosa sonis*: this magnificent couplet, with its alliterative, hissing sibilants and reiterated *i*, is packed with innuendo and Virgilian allusion. Juno, disguised as a maenad, goads (*instimulat*, 508) the Arcadians to violence, just as, disguised as Beroë, she instigated the burning of Aeneas' ships (Virg. *Aen.* 5. 620–40). The two words chosen to describe Juno, *dissimulata* and *insidiosa*, suggest the destructive nature of this dangerous goddess. It has been suggested that both Virgil (*Aen.* 5. 606) and Ovid (*Met.* 9. 176–8) play on a possible etymological connection between *Saturnia* and words implying Juno's insatiability, such as *satiare* and *saturata* [see J. J. O'Hara, 'Virgil's Best Reader? Ovidian Commentary on Vergilian Etymological Wordplay', *CJ* 91 (1996) 255–76].

509. ***o toto pectore captae*****:** Juno's outpouring of scorn for the naivety of the Arcadian women echoes a phrase in a duplicitous speech by Virgil's Juno, who claims that Venus has *tota quod mente petisti* because she has driven Dido mad with a passion for Aeneas, which is later described using the simile of Bacchic possession (Virg. *Aen.* 4. 300–3), imagery which Ovid may have intended to recall here.

512. ***quo possit poenas pendere, pignus habet*****:** Juno's suggestion that they seize Melicertes to punish Ino for spying on the sacred rites, *sacrique parat cognoscere ritum* (511), evokes Pentheus' fate. The goddess makes her sinister intention more emphatic by alliteration in the pentameter. The word *pignus*, often used of children, primarily meant a pledge, a guarantee or, if it was a person, a hostage (*OLD* s.v. 1*b*). *pignus habet* is a double entendre, Melicertes is the 'proof' of Ino's marriage and motherhood. For Juno he could be a hostage on which vengeance could be wreaked if his mother were found, like Pentheus, guilty of spying on the sacred rites.

513–14. ***complent ululatibus auras* | *thyiades, effusis per sua colla comis*****:** exotic sound patterns and assonance in *ululantibus* and *thyiades, effusis* evoke Dionysiac abandon. The Arcadian maenads follow the traditional literary manifestation of Bacchic frenzy which closely mirrors the wording of Virgil's description of Amata and her companions, who loose their hair (*ventis dant colla comasque*, *Aen.* 7. 394) and fill the air with howls (*ululantibus aethera complent*, 395).

515. ***puerumque revellere pugnant*****:** the word *revellere*, meaning 'to tear away', implies here that the maenads struggle (*pugnant*) to wrench Melicertes from his mother's arms. There may be a hint of intended *sparagmos* in Ovid's choice of a word found in an Ennian phrase, *caput a cervice revulsum* (fr. 483 Sk.), which Virgil transposes into a Bacchic context in which Orpheus' head is ripped off by maenads (*G* 4. 520–2).

517. ***'dique virique loci'*****:** a sequence of sharp assonance gives a shrillness to Ino's invocation of the divine and human inhabitants of the land, whom Ovid links with the traditional epic *que*... *que* (cf. Ovid *Am.* 1. 2. 37, *Met.* 14. 807).

518–22. ***clamor Aventini saxa propinqua ferit.* |... *femineae terga dedere fugae*****:** in these six lines Ovid reduces to an elegiac level both Virgil's and his own earlier account of Hercules' epic confrontation with Cacus (Virg. *Aen.* 8. 213–67, Ovid *Fast.* 1. 543–78). *Aventini saxa* (518) conjures up the site of Cacus' cave (*Aen.* 8. 231, *Fast.* 1. 551). Hercules, described not as Amphitrionidas (cf. *Aen.* 214) nor *claviger* (*Fast.* 1. 544), but Oetaeus, an allusion to his death, arrives driving, not oxen from the herd of Geryon (*boves... Erytheidas*, *Fast.* 1. 543), but 'Spanish cows' (*vaccas Hiberas*, 519). In the earlier accounts Hercules' fight with Cacus is sparked by the lowing of the stolen bulls (*Fast.* 1. 548), who fill the whole grove and surrounding hills with their clamour (*Aen.* 8. 216). In this passage Ino's wails bring Hercules face to face with a group of women who turn tail at the very sight of the hero: *turpia femineae terga dedere fugae* (522). The elegiac scene is reminiscent of Prop. 4. 9, where Hercules scatters the priestesses who refuse him a drink of water at the shrine of the Bona Dea. [On the heroic register of Ovid's version of the Cacus story in *Fasti* 1, see Miller (2002) 189–92, Green (2004*a*) 247–50.]

523. *cognorat enim*: 'for he knew (it was Ino).' This parenthetical aside implies that since Ino and Hercules both belong to Theban mythology, they must be conversant with each other's story. Ovid humorously extends this knowledge to physical recognition.

523. *matertera Bacchi*: *matertera* signifies a maternal aunt as opposed to *amita*, a paternal aunt, whose relationship with her brother's children was usually less close than that of their mother's sister [see Bettini (1991) 77–99, Boëls-Janssen (1993) 263–4, 351–2]. *matertera* is a key word in a passage which celebrates the patron goddess of Roman aunts, but the harmonious domesticity evoked by *matertera* sits uneasily with the untameable *Bacchi.* There is a touch of the same incongruity in *Metamorphoses* 3. 719, where Pentheus, confronted by his mother and her maenad sisters, appeals vainly to Ino: '*fer opem, matertera.*' Hercules' meeting with the goddess of Roman aunts foreshadows the ending of *Fasti* 6, where Hercules endorses (*adnuit*, 812) Clio's eulogy of Atia, *matertera Caesaris* (809), in the temple of Hercules Musarum.

524. *'an numen, quod me, te quoque vexat?'*: Ino's sister, Semele, and Alcmene, Hercules' mother, both attract the lust of Jupiter and bear his sons. As innocent victims of Juno's jealousy, Ino and Hercules share the same misfortune of being driven by madness to kill their own children. Expiation of this guilt has brought each to the shores of

Italy where their paths intersect in the Forum Boarium, the location of the cults of Mater Matuta and of Hercules. Ovid emphasizes their shared circumstances by the word order of this pentameter, where the juxtaposed *me te*, euphoniously framed by *quod... quoque*, stand between the subject (*numen*) and verb (*vexat*). Hercules' heavy admission of his unnatural crime is conveyed by ponderous spondees in the first half of the line.

Ino visits Carmentis, who prophesies her apotheosis

525–36: *Ino told him part of her story, suppressing, in front of Melicertes, her attempted infanticide. The rumour spread quickly: how Ino had visited the home of Carmentis who had baked cakes for her and how delighted she had been. Even today the goddess enjoys cakes at the* Matralia. *Then Ino urged Carmentis to reveal what Fate had in store for her.* **537–50:** *As inspiration came upon her, Carmentis grew in stature. She told joyful news, 'You and your son will become deities of the sea. You will be Leucothea to the Greeks and Matuta here in Rome. Your son will have power over harbours. We shall call him Portunus—Palaemon in his own tongue. Farewell and, I pray, look kindly on us!' Ino, now a goddess, assented.*

525–6. *illa docet partim, partim praesentia nati | continet*: the key word here is *partim*, which Ovid accentuates by repetition on each side of the third-foot caesura. Despite her unnerving encounter with the maenads, the presence of her son ensures that Ino regains enough self-control to be economical with the truth, and she responds to the sympathetic complicity inherent in Hercules' remark by suppressing any reference to infanticide. Ovid's portrait of Ino in *Fasti* 6 offers an artistic contrast with the bacchant Ino whom Ovid describes in a dark Theban context (*Met.* 4. 416–562), whose demeanour lacks none of the traditional signs of Bacchic possession. In stark contrast to Ovid's earlier Ino, who is still whooping '*euhoe, Bacche!*' as she leaps over the cliff, the future Mater Matuta stoically prepares a decent funeral (*omnia iusta, Fast.* 6. 492) for her murdered elder son, Learchus, and betrays no outward sign of frenzy (*huc venit*, 497) when she reaches the place of suicide with her remaining child.

526. ***furiis in scelus isse pudet*****:** *pudet* refers to Ino's own shame at being driven to unnatural crime (*in scelus isse*). The avenging Furies with their whips are evoked by Ovid's striking alliteration of *s* across the middle of the pentameter.

527. ***Rumor, ut est velox, agitatis pervolat alis*****:** Ovid's *rumor* is swift and winged, like Virgil's Fama (*qua non aliud velocius ullum*, *Aen.* 4. 174). However, unlike *fama, fertur* or even *diceris* (530), *rumor* has the connotation of an unsubstantiated report (cf. Ovid *Met.* 12.55). This does not represent an Alexandrian footnote but a mistier oral tradition associated with the holy places of the Forum Boarium. By alluding to Virgil's striking personification of *Fama*, who initiates cataclysmic events by proclaiming false rumours through the cities of Libya, Ovid humorously adapts an epic motif to an elegiac context: the news of Ino's arrival spread through Evander's tiny settlement like wildfire, which is made clear in the pentameter: *estque frequens, Ino, nomen in ore tuum* (528). But which part of Ino's story provided gossip for Evander's settlers? Ino's Theban past and her infanticide were wholly incompatible with her new role as a Roman kourotrophos goddess. Besides, she had been symbolically cleansed by her rite of passage through the sea (see note on 499–50). In the subsequent distich (529–30) the poet uses imagery which demonstrates clearly Ino's new role by elevating her to the stature of the archetypal sorrowing mother goddess, Ceres.

529–30. ***hospita Carmentis fidos intrasse penates | diceris et longam deposuisse famem*****:** 'They say you came as a guest to Carmentis' honest home and broke your long fast.' Ino appears as a majestic grieving mother figure through verbal reminiscences of Ovid's description of Ceres entering the humble home of Triptolemus (*parvos initura penates*, *Fast.* 4. 531. Cf. *Met.* 8. 637) and there ending her grief-induced fast after the disappearance of her daughter (*longam ... exsoluisse famem*, *Fast.* 4. 534). The narrative in historic present is varied here by a series of historic infinitives: *intrasse ... deposuisse ... dedisse.* Ovid suggests a comparison with Ceres by implying that this is the first food that Ino has tasted since the death of Learchus.

531. ***Tegeaea sacerdos*****:** Carmentis and her son Evander were exiles from Tegea in Arcadia. Carmentis is described as *sacerdos* in her capacity as *vates* (533) who can utter prophetic truth. Carmentis had a double festival on 11 and 15 January. Ovid celebrates her first as a prophetess (*Fast.* 1. 461–586); this is Carmentis' primary role in *Fasti* and her name derives from *carmen*, a prophetic utterance (*OLD* s.v. 1*c*). She is described by Virgil as *vatis fatidicae* (*Aen.* 8. 340. Cf. Liv. 1. 7. 8). On 16 January she is honoured as a goddess concerned with childbirth (617–36), who was invoked by expectant mothers (Gell. 16. 16. 4). The same dichotomy exists in the cult of Fortuna of Praeneste who was honoured both as an oracular and a fertility goddess [see Champeaux (1982) 1. 249–332]. In this way three goddesses associated with the *Matralia*, Carmentis, Mater Matuta, and Fortuna, are united by the propinquity of their sanctuaries and the similar spheres of influence of the two goddesses, Carmentis and Mater Matuta, who are both associated, directly or indirectly, with prophecy, childbirth, and fecundity. The Porta Carmentalis was set in the Servian Walls at the point where they intersect the Vicus Iugarius; there seems to have been a shrine to Carmentis very close to the temples of Mater Matuta and Fortuna, although no remains have been found [Richardson 72, Steinby 1. 240–1].

533. *nunc quoque liba iuvant festis Matralibus illam*: the cakes baked by Carmentis provide the aition for the custom of eating cakes at the *Matralia.* To give a sense of fictional reality to this prequel to Virgil's story of Evander's meeting with Aeneas, Ovid imposes a chronological sequence. Virgil's story of the ageing King Evander in *Aeneid* 8 takes place when Hercules' defeat of Cacus has already become a legend. When Evander and Carmentis arrive in Italy, Evander is a callow youth, despondent in exile (*Fast.* 1. 479–50), who needs the reassurance of his strong-minded and athletic young mother (503–8). Carmentis' encounter with Ino in *Fasti* 6 takes place many years later, at the time of Hercules' arrival with the cattle of Geryon when Evander has become a ruler (*sceptra tenere loci*, 506) and Carmentis, baking cakes in her cottage, is now an elderly woman living alone. (529–34). Carmentis' son, Evander, is also a cult founder, for he brings from his native Arcadia the worship of Faunus which leads to the cult of the Luperci (*Fast.* 2. 279–80, 5. 91–100) as well as the cult of Hercules at the Ara Maxima.

534. *rustica sedulitas gratior arte fuit*: 'her rustic welcome gave Ino more pleasure than her (culinary) skill.' Coupled with *rustica*, the word *sedulitas* which describes Carmentis' domestic diligence suggests a comparison with Anna of Bovillae, *pauper et multae sedulitatis anus* (*Fast.* 3. 668). Both belong in the tradition of humble hosts, who prepare food as an essential part of the hospitality extended to visiting gods or heroes, such as Callimachus' Hecale and Ovid's Philemon and Baucis (*Met.* 8. 626–724) and Hyrieus (*Fast.* 5. 495–534).

535. '*venientia fata resigna*': 'reveal my future destiny!' Ino uses language to suit Carmentis' dignity as a prophetess. Usually in such circumstances, the divine guest offers a gift to the humble host in gratitude for hospitality (*Fast.* 4. 550–2, 5. 523–4, *Met.* 8. 704–5). At this point in the story, however, the seer Carmentis' powers are greater than Ino's, whose apotheosis has not yet been accomplished.

538. *fitque sui toto pectore plena dei*: the expression *plena dei* was a common way of describing a seer in the grip of inspiration from Apollo or Bacchus (Hor. *Carm.* 3. 19. 6, 3. 25. 1–2. Cf. *deo plenus*, Luc. 9. 564, Stat. *Theb.* 10. 624). The word *plenus* appears in the same context in the companion passage, *Fast.* 1. 473–4, where Carmentis prophesies the future greatness of Rome, speaking *ore pleno carmina vera dei.*

539–40. *vix illam subito posses cognoscere, tanto | sanctior et tanto, quam modo, maior erat*: to announce the apotheosis of Ino and her son into new Roman deities Carmentis must shed her image of a humble old woman baking cakes and become an awesome deliverer of prophecy. Soon she is barely recognizable (*vix illam . . . posses cognoscere*, 539) and her remoteness and mystery are summed up by the word *sanctior*, more like a goddess (cf. *OLD* s.v. 3*b*). She becomes taller (*maior*, 540) in the same way as Virgil's sibyl when she comes under the influence of Apollo (Virg. *Aen.* 6. 49). When the young Carmentis prophesies the greatness of Rome, Ovid dwells on her dishevelled hair and stamping feet (1. 503–8). Here, much older, she presents a huge and majestic figure to Ino.

543. *numen eris pelagi, natum quoque pontus habebit*: Ino and Portunus' connection with the sea (*pelagi . . . pontus*) was appropriate for deities whose shrines were found among the harbour sanctuaries. These were, like the cult of Hercules, popular with foreign traders because their origins were Greek. The cult of Leucothea at Pyrgi has the same origin and associations. Carmentis hails Italy as *novos caelo terra datura deos* (*Fast.* 1. 510). As Rome's earliest seer, Carmentis is the right goddess to prophesy the apotheosis of Rome's three new gods: Hercules (1. 583–4), Ino, and Portunus (6. 543–50).

544. ***in vestris aliud sumite nomen aquis*:** 'In (Roman) waters, which are your own, take another name.' Carmentis seems also to imply that Ino lost her old name in the rite of passage which brought her under the waves from the Isthmus of Corinth to the Lucus Stimulae.

546–7. ***in portus nato ius erit omne tuo: | quem nos Portunum, sua lingua Palaemona dicet*:** Palaemon's Roman name, Portunus, is said to be derived from *portus.* Portunus was given a temple in the Forum Boarium, a flamen (Fest. 238L), and a festival, the *Portunalia*, which was celebrated on 17 August. This etymology is also given by Virgil (*Aen.* 5. 241–2, *et pater ipse manu magna Portunus euntem | impulit*).

549. ***adnuerat*: *promissa fides*:** Ino's first action as Mater Matuta is to agree to deal justly with the people of Rome. Tying up the remaining loose ends in a couplet of terse parataxis and asyndeton, Ovid ends this complex and colourful narrative with a snappy conclusion [cf. Murgatroyd (2005) 275]. For the sense pause at the 'strong' caesura in the second foot of the hexameter compare Virg. *G.* 4. 497: *iamque vale: feror ingenti circumdata nocte.*

Two distinguishing features of Mater Matuta's cult

551–568: *You ask why Matuta bans serving women from her shrine? One of her maids became a concubine of her husband Athamas, and she told him how Ino had given the farmers burnt seeds (to cause a famine). So rumour tells, but Ino herself denies it. A good mother does not pray to Matuta for her own child but for another woman's child. The goddess was a better aunt than she was a mother.*

551. ***cur vetet ancillas accedere quaeritis?*:** this question, raised by Plutarch (*Quaest. Rom.* 16. 267*d*, *Cam.* 5. 2), has found no consensus of explanation (see note on line 481).

551–2. ***odit | principiumque odii, si sinat illa, canam*:** 'Ino hates (serving maids) and I will relate the reason for her hatred, if she will allow it.' Revisiting once more Ino's former Theban persona for the solution to the exclusion of female slaves on Matuta's festal day, the poet signals the ill-omened city by addressing Ino as *Cadmei*, daughter of Cadmus, in line 553.

555–6. ***ab illa | comperit agricolis semina tosta dari***: 'from the maid Athamas discovered that burnt seeds had been given to the farmers.' Here Ino's Theban slave girl reveals to Athamas plainly the cause of the famine. On another occasion Ino's identity is made perfectly clear by the periphrasis *quae ruricolis semina tosta dedit* (*Fast.* 2. 628), which links her with Medea as an archetypal wicked stepmother and unwelcome guest at the Roman family celebration of the *Caristia*. Again, Ovid juxtaposes *scelerata noverca* with *semina tosta* in his aition for the zodiacal Aries, which is also set in Thebes (*Fast.* 3. 853), so that burnt seeds become Ovid's code for the famine which Ino brings about to get rid of her unwanted stepchildren, leaving the succession open for her own offspring. Mater Matuta's festival occurs in midsummer, and consequently there may be some agricultural significance in the transformation into a propitious fertility goddess of one who has in the past deliberately vitiated the natural process of growth and harvest [see Dumézil (1980) 176–205].

559. ***non tamen hanc pro stirpe sua pia mater adoret***: 'Not for her own offspring will a scrupulous mother invoke this goddess.' Mater Matuta was invoked by women on behalf of their sister's children entirely on the basis of Ino's mythological credentials which make her a poor example for mothers (*felix parum . . . parens*, 560) but a more promising aunt (*utilior Bacchi*, 561). There seems to be no clear anthropological nor religious explanation why mothers should not appeal directly to Mater Matuta [see Frazer (1929) 4. 281–3, H. J. Rose, 'Two Roman Rites', *CQ* 28 (1934) 156–8, Dumézil (1980) 179–83]. The prayers offered for newborn babies by Roman aunts and grandmothers are graphically described by Persius (*Sat.* 2. 31–5).

563–8: *They say that you told the consul Rutilius that he would be killed by the Marsi on your feast day. And so it happened and the River Tolenus ran red with blood. On the next anniversary of the* Matralia *the death of T. Didius doubled the strength of the enemy.*

563. ***quo properas . . . Rutili?***: Ovid is our only source for the date of this battle in the Social War, 90 BC, in which P. Rutilius Lupus (*cos.* 90 BC) was defeated and killed by Vettius Scato, leader of the Marsi (*ab* *hoste Marso*, 564. See Liv. *Per.* 73). The implication of haste in *quo properas* might suggest recklessness since Rutilius Lupus and his men were ambushed by the Marsi when they crossed a bridge which they had constructed over the River Tolenus. Lupus is addressed here by Mater Matuta herself because he is killed on 11 June (*mea luce*, 564), but perhaps also because Matuta may have been worshipped as a dawn goddess with power to influence military engagements at daybreak. That Mater Matuta might be considered, even peripherally, as a deity associated with war, like Juno, Iuventas, Bellona, Mars, and Fortuna, is obviously highly pertinent to the war theme in *Fasti* 6 [see Dumézil (1980) 53–69, 105–21, who attributes Camillus' cult of Mater Matuta to battles won at dawn particularly during the period of the summer solstice]. For Camillus' dedications to Mater Matuta see Liv. 5. 19.6, 23. 7.

565. ***flumenque Toleni | purpureum mixtis sanguine fluxit aquis***: at the Battle of the River Tolenus Lupus and some 8,000 Romans were slaughtered after they crossed the river. C. Marius, Lupus' second-in-command, realized what had happened when he noticed Roman bodies floating downstream, and launched a successful counter-attack (Liv. *Per.* 73, Vell. 2. 16. 4, App. *Bell. Civ.* 1. 43).

567. ***proximus annus erat; Pallantide caesus eadem***: 'killed on the anniversary in the following year.' For metrical convenience Ovid, on several occasions, names Pallas as the father of Eos/Aurora (*Met.* 9. 421, 15. 191, 700). Hesiod (*Theog.* 371–4) gives the more traditional identification of Dawn as the child of Pallas' brother, Hyperion.

568. ***Didius***: T. Didius (*cos.* 98 BC) was granted a triumph in 93 BC after a successful campaign in Spain (98–94 BC) and in 89 BC took Herculaneum during the Social War (Vell. 2. 16. 4). Only Ovid records the death of this renowned *triumphator* on the battlefield, which would no doubt have redoubled (*ingeminavit*, 568) the enemy's resources, no less than the encouraging news of two Roman defeats in the Social War on the same day.

Fortuna, 569–636

[Boardman (1972), Castagnoli (1979) 152–4, Champeaux (1982) 1. 199–207, 243–332, Richard (1987) 205–25, Coarelli (1988), 301–28,

Boëls-Janssen (1993), 342 ff., Herbert-Brown (1994) 145–56, Cornell (1995) 130–50, 156–72, Newlands (1995) 222–7, Mertens-Horn (1996), Vernole (2002), Littlewood (2002) 191–211, Murgatroyd (2005), 201–5.]

Fig. 14 Two Fortunae at a lectisternium, marble sculpture, Museo Archeologico, Palestrina. The two figures are represented on a couch which, as the snake suggests, may also be the marriage bed which was the particular responsibility of the goddess Fortuna. (Photograph courtesy of D.A.I. Rome, Inst. Neg. 1969. 1140.)

1. *Fortuna, goddess of marriage and fecundity*

Fortuna, in archaic Roman and Etruscan religion, was a fertility goddess who presided over the rite of passage of young girls from virginity to the married state. She was also associated with 'king-making', particularly in connection with Servius Tullius. Fortuna's union with Servius, described elegiacally in Ovid's account of her *furtivi amores* (*Fast.* 6. 573), may also be associated with the tradition of goddesses who had a simultaneous charge over fertility and royalty. Champeaux (1982) 1. 154, describes a dyad of Fortunae at Antium, one representing fecundity as a *matrona* and the other a warrior goddess. As Fortuna in Algido, Fortuna was honoured with Juno, Iuventas, and Hercules in 218 BC in an attempt to bring the divine powers on to the Roman side in the struggle with Carthage. This duality, found in Juno Seispes Mater Regina of Lanuvium, existed also in Juno's Etruscan counterpart: in the Pyrgi inscription (*c.*500 BC) the Etruscan ruler of Caere, Thefarie Velianas, dedicates a temple to the Etruscan goddess Uni because she has elevated him to his position of power. Like Servius' temple to Fortuna in the Forum Boarium, the Caeretan temple is paired with a second honouring Leucothea/Mater Matuta.

Fortuna has a historical counterpart in Tanaquil, the queen of Tarquinius Priscus. Tanaquil's distaff and spindle were preserved in the temple of Semo Sancus (Plin. *Nat.* 8. 194), a deity believed by some to be none other than Hercules (Var. *L* 5. 66). Vernole (2002: 88–96) suggests a connection between the archaic temple of Semo Sancus, founded by Tarquinius Priscus on the Quirinal, and the temple of Fortuna, founded by Servius in the Forum Boarium, because the former contained Tanaquil's spindle and distaff and the latter the toga which she is said to have woven for Servius. Tanaquil was regarded as a model for young, soon-to-be-married, women. Her name in this role was sometimes given as Gaia Caecilia (Plin. *Nat.* 8. 194, Fest. 85L), which associates her with the Roman marriage formula uttered by a bride married by the ritual of *confarreatio*: *ubi tu Gaius, ego Gaia.* Tanaquil's connection with both clothing and brides points to Fortuna's role as a goddess who watched over young women's sexuality in the early weeks of marriage.

2. Fortuna the king-maker

Divine care for the survival of the Roman race and its ruler is expressed in different ways in *Fasti* 6: in Carna's protection of Proca, the Alban heir to the throne; in Vesta's miraculous provision of bread to avert the Gallic siege, a manifestation of Vesta's cult ensuring the survival of the Roman state; and in Fortuna's 'sacred marriage' to Servius and the retribution she brings to his parricide daughter. The dual cult of Mater Matuta and Fortuna, the divine powers that watch over the perpetual life-cycle from birth to marriage, were closely allied to the potency of the ruler which was measured by his success in war and the prosperity of his people.

The fragments of terracotta decoration from the archaic temple believed to be founded by Servius in the Forum Boarium show iconography associated with tyrant rule in the city states of Central Italy where, as in Greece, the tyrants who seized power surrounded their origins and their achievement with legend of divine support and increased their prestige by temple-building. Servius' legend is stamped with the hallmarks of the archetypal archaic tyrant. The emperor Claudius, identifying Servius with the Etruscan warlord and adventurer, Mcstrna (*ILS* 212. 1. 8–27), says simply: *mutato nomine ... regnum ... obtinuit* ('he changed his name and achieved kingship'). Etruscan history was one of Claudius' areas of historical expertise, and his description of roving aristocrats in command of private armies finds some support in the late fourth-century frescos in the François tomb at Vulci. When Ovid wrote on the cults of the Forum Boarium and in particular the association of Servius and Fortuna, he must have been aware that Verrius Flaccus' distinguished research into *Res Etruscae* included discussion of Servius/Mcstrna in connection with the Vicus Tuscus which, according to Verrius, took its name either from the Etruscans left behind after Porsenna's siege of Rome or from the Vibenna brothers of Vulci who came to Rome with Mcstrna (cf. Var. *L* 5. 46, Fest. 486L, D.H. 2. 36. 2).

Fortuna's love for King Servius

569–86: *Fortuna's temple was founded in the same place on the same day. But who is that covered by togas? It is generally believed to be King Servius. The* *reason for this is not certain. The goddess was ashamed that she loved a mortal—Fortuna cherished a blind passion for Servius—and now hides her lover under a royal toga? The king's face was veiled after his death to avoid demonstrations of grief by the plebs? I will offer a third possibility.*

570. ***sed superiniectis quis latet iste togis?***: 'but who is that hiding with togas flung over him?' Both the identity of the cult statue and the ownership of the garment is in question here. Religious custom would indicate that the ancient gilded cult statue in Fortuna's temple represented Fortuna herself, a view held by Pliny (*Nat.* 8. 197), Dio (58. 7. 2), Varro (Non. 278L). Examples of veiled terracotta statuettes of Fortuna Primigenia are to be seen in the Villa Giulia, Rome (Inv. nos. 13551, 27176, 13547, 13510). If the statue represented Fortuna, then it might be suggested that the plural *togis superiniectis* correspond to the *togulae* traditionally offered to Fortuna Virgo on the eve of marriage by Roman girls, who wore what, in early Rome, was regarded as a unisex outer garment until marriage permitted them to wear the *palla* of the Roman *matrona* (Var. Non. 867L: *ante enim olim toga fuit commune vestimentum et diurnum et nocturnum et muliebri et virile.* Cf. Plut. *Mor.* 10. 322*f*–323*a*). However, Champeaux (1982) 1. 291–302 makes a clear distinction between Fortuna, goddess of the Forum Boarium, who is responsible for both royalty and married women, and Fortuna Virgo, to whom pre-nuptial girls offer their *togulae.*

If, as Ovid, Dionysius (4. 40. 7), and Valerius Maximus (1. 8. 11) claim, the statue represents Servius Tullius, the drapery should be a (single) toga, supposedly the one woven by Tanaquil herself for King Servius: *factam ab ea (Tanaquil) togam regiam undulatam in aede Fortunae qua Servius fuerat usus* (Plin. *Nat.* 8. 194). It was not uncommon for ancient cult statues to be dressed in garments created for this purpose. The antiquity of the garments enhanced the holiness and efficacy of the statue. The royal toga was described as *undulata*, 'falling in folds', and *praetextata*, 'with a purple border', by Varro (Non. 278L). A third possibility is that a man's toga was draped over Fortuna's statue to symbolize the transvestism practised in ancient societies to avert evil from the bride's potential fecundity, which was the particular concern of Fortuna in Roman marriage. [See I. Kajanto, *Fortuna*, *ANRW* II. 17. 1 (1981): 502–58,

L. Bonfante, *Etruscan Dress* (1975) 46–50, 90–3, Boëls-Janssen (1993) 357–70, Champeaux (1982), 1. 296–301.]

571. ***Servius est, hoc constat enim***: it would be hard to imagine that Ovid was not perfectly aware that, far from being 'agreed' (*constat*) that the statue represented Servius, the identity of the ancient gilded cult statue was much debated until it was examined and proved to be Fortuna (D.H. 4. 40. 7). Confessing uncertainty as to why the statue was veiled, the poet focuses on explanations which are all generically appropriate to elegy, each being driven by emotion: Fortuna veils her lover out of shame (*concubuisse pudet*, 574), the Roman people cover the king's face in an outpouring of public grief (581–4), as, alternatively, the outraged statue of Servius demands to be screened from the sight of his parricide daughter (615–16).

573. ***furtivos... amores***: Ovid's vocabulary in the first two couplets (573–60) transpose the cultic association of Servius and Fortuna into the world of amatory elegy. The customary secrecy which attended illicit love intrigues in Roman elegy made *furtivus* a conventional adjective to describe *amores* (cf. Ovid, *Am.* 2. 8. 8, *Ars* 1. 275, 2. 246). Adulterous love affairs could succinctly be described as *furta* (Cat. 68. 136, Tib. 1. 2. 34). Traces of both mime and *praetexta* have been detected here. Fortuna's confession (*profitetur*, 573) of her love might have featured in mimes about Servius and Fortuna in which a veiled head might suggest an amorous intrigue. Above all, however, there is a tragedy, a *praetexta*, within the frame of the story of Servius' deposition, a *togata* centred on the familiar tragic themes of parricide and regicide (cf. Cic. *Rosc. Am.* 67). As in Livy's narration of the same story, Ovid's narrative suggests several clearly demarcated scenes: Tullia incites Tarquinius (589–96), Tarquinius takes his seat on Servius' throne (597–600), Tullia urges her *auriga* to violate her father's corpse (603–8), Tullia is confronted by Servius' statue and Fortuna (611–20). Fortuna might deliver the prologue in such a play, which would end, like Ovid's story, with the voice of Fortuna in her own temple, proclaiming the virtue of Pudicitia. [See Wiseman (1998) 27–30, (2002) 275–99.]

574. ***caelestemque homini concubuisse pudet***: Ovid makes repeated allusions to Pudor (*pudet*, 574... *pudet*, 579... *pudoris*, 620), which contrasts with the amatory language which he uses to describe Fortuna's liaison with Servius. The opposition of Pudor and Amor is found in Ovid, *Am.* 3. 10. 28, *Met.* 7. 72–3. Livy gives the title of Pudicitia to Fortuna Virgo (Liv. 10. 23. 3).

575. ***arsit enim magno correpta cupidine regis*****:** Ovid continues to use the language of Roman amatory elegy. The metaphorical *ardere*, 'to burn with love', has an additional resonance when applied to Fortuna's affection for Servius, who is associated with fire through his alleged divine parent, Vulcan (*Fast.* 6. 626–7), his miraculous conception from a phallus in the hearth (631–4), and the flames of destiny which appear in his hair (635–6. Cf. Liv. 1. 39. 1–3). Ovid's other amatory cliché, *correptus amore*, is more commonly used to describe epic passion (cf. *Met.* 3. 416, 4. 676, 9. 455, 734).

576. ***caecaque in hoc uno non fuit illa viro*****:** 'in the case of this one man (Fortuna) was not blind.' In ancient literature blindness was attributed to both Love (Ovid *Tr.* 2. 375) and Fortuna (Cat. 67. 25, Ovid *P* 4. 8. 16). Here Ovid suggests that Fortuna selected Servius for his merits, an allusion to the historical tradition that the king was distinguished above all by personal merit, demonstrated by his legendary rise to distinction from obscure origins (cf. Plut. *Mor.* 322*c*–323*d*).

577–8. ***nocte domum parva solita est intrare fenestra | unde Fenestellae nomina porta tenet*****:** the palace of Tarquinius and Tanaquil is said to have stood near the temple of Jupiter Stator with its windows overlooking the Nova Via (Liv. 1. 41. 4, Plin. *Nat.* 34. 29, Plut. *Quaest. Rom.* 36). It has been deduced from archaeological evidence that the Porta Fenestella, meaning 'The Gate of the Little Window', was a local name for the Porta Mugonia because of an adjacent window sited in the sixth-century palace from which Tanaquil addressed the crowds after Tarquinius' murder and through which Fortuna reputedly entered Servius' chamber (Liv. 1. 41.4–6, D.H. 4.5.1, Plut. *Mor.* 273*b*–*c*) [see Wiseman (1998), 25–34]. The tradition that the same window served both purposes (Plut. *Quaest. Rom.* 36) either suggests an allegorical interpretation of Fortuna's entry or points to an instance of the 'sacred marriage', familiar in ancient Eastern kingdoms, where the king lies with a goddess of fertility, represented by a temple prostitute, and an announcement is made from a window that the marriage has been consummated. This latter view is strengthened by Fortuna's origins as a fertility goddess, and evidence of this practice during the archaic period can be found at the temples of Ino/Leucothea and Uni/Astarte at Pyrgi, where the cells of the temple prostitutes were decorated with antefixes representing Hercules, Ino, Juno, and maenads. In Ovid's literary account it seems more likely that the poet is using a tradition where Fortuna allegorically represents the good fortune, particularly in his ally, Tanaquil, which advanced Servius to his initially unassailable position in the Tarquin household.

581–3. ***post Tulli funera plebem | confusam placidi morte fuisse ducis |... crescebat imagine luctus***: the outpouring of public grief at the death of Servius was part of the legend of Servius, a king dedicated to the well-being of the common people (D.H. 4. 40.5). This idea gained popularity among supporters of the Gracchi in the late Republic [see Richard (1987) 208–14, Ridley (1975) 170]. Conversely, a few decades later other aspects of the Servius myth, including Fortuna's patronage and Servius' plan to abdicate, were adopted by Sulla's supporters.

586. ***nos tamen adductos intus agemus equos***: 'I shall relate a shortened version of the story.' Ovid uses a metaphor from the Circus Maximus, where a charioteer looking for the shortest way round the track would guide his horses along the inside lane (*intus*). The dramatic imagery of the chariot race, which had been popular with ancient poets since Pindar, empowered writers to convey effectively grandeur and audacity, restraint and moderation, and illustrated the poet's professional skill to select the right register for the occasion (cf. Virg. *G* 3. 18). The imagery was popular with Ovid (cf. *Am.* 3. 15. 18, *Ars* 2. 426, *Fast.* 2. 361). By describing the striving and elation of horses and charioteer, poets evoked the exhilaration of poetic inspiration and the poet's literary ambition: *tantis amor laudum, tantae est victoria curae* (Virg. *G* 3. 103–12. Cf. Lucr. 2. 263). Callimachus (*Aet.* fr. 1. 25–8 Pf.) used the metaphor of driving a chariot alone for writing original poetry, which was later adapted by Manilius (2. 136–44).

Tullia's parricide: a Roman tragedy

587–96: *After Tullia had murdered and married, she used to goad her husband. 'If we had wished to live unsullied lives, we should not have cleared the path to our marriage by murdering your brother and my sister. As my dowry I offer you my father's throne. Take it—if you are a man! Crime is a royal prerogative.'*

597–610: *L. Tarquinius, Tullia's husband, sat on Servius' throne. Riots followed. Old Servius, murdered below his own palace, lay bleeding in the street. Tullia saw him on her way home in her carriage and ordered her grieving driver to drive over the corpse. That street is now called Criminal.*

587. *coniugio sceleris mercede peracto*: this aetiological narrative celebrates a goddess responsible for women's transition into marriage, whose cult is practised by *bonae matres* and *univirae.* By announcing at the outset that Tullia's marriage has been contracted 'at the price of a crime', the poet foreshadows the coming catastrophe. In Livy's narrative noun polyptoton underlines the word *scelus*: *ab scelere ad aliud spectare mulier scelus* (Liv. 1. 47. 1).

587–8. *Tullia*...| *his solita est dictis exstimulare virum*: Ovid's version of Livy's longer narrative (Liv. 1. 46.1–48. 7) opens with Tullia, who is the instigator of the regicide, for she is the central mover in the tragedy. The verb *exstimulare* signals a loose symmetry between the two passages celebrating the cults of 11 June. As the story of Ino in Italy opens with Juno goading (*instimulat*, 508) the Arcadian maenads of the Lucus Stimulae to seize the infant Melicertes, so Tullia, in the second passage, is first seen goading (*exstimulare*, 588) her husband Tarquinius to murder her father, Servius. Whilst Juno's machinations are foiled by the arrival of Hercules, Tullia, who successfully manipulates her husband, is eventually punished by public condemnation from the goddess Fortuna in her temple. Ovid's reiteration of the theme of goading women in this passage (cf. *instinctus*, 597) serves as a reminder here, in the context of women's cult, of women's influence in the promotion or destruction of civic order.

589. *'quid iuvat esse pares*...|...*si pia vita placet?'*: the moral implication of *pares* is apparent in Livy's description of the two daughters of Servius, who are *dispares moribus* (Liv. 1. 46. 5). By giving Tullia an extended passage of direct speech (589–96) in which to unfold her plot, Ovid reduces Tarquinius' guilt to meek acquiescence, making Tullia entirely responsible for her father's murder, so that the full burden of retribution awaits her in Fortuna's temple. Tullia's obvious scorn for *pia vita* implies that her violation of marital *pietas* was simply the first step to two further breaches of *pietas*, parricide and regicide.

589–91. *'te nostrae caede sororis | meque tui fratris ... | ... vir meus et tua coniunx'*: Tullia and L. Tarquinius are *pares caede*, because each has murdered the other's sibling, respectively *vir meus et tua coniunx* (591). Having been brought up with the sons of Tarquinius Priscus, Servius Tullius is said to have reigned for forty-four years (Liv. 1. 48. 8). His daughters' husbands must therefore have been not the sons but the grandsons of Tarquinius. Juxtaposed and reiterated possessive pronouns help to accentuate the family relationships in this double murder. In the iconography of Augustan Rome after Actium marital murder took on the heightened significance of a barbaric and unnatural crime; the statues of the Danaids, which stood in the portico of the temple of Palatine Apollo, represented a characteristically Egyptian crime. [See Zanker (1988) 85–6, Kellum (1985) 172–5, Stephen J. Harrison, 'The Swordbelt of Pallas: Moral Symbolism and Political Ideology,' in Stahl (ed.) (1998) 222–40.]

593. *'et caput et regnum facio dotale parentis'*: 'I give you the life and throne of my father.' Although, legally, a Roman woman was permitted to name her dowry (Ulp. *Reg.* 6. 2), to claim as dowry a throne which depended on the murder of her father was an ill-omened beginning to a marriage. Tullia's argument that Tarquinius has a right to 'claim' (*exige*, 594) the kingship, as payment of his new wife's dowry (*regnum ... dotale*), is obviously flawed and offers a contrast with the honourable expectation of dowry payment under similar circumstances formulated by Aeneas to his future father-in-law, Latinus: *socer arma Latinus habeto | imperium sollemne socer* (Virg. *Aen.* 12. 192–3). Livy's Tullia argues more convincingly that Servius' throne is Tarquinius' inheritance from his own father: *di te penates patriique et patris imago et domus regia et in domo regale solium et nomen Tarquinium creat vocatque regem* (Liv. 1. 47. 4).

594. ***'si vir es, i, dictas exige dotis opes'***: the dramatic impact lies in the blunt crudeness of the four opening monosyllables (cf. Liv. 1. 47. 3. *si tu is es*...). The second half of the pentameter simply recapituates the idea from the previous hexameter.

595. ***'regia res scelus est'***: 'A royal house is ever steeped in blood' might convey the spirit of Ovid's epigram, which encompasses two marital murders already committed and a parricide-regicide now well in hand. Its less pithy Livian counterpart (*Romana regia sceleris tragici exemplum*, Liv. 1. 46. 3), also carries the suggestion that the royal palace in Rome, no less than in Mycenae or Thebes, might also provide a theme for a tragedy. This idea is borne out by the second half of Ovid's hexameter, which succinctly defines the full impiety of Tarquinius' treacherous regicide: *socero cape regna necato.* This offers a defiant contradiction of Concordia's claim (95) that June derives its name from the happy cooperation of an earlier *gener/socer* pair, Romulus and Tatius, who followed Virgil's model, Aeneas and Latinus. Given the network of allusions characteristic of his *Fasti*, there may be an allusion here to Accius' tragedy 'Brutus', in which Servius Tullius and Tarquinius Superbus both had a role. 'Brutus' owed its conception to the fact that Accius' patron was D. Iunius Brutus Callaicus (*Fast.* 6. 461–2), the descendant of Brutus the Liberator. Since both Servius and Brutus' father had married daughters of Tarquinius Priscus, Servius was, by marriage, both the uncle of the Liberator and an ancestor of Callaicus. This link had potential for later political propaganda, for it should be remembered that Accius' 'Brutus' belongs to the Gracchan era when Servius was celebrated for his democratic policies, as the single fragment referring to the king suggests: *Tullius qui libertatem civibus stabiliverat* (Accius fr. 674 Dangel) [see Richard (1987) 205–25, Ridley (1975) 152]. The custom among the great families of the late Republic of dramatizing the heroic deeds of their ancestors in *fabulae praetextae* offered to *novi homines* a good way of offering to the electorate an encomiastic picture of their forebears [see Wiseman (1998) 195 n. 12].

596. ***'et nostras patrio sanguine tingue manus'***: Tullia ends her impious speech with a shocking image of bloodshed which is picked up by *cruor et caedes* (599) and *sanguinulentus* (602).

597. ***solio privatus in alto | sederat*****:** Tarquinius' outward and visible gesture of usurping the throne is dramatized by Ovid's enjambement of *sederat*, followed by a sense pause suggesting the momentary hesitation of the shocked citizenry (*attonitum vulgus*). Livy describes Tarquinius *in rege sede... sedens* (1. 47. 7) in response to his wife's nagging, *muliebribus instinctus furiis*, cf. Ovid's *talibus instinctus* (597).

599. ***cruor et caedes*****:** juxtaposed with *infirmaque vincitur aetas*, the alliterative phrase underlines the pathos of the murder of an ageing monarch by a young and ruthless usurper, of which the archetypal example was the death of Priam at the hands of Neoptolemus (Virg. *Aen.* 2. 509–53). Livy, who makes the same point—(*Tarquinius*) *multo et aetate et viribus validior* (1. 48. 3)—goes on to describe how Tarquinius hurls Servius down the senate steps before sending hired assassins to finish the job. Ovid, who is solely concerned with Tullia's crimes, merely says that Tarquinius seized the crown, confining his moral judgement to the juxtaposed *gener socero.*

601. ***ipse sub Esquiliis, ubi est sua regia, caesus*****:** both Livy (1. 44. 3) and Dionysius (4. 13. 2) put Servius' palace on the Esquiline Hill, close to the site of Augustus' Porticus Liviae, which was reached by continuing along the Clivus Urbius and the Clivus Pullius, which run in the same direction. Carmine Ampolo ['La Casa di Servio Tullio, L'Esquilino e Mecenate', *PdP* 286 (1996) 27–32] suggests that Maecenas, antiquarian and descendant of Etruscan kings, consciously chose for his own palatial house and gardens the site of Servius' palace, just as his friend Augustus had made a political statement by establishing his home near the *casa Romuli.*

602. ***sanguinulentus*****:** the pentasyllabic *sanguinulentus* recurs five times in Ovid's *Fasti* in this *sedes*, the penultimate word of the pentameter. The overbearing emphasis on bloodshed in all these five lines has the insistence of a leitmotiv. In his *Fasti* Ovid describes three figures from Rome's regal period, Lucretia (2. 832), Remus (4. 844, 5. 470), and Servius (6. 602), falling to the ground in their death agonies, bleeding and vanquished. Like the image of Turnus falling to his knees at the end of his duel with Aeneas, this presents an iconographic image of defeat. Even as ghosts, Dido (3. 640) and Remus (5. 470) are described as *sanguinulentus*, bloodstained by their conflict with Rome's destiny.

603. *filia carpento*: these juxtaposed words contrast Tullia in her carriage with her father, King Servius, in the previous line *sanguinulentus humo.* Livy's narrative mentions Tullia's arrival in a *carpentum*, the light two-wheeler permitted to Roman women at festivals, to describe her determination to be the first to hail her husband as king [Maltby 111 *carpentum*]. The word *carpentum* had the resonance of moral laxity. During the Second Punic War it was decreed (Lex Oppia) in 215 BC that the women of Rome should forgo their privilege (Liv. 34. 1. 3), and Ovid uses this episode to begin his second celebration of the *Carmentalia* on 15 January. Angered by the loss of their carriages, the Roman women retaliate by aborting their own babies. Carmentis intervenes and is honoured by the cult of a kourotrophos goddess. The ill-omened *carpentum*, a symbol of *luxuria* and arrogance, is therefore associated, in *Fasti* 1 and 6, with two episodes in Roman history in which Roman women are guilty of violating family *pietas* through infanticide or parricide, both of which belong to a celebration of women's cult connected with Carmentis. The two Carmentis celebrations in *Fasti* 1 show Carmentis first as a prophetic goddess and second as a kourotrophos, while in *Fasti* 6 the cult of Mater Matuta, the kourotrophos, precedes that of Fortuna, who is associated with prophecy.

603. *patrios initura penates*: as daughter of Servius Tullius, Tullia's *patrii penates* belonged in her father's palace on the Esquiline Hill (Liv. 1. 44.3. Cf. D.H. 4. 13. 2). The family gods of her husband would be found in the palace of the Tarquinii which stood near the temple of Jupiter Stator on the Velia (Plin. *Nat.* 34. 29, Liv. 1. 41. 4).

604. *ibat per medias alta feroxque vias*: *ibat* in this *sedes* is frequently used by Ovid to describe majestic progress of a deity or heroic figure, e.g. *Fast.* 2. 309 (Omphale), 3. 737 (Liber), 5. 233 (Juno), and 6. 341 (parodically, Priapus). The physical height signified by *alta* suggests hauteur, as it clearly does in Ovid's description of Niobe (*Met.* 6. 169) and Tragedy (*Am.* 3. 1). *Ferox*, on the other hand, points forward to Tullia's final impiety of driving across her father's face.

605–6. *corpus ut aspexit, lacrimis auriga profusis | restitit*: the enjambement of *restitit* effects a pause, reflecting the driver's hesitation which increases Tullia's anger (*hunc... corripit*, 606). Tullia's driver's display of grief (*lacrimis... profusis*) reflects the affection in which Servius was reputedly held by the common people, which Ovid alludes to in line 589.

607. *'vadis, an exspectas pretium pietatis amarum?'*: Tullia tells her coachman that punishment (*pretium . . . amarum*) will be the reward for his loyalty to Servius. The word *pietas* draws attention to Tullia's own violation of filial loyalty.

608. *'duc, inquam, invitas ipsa per ora rotas'*: 'Drive on, I say, over his very face, though the wheels (themselves) be unwilling!' Short bursts of direct speech are an important element of Ovid's narrative style. Here, as in line 595, Ovid chooses shockingly brutal language to accentuate Tullia's unwomanly ruthlessness and inhumanity. Spondees heighten the drama of the first three words. The elegiac pathos of the vehicle's 'reluctant' wheels foreshadow the speaking statue and the supernatural voice of Fortuna.

609. *dictus Sceleratus ab illa | vicus*: Tullia came upon her father's body in the Clivus Urbius, which she turned into at the top of the Vicus Cyprius where there was a shrine to Diana (Liv. 1. 48. 6–7. Cf. Var. *L* 5. 159). The proximity of the Dianium suggests that Clivus Urbius may once have been Clivus Virbius, which recalls another name for Hippolytus, whom Diana was said to have rescued and restored to health in her sacred grove at Aricia [see Richardson 422].

610. *aeterna res ea pressa nota*: 'this (deed) is inscribed with an indelible mark.' Following the wheels on Servius' face, this imagery is intentionally unpleasant. Since *nota* has the connotation of a shameful mark, *pressa* might suggest the metaphor of branding a slave. *nota* occurs frequently in Ovid's *Fasti* to signify a calendric notation (*Fast.* 1. 596, 3. 429, 5. 727, 6. 87, 649). Juno was honoured on the Kalends, Jupiter on the Ides (*Fast.* 1. 55–6). The Nones lacked a tutelary deity, and the plebs, believing that Servius' birthday fell on the Nones but not knowing in which month, honoured the king on this day all through the year (Macr. 1. 13. 17).

The retribution of Fortuna: a miracle

611–24: *Afterwards Tullia dared to enter her father's temple of Fortuna. They say Servius' statue covered its face with its hands, saying, 'Let me not set eyes on* *my impious daughter!' The statue was veiled and Fortuna spoke within the shrine, 'If his face is uncovered, there will be no more modesty in Rome. May it always be veiled by a Roman toga.'*

611. ***ausa est templum monimentum parentis | tangere*:** 'she had the nerve to set foot in Fortuna's temple, a monument (built by) her father.' Tullia brings retribution upon herself by the act of sacrilege which she commits in entering the temple of Fortuna, founded by her father. By murdering her first husband in order to be able to facilitate the regicide she has violated Pudor. She has also destroyed a king who was Fortuna's favourite, thus violating the 'sacred marriage' of Servius and Fortuna.

612. ***mira quidem sed tamen acta loquar*:** that the story of Tullia's parricide provided a drama for 11 June is strengthened by Ovid opening his final scene with the words *mira quidem, sed tamen acta loquar*, which may be loosely paraphrased: 'A miracle, yes, but I shall relate (what you have seen) on the stage' (cf. *OLD* s.v. 25). It is characteristic of Ovid's humour that he bases the veracity of a miracle on the fact that it is the focus of a miracle play! (Cf. *Fast.* 4. 326: *mira sed et scaena testificata loquar.*)

613. ***signum erat in solio residens sub imagine Tulli*:** 'There was a statue in the likeness of Servius sitting on a ceremonial seat.' The first question that arises here is the nature of the statue. If we take the *signum sub imagine Tulli* to be an honorific ancestral image of Tullia's dead father, the previous king and the founder of the temple, and translate this concept into archaic terms, we will have a seated ancestral figure similar to those sometimes found in sixth-century Etruscan tombs. In Augustan Rome the archaic style resurfaced in statues of the gods which were created in this style to represent Roman *pietas* as a truly ancient attribute of the Roman race. Romans of Ovid's day had a fund of antiquarian knowledge, which became fragmentary in subsequent ages. The poet's day-to-day contact with ancestral Roman *imagines* made it easy for him to formulate, as an archaic version of this, a seated image of the sort which was still being used by families with Etruscan roots [see Flower (1996) 339–51].

There was a contemporary precedent for the statue of a previous (and murdered) ruler occupying a place of honour in a Roman temple: a statue of Divus Iulius stood beside those of Mars and Venus in the temple of Mars Ultor, implying the special relationship of the Gens Iulia with Mars Ultor, the founder of the race. Servius' *solium*, placed in the sanctuary of Servius' patron goddess, should be taken as a seat of honour (*OLD* s.v. 1) rather than a royal throne (*OLD* s.v. 2).

614. ***dicitur hoc oculis opposuisse manum***: 'this (statue) put its hand in front of its eyes.' A gesture of horror. The sight of the Vestal Ilia giving birth to Romulus induces the same reaction in Vesta's cult statue (*Fast.* 3. 46. Cf. 4. 178).

615–16. ***et vox audita est***: '*voltus abscondite nostros* | *ne natae videant ora nefanda meae!*': Ovid's description of Servius' paternal shame had a topical resonance in the decade following Augustus' banishment of his daughter Julia for her violation of marital *pudor* [see Herbert-Brown (1994) 145–56, Newlands (1995) 222–9].

617. ***veste data tegitur***: the exact nature of the garment (*veste*) is here not actually specified. Pliny (*Nat.* 8. 194) claims that Servius' royal toga was kept in Fortuna's temple. In dramatic terms Ovid's phrase, *superiniectis togis* (570) would add to the entertaining elegiac drama, for an easily divested outer garment would be the obvious way of silencing the voluble statue unless, however, the occasion was the women's festival of the *Matralia* on 11 June, when only *matronae*, all clad in *palla* and *stola*, should have been present. If this were taken literally, the only possible solution would be that Ovid is making a conscious reference to an earlier period when the toga was worn by both men and women (Var. Non. 867L).

619–20. ***'ore revelato qua primum luce patebit* | *Servius, haec positi prima pudoris erit'***: 'The day when Servius appears with his head unveiled will mark the abandonment of modesty.' Fortuna has the last word and alliteration enhances the oracular nature of her pronouncement. It is appropriate that this should relate to her sphere of influence in women's cult. *pudor* can be taken here in the sense of sexual propriety in marriage. The word is used twice by Virgil's Dido to refer to the virtue which she will violate (her loyalty, as *univira*, to Sychaeus) if she yields to her passion for Aeneas. The connection between Fortuna and Pudor is indicated by the existence of a sacellum to Pudicitia near to the round temple of Hercules Victor in the Forum Boarium which '*quidam Fortunae esse existimant*' (Liv. 10. 23.

3, Fest. 282L). The statue's covered head is a symbol of *pudor* which Fortuna herself encourages in married women. Although Ovid's aition requires that the statue be Servius, *pudor* would be more appropriately represented by a veiled cult statue of Fortuna herself.

623–4. ***sitque caput semper Romano tectus amictu | qui rex in nostra septimus urbe fuit*****:** the couplet begins and ends with a form of *esse* which forms a frame. This is a common device in Ovid's elegiac verse (cf. *Fast.* 5. 149–50, 6. 219–20, with *esse*, and more exotically, *Fast.* 2. 235–6, *una dies*, *P* 2. 9. 25, *Iuppiter*, *Rem.* 705–6, *Phoebus adest*). [See, too, Wills (1996) 431.] Servius is the seventh king of Rome if Titus Tatius, ruling jointly with Romulus, is counted as the second.

Servius' divine origin is revealed in the burning of Fortuna's temple

625–36: *When this temple burnt down, Mulciber rescued the statue of his son. For the father of Servius was Volcanus, his mother Ocresia, a lady of Corniculum. When Tanaquil ordered her to pour a libation in the fire, a male member appeared among the ashes. From this Servius was conceived. Flame playing in the child's hair was the sign of his paternity.*

625. ***arserat hoc templum: signo tamen ille pepercit | ignis*****:** the ancient cult statue survived the fire which destroyed the temple of Fortuna in 213 BC (Liv. 24. 47. 15, D.H. 4. 40. 7). The temple was restored in the following year (Liv. 25. 7. 6, D.H. 4. 40. 7). To describe Volcanus sparing the statue of his son, Ovid uses the euphemistic Mulciber, which refers to the god's ability to mould metal: *a moliendo ferro* (Fest. 129L).

627. ***pater Tulli Volcanus, Ocresia mater*****:** most of the Latin sources deriving from Fabius Pictor identify Servius' mother as a captive woman taken into the house of Tarquinius Priscus (Liv.1. 39. 5, D.H. 4. 1. 2). The story of Servius' conception from a phallus on the hearth (Liv. 1. 39. 5, D.H. 4. 2. 1–3) is told of at least three other founder figures: Romulus (Plut. *Rom.* 2), Caeculus, the founder of Praeneste (Virg. *Aen.* 7. 678), and Modius Fabidius, founder of Cures (D.H. 2. 48).

629–31. ***hanc secum Tanaquil | ... obsceni forma virilis*****:** Tanaquil's part in the story of the phallus on the hearth is closely echoed by Plut. (*Mor.* 323*b*). Verrius Flaccus was one of Plutarch's sources for his *Quaestiones Romanae*, which he wrote almost a century after Ovid's *Fasti*, and it is possible that Verrius was also Ovid's source for the story. Livy, on the other hand, introduces Servius Tullius for the first time as a sleeping child in the royal palace, whose head is miraculously engulfed in flames, a favourable portent which is immediately recognized and interpreted by Tanaquil (Liv. 1. 39. 1–2).

634. ***aut fuit aut visa est: sed fuit illa magis*****:** the sequence of thought, 'she saw—or thought she saw', is found in Ovid, *Her.* 18. 32: *aut videt aut acies nostra videre putat.* A parallel with the second half of the line is *Met.* 9. 782, where Telethusa realizes that the altar has actually been moved: *visa dea est movisse suas—et moverat—aras.* The purpose of the device is to create suspense by delaying the action through the disbelief of the onlooker.

635–6. ***signa dedit genitor... | ... inque comis flammeus arsit apex*****:** Servius' destiny is signalled by the flames which play harmlessly in his hair (Liv. 1. 39. 1–4, D.H. 4. 2. 4) where Tanaquil finds the sleeping child Servius with his hair ablaze. The portent is used by Virgil for Ascanius (*Aen.* 2. 682), Aeneas (*Aen.* 10. 270–2), and Augustus (*Aen.* 8. 680–1).

Coda: two Augustan monuments: Aedes Concordiae and Porticus Liviae, 637–648

[Flory (1984) 307–30, Purcell (1986) 78–105, Kellum (1990) 277–8, Edwards (1993) 165–71, Herbert-Brown (1994) 145–56, Newlands (1995) 226–9, (2000) 171–202, Barchiesi (1997*a*) 90–2, Littlewood (2002) 209–11.]

The Aedes Concordiae and Porticus Liviae

On 11 June—the year is not known—Livia dedicated a shrine to Concordia, probably in the form of an open-air altar, as a token of the harmony of her marriage to Augustus (*quam caro praestitit ipsa viro*, 638). It was an appropriate gesture on a day devoted to the cult of two female divinities who watched over the essential aspects of married life. Livia's altar to Concordia stood inside Augustus' Porticus Liviae, which was dedicated by Livia and her son Tiberius in early January 7 BC, possibly on the occasion of Tiberius' triumph (Dio 55. 8. 2), on the same day that Tiberius began to rebuild the Aedes Concordiae Augustae which was eventually dedicated in AD 10 on 16 January (*Fast.* 1. 637–50). Situated on the Esquiline, not far from Maecenas' gardens, the Porticus Liviae was adorned with antique paintings (Ovid *Ars* 1. 71) and provided a pleasant walkway. Ovid's decision to mention Livia's shrine to Concordia, celebrating the marital harmony of the imperial couple, would seem, at first glance, an entirely apposite finale to the *Matralia.* The public *exemplum* provided by Livia's demonstration of long-standing marital loyalty has a bearing on Fortuna's influence over newly married women, which is so flagrantly violated by Tullia in the second passage. Any celebration of Concordia in the Domus Augusta, as an artistic contrast to dynastic intrigues of Servius' house, was seemly, even of good augury, when quite plainly all Rome was aware that dynastic tensions had increased through the estrangement within the dynastic marriage of Tiberius and Julia. If Ovid's story of the palace intrigues which precipitate Servius' murder seems 'destabilizing', it should be remembered that his emphasis is on Tullia's unmitigated lack of *pietas* which is punished, publicly, by Fortuna herself.

Livia's Aedes Concordiae leads naturally into the encircling Porticus Liviae built by Augustus, who had prudently obliterated the embarrassing monument to Pollio's *luxuria* which he had inherited. On several occasions in *Fasti* 6 Ovid draws attention to points of similarity between Servius and Augustus. Like Augustus, Servius is a temple founder and *dux placidus* (582, cf. Augustus in line 92); he is marked out by the portent of flames in his hair (635–6, cf. Augustus, Virg. *Aen.* 8. 680–1); less auspiciously, he expresses the wish never to set eyes on his daughter again (615–6). In view of this, Ovid's comment, *sic agitur censura*, 'for this was a personal act of censorship', might seem to suggest Servius' most significant, but generically unapproachable, achievement: the organization of Rome's first census (Liv. 1. 42. 4–44), a military reorganization of Rome's *iuvenes* designed to furnish Rome with an effective hoplite army. Iuventas' allusion in the proem (83–4) to Romulus' earlier division of the populace into *iuniores* and *seniores* indicates its importance to the military theme of the book (see Introduction 5). Ovid's passage on the pipers at the *Quinquatrus* (637–92) also offers a tenuous link to 11 June through judicious censorship for the public good. As Augustus performs an unofficial act of censorship in demolishing an ostentatious private house to make space for a public portico, so on 14 June a censor, lenient this time, allows the flute-players to practise their art freely in Rome on their return from a voluntary exile caused, according to Livy, by his harsher colleague. In this case, the word *censura*, in its widest sense, engenders another web of indirect association over roughly 100 lines of *Fasti* 6: Augustus' censorship of *luxuria*, Servius' unmentioned military census, and the two censors of the *Quinquatrus*.

637–48: *Livia presented her husband with an altar dedicated to marital harmony. Posterity, learn from this! A vast dwelling occupied the space of the Porticus Liviae—a house the size of a walled city! It was razed, not because of a charge of treason, but because it was a monument to extravagant living. Although it was bequeathed to him, Caesar paid for the demolition and the building work. That is true censorship—when the censor bows to his own decree.*

637–8. ***te quoque magnifica, Concordia, dedicat aede | Livia*:** emphasis is given to the words *Livia* and (640) *porticus* by enjambement directly followed by a sense pause. The passage which began by summoning *bonae matres* to the *Matralia* (475) ends with an altar to marital fidelity, possibly on the very site of the temple founder's former palace.

639. ***disce tamen, veniens aetas*:** this somewhat portentous address to coming generations of Romans (*veniens aetas*) sets the moralizing tone of the next four couplets, which are devoted to Augustus' refusal to benefit from the tainted legacy of P. Vedius Pollio, an *eques* who had bequeathed his *inmensae domus* (640) to his old friend. Through his ostentatious extravagance and notorious cruelty (D.S. 54. 23. 1–4) Pollio's friendship may have become an embarrassment to Augustus long before the former's death in 15 BC; his lifestyle was incompatible with a regime which supported the values of frugality. Pollio's will had indicated that a public monument should be built in his name (D.S. 54. 23. 6), and the Porticus Liviae might be said to represent the spirit of the will. It was in keeping with the policy of Augustus that his Porticus should be dedicated by representatives of the ruling house, Livia and Tiberius. [See R. Syme, 'Who Was Vedius Pollio?', *JRS* 51 (1961) 22–30, Herbert-Brown (1994) 151–3, Newlands (2002) 231–43.]

639–40. ***ubi Livia nunc est | porticus, immensae tecta fuere domus*****:** the implied contrast between the public *porticus* and the private *domus* is accentuated by the word order in the pentameter, which is framed by *porticus* and *domus*, with *immensae*, defining *domus*, in a dominant central position at the end of the first half of the line, and *porticus* isolated from the rest of the line by its enjambement.

641–2. ***urbis opus domus una fuit spatiumque tenebat | quo brevius muris oppida multa tenent*****:** this striking description of Pollio's house, 'more extensive than many walled cities', furnished, like *adscitas dapes* (172), another popular focus for Roman *luxuria* [see Edwards (1993) 137–72]. The hubristic immensity of the mansion which is implied by the wording of Ovid's description, *urbis opus*, has been compared to Virgil's description of the monstrous ship *Chimaera*, Virg. *Aen.* 5. 118–19 [see Newlands (2002) 237–43]. The end-of-line repetition, *tenebat* . . . *tenent*, is a form of repetition which Ovid uses extensively in hexametric and elegiac poetry (cf. *Fast.* 2. 137–8, *habebas* . . . *habet*, 3. 163–4, *diebus* . . . *die*, 4. 593–4, *tulissem* . . . *tuli*, 6. 56–7, *honor* . . . *honorem*). [See Wills (1996) 422–3.]

643. ***haec aequata solo est, nullo sub crimine regni*****:** 'through no conviction of treason.' Unlike M. Manlius Capitolinus (see line 187), whose house on the Capitol was razed after he was condemned to death in 384 BC for inciting the plebs to rebellion (Liv. 6. 11.7), Pollio's crime appears to be *luxuria* in the opulence of his house. Ovid seems to point to the hubris which ultimately destroyed both the reputation of the Republican hero and the monument to the successful equestrian's wealth.

645–6. ***sustinuit tantas operum subvertere moles | totque suas heres perdere Caesar opes*****:** 'His heir, Caesar, bore the cost of demolishing such a vast edifice and the loss of so much wealth.' Ovid seems to present this naive assessment of Augustus' use of his legacy with tongue in cheek. The legacy of a prime area of urban real estate provided Augustus with a welcome opportunity to erect another dynastic monument which would offer to the people of Rome a generous civic amenity. A similar example is the Flavians' appropriation of Nero's Domus Aurea and its grounds to provide Baths and the Colosseum, contrasting their public spirit with the unwholesome *luxuria* of the last of the Julio-Claudian dynasty. Augustus' comparatively modest house on the Palatine was surrounded by monuments significant to his own *imperium*: the temples of Apollo, Cybele, and Victory and the *casa Romuli.* The Esquiline residence was entirely superfluous to his needs as well as being totally out of keeping with his political ideology; however, he was happy enough to use the country villa which he inherited from Vedius Pollio at Pausilypon.

647–8. ***sic agitur censura, et sic exempla parantur***: *exempla* may include both Livia and Augustus, for by her marital fidelity Livia sets an example to Roman women who gather to celebrate the *Matralia.* However, *censura* can only refer to Augustus who has, like Servius the original temple founder, provided a building for the public good. Augustus has displayed the virtue of a model censor in obliterating the unwholesome monument to Pollio's *luxuria.* This type of *censura* would seem to have little to do with Servius' census, which was a military reorganization aimed at providing the Roman state with a model army. However, thematic correspondence would contribute to the structural architecture of Ovid's *Fasti.* I would suggest that Ovid selected the Porticus Liviae as the central theme of his coda because it drew together a number of themes which look back to the *Matralia* but also forward to the *Quinquatrus.* Augustus' *censura* points forward to the *Quinquatrus* on 13 June, where Ovid relates how Rome's flute-players demonstrate against the edict of a harsh censor, Appius Claudius Caecus, by going into voluntary exile at Tibur, but, brought back by a trick, are then mollified by the actions of Appius' more lenient colleague.

648. ***cum iudex, alios quod monet, ipse facit***: the reading of *U*, *iudex*, preferred by Bömer, is convincing because Ovid focuses here on the action of a censor, which was to pass judgement on extravagance. However, *vindex*, which is the reading of several less important mss and the choice of Merkel and *AWC*, has the sense of correcting a social injustice (*OLD* s.v. 3), a fair description of Augustus demolishing Pollio's mansion to create the Porticus Liviae for public enjoyment.

C PR. EID. IUN. N, 649–650

12 June has no distinguishing mark. On the Ides a temple was dedicated to Unconquered Jupiter.

649. ***nulla nota est veniente die quam dicere possis***: unlike the previous day, which marked the *Matralia*, 12 June, is unmarked on the calendar (cf. *Fast.* 3. 42, 6. 206). Although no deity or anniversary was commemorated, the day is *feriatus* because sacrifices must be made on the days preceding the Ides, which consequently were designated N.

650. ***Idibus Invicto sunt data templa Iovi***: Richardson (227) points out that Ovid's Iuppiter Invictus here is not the same as Jupiter Victor on the Quirinal to whom Q. Fabius Rullianus vowed a temple before the Battle of Sentinum (Liv. 10. 29. 14). Since the Ides of every month were sacred to Jupiter, June's, at the peak of the fighting season, would have been an appropriate occasion for a dedication in honour of Unconquered Jove. There seems to be no record of a temple dedicated on 13 June, although both the Republican *Fasti Tusculani* and the Augustan *Fasti Venusini* annotate 13 June with the words N *Feriae Iovi.* 13 April, the *natalis* or dedication day of both the Aedes Iovis Libertatis on the Aventine and Rullianus' temple to Iuppiter Victor, is damaged in the *Fasti Praenestini* but appears as NP *Iovi Victori* in the Republican *Fasti Antiates Maiores*, and this is confirmed by Ovid, *Fast.* 4. 621–2. Ovid inexplicably confuses the Aedes Iovis Libertatis with the Atrium Libertatis, which was the archive of the censors in the Forum and not a religious building at all [see Richardson (1992) 221 and Fantham's (1998) note on lines 623–4]. The most illustrious Ides were probably 13 September, the *natalis* of the Capitoline temple of Iuppiter Optimus Maximus.

D EID. IUN. NP, *QUINQUATRUS MINUSCULAE*, 651–710

[On politics and *Ludi*, see Gruen (1990) 188–221, Wiseman (1994) 68–85, Oakley (1997) 40–62, *BNP* 1. 66–8, 99–101. On the censors in

Livy's account, see R. E. A. Palmer, 'The Censors of 312 BC and the State Religion', *Historia* 14 (1965) 293–324, Bruce MacBain, 'Appius Claudius Caecus and the Via Appia', *CQ* 30 (1980) 356–72. See also Levene (1993) 230–2, Wiseman (1994) 23–36, Pasco-Pranger (2002) 251–5, Habinek (2005) 36–44.]

Minerva tells of a calamity which drove the Roman pipers into voluntary exile at Tibur

1. *The* Quinquatrus Minusculae

It is uncertain whether the *natalis* of the Aedes Minervae on the Aventine was on 13 or 19 June. Augustus claims to have rebuilt the three Aventine temples of Minerva, Jupiter Libertas, and Juno Regina, which he groups together (*RG* 19) as though in response to the Capitoline triad. The temple of Minerva was already in existence during the Second Punic War, when a portent was expiated or, more probably, M. Livius Salinator's victory at the River Metaurus celebrated by a hymn, composed by Livius Andronicus, which a choir is said to have rehearsed in the temple of Jupiter Stator in 207 BC. After the public performance this *carmen* was ceremonially attributed to Livius by the guild in Minerva's Aventine temple, which was the headquarters of the guilds of writers and actors, and may have included professional *tibicines* (Fest. 446–8L).

Minerva's principal festival was the five-day *Quinquatrus Maiores* beginning on 19 March, which opened the fighting season and honoured Minerva in her capacity as *bellica dea* (Ovid *Fast.* 3. 809–49). The first day was thought to be the *natalis* of the goddess' Aventine temple (*Fasti Praenestini*, Degrassi 427). Four more days were given over to *Ludi* in the mistaken belief that the word *Quinquatrus* meant 'five day' rather than 'the fifth day (after the Ides)' (Var. *L* 6. 14, Fest. 304, 306L). The ceremony of the Purification of the Trumpets of War, the *Tubilustrum*, on 23 March coincided with the last day of Minerva's festival (*Fast.* 3. 849–50). Ovid humorously highlights Minerva's contiguity with Mars, the patron of the month, in his tale of the passion of one *armifer* for another (681–3). The *Quinquatrus Minusculae* on 13 June honoured Minerva in her capacity as the patron goddess of craftsmen; it was celebrated by those who claimed her as a patron of their art, including doctors, schoolmasters, and musicians as well as artisans and military technicians.

2. *Appius Claudius Caecus and the pipers' walk-out to Tibur*

By the fourth century BC when Ovid's story takes place, professional pipers, who had brought their art from Etruria, were regularly hired to perform in religious ceremonies, particularly during sacrifices, at *Ludi Scaenici*, and private funerals (Liv. 7. 2. Cf. Ovid, *Ars* 1. 111). These three types of performance are listed twice by Ovid (*Fast.* 6. 659–60, 667–8). Although Ovid's version of the story does not correspond in every detail to that of Livy, an essential point of both versions is that unfair restrictions were imposed on the *tibicines*, who expressed their dissatisfaction by staging a 'walk-out' to neighbouring Tibur. The story of the musicians' strike in 312 BC is told by Livy (9. 30. 5–10), Valerius Maximus (2. 5. 4), and Plutarch (*Quaest. Rom.* 55) as well as by Ovid. It is made clear by all four writers that the disagreement between the flute-players and the Roman authorities was a religious matter. Livy claims that this is the only reason why he records the story: *ad religionem visa esse pertinere* (cf. Val. Max. 2.5.4, *senatus ... a Tiburtibus petiit ut eos ... Romanis templis restituerent*). Livy makes the censors directly responsible for the musicians' action, by forbidding them to participate in a banquet at the temple of Jupiter (*prohibiti ... erant in aede Iovis vesci*, Liv. 9. 30. 5). A solemn banquet, *Epulum Iovis*, was held twice annually, in the course of the *Ludi Romani* and *Ludi Plebeii*, both of which honoured Jupiter Optimus Maximus. The banquet followed a ceremonial sacrifice and *Ludi Scaenici*, both accompanied by *tibicines*, who were then allowed to join in the banquet with the *sodales*, the priesthood, in the evening. Strictly speaking, dining rights were exclusive and the *ius publice epulandi* was restricted to senators, as they were at the *Ludi Megalenses*, *Ludi Ceriales*, and *Feriae Latinae*. The character and motives of Appius Claudius Caecus emerge rather ambiguously from ancient sources, which has led to variance among modern historians. Appius' uncompromising patrician views in religious matters led him to oppose the *Lex Ogulnia*, which opened the priesthood to plebeians in 300 BC. As censor in 312 BC he reorganized the cult of Hercules at the Ara Maxima so that the rites were in future performed by public slaves instead of by the Potitii and Pinarii (Liv. 9. 29. 9. Cf. Virg. *Aen.* 8. 269–70). If, in the same year, Appius Claudius banned the *tibicines* from the *Epulum Iovis*, he would seem to have been acting in character both in interfering in religious matters and in reinforcing restrictions limiting the participants. In 296 BC he vowed a temple to Bellona in Rome (see note on line 201) and another in Forum Appii, which he had founded on the route of his new aqueduct.

Appius' censorship in 312 BC was supposedly marred by the inclusion of large numbers of the urban proletariat, a 'populist' move which caused the resignation of his more conservative colleague C. Plautius (Liv. 9. 29. 7: *ob infamem atque invidiosam senatus lectionem.* For an alternative version, see D.S. 20. 36. 1–6). MacBain suggests that this influx into the electoral roll represented Appius' newly acquired *clientela* from the communities of Campania along the 132 miles of his new aqueduct. In Ovid's version of the story, Plautius, who may have been C. Plautius Venox, who held the office of censor in the same year as Appius Claudius Caecus, appears to be the more lenient of the two censors. The intricacies of the historical situation and conflicting evidence concerning the character of Appius Claudius Caecus should not divert us from the essential point of the story. The importance of the *tibicines* in Roman religion and their dispute over the formalities of religious ritual are appropriate material for Ovid's *Fasti.* For the sake of a more entertaining story, Ovid focuses not on the political motives of Appius Claudius, but on a relatively trivial aition, the costume of the *tibicines* at the *Quinquatrus.* In ancient religious ritual clothing sometimes played a symbolic role. A similar example is *Fasti* 2. 303–58, where Ovid answers the question why the Luperci run naked with a *fabula plena ioci* (304), embedded in which tale is the ritual transvestism of Hercules and Omphale. The masks and *stola* worn by the *tibicines* evoke a carnival atmosphere, but there is also a hint of disguise and transvestism which would have more ancient roots than the walk-out described by Ovid and Livy.

3. *Flute-playing in Roman religious ritual*

Numa, traditionally the founder of Roman religion, was also considered to be the founder of Roman music (Cic. *de Orat.* 3. 197, Plut. *Num.* 17. 3, *Quaest. Rom.* 55), which before the fourth century BC was considered an honourable pursuit for freeborn Roman youth. Under the Tarquin dynasty young Roman patricians were chosen to provide music for the *Ludi Romani*, which corresponds to Horace's description of early Roman religious festivals where there is no suggestion that the *tibicines* are not freeborn Romans (Hor. *AP.* 202–19). Cicero, quoting Cato's *Origines* and the Twelve Tables, describes choral music accompanied by *tibia* at aristocratic banquets and religious festivals (Cic. *Tusc.* 4. 3–4. Cf. 1. 3) [see Zorzetti (1991) 311–29, (1990) 289–307]. The belief that the gods should be honoured by *Ludi* organized solely by patricians continued until the fourth century. In 366 BC, the first year in which a plebeian was elected to the consulate, the curule aedileship was created as a patrician office so that the patricians might continue to be in charge of musical performances at the Roman religious festivals (Cic. *Agr.* 2. 93).

According to Livy's famous digression on the origin of the *Ludi Scaenici*, it was during the years following the plague and *lectisternium* in 364 BC that the *Ludi Scaenici* developed out of solemn Etruscan dances performed by masked dancers accompanied by *tibicines* to appease the gods (Liv. 7. 2. 1–13). These musicians, first Etruscan and later Roman, were always paid professionals. By 311 BC, when Ovid's tale takes place, there were three different *Ludi* (*Megalenses*, *Romani*, and *Plebeii*). The organization of the *Ludi* was divided between two curule and two plebeian aediles, who were held responsible for the religious success of the occasion (cf. Cic. *Ver.* 2. 5. 14). Not only aediles, mentioned in Ovid's account (663), but also censors (mentioned by Livy) had the job of engaging *tibicines.* Augustus later reintroduced into civic religion the religious formalities surrounding the solemn act of enumerating the citizen body (*RG* 8): the censors began by taking the auspices (Var. *L* 6. 86–7) and, on completion of the census, performed a *lustratio* followed by the sacrifice of the *suovetaurilia* (pig, sheep, and bull); neither of these two religious rituals could be properly performed without *tibicines.*

651–68: *Assist me, Minerva. I must describe the* Lesser Quinquatrus. *Why do the pipers roam the city wearing masks and women's dress? The goddess laid aside her spear and said, 'The flute was heard in the temples, at religious plays and funerals. The pipers were well satisfied with work and fee. Then came a* *terrible blow and, in addition, their numbers were restricted at funerals. They fled to Tibur and were greatly missed.'*

651. ***Quinquatrus iubeor narrare minores*****:** Ovid replaces the metrically problematic *minusculae* with *minores.* Similarly he indicates by his choice of words, *Parilia poscor*, that he is writing in response to a patron's request or approval (*Fast.* 4. 721. Cf. Virg. *G* 3. 41, *haud mollia iussa*, Prop. 3. 9. 52, *sub tua iussa*). In this instance Ovid's direction comes from the Roman calendar itself.

652. ***nunc ades o! coeptis, flava Minerva, meis*****:** Ovid uses the hymnic invocation *ades* several times (cf. *Fast.* 1. 67, 69, 3. 2, 5. 183). Here, as in 4. 192, *adesse*, followed by a dative, means 'support' (*OLD* s.v. 13*b*). As Ovid's informant about her festival, Minerva provides a link between the two aitia of the *Quinquatrus*, the reason for the long dress (*stola*) and masks (*personae*) worn by the flute-players, and secondly, Minerva's invention of the flute and the story of Marsyas, the first artiste.

653–4. ***'cur vagus incedit tota tibicen in urbe? | quid sibi personae, quid stola longa volunt?'*****:** The idiom (*sibi*) *velle*, meaning 'signify' (*OLD* s.v. 17), appears earlier: *Pistoris quid velit ara Iovis?* (*Fast.* 6. 350). Ovid asks a double question which concerns, first, the pipers' apparently desultory progress through the city (*vagus incedit*, 653), and secondly, their costume at the *Quinquatrus.* Livy, who does not comment on the nature of their costume, mentions that on their return to Rome the flute-players were allowed to wander freely round the city, in costume, for the period (*triduum*) of the *Quinquatrus*: *vagarentur per urbem* (Liv. 9. 30. 10. Cf. Val. Max. 2. 5. 4, Plut. *Quaest. Rom.* 55).

655. ***sic ego. sic posita Tritonia cuspide dixit*****:** Minerva's weaponry surrounds her heroic epithet Tritonia, which belongs to Minerva's warlike role in epic (cf. Virg. *Aen.* 2. 615, 5. 704, 11. 483, Ovid, *Met.* 2. 783). The pursuit of war and poetry are incompatible, and she puts down her lance before she answers the poet. Similarly Ovid suggests that Mars disarm before he offers a suitably elegiac contribution to his month (*Fast.* 3. 171). [See Wills (1996) 118–19.]

656. ***possim utinam doctae verba referre deae!*****:** Ovid usually signals the individuality of his informants with a reference to their salient characteristics. Since Minerva is, like Erato (4. 195), *docta*, the poet suggests that he cannot aspire to emulate her scholarly turn of phrase.

657–8. '*temporibus veterum tibicinis usus avorum* | *magnus*': 'In the days of our ancestors there was a great deal of flute-playing.' What period did Ovid consider to be *temporibus veterum avorum*? It is clear from line 661 that he is referring to a time when flute-playing for religious festivals and funerals was undertaken by paid professionals, to a time before the exodus of the flute-players, which Livy sets in 311 BC. The *tibia* was held in great honour (*in magno semper honore*, 658) because of its close associations with religious ritual (667–8, 659–60). Piping was an essential accompaniment to the Roman ritual of sacrifice, as important as the words of the prayers; if the piper hesitated or fell silent, a sacrifice or ritual had to be repeated (Cic. *Dom.* 48. 125, *Har.* 11. 23).

659–60. '*cantabat fanis, cantabat tibia ludis,* | *cantabat maestis tibia funeribus*': the almost entirely spondaic hexameter, combined with the triple anaphora *cantabat*... *cantabat*... *cantabat*, seems to emulate the dirge-like sound of the flute. Ovid sums up the civic duties of the Roman *tibicines* who played at religious ceremonies (*fanis*), at *Ludi Scaenici*, and at funerals (*funeribus*), which were regarded as religious ritual purification from the pollution caused by death. Funerary reliefs suggest that *tibicines* played beside the bier during the lying-in-state and then as they accompanied the procession of mourners and *imagines* to the place of burial or cremation (cf. Ovid *Tr.* 5. 1. 48: *tibia funeribus convenit ista meis*).

661. '*dulcis erat mercede labor*': Ovid sums up the attitude of a professional performer: 'the task was (made) agreeable by the fee.'

661–2. '*tempusque secutum* | *quod subito gratae frangeret artis opus*': 'The subsequent period inflicted, abruptly, a crushing blow on the practice of a delightful art.' *subito* suggests the sudden and unexpected promulgation of the edict excluding them from the sacrificial banquets at the temple of Jupiter. The flute-players responded with strike action to what they clearly perceived as an indignity.

663. '*adde, quod aedilis pompam qui funeris irent* | *artifices solos iusserat esse decem*': it was laid down in the Twelve Tables that only

Fig. 15 Marble relief from a late Republican grave monument from Amiternum, Museo Aquila. The depicts a Roman funeral procession. In the centre, propped on her elbow, is a woman on the bier preceded by hired mourners and seven musicians, including four pipers with diauloi. The eighth figure, touching the bier, is the *dissignator* or funeral director. Family mourners, including children, follow. (Photograph courtesy of D.A.I. Rome, Inst. Neg. 1961. 3.)

ten flute-players should accompany a Roman funeral cortège (Tab. X. 3 in Cic. *Leg.* 2. 23. 59). Responsible for enforcing this regulation was an aedile, whose job it was to organize the music for civic processions. After saying in the previous couplet that the flute-players suffered a sudden misfortune (662) without defining the calamity, Ovid continues: *adde, quod aedilis*, 'and, in addition, the aedile . . .'. The wording suggests that the aedile's insistence on the legal quota of pipers at the funeral processions followed some other, previously mentioned, act of injustice. The most convenient and sensible solution is to accept Pighi's conjecture, supported by Frazer and Bömer, that there is a lacuna after line 662. A reduction of the numbers of *tibicines* at funerals, particularly to the recognized legal limit, would seem an inadequate reason for the walk-out unless this was compounded with another, more serious, restriction: that, as Livy explains, the *tibicines* had been excluded from the honour of participation in the *Epulum Iovis.*

665–6. '*exilio . . . exilium*': the anaphora and noun polyptoton, *exilio . . . exilium*, at the beginning of both lines in this couplet, no less than the pointed observation in the pentameter, *exilium quodam tempore Tibur erat* (666), suggest that the couplet may have been reworked in Tomis. In *P* 1. 8. 81–2 Ovid again refers to Tibur as a place chosen for exile from Rome in ancient times. Ovid's propensity for adding pointed comments on the subject of exile is apparent in his revised *Fasti* 1. 481–2, where Carmentis tells Evander: *nec te tua culpa fugavit | sed deus; offenso pulsus es urbe deo* (cf. 5. 653, 1. 540, *felix exilium cui locus ille fuit*, and 4. 79–82, where the poet addresses Germanicus directly on the wretchedness of the exile's lot). Whilst Ovid did not revise his *Fasti* comprehensively beyond Book 1, he appears to have tweaked almost every passage which contained some allusion to exile.

667. '*quaeritur . . . quaeritur*': the anaphoric repetition balances *cantabat . . . cantabat* in line 659. In contrast, however, the hexameter of this matching couplet is predominantly dactylic. These two hexameters describe the *tibicines* performing at religious festivals. While *scaena* in line 667 corresponds to *ludis* in line 659, both referring to the *Ludi Scaenici, aris* (667) corresponds to *fanis* (659) and refers to piping before and during the performance of a ritual sacrifice (cf. Cic. *Agr.* 2. 93).

668. '*nenia nulla*': this alliterative phrase occurs in a couplet already distinguished by the alliteration of *qu . . . c . . . c . . . qu* in the hexameter. *nenia* signified a lament or dirge to be sung with flute accompaniment, which would glorify the deeds and ancestry of the deceased (cf. Hor. *Carm.* 2. 1. 38, 20.21). According to Varro (Non. 93L, 212L), *neniae* were best sung by a woman. Both pentameters, 660 and 668, which describe the *tibicines* playing at funerals, are distinguished by slow spondees in the first half of the line: *ducit supremos* (668), *cantabat maestos* (660). [See Habinek (2005) 233–49.]

The pipers are tricked into returning to Rome

669–84: *A certain freedman, respected in the town of Tibur, invited the pipers to a country feast. When night fell, the musicians were the worse for wine. Then came a message, prearranged: 'Break up the party! Your old master's here!' The host at once ordered the befuddled pipers to depart. They were tossed into a wicker farm cart, where wine and motion kept them sleeping all the way to Rome.*

669–70. *'servierat quidam quantolibet ordine dignus | Tibure, sed longo tempore liber erat'*: in Livy's version of this story civic religion has come to a standstill in Rome without the *tibicines* and the Roman senate negotiates their immediate return with the Tiburtine authorities. A plot is quickly hatched to invite the unsuspecting pipers to perform at a country party, with the express intention that they should be plied with wine until they are incapable of resisting being thrust into a nearby waggon. Ovid's witty vignette of the parvenu freedman is his own invention, and we should assume that every detail in this couplet is important to Ovid's social comedy. Once a slave (*servierat*, 670), Ovid's freedman has been free for a long time (*longo tempore*, 671), enabling him to accrue a measure of respect in the community so that he is now worthy to be included in any level of Tiburtine society (*quantolibet ordine dignus*, 670). That an entire distich separates the framing words *servierat* and *liber erat* suggests years of working his way upwards. With the dramatic flair of an accomplished storyteller, Ovid omits to say whether the town councillors of Tibur revealed their plot openly to the freedman or simply highjacked his party for their own purposes, deviously manoeuvring the socially self-conscious freedman into engaging a band of classy Roman pipers.

671–2. *'rure dapes parat ille suo, turbamque canoram | convocat: ad festas convenit illa dapes'*: the freedman hosts the party at his own country estate and invites the Roman *tibicines* for the purpose of providing music, which was a regular part of country festivals (Virg. *G* 1. 349–50, Hor. *Carm.* 3. 18. 15, Tib. 2. 1. 51–6, 2. 5. 87, Ovid *Am.* 3. 10. 47, *Ars* 1. 111–12). The ostensibly simple paratactic narrative is enhanced by using the keyword *dapes* to frame the distich, and by the symmetrical allusion to the main characters in the drama as *ille* (the host) and *illa* (the musicians). *turba* signifies a large group with common interests, soldiers, philosophers, lovers, satyrs (*OLD* s.v. 5*a*), which may be unified by an appropriate adjective such as *canora*. In Book 2 the throng of relatives going to the Caristia party are described as *turba propinqua* (*Fast.* 2. 618. Cf Ovid *Her.* 5. 135–6, *Fast.* 4. 142, *satyri . . . turba proterva*).

673. '*vinis oculique animique natabant*': 'under the influence of wine, they were unable to focus their eyes or their minds.' *natare* is regularly used with *oculi* to indicate an inability to maintain a steady gaze (*OLD* s.v. 4*b*). Ovid extends the metaphor to include the concentration (*animi*) of the pipers.

674. '*praecomposito nuntius ore*': 'a messenger with a prearranged message.' The artifice is emphasized by the double prefix of *prae-com-posito.* But who, in Ovid's account, was party to the plot? The anecdote gains in humour if the freedman had, in all innocence, welcomed the Roman *tibicines* to oblige the dignitaries of Tibur, and was then thrown into a panic at the prospect of his former master finding him hosting a gathering where even the paid musicians were too intoxicated to perform. Surely the message, 'Your former master is approaching', could only have been devised by Rome's Tiburtine accomplices, who knew full well that this was a sure way to startle the upwardly mobile freedman into getting rid of his disreputable guests with all speed. It was they who had arranged that a farm cart should be standing conveniently on hand with directions to carry the pipers back to Rome.

675. '*quid cessas convivia solvere*': 'Quick, break up the party . . . !' A loose translation is appropriate. The colloquial idiom *quid cessas* followed by an infinitive, which means, literally, 'Why do you hesitate to . . . ?' occurs frequently in Roman comedy and in humorous passages of Cicero's speeches (*OLD* s.v. 3).

676. '*auctor vindictae nam venit ecce tuae*': 'for, look! the man who freed you is coming!' The word *vindicta* described the official act of freeing a slave, *vindictam imponere.* The ceremony required the presence of the slave himself, his owner, and a magistrate who pronounced the formula: *hunc ego hominum liberum esse aio ex iure Quiritium.*

677–8. *'convivae valido titubantia vino | membra movent, dubii stantque labantque pedes'*: 'under the influence of strong wine, the guests stagger, pause unsteadily and lurch about.' The pipers' drunken state is crucial to the story, and Ovid devotes a further distich (677–8) to describing their tottering steps (*titubantia... membra, labunt pedes*), their inability to concentrate (*dubii... morantes*), and the strength of the wine (*valido... vino*). The description is enhanced by alliteration and the staccato and almost onomatopoeic assonance of *stantque labantque.*

679–80. *'at dominus "discedite" ait, plaustroque morantes | sustulit'*: 'What of the master? "Get moving!" he yells and bundles the stragglers into the cart.' Ovid enhances the confusion of the drama in a disjointed hexameter with an unusual elision across the main caesura which produces a striking coincidence of accent and ictus in the third foot, at the key word *discedite* (cf. *Fast.* 5. 247, and see Platnauer 84). The musicians offer little resistance (*morantes*) as they are heaved into the waggon. The enjambement of *sustulit* effects a slight pause before the reader's attention is directed to a description of the waggon. At greater length Livy explains that they were already asleep and could therefore be tossed in oblivious: *vino... oneratos sopiunt atque ita in plaustra somno vinctos coniciunt* (Liv. 9. 30. 9).

680. *'in plaustro scirpea lata fuit'*: 'in the waggon was a spacious compartment woven out of rushes.' This rural cart has sides made of interwoven reeds, which prevented the flute-players from seeing where they were going as it became light.

683. *'iamque per Esquilias Romanam intraverat urbem'*: approaching Rome from Tibur, the pipers entered the city through the Porta Esquilina in the Servian Wall before descending, *per Esquilias*, the Clivus Suburanus and the Argiletum into the Forum. Their dawn arrival in the Forum is described in a succinct, alliterative pentameter: *et mane in medio plaustra fuere foro* (684).

Why the pipers disguise themselves on the *Quinquatrus*

685–92: *To mislead the senate Plautius ordered the pipers to conceal their identity by wearing masks and, by putting on women's robes, to increase their* *numbers by including female pipers. They agreed and on the Ides of June they are allowed to wear this novel costume and sing ribald ditties.*

685. *Plautius*: although the mss without exception have the reading *callidus* or *Claudius*, *AWC* subscribes to the conjecture *Plautius*, supported by Merkel (1841) and Pighi. In Livy's account, C. Plautius Venox appears to have been the less intransigent censor. It is possible that Ovid may have written Claudius; the verb *imperat* (686) suits the personality accredited to Appius Claudius Caecus, and this would fit Livy's claim that Plautius had resigned from the censorship because he disagreed with Claudius' over-inclusive census (Liv. 9. 29. 7–8). The two censors must have been in agreement over the current impasse which Livy describes, and therefore connived with the senate at the enforced repatriation of the *tibicines*.

685–6. *'ut posset specie numeroque senatum | fallere, personis imperat ora tegi'*: Plautius gives two different reasons for the two forms of disguise that he suggests. The first is that the flute-players are to cover their faces with masks (*personis*), 'to deceive the senate in respect to their appearance and their number'. The masks achieve the first objective, which is to avoid recognition, and possibly unfair discrimination against the ringleaders. Frazer (1929: 4. 306) cites numismatic evidence to suggest that the flute-players wore Gorgon masks, which suggests that their function at Minerva's festival was partly apotropaic, like the *verba iocosa* (692). For the same reason, grotesque faces of gorgons and *sileni* were traditional subjects for terracotta antefixes in temples across Central Italy [see D. Wiles (1991), *The Masks of Menander: Sign and Meaning in Greek and Roman Performance* (Cambridge), 131–49]. The second form of disguise, the long robes (*longis vestibus*, 698), allow them to include flute-players of both genders; this will make it impossible to tell which of this large number of musicians belonged to the group who left for Tibur.

687. *'admiscetque alios'*: *admiscere* implies the inclusion of a different class of performer. They all wear long dresses for the express purpose of making it unclear which are male and which female performers (*ut hunc tibicina coetum | augeat*, 687–8). Female flute-players are found in Roman literature (Plaut. *Aul.* 332, Hor. *Epist.* 1.

14. 25). Their role was to enliven private parties, and possibly play for funerals, but not to perform at sacrifices or be included in the ensuing sacrificial banquet.

689. *'sic reduces bene posse tegi'*: a continuation, in reported speech, of what Plautius said to the flute-players: 'in this way those who have returned can be effectively disguised.'

689–90. *'ne forte notentur | contra collegae iussa venire sui'*: 'in order that they should not run the risk of being penalized for having opposed the orders of his colleague.' The words *collegae iussa* refer to the working conditions with which the striking pipers refuse to comply. The reading of *M*, *collegae iussa*, can only refer to the orders of Plautius' colleague, Appius Claudius Caecus. This reading has the support of Merkel (1841). The alternative is *collegi* in *U* and *G*, which is the choice of *AWC*. If this means *collegii tibicinorum*, it is suggested that, in going to Tibur, the pipers contravened a decision of their own guild. In this case the rest of the guild stayed in Rome and therefore would not need the errant guildsmen to be brought back so urgently. Alternatively, *collegium* could mean 'the collegiate office of two censors' (*OLD* s.v. 4) and *collegii iussa* orders issued jointly by Plautius and Claudius, which would be impossible if Plautius had already resigned from the censorship.

691. *'cultuque novo licet Idibus uti'*: the *tibicines* were allowed to wear their new costume, masks and women's robes, only on the Ides of June. This meant that all Roman *tibicines*, male and female, could celebrate Minerva's festival together.

692. *'et canere ad veteres verba iocosa modos'*: like the *Floralia* (Ovid, *Fast.* 5. 183–378), the *Quinquatrus* was a festival on which *verba iocosa* might be included in old songs (*ad veteres modos*) with impunity; salty jests, part of *Ludi Scaenici* from their origins (Liv. 7. 2. 3–3. 2), were considered apotropaic.

A MIME: MINERVA AND MARSYAS: THE INVENTION OF PIPING, 693–710

[J. D. Small, *Cacus and Marsyas* (Princeton, 1982), Wiseman (1994) 68–85, Newlands (1995) 197–200, Barchiesi (1997*a*) 89–92.]

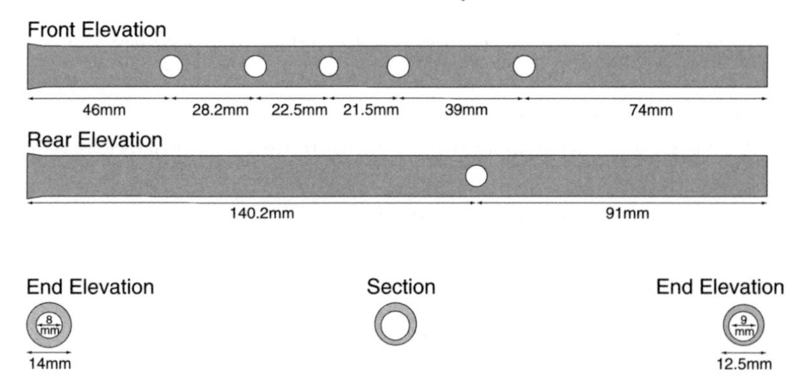

Fig. 16 Drawing of a diaulos taken from the Greek-Etruscan shipwreck in 580 BC near the island of Giglio off Etruria. In addition to a cargo of olives, wine, and Corinthian *aryballoi*, the ship was carrying banqueting equipment including silverware and pipes made of boxwood and ivory and a boxwood writing-tablet, testifying to an aristocratic lifestyle which had spread to Rome at the time when the archaic temple of the Forum Boarium was being redecorated. (I am indebted to Mensun Bound, St Peter's College, Oxford, for lending me a plan of the flutes with technical specifications reproduced here in graphic form by Julian Littlewood.)

Minerva invents the *tibia* which causes the downfall of Marsyas

A rustic mime

Ovid's story of 'The Invention of the Flute' has the dramatic potential for a mime for Minerva's festival. The scene is set in rustic surroundings and scenes featuring Minerva, Marsyas, and Apollo might be interspersed by choruses of dancing nymphs or satyrs. Like the story of the exodus of the flute-players, Marsyas also had associations with political power-struggles in the fourth century. According to Servius (on Virg. *Aen.* 3. 20, 4. 57), statues of Marsyas, a companion of Liber, were erected in other cities as an indication of civic liberty. Roman poets liked to associate with the nearby praetor's tribunal a statue of Marsyas which was believed to have been set up in the Forum by Cn.

Marcius Rutilius during his censorship (294 BC), possibly to commemorate his election, as one of the first plebeians, to the college of augurs, for Marsyas was said to be the inventor of augury (Hor. *Serm.* 1. 6. 120, Juv. 1. 128, Mart. 2. 64. 8), or simply to honour the mythological founder of the Gens Marcia, which accounts for Marsyas' depiction on the coins of L. Marcius Censorinus (from *c.*82 BC) with a female figure which may have represented Minerva. In Augustan times Marsyas represented another aspect of the victory of Apollo, and for this reason a painting of Marsyas Bound, possibly based on Zeuxis' famous original, was placed in the Aedes Concordiae Augustae [see Kellum (1990) 81–2].

693–710: *Asked why the Quinquatrus was so named, Minerva said, 'That is the name of my March festival. The pipers are associated with another of my inventions. I was the first to create a flute and enjoy its music. But when I saw my bulging cheeks, I threw it away. Marsyas found it, learnt how to play and showed off his skill to the nymphs. He even challenged Apollo—to his cost. But I am the inventor of the flute and the pipers keep my festival.*

695. ***Martius.*** Minerva answers Ovid's question why the *Quinquatrus* is so named by referring to the *Quinquatrus* on 19 March (*Fast.* 3. 809–36), which took place five days after the Ides of March.

696. ***'estque sub inventis haec quoque turba meis'*****:** in this context *turba* signified a crowd of cult followers, the musicians and other performers who might celebrate Minerva's festival (*OLD* s.v. 3. Cf. Tib. 2. 1. 16, *candida turba*, and *Fast.* 1. 42, 6. 671). *Inventis meis* points forward to the story of Minerva's invention of the flute. This elegiac version here has the comedy of a mime; when Ovid tells the same story in his *Metamorphoses*, the emphasis is entirely on the sufferings of Marsyas' and Minerva is mentioned only for her invention: *Tritoniaca harundine* (*Met.* 6. 384).

697. ***'terebrato per rara formamina buxo'*****:** 'I bored the boxwood with spaced holes and made the long flute sing.' The artisans' goddess speaks in her worshippers' idiom. Ancient *tibicines* usually played two pipes together as a *diaulos.* These pipes could be made from ivory, reed, wood, bone (often the tibia of a goat), or even metal or a combination of metal with bone or wood. There would be five or six holes, not evenly spaced, the second from the top being placed underneath the pipe for the thumb. If there were a sixth hole, it would be bored further down the pipe as a vent-hole. Popular in Greece and across the Middle East, the *diaulos* came to Etruria during the Orientalizing period and it is probable that *tibicines* formed part of the banqueting tradition in Rome also during the archaic and regal period. When Livy relates (7. 2. 1–13) that the art of piping was brought to Rome by Etruscan dancers during the early fourth century BC, he is concerned with *tibicines* who accompany religious ritual. [Details concerning the musical range and limitations of the *diaulos* are to be found in M. L. West, *Ancient Greek Music* (Oxford 1992) 81–107.]

699. *'vox placuit: faciem . . .'*: the pause at the caesura accentuates the contrast between the beautiful sound and Minerva's distorted face. Confronted with the displeasing spectacle of his own distorted features, Alcibiades is said to have reacted in the same way (Plut. *Alc.* 2. 5).

701. *'ars mihi non tanti est'*: discarding the newly discovered instrument because it spoils her beauty, the patroness of *tibicines* observes dismissively, 'Art isn't worth the effort!' Ovid adapts this line and situation from a passage in his *Ars*, where he advises women not to distort their features by playing musical instruments if they aim to please (*Ars* 3. 505. Cf. *Met.* 6. 386). In his *Metamorphoses* version of the Marsyas story Ovid, who is concerned with Marsyas' torture, remarks that music is not worth the pain: *non est tibi tanti.* Barchiesi (1997*a*: 90) suggests a double entendre in Apollo's punishment of Marsyas *arte superbus* through the association of elegy and flute-playing; Ovid, too, might be considered, with reference to his *Ars Amatoria*, to be *Arte superbus*, which led to his punishment by the Apolline Princeps.

702. *'excipit abiectam caespite ripa suo'*: Ovid describes a rural setting characteristic of satyr drama: a grassy bank beside a stream, the haunt of nymphs, which recalls Lucretius' description of the invention of piping (Lucr. 5. 1379–87).

703–4. *'inventam Satyrus primum miratur, et usum | nescit et inflatam sentit habere sonum'*: Ovid exploits the scene's dramatic potential. Minerva has flounced off, leaving the flute in the grass.

Enter Marsyas, who picks it up, wondering what it is (*inventam miratur*). Whilst he has no idea what to do with it (*nescit usum*), he thinks, if he blows it (*inflatam*), it might make a noise (*sentit habere sonum*).

705–6. '*et modo dimittit digitis, modo concipit auras,* | *iamque inter nymphas arte superbus erat*': 'now Marsyas uses his fingers to release air, now he sucks it in. Before long he was showing off his skill among the nymphs.' This couplet splendidly replicates Marsyas' clumsy attempt to make music. Beginning with the tongue-twisting alliteration of *modo dimittis digitis* (705), with its insistently repeated *i*, the sounds broaden out from *auras* to the euphonious Greek *nymphas*, ending with a flourish at the end of the line, *arte superbus erat*, which suggests Marsyas' self-assured mastery of his instrument.

706. '*inter nymphas arte superbus erat*': surrounded by admiring nymphs, the satyr is incapable of modesty and coming events are foreshadowed by Ovid's use of an epic phrase, *superbus* with ablative of source of pride (cf. Virg. *Aen.* 2. 556, 9. 324, 12. 326).

707. '*provocat et Phoebum: Phoebo superante pependit*': chiastic word order enhances the meaning. The first word, *provocat*, initiates Marsyas' downfall which is graphically evoked by the final *pependit*, evoking his characteristic pose in Roman art following his defeat by Apollo. The sense pause at the central caesura marks the watershed of Marsyas' fortunes, whilst the juxtaposition and polyptoton *Phoebum: Phoebo* conveys role reversal, as Phoebus challenged becomes Phoebus victorious [see Wills (1997) 273–4].

708. '*caesa recesserunt a cute membra sua*': the physical reality of the flaying of Marsyas which Ovid explores in greater detail in *Metamorphoses* 6 (385–96) is suggested both by the combined alliteration of *c* and *s*, beginning with the onomatopoeic *caesa*, and by the pun *a cute* suggestive of the sharp shearing of skin from flesh (*acute*).

709. '*sum tamen inventrix auctorque ego carminis huius*': Ovid uses *carmen* here to signify the music of the flute.

E XVIII KAL. IUL. EN, 711–712

Rising of the Hyades

711–16: *The Hyades appear on the night before Vesta's impurities float down the Tiber.*

711–12. *Tertia lux veniet, qua tu, Dodoni Thyone | stabis Agenorei fronte videnda bovis*: Ovid conjures up an imaginatively graphic image of Thyone, one of the Hyades, nymphs from Dodona in northern Greece, standing by the head of the bull of Europa, daughter of Agenor, whose story is told on 14 May when the constellation Taurus appears (*Fast.* 5. 603–20). The assonance in *Dodoni Thyoni* followed by pentasyllabic Greek patronymic *Agenorei* makes this a particularly mellifluous astronomical note. This is Ovid's fourth allusion to the rising of the Hyades, which he notes three times in May (*Fast.* 5. 163, 603, 734), entirely at variance with Pliny and Columella [see Ideler (1825) 153–5]. Their setting on 17 April (*Fast.* 4. 677) is in line with Pliny (*Nat.* 18. 247) and a day earlier than Columella (11. 2. 36).

F XVII KAL. IUL. Q. ST. D. F., 713–716

Impurities from Vesta's temple are cast into the Tiber

713–14. *haec est illa dies qua tu purgamina Vestae | Thybri, per Etruscas in mare mittis aquas*: after Vesta's storeroom was closed on 14 June, the 'impurities' were removed and, on 15 June, thrown into the Tiber, which would carry them down to the sea. This explains the letters Q. ST. D. F.: *quo stercus delatum fuit.*

715. *Zephyro date carbasa, nautae*: the didactic poets Hesiod and Virgil characteristically added to notices of rising and setting constellations some practical advice for seamen and farmers relevant to the anticipated weather. In Ovid's poem of the first half of the Roman year these warnings come most frequently in February, when longed-for signs of spring might prove to be treacherous: *Fast.* 2. 147–8 (wind), 151–2 (frost), 453–4 (wind), 853–4 (swallows). Cf. 4. 625–6 (storms at sea).

H XV KAL. IUL. C, 717–720

A XIV KAL. IUL. C, 721–724

Orion in the closing sequence of katasterism and apotheosis

Orion, son of Hyreius, was a mighty hunter, renowned for his strength, impetuousness, and amorous exploits (Hom. *Od.* 11. 572–5). [See J. Fontenrose, *Orion: The Myth of the Hunter and the Huntress* (Berkeley, 1981), Phillips (1992) 55–82, Newlands (1995) 111–15.] Among many causes cited for his katasterism was his assault on the virtue of Artemis, who was saved by the appearance of a giant scorpion (Arat. *Phaen.* 634–46). In *Fasti* 5 Ovid transforms Orion into Diana's loyal companion, who is destroyed by the Scorpion because he boasts of his hunting prowess: *'quam nequeam' dixit 'vincere nulla fera est'* (540). This hubristic boast links thematically Orion with Marsyas (*Fast.* 6. 707–8) and Aesculapius (745–62). Since it is not strictly necessary for Ovid to signal the rising of Orion when only his arms appear, it might be suggested that the Orion myth is mentioned because it forms a link with the story of the huntress Carna, as well as being part of the web of thematic correspondences in a group of myths concerned with katasterism and apotheosis at the end of *Fasti* 6.

The epilogue of *Fasti* 6 begins, in a sense, in line 719 with *proles Hyriea*, for this anticipates the first of Ovid's numerical statements counting the days to the end of June in line 725. Their closural force is enhanced by two allusions to garlands hung on boats (779) and on the shrine of the Lares (792), possibly with literary significance, and by a series of myths of apotheosis or katasterism. In the language of Augustan panegyric, the theme of apotheosis when applied to Quirinus and Hercules had a direct relationship to Augustus. Within the epilogue of *Fasti* 6 occurred an important dynastic anniversary which the poet fails to mention: the adoption of Tiberius as Augustus' heir on 26 June, the summer solstice. It might seem that Ovid's closural sequence of katasterism and apotheosis should have some bearing on this, especially as 26 June falls in the intervening passage between the myths of Aesculapius and Hippolytus and those of Quirinus and Hercules. Adoption as Augustus' heir raised Tiberius to the sure expectation of immortality, however disapproving his own views may have been on imperial apotheosis. In the absence of anything other than a suspicion that Ovid intended the epilogue of *Fasti* 6 to convey more than he actually says, another line might be added to the corpus of ambiguous and potentially 'Augustan' utterances, *fieri quod vetat, ipse (Iuppiter) facit* (*Fast.* 6. 762).

Orion and the Dolphin rise

717–24: *Orion and the Dolphin appear on the anniversary of the Battle of Mount Algidus, when A. Postumius Tubertus triumphed over the Volsci and the Aequi.*

717–18. ***at pater Heliadum . . . | . . . cinget geminos stella serena polos***: Ovid describes sunset with a particularly prolix periphrasis: 'Now when the father of the daughters of the Sun . . .'

719. ***tollet humo validos proles Hyreia lacertos***: Ovid records Orion's setting during the *Megalensia* on 9 April (*Fast.* 4. 545–8) and notes that it is still invisible in the night sky during the *Lemuria* (9–13 May, *Fast.* 5. 493–4). Implying that Orion is a large constellation, Ovid observes that only the arms appear over the horizon on 17–18 June, and seven nights later an inebriate on his way home cannot yet see Orion's belt (*zona latet tua et cras fortasse latebit*, 6. 787), which will be visible only on the following night (*dehinc erit, Orion, aspicienda*, 788). Cf. Plin. *Nat.* 18. 256. Orion's size was legendary (Hom. *Od.* 11. 308; Ovid *Fast.* 5. 537 and see Bömer *ad loc.*).

720. ***continua Delphin nocte videndus erit***: here Ovid is in agreement with Pliny (*Nat.* 18. 256) and Columella (11. 2. 45), who also have the Dolphin rise four days before 10 June (cf. *Fast.* 6. 471–2). All three writers differ marginally on the Dolphin's rising in January (*Fast.* 1. 457–8) and setting in February (2. 79) [see Ideler (1825) 148–9]. Ovid, in his *Fasti*, prefers the nominative *Delphin* to the Latinized *Delphinus* (cf. *Fast.* 1. 457, 2. 79, 113).

721. *scilicet hic olim Volscos Aequosque fugatos | viderat in campis, Algida terra, tuis*: Ovid's abrupt return to Roman wars is signalled by his witty use of sound-effects to entertain his readers. The cacophonous internal rhyme and alliteration in *Volscos Aequosque fugatos* contrasts with the euphonious Greek tetrasyllabic *Heliadum* and *Hyreia* in the previous couplet, hinting perhaps at the barbaric rusticity of the Italian tribes. During the fifth century Rome skirmished with her neighbours, the mountain tribes of the Aequi and Volsci. The crucial battle took place in a valley below Mount Algidus in 431 BC. Defeated earlier as a result of disunity between the consuls, the Romans decided to appoint as dictator A. Postumius Tubertus, who led the capture of the Volscian camp and celebrated a triumph before abdicating (Liv. 4. 26–9).

724. *vectus es in niveis postmodo victor equis*: Ovid's statement that Tubertus was carried in a *quadriga* of white horses is our only source for a triumphal refinement which was censured as hubristic some forty years later, when Camillus was given a triumph for his conquest of Veii (Liv. 5. 23. 6, Plut. *Cam.* 7. 1). The Roman *triumphator* was normally carried along the triumphal route in a chariot drawn by dark horses, white horses being sacred to Jupiter. Any mention of white horses tended to imply the divine status of the *triumphator*, who, by using four white horses, became part of a tradition. To this belongs Anchises' interpretation of the sighting of four white horses as a (propitious) omen of war, but also *spes et pacis* (Virg. *Aen.* 3. 537–43). Cf. Romulus (Prop. 4. 1. 32), and perhaps Latinus (Virg. *Aen.* 12. 161). Although Camillus had been accused of religious impropriety for arrogating to himself the white horses of Jupiter, they may have been used in Caesar's quadruple triumph in 46 BC (Dio 43. 14. 3). Part of the legendary trappings of the Aeneadae, white horses seem later to have become a conventional part of the dynastic triumph: Ovid uses the image of white horses for Tiberius' triumph over the German tribes (*P* 2. 8. 50) and for the prospective triumph of Gaius Caesar over the Parthians (*Ars.* 1. 214) [see Weinstock (1971) 68–75].

B XIII KAL. IUL. C, *MINERVAE IN AVENTINO*, 725–728

725–8: *When thirteen days of June remain, the sun passes from the sign of the Twins to the Sign of the Crab. This is the festival of Minerva on the Aventine.*

725. ***iam sex et totidem luces de mense supersunt | huic unum numero tu tamen adde diem*****:** this is the first of five allusions to the approaching end of June (cf. 6. 768, 771–2, 795, 797). Here Ovid counts thirteen days before 1 July, so that, by inclusive reckoning, it is now 19 June.

726–7. ***sol abit a Geminis, et Cancri signa rubescunt*****:** 'the sun is passing from the sign of the Twins and the constellation of the Crab begins to glow red.' Ovid makes a point each month of alluding to the passage from one zodiacal sign to another (*Fast.* 1. 651–2, 2. 457–8, 3. 851–76, 4. 713–20, 5. 693–5). The twelve constellations of the Zodiac were recognized as the basis of a solar calendar at the time of the appearance of the parapegma of Meton and Euctemon (430 BC). It seems to have been customary for astronomical writers to present a list of the twelve (Arat. *Phaen.* 545–94, Manil. 1. 263–74).

728. ***coepit Aventina Pallas in arce coli*****:** this peripteral temple stood on the Aventine, adjacent to the temple of Diana, and was a focus for those engaged in music or drama. Here the singers' guild formally registered Livius Andronicus' hymn which he wrote either to expiate a portent (Liv. 27. 37. 7) or to celebrate the victory of his patron M. Livius Salinator at the Battle of the Metaurus in 207 BC (Fest. 446–8L). Although the *Fasti Praenestini* gives the temple's *natalis* as 19 March, 19 June is the *natalis* marked in the *Fasti Esquilini* and *Amiternini.* Frazer (1929: 4. 317) suggests that the June date celebrated a new dedication following the restoration of the temple by Augustus (*RG* 19).

C XII KAL. IUL. C, *SUMMANO AD CIRCUM MAXIMUM*, 729–732

729–32: *They say Summanus, whoever he is, was given his temple in the days when Pyrrhus was a threat to Rome.*

729. *iamque tua, Laomedon, oritur nurus*: Aurora, being the wife of the Trojan prince Tithonus, was the daughter-in-law of Tithonus' father, Laomedon, king of Troy.

731–2. *reddita, quisquis is est, Summano templa feruntur*: Of Sabine origin (Var. L 5. 74), Summanus was a personified aspect of Jupiter's control over the weather akin to Tonans or Pluvialis. He was believed to govern nocturnal lightning and received black victims as a sacrifice (Cic. *Div.* 1. 16, Plin. *Nat.* 2. 138). Daytime lightning was considered to be controlled by Jupiter himself (Plin. *Nat.* 2. 138). A temple was built for Summanus on the Aventine during the wars with Pyrrhus.

732. *tum, cum Romanis, Pyrrhe, timendus eras*: Pyrrhus, king of Epirus, had been summoned by the Greek cities of southern Italy to spearhead resistance to Roman expansion. The story that Pyrrhus represented himself as Achilles' descendant intent on wreaking havoc among the Trojan Romans is vitiated by his family's boast that they were also descended from Andromache [see Erskine (2001) 157–61]. Equipped with huge forces, Pyrrhus defeated Roman armies at Heraclea and Ausculum in the years 280–279 BC. These were, however, 'Pyrrhic' victories, and he returned to Epirus in 275 BC with only one-third of his original force. The topic of Pyrrhus' invasion evokes the figure of Appius Claudius Caecus, who opposed Pyrrhus' peace initiatives (Plut. *Pyrrh.* 19, Cic. *Brut.* 55, 61).

D XI KAL. IUL. C, 733–762

The myths of Hippolytus and Glaucus

733–54: *During the next night the youth Aesculapius appears holding two snakes. Cursed by his father, the dutiful Hippolytus was flung from his chariot* *as he travelled to Troezen. He died, to the chagrin of Diana. Aesculapius promised her that he would restore the youth to life. He used the herb which had once saved Glaucus after the augur Polyeidus observed it being used by one snake to cure another.*

733. ***hanc quoque cum patriis Galatea receperit undis***: an Ovidian variant description for sunset. The sea nymph Galatea is said to receive the day (*hanc*) into her father Neptune's waves.

735. ***surgit humo iuvenis telis adflatus avitis***: On 21 June a constellation appeared in the night sky known as Ophiuchus or Anguifer, the boy holding two snakes: *gemino nexas porrigit angue manus*, 736 (cf. Cic. *Nat.* 2. 109, Arat. *Phaen.* 74–6). In fact this was part of a pair of constellations, the second being the Snake. From five alternative mythological figures who might be identified with Ophiuchus (Hyg. *Astr.* 2. 14) [see Newlands (1995) 192–6], Ovid selects Aesculapius, the son of Apollo, who was destroyed by Jupiter's thunderbolt (*telis adflatus avitis*) after he had brought Hippolytus back to life using the medical skill given to him by his father Apollo. It was believed that when the ship bringing the cult of Aesculapius from Epidaurus to Rome approached the harbour, a serpent swam from the ship to the Tiber island where the Romans, in response to this omen, built a temple to Aesculapius in 291 BC (Val. Max. 1. 8. 2). This passage forms, with Ovid's allusion to Aesculapius in *Fasti* 1. 289–94, another of the ring-compositional 'frames' which link Books 1 and 6. A sense of impending closure of the first half of the year, if not of Ovid's calendar poem, is accentuated by his concentration of myths of apotheosis at the end of this book (735–812). Aesculapius first appears as the constellation Ophiuchus (735), his reward for restoring Hippolytus to life as Virbius: *Phoebe, querebaris: deus est!* (761). The snake, which represented Aesculapius when it swam to the Tiber island, is itself a symbol of rebirth, for it is reborn when it sloughs its skin (Macr. 1. 20. 2). Ovid carefully constructs his retelling of this myth in *Fasti* 6 by interweaving the themes of *anguis* and *anguifer* with a multiplicity of motifs of rebirth and apotheosis. When Aesculapius promises Diana to restore Hippolytus to life, *sine vulnere* (747), he resorts to a herb which brings about the rebirth of the snake in the esoteric myth of Glaucus (751–20).

737. ***notus amor Phaedrae, nota est iniuria Thesei***: the two motives which drive Phaedra and then Theseus unwittingly to cause

Hippolytus' death are essential to the tragedy of Hippolytus. Ovid uses the anaphora *notus*... *nota* to indicate an Alexandrian footnote (cf. *memorant*, *Fast.* 3. 729), and the reader is reminded that the full story is told elsewhere [see Hinds (1998), 1–5. The differences and similarities in the treatment of this part of the story in Euripides, Seneca, and Ovid are discussed by W. S. Barrett in his commentary on *Euripides' Hippolytus* (Oxford, 1964) 29–45.]

738. *devovit natum credulus ille suum*: 'too easily convinced (of his guilt), he curses his son.' The word *credulus* mirrors *credulitate* (*patris*, *Met.* 15. 498), just as *devovere* has the same meaning (*OLD* s.v. 5) as *detestari*, which is Ovid's choice in his *Metamorphoses* version of the story.

739. *non impune pius iuvenis Troezena petebat*: *non impune* goes closely with *pius*, which is repeated in line 747. Because Hippolytus has rejected his stepmother's advances out of loyalty to his father, he has been denounced by Phaedra and punished by Theseus. In the *Metamorphoses* version of the story, Ovid uses the same line ending, *Troezena petebat* (506), to describe Hippolytus fleeing from his father's palace in Athens to his grandfather's kingdom in Troezen.

740. *dividit obstantes pectore taurus aquas*: a single graphic pentameter summarizes Ovid's epic description of the bull's chest thrusting through the waves (cf. *Met.* 15. 508–18).

741–4. *solliciti terrentur equi frustra retenti* | ... *lacero corpore raptus erat*: the extended descriptions of Hippolytus' dismemberment in Euripides, Seneca, and Ovid's *Metamorphoses* are succinctly pruned to two couplets recounting the basic facts: the terrified horses bolt (*frustra retenti*, 741). Hippolytus is thrown from his chariot onto the shore (*exciderat curru*, 743), where he is dragged over the rocks entangled in the reins (*lorisque morantibus*, 743). An onomatopoeic impression of galloping horses is suggested by a high proportion of dactyls, the chariot's jolting progress suggested by alliteration which passes from *t* to *d* to *c* to *t* again.

745. *reddideratque animam multum indignante Diana*: Ovid adapts here, in the same context and *sedes*, Virgil's use of *indignatus* to describe the rage and resentment of Jupiter when he finds Hippolytus has been restored to life (*Aen.* 7. 770–3).

746. *'nulla' Coronides 'causa doloris' ait*: Aesculapius was the son of Apollo and a nymph, Coronis, whom Apollo destroyed when she contracted a second union with Ischys, son of Elatus (cf. *Fast.* 1. 291).

747. *'vitam sine vulnere reddam'*: Aesculapius' promise to give Hippolytus life *sine vulnere* recalls *Metamorphoses* 15. 529, where the youth's shattered limbs are described as 'all one wound', *unumque erat omnia vulnus.*

749. *gramina*: Virgil describes Hippolytus as restored to life 'by Aesculapius' herbs and Diana's love' (*Aen.* 7. 769).

750. *profuerant Glauci manibus illa prius*: 'on a previous occasion these herbs had restored the dead Glaucus.' Glaucus was the son of Minos and Pasiphae. As a child, he was restored to life by means of herbs by Polyeidus, an augur. While seeking a remedy, Polyeidus killed a snake which threatened the dead child. A second snake, carrying a herb, brought the first to life, proving the herb's magical power (*auxilio est anguis a angue dato*, 751). The story is told by Hyginus (*Astr.* 2. 14. 5). The theme of restoring a princely child to life by means of a plant and a thrice-repeated magic formula forms another frame with the story of Crane's resuscitation of Proca (*Fast.* 6. 155–62), and at the same time relates to the theme of protecting the life and *viscera* of Roman *iuvenes*, the responsibility of the Roman goddess Carna. To emphasize by repetition the subject of dead princes during the years immediately following the premature deaths of Augustus' heirs and grandsons, Gaius and Lucius, has an Augustan resonance (see Introduction 4.4). Adverbs, as *prius* here, are seldom found as the last word in a pentameter [see Platnauer 40–1].

753. *pectora ter tetigit, ter verba salubria dixit*: three times Aesculapius touches Hippolytus and utters the words of a spell, as Carna protects Proca by touching the doorposts three times and reciting the spell (*Fast.* 6. 155–62). Alliteration enhances the formulaic expression.

The Katasterism of Aesculapius

755–62: *Diana hid Virbius in her sacred grove. However, Pluto and the Fates protested and Jupiter, fearing the precedent, made Aesculapius a constellation. You grieved, Apollo? Be reconciled with your father, who has overridden his own laws for your sake.*

756–7. *lucus eum nemorisque sui Dictynna recessu | celat: Aricino Virbius ille lacu*: enjambement accentuates the importance here of *celat.* Virbius is concealed within a sacred precinct (*lucus*), in the remoteness (*recessu*) of Diana's wood, beside her lake at Aricia, and finally by his new name, Virbius (cf. Virg. *Aen.* 7. 774: *secretis alma recondit sedibus*). Virbius' association with Diana's grove at Aricia is underlined by juxtaposition. The story of Hippolytus' transformation into the Italian Virbius is told by Virgil (*Aen.* 7. 761–82) and Ovid (*Met.* 15. 536–46). Serv. (*ad Aen.* 7. 778), also cites Callimachus (*Aet.* fr. 190 Pf.).

757. *at Clymenus Clothoque dolent*: Ovid unites in *dolent* Clotho, one of the Parcae, who now has to spin a second life-thread for Hippolytus, and Clymenus, or Hades, who is displeased that the laws of his realm are being taken lightly (*fieri regni iura minora,* 758). The line is textually problematic. It is clear from what follows, *haec... hic,* that there must be two names: a Fate and Clymenus, which is a name used for Hades by Callimachus (fr. 285 Pf.). Clymenus is Heinsius' conjecture for the reading *climen-s* in *M,* which is supported by Merkel (1841) and *AWC.* The reading *at Clymenus Clothoque* seems better than *Lachesis Clymenusque,* which is found in *U.* Of the three Fates, Clotho, Atropos, and Lachesis, Clotho would be the apt choice in this context because her name derives from her traditional activity, the Greek word meaning 'to spin' [see Frazer (1929) 4 *ad loc.*]. Further, the sense of the line is enhanced by the addition of the particle *at,* which indicates the turning-point in the story when divine opposition to Aesculapius' action begins: 'But Clymenus and Clotho...'

757–8. *dolent, haec fila reneri | hic fieri regni iura minora sui*: '(The gods) are aggrieved: she (Clotho) that a thread of life is spun a second time; he (Clymenus) that the laws of his realm are undermined.' *dolent* here governs two accusative and infinitive clauses, defining the grievances, respectively, of Clotho and Clymenus. In this instance Bömer's retention of the conjecture *reneri* seems preferable to *AWC*'s less picturesque *teneri.* The Fates were inflexible where respinning the threads of life was concerned. Bömer aptly quotes, in support of *reneri,* a similar occasion in Statius' *Thebaid*: *immites scis nulla revolvere Parcas stamina* (7. 774).

759–60. *derexit in ipsum | fulmina qui nimiae moverat artis opem*: '(The god) aimed his thunderbolt at the man who achieved his power through superhuman art.' Jupiter punishes Aesculapius because he has used his skill in a way which seems to compete with Jupiter himself. Competition with Apollo himself led to the punishment meted out to Marsyas in the previous passage, where the satyr's ruin is precipitated by his innocent boasting among the nymphs. The question arises whether we should see a significance in the recurrence of myths with an ominous emphasis on divine retribution and a comparison, in the divine punishment of Marsyas and Aesculapius, with the punishment which destroyed an over-confident poet who imagined that his poetry would transcend mortal judgement (see note on line 701). The interlocking narratives of Theseus–Hippolytus–Diana and Aesculapius–Apollo–Jupiter, linked by the myth of Glaucus, introduce the cycle of apotheosis myths which heralds the closure of *Fasti* by reflecting the closure of the *Metamorphoses*. Whilst Ovid's *Metamorphoses* end with Augustus achieving heroic apotheosis and Ovid poetic immortality, the literary and Augustan discourse intermittently discernible in the last eighty lines of *Fasti* remains, as the poet seems to have intended, tantalizingly difficult to decipher. The striking Augustan resonance of lines 759–60, however, offers a compelling invitation to make some attempt. Indeed, a particularly illuminating interpretation of this passage may be found in Newlands' examination of Ovid's self-portraiture in *Fasti* [see Newlands (1995) 175–208]. Newlands underlines the significance of the association between Apollo's complementary healing arts of medicine and poetry, and this should be regarded as the basis of an investigation of possible parallels between Aesculapius and Ovid, the practice of whose arts is cut short by 'Jupiter's thunderbolt'. This thread of literary discourse is accentuated by a 'frame' linking this story of Aesculapius, the final katasterism in *Fasti*, with Ovid's first star myth, the story of Arion (*Fast.* 2. 79–118), where Apollo's poetic art is recalled by the imagery of lyre and swan. The salient components of Ovid's Aesculapius narrative, two acts of destruction by two figures jealous of their paternal authority, are accentuated by a chiasmic structure: Theseus' paternal wrath and indignation destroy Hippolytus, who is mourned by Diana; meanwhile Apollo's gifted son, Aesculapius, is blasted into—not oblivion, but immortality by Jupiter, whose supreme power has been threatened 'by excessive art'. This passage illustrates cogently how the poetics of closure in *Fasti* appear to mirror the conclusion of Ovid's own poetic career.

E X KAL. IUL. C, 763–768

[Fantham (1985) 272–3, Newlands (1995) 203.]

763–8: *Whatever your haste, Caesar, delay if the auspices are unfavourable, as Flaminius and Lake Trasimene may testify! His reckless anniversary falls ten days before the end of the month.*

763. ***non ego te, quamvis properabis vincere, Caesar*:** arguing from the viewpoint that Book 6 is largely unrevised, Bömer cites this reference to 'Caesar' as an instance where the poet apostrophizes Augustus as though he were still alive (cf. *Fast.* 2. 15, 60, 127, 637, 3. 419, 710, 4. 19, 949, 5. 578 [see Bömer (1957) Introduction 18). Le Bonniec concurs. In AD 8 Augustus was 70 years old and for several decades Roman armies had been led by Tiberius, Germanicus, and, until his premature death, by Gaius Caesar. Augustus in the context of 'hastening to conquer' may be intended symbolically, with the understanding that his armies would be physically led by a young and more impetuous Caesar for whom the words *properabis vincere* would be appropriate. If we are to take Caesar literally here, then it makes better sense to assume that Germanicus is meant and that the couplet was inserted or altered after *Fasti* was rededicated.

765. ***sint tibi Flaminius Trasimenaque litora testes*:** the general and the battlefield are significantly juxtaposed (Liv. 22. 7. 5). On the Ides of March Ovid calls on both the battlefield and its dead (*Fast.* 3. 707: *testes estote, Philippi*) to bear witness to an act of sacrilege, the murder of the Pontifex Maximus, which led to a Roman military disaster. In calling to witness Flaminius and Lake Trasimene, the vanquished general and the place of his defeat, Ovid echoes Horace's line, *testis Metaurum flumen et Hasdrubal* (*Carm.* 4. 4. 38). Horace's poem culminates dramatically in Hannibal's lament for his brother

Hasdrubal's suicide. Ovid's terse reference to the military victory at the River Metaurus, *postera lux melior... cecidit telis Hasdrubal ipse suis* (769–70), seems consciously reminiscent of Horace's *occidit, occidit... Hasdrubale interempto* (*Carm.* 4. 4. 70–2), for it also clearly recalls Horace's imagery of the new dawn for the Romans which is heralded by the suicide of the Carthaginian general: *pulcher fugatis | ille dies Latio tenebris* (4. 4. 39–40). Before the Battle of the Metaurus, M. Livius Salinator vowed a temple to Iuventas, motivated by the knowledge that a lustrum held during the previous year had recorded a severe drop in the number of *iuvenes* who could be thrown into the field against the Carthaginians. However, after the victory the Carthaginians released Roman prisoners, which swelled the numbers of the *iuvenes*. The temple was dedicated in 191 BC and *Ludi Scaenici* were celebrated in honour of Iuventas (Liv. 36. 36. 5–7). The Second Punic War saw a rise in the popularity of the cult of Iuventas, which regained momentum when the temple was restored in 16 BC, as part of his encouragement of Roman youth, by Augustus, a strong supporter of the *Lusus Troiae*, which were cavalry exercises designed to prepare young Roman nobles for military service (Suet. *Aug.* 43. 2. Cf. Virg. *Aen.* 5. 553. Cf. Hor. *Carm.* 1.8, 3.2, 24). [See also Neraudau (1979) 187–90, Weinstock (1971) 88–90.]

767. *tempora si veteris quaeris temeraria damni*: Flaminius was said to have shown a reckless disregard for the unfavourable auspices before being defeated by Hannibal at Lake Trasimene in 217 BC (Liv. 21. 63. 7–10, 22. 3. 11–13. Cf. Cic. *ND* 2. 8). As *vates* of Roman religion, Ovid points out that Roman generals ignore or abuse the gods and their ministers at their peril. Ovid has added this couplet largely for the purpose of pointing out that the anniversary falls just ten days before the end of the month, *quintus ab extremo mense bis ille dies* (768).

F IX KAL. IUL. C, 769–770

769–70: *The next day is more propitious: Masinissa conquered Syphax and Hasdrubal fell on his sword.*

769. ***postera lux melior: superat Masinissa Syphacem***: customary juxtaposition of conqueror with conquered. For the first time Ovid records an event in the Third Punic War, in 203 BC, when the combined forces of Scipio Africanus and his ally, Masinissa, defeated a Carthaginian army led by Syphax outside the city of Cirta (Liv. 30. 12).

770. ***et cecidit telis Hasdrubal ipse suis***: another allusion to the Roman victory of the consuls M. Livius Salinator and C. Claudius Nero at the Battle of the Metaurus in 207 BC. Hasdrubal's suicide is not recorded in Livy's account, where Hannibal's brother dies fighting courageously (28. 12. 6, cf. Hor. *Carm.* 4. 4. 38). Livy's Book 27 is structured around this battle, beginning with Hasdrubal's arrival in Italy and, after devoting the last third to the battle, ending with Hannibal's grief for his dead brother and the dawning realization that he will never conquer Rome (27. 51. 12). Horace (*Carm.* 4. 4. 37–76) also visualizes the battle through the anguish of Hannibal, who rails against the victorious Claudii Nerones and the race 'risen from the ash of Troy'.

G VIII KAL. IUL. C, FORTI FORTUNAE TRANS TIBERIM (AD MILLIARIUM) PRIMUM ET SEXTUM, 771–784

Aquatic revelry at the feast of Fors Fortuna

771–84: *We grow old as time slips by. How quickly the festival of Fors Fortuna has come round! June will be over in seven days. Celebrate, Romans! Fortuna's temple was given by a king. Go downstream on foot or by boat. Don't be ashamed to come home the worse for wine! Bring the revellers downriver, you garlanded boats! Fortuna is worshipped by men of lowly station like the founder of her temple.*

771–2. ***tempora labuntur, tacitisque senescimus annis***: this third reminder of passing time before the end of the month of June has a mournful tone reminiscent of Ovid's exile poetry. Literary discourse is suggested by Ovid's choice of the word *tempora*, the central and opening theme of *Fasti*: the poem itself is moving on towards its completion. The image of time slipping past silently appears in *Fast.* 1. 65, *anni tacite labentis origo*, and *Tr.* 4. 10. 27. Ovid compares time's ceaseless flow to a river: *labuntur tempora motu | non secus ac flumen* (*Met.* 15. 179–80. Cf. *Am.* 1. 8. 49 and Hor. *Carm.* 2. 14. 1–4). [Newlands (1995) 204 sees a closural force in this motif of age and decay and the sequence of deaths: of Marsyas, Flaminius, Aesculapius, Hippolytus, and Glaucus.]

773. *quam cito venerunt Fortunae Fortis honores!*: on the far bank of the Tiber stood two temples to Fors Fortuna situated at the first and the sixth milestone along the Via Portuensis. According to the *Fasti Esquilini, Amiternini*, and *Magistrorum Vici* both celebrated a festival in honour of Fors Fortuna. The further temple, which was probably too far for city revellers to reach on foot, was founded in 296 BC by Sp. Carvillius Maximus (Liv. 10. 46. 14). The temple at the first milestone was believed to have been founded by Servius Tullius (Varro *L* 6. 17, D.H. 4. 27. 7), and this is far more likely to have been the goal of Ovid's urban plebs on 24 June. [On this cluster of temples see S. H. Savage, 'The Cults of Trastevere', *MAAR* 17 (1940) 26–56.]

774. *post septem luces Iunius actus erit*: the fourth (temporal) milestone: June has but seven more days.

775. *ite, deam laeti Fortem celebrate, Quirites*: Ovid's word-order here enhances the key ingredients of his invitation to Fortuna's festival. The assonance and the repetition of *ite*, in the framing words *ite . . . Quirites*, is insistent: the worshippers must hurry to Fortuna's temple. The goddess herself, occupying the central position in the line as she does in the festival, is surrounded by an inner alliterative frame, *laeti . . . celebrate*, where both words point to the merriment and the wine which will be the main focus of the day, for the word *celebrare*, like the English cognate 'celebrate', could be directly associated with festal drinking (*Fast.* 3. 542, 656, Hor. *Serm.* 2. 2. 60, Tib. 2. 1. 29).

776. *in Tiberis ripa munera regis habet*: the grassy Tiber bank near the temple (*munera regis*) was an ideal location for the urban plebs to celebrate Fors Fortuna's midsummer festival, where they could drink, dance, and make love as they did at the springtime festival of Anna Perenna: *non procul a ripis, advena Thybri* (*Fast.* 3. 523–4).

777. *pars pede, pars etiam celeri decurrite cumba*: the anaphora *pars...pars* gives an impression of numbers streaming across the river to Fortuna's temple on the far bank, some walking across the bridges, others crossing the river in small boats (cf. *Fast.* 3. 527–9). *celeri cumba* suggests a fast current, which is supported by numerous references in Latin authors to the Tiber's eddies and sand-churning (*flavus*) waves (cf. Hor. *Carm.* 1. 2. 13, 1. 8. 8, 2. 3. 18, Virg. *Aen.* 7. 30, Ovid *Fast.* 6. 228, *Tr.* 5. 1. 31).

778. *nec pudeat potos inde redire domum*: 'let it be no disgrace to return home in your cups!' The word *potare* implies drinking more serious than simply quenching thirst, for which the proper word is *bibere* (*OLD* s.v. 4). The gods are honoured by festal drinking, and Ovid comments that people who encounter the intoxicated procession staggering home on the feast of Anna Perenna 'call them blessed' (*fortunatos obvia turba vocat*, *Fast.* 3. 540). The *primitiae* of the vineyard traditionally belonged to Jupiter, whose name, in its Etruscan form, Tinia, is related to the Etruscan word for wine [see Dumézil (1970) 183–6]. This gives point to Mezentius' arrogance in demanding for himself the *primitiae* in Ovid's aition for the *Vinalia* (*Fast.* 4. 877–900).

779. *ferte coronatae iuvenum convivia lintres*: a well-known feature of this festival was the *Tiberina descensio* which described how revellers reached the temple by boat. The garlanded boats suggest festivity, like the garlanded donkeys at the Vestalia (311), and hint at literary closure, like the hares' garlands (792). Cicero uses this merry progress of revellers floating downstream on 24 June as a point of comparison with the solemn but triumphant journey upstream of L. Aemilius Paullus in 167 BC, when he brought back to Rome the captive king, Perseus of Macedon (Cic. *Fin.* 5. 24. 70, cf. Varro, Non. 209L, 687L). Depicted with a rudder on coinage, Fortuna's association with boats and the sea continued into Augustan times [see Nisbet and Hubbard (1970) 390–1, Weinstock (1971) 121–6]. Frazer (1929:4. 333) draws attention to the importance of rituals involving water at the summer solstice.

780. ***multaque per medias vina bibantur aquas*****:** Ovid's humorous 'reformulation of the more usual festal associations of wine and water' is observed by Miller (1991: 135).

781. ***plebs colit hanc*****:** similar phrasing (*plebs venit ac*) in the same *sedes* in the line (*Fast.* 3. 525) emphasizes a similarity in the character of the 'worshippers' at the festivals of Fors Fortuna and Anna Perenna. Although Servius' popularity with the urban plebs became a political catch-phrase during the Gracchan period [see Richard (1987)], Ovid's description of the festival is simply a colourful evocation of tradesmen and artisans having a good time on a Roman holiday.

783. ***convenit et servis, serva quia Tullius ortus*****:** Ovid's polyptoton, *servis, serva,* emphasizes a feeling of commonality between the legendary servile birth of the temple founder, Servius Tullius, and the goddess' devotees, an oversimplification appropriate to the slaves and urban plebs who come to the festival. This is supported by votive deposits of terracotta figurines wearing the pileus and by dedications on this theme found near the site of the temple to Fors Fortuna which was built in 293 BC [see Champeaux (1982) 1. 209]. Ovid's more elevated explanation of Servius' parentage, based on 'historical' sources, is to be found in lines 626–36.

784. ***constituit dubiae templa propinqua deae*****:** '(Servius) founded the nearby temple of the changeable goddess.' The word *dubiae* expresses the changeful nature of Fortuna as Tyche, an aspect of Fortuna which developed during the Hellenistic period and was certainly present in the various cults of Fortuna favoured by Roman generals [see Weinstock (1971) 112–27].

H VII KAL. IUL. C, 785–790

The musings of an inebriated stargazer

785–90: *And look! Here's an inebriate on his way home. 'Your belt, Orion, is not to be seen now or tomorrow. After that it will be visible to me.' If he had been sober, he might have mentioned the coming solstice too.*

789–90. ***Si non esset potus, dixisset … | … solstitiale die***: in addition to the summer solstice in June Ovid makes a point of noting other seasonal markers: the middle of winter on 10 January (1. 459–60), the beginning of spring in February (2. 149–50), the spring equinox (3. 877–8), the middle of spring in April (4. 901–2), and the beginning of summer in May (5. 601–2). In tune with the spirit of the festival and Ovid's recommendation in line 778: *nec pudeat totos inde redire domum*, one of Fortuna's worshippers staggers home *male sobrius* in the early hours of 25 June. His condition has rendered him incapable of discerning Orion's belt in the night sky (787–9) and even of remembering the summer solstice the following day: *si non esset potus, dixisset…| venturum tempus solstitiale die* (789–90). Nor, certainly, Ovid might have added, would such a man have any recollection of the momentous dynastic settlement of 26 June AD 4: Augustus' adoption of Tiberius and Agrippa Postumus as his heirs. It is tempting to suggest that Ovid has deliberately used this dramatic scenario as a witty way to avoid mentioning directly the adoption of Tiberius. The day of his adoption of Tiberius will have been carefully chosen by Augustus. His choice of the summer solstice, believed to occur on 26 June, would harmonize with Augustus' own 'complex of time' in the Campus Martius, where the shadow cast by the obelisk of the Horologium Solare touched the centre of the Ara Pacis on Augustus' birthday, the autumn equinox [see Wallace-Hadrill (1987), E. Buchner, *Die Sonnenuhr des Augustus* (Mainz 1982)]. The adoption of Tiberius was unwelcome to a number of people belonging to the circle of the younger Julia, in which Ovid was now moving. Continued opposition to Tiberius was evident in the civic disturbances during the years AD 6–8 [see Levick (1976)]. Besides, Tiberius' adoption was precipitated by the recent and tragically premature deaths of the sons of the still popular elder Julia, which may have discouraged displays of overt jubilation even among the supporters of Tiberius.

Syme used Ovid's omission of Tiberius' adoption to support his argument that Ovid must have completed his *Fasti* before 26 June AD 4. Herbert-Brown points out that there is no surviving fragment of epigraphic evidence that 26 June was designated a public holiday from any of the surviving *Fasti* datable between AD 4 and AD 14 [Herbert-Brown (1994) 230]. In Verrius' *Fasti Praenestini* all references to Tiberius were added in a different hand some time after AD 10. [see Degrassi 141–2]. There is no extant fragment of the month of June from the *Fasti Praenestini*, but the *Fasti Amiternini* of AD 20 designates 26 June as NP and records the adoption fully as follows: A VI [Kal. Iul.] NP *Feriae ex senatus consulto, quod eo die Imp. Caesar Augustus adoptavit sibi filium Ti. Caesarem. Aelio et Sentio consulibus* [Degrassi 474]. The accounts of Suetonius (*Aug.* 65. 1–3) and Velleius (2. 103) mention public rejoicing on 26 June AD 4, but do not allude to Agrippa Postumus, Tiberius' junior co-heir, which suggests that they were clearly written later when Tiberius' succession was unchallenged and Postumus had been conclusively eliminated [see Herbert-Brown (1994) 229–33]. The contiguity of the urban festival of Fors Fortuna, honouring a goddess associated with a ruler of lowly status, as compared with Tiberius' aristocratic Claudian lineage, was evidently considered entirely irrelevant [see Syme (1978) 33–4, Newlands (1995) 221].

B V KAL. IUL C/C IV KAL. IUL. C, 791–794

Anniversary of the temple of Jupitor Stator

791–4: *Tomorrow carefully woven garlands are placed at the temple of the Lares. It is also the anniversary of the temple Romulus built for Jupiter Stator by the Palatine.*

791. ***Lucifero subeunte Lares delubra tulerunt*:** the temple to the Lares which stood on the Velia was burnt down in 106 BC and rebuilt in 4 BC by Augustus (*RG* 19: *aedem Larum in summa sacra via feci*). He donated a pair of statues of the Lares, the base of which was found at the top of the Via Sacra and is now in the Museo Archeologico in Naples (Inv. 2606). It is inscribed *laribus publicis* (*CIL* 6. 456), which makes it clear that, unlike the *Lares Compitales*, which were administered by the *vicomagistri augustales* of the *vici*, the cult of the *Lares publici* was part of the state religion [see Gradel (2002) 130]. The original shrine, said to have its origins in the archaic period, stood near the Porta Mugonia (Var. Non. 852.20L) which was adjacent to the palace occupied first by Ancus Marcius and later by the Tarquin dynasty.

792. *si non esset potus, dixisset*...|... *solstitiale die*: 'in the place where many a garland is woven by skilful hands.' Making no distinction between *Lares Compitales* and *Lares publici*, Suetonius claims that on 1 May (*Fast.* 5. 129–47) and 27 June (*Fast.* 6. 791–2), immediately after the summer solstice, the shrines of the *Lares Compitales* should be garlanded with flowers (Suet. *Aug.* 31. 4). Mention of garlands may suggest poetic discourse (cf. Ovid *Am.* 3. 11. 29–30). Since Ovid prefaces 28 June with no allusion to the days remaining to June, it is possible that *corona* and *docta manu* may themselves carry some closural significance. The *doctus poeta* has 'hung a garland, cleverly fashioned, on the Lares' shrine', in other words, he is about to conclude (at any rate the first half of) his work on Roman religion. If this were so, then closure must surely also be anticipated by the garlanded boats in line 799, which evoke the symbolism of a completed, literary voyage (cf. Prop. 3. 24. 15, Ovid *Am.* 3. 11. 29, *Rem.* 811).

793. *tempus idem Stator aedis habet*: the temple to Iuppiter Stator stood near the Porta Mugonia, which had been the ceremonial entrance to the Palatine from the Via Sacra during the early archaic period (D.H. 2. 50. 3). The word Stator or 'Stayer' implied that Jupiter had strengthened the minds of the Roman troops to stand firm against their enemies, and traditionally Romulus vowed the temple when seeking Jupiter Stator's assistance in strengthening the flagging Romans in a battle at the Porta Mugonia (Liv. 1. 12. 3–6, D.H. 2. 50. 3). The temple was, however, not built until 294 BC, having been vowed a second time by M. Atilius Regulus in a battle against the Samnites (Liv. 10. 36. 11).

D IV KAL. IUL. F, 795–796

Anniversary of the temple of Quirinus

795–6: *Quirinus received his temple when June's remaining days equal the number of the Fates.*

795. *tot restant de mense dies quot nomina Parcis*: Ovid's fifth countdown to July observes that the remaining days of the month equal the number of the Fates.

796. *cum data sunt trabeae templa, Quirine, tuae*: the temple to Quirinus was believed to be of great antiquity (Plin. *Nat.* 15. 120) and for this reason might have been thought to contain the king's royal *trabea*, a short toga or *tebenna* of Etruscan style and origin. It had a reddish-purple border and was fastened on the shoulder with a fibula, rather than simply draped. The short *trabea* depicted on archaic Etruscan statues of gods or people engaged in religious ritual was sometimes reproduced on statues of a Roman Genius [see L. Bonfante-Warren, 'Roman Costume. A Glossary and some Etruscan Derivations', *ANRW* I. 4 (1973) 592]. The temple commemorated Iulius Proculus' sighting of the deified Romulus on the Quirinal (*Fast.* 2. 499–512) and was said to have been first dedicated on 17 February in the mid-sixth century BC. Rebuilt more splendidly by Augustus in 16 BC, it was rededicated on 29 June. The surviving fragment from its pediment, showing Romulus and Remus taking the auspices for the founding of Rome, may perhaps be related to Ovid's treatment of the founder legend in *Fasti* 2 and 5 [see Littlewood (2001) 928–35].

E PR. KAL. IUL. C, HERCULIS MUSARUM, 797–812

[L. Richardson, 'Hercules Musarum and the Porticus Philippi in Rome', *AJA* 81 (1977) 355–61, Syme (1978) 143–51, M. Martina, 'Aedes Herculis Musarum', *Dialoghi di Archeologia* N.S. 3:1 (1981) 49–68, M. Gray-Fow, 'A Stepfather's Gift: L. Marcius Philippus and Octavian', *Greece & Rome* 35: 2 (1988) 184–99, Newlands (1995) 212–36, Rüpke (1995) 331–68, Barchiesi (1997*a*) 266–72, (1997*b*).]

History of the temple to Hercules and the Muses

The month closes on 30 June with the *natalis* of the temple of Hercules Musarum. The circular temple of Hercules Musarum was built by M. Fulvius Nobilior in 189 BC on his return from campaign in Ambracia, for which he had a triumph in 187 BC (Cic. *Arch.* 11. 27). Nobilior decorated the interior of the temple with statues of the nine Muses which he had brought back from Greece (Plin. *Nat.* 35.

66), possibly with the booty from his campaign (Liv. 39. 5. 14). Rüpke suggests that the senate criticized his plundering of Ambracia, which may account for the delay in building the temple, which celebrated its *natalis* only in 178 BC. The statues of Hercules playing the lyre and the nine Muses were thought to be mutually beneficial: Hercules guards the Muses who, in turn, have the skill to sing his praises (*Musarum quies defensione Herculis et virtus Herculis voce Musarum*, Eumenius *Paneg.* 9. 73). The temple is a monument to the wave of Hellenistic culture which was gaining popularity in Rome at this time. Hercules' association with musical instruments goes back to the archaic period, when he is depicted holding a lyre or flute on black-figure vases. As Fox points out (2004: 124–5, n. 52), Ovid would no doubt be fully aware of the conjunction of Hercules and Lyra in the night sky on 30 June AD 5. According to Pausanius (4. 31. 10) a statue of Hercules was placed among those of the nine Muses in the temple of Asclepius in Messene.

A most sacred relic was added to the temple treasure in the form of a small shrine to the Camenae which was believed to date back to the time of Numa. Nobilior composed and installed in the temple a copy of 'Roman Fasti', which included etymological explanations of the names of the months and a basic chronicle of Roman temple *natales* and their aristocratic founders, over which the poet Ennius had possibly cast a critical eye (Macr. 1. 12. 16, 13. 21). Nobilior was accompanied on campaign by Ennius, who celebrated the events with a *fabula praetexta* called 'Ambracia' which may have been performed at the *Ludi Votivi* in 186 BC (Liv. 39. 5, 22. 1–2), if not at the celebration of the temple's *natalis* [see Flower (1995) 184–6]. If Ennius had used Nobilior's victory at Ambracia as the culminating event in Book 15 of his *Annales*, he would surely have incorporated the transference of the Muses to their Roman temple. [On the ending of Ennius' *Annales* see O. Skutsch, *Studia Enniana* (London, 1968), Barchiesi (1997*a*) 270 n. 16.] A set of ten *denarii* struck in 66 BC by Q. Pomponius Musa, which are now in the British Museum, show on their obverse side a picture of each Muse and Hercules Musarum himself [these are shown in T. P. Wiseman, *The Myths of Rome* (Exeter, 2004) 184, fig. 71]. The *natalis* on the final day of June of this particular temple with its Ennian associations provided Ovid with an appropriate literary motif of closure for the first half of his *Fasti*.

In 29 BC the temple of Hercules Musarum was splendidly restored by the son of L. Marcius Philippus [*PIR* M241*a*] and rededicated on 30 June (Suet. *Aug*. 29. 5). The wife of the elder Philippus was Atia, mother of the young Octavian, who had grown up in his stepfather's house. Here Caesar visited Philippus on 19 December 45 BC, possibly to acquaint him with the contents of his will and its implications for Octavian. The restorer of the temple, Octavian's stepbrother, had a daughter, Marcia [*PIR* M257], who married Paullus Fabius Maximus [*PIR* F47] some time after 11 BC. Marcia was a close friend of Ovid's wife (*P* 1. 2. 136) and Ovid counted her husband among his friends even after the poet's relegation to Tomis (*P* 3. 3, 1. 2). Whilst the initial foundation of the temple celebrates the arts, its restoration is associated with a family close to Augustus with links to the poet. The conjunction of the temples honouring Romulus/Quirinus and Hercules on 29 and 30 June balances Iuventas' speech in the prologue where she offers Hercules and Romulus as parallel *exempla* for Roman *iuvenes*. Beyond the challenge of conquest which tests only physical prowess, the paradigmatic hero requires divine opposition to test his constancy. Juno, the second most potent force in the divine hierarchy, obstructs his masculine heroism with feminine scheming, deviousness, and jealousy. She is, in short, an unwelcome but essential concomitant which stimulates the hero to surpass human limitation and achieve apotheosis. In Ovid's first question to the Muses concerning their seemingly odd conjunction with Hercules, the hero is designated at the moment when Juno, who has opposed his toiling progress to immortality at every step, is forced to welcome him among the Olympians (800).

Epilogue: a celebration of the temple's founder L. Marcius Philippus and his daughter, Augustus' cousin Marcia

797–812: *Tomorrow is 1 July. Add an epilogue to my poem, Muses! And tell me who united you with the one reluctantly accepted by his stepmother. Clio answered, 'This was built by Philippus, the father of Marcia. She was descended* *from priestly Ancus and endowed with beauty, wit, and nobility in equal measure. It is not a sin to praise her beauty when we praise the charms of mighty goddesses. Philippus married Caesar's aunt, an adornment to her noble family!' So sang Clio, her sisters agreed and, in assent, Hercules struck a final chord.*

797–8. *tempus Iuleis cras est natale Kalendis: | Pierides, coeptis addite summa meis*: the opening spondees suggest a portentous announcement of the approaching month of July. The pentameter might be translated 'You Muses, add an epilogue to the work which I began'. *coepta*, 'the work I have begun', is used by Ovid on several occasions midway through a work (*Met.* 8. 200–1, *Ars* 1. 771). *summa* is used by Quintilian, in the expression *summus liber* (*Inst.* 3. 8. 42), to refer to his final volume. Although no other month offers a similar countdown to the next, the first three books of Ovid's *Fasti* end with a couplet announcing that the poet has reached the end of the month (1. 723–4, 2. 863–4, 3. 883–4).

799–800. *quis vos addixerit isti | cui dedit invitas victa noverca manus!*: a mood of closure is achieved by the resolution of differences indicated elsewhere in Ovid's *Fasti.* Book 5 begins with a disagreement among the traditionally harmonious Muses (*dissensere deae*, 9) who are reconciled in the last lines of *Fasti* 6: *doctae adsensere sorores* (811). Book 6, which opens with discord between Juno and Iuventas and goes on to allude to Juno's persecution of Hercules (524), in the closing passage shows Juno offering her hands, grudgingly (*invitas*), to her stepson Hercules. In closure lines must be drawn under long-running animosity and characters brought to reconciliation. The reference to Juno's reconciliation to Hercules is also an allusion to Hercules' apotheosis and his entry into the Assembly of the Gods. Each of these is, in itself, a closural theme: the gods assemble to witness, but also pronounce on, the denouement of an epic while apotheosis, which contains much of the same iconography as a triumph or a funeral procession, marks the end of life's journey.

A further closural link is often perceived between the last poem of Propertius' Book 4 and Ovid's finale for *Fasti* 6, both of which are devoted to the praise of Roman noblewomen. Propertius' Cornelia, newly deceased, encourages her children to win the good-will of a prospective stepmother by a cheerful acceptance of their father's remarriage: *capta dabit vestris moribus illa manus* (Prop. 4. 11. 88). Hercules is received by his stepmother who has been 'brought round' (*victa*) against her stepmotherly instincts. Verbal similarities in Ovid's line draws the reader's attention to Marcia's affinities with Propertius' Cornelia, who is distinguished, like Marcia, by her nobility and virtue, but related to the Domus Augusta somewhat more tenuously as the daughter of Augustus' first wife Scribonia and therefore the half-sister of his daughter, Julia. The two women have in common their generosity of spirit and their propinquity to Augustus, whom Propertius describes as weeping at Cornelia's funeral (4. 11. 6). The purpose of Propertius' poem is Cornelia's autobiographic epitaph: the death of a Roman woman makes this a poem of closure, in the same way as Turnus' death at the end of Virgil's *Aeneid* gives absolute finality to the last line. It might be added, in conclusion, that Marcia's husband, Paullus Fabius Maximus, and Cornelia's son, L. Aemilius Paullus, were both eventually destroyed in political intrigues directed against Tiberius in AD 14 and AD 8 respectively, although this contributes nothing to Ovid's poetics of closure, since both misfortunes occurred nearly a decade after each poem was written.

803. '*Marcia, sacrifico deductum nomen ab Anco*': 'Marcia, who takes her name from priestly Ancus'. The name is repeated (802–3) in epanalepsis [cf. Wills (1996) 161]. Ancus Marcius was the son of Numa, the founder of Roman religion. Like Numa, Ancus is designated here as a priest-king, and his descendant, Marcia, a member of a *sacra domo* (810). In 68 BC, in his funeral speech for his aunt Julia, Caesar claimed that she was descended from both Venus on her father's side and the Marcii Reges on her mother's (Suet. *Caes.* 6. 1). Augustus, as head of the Gens Iulia, is presented in art, and indeed in Ovid's *Fasti*, as the heir of Aeneas who brought the *sacra* from Troy; his cousin Marcia is also descended from the Roman priest-kings through Ancus, the descendant of Numa, the founder of Roman religion. These lines conclude the first half of Ovid's work on Rome's dynastic religion, so it is appropriate that Ovid begins Marcia's encomium by setting her in the religious hierarchy of the Domus Augusta.

806. ***'et genus et facies ingeniumque simul'***: Marcia is distinguished by her noble birth, her physical beauty, and her intellectual gifts, each quality being equal to the other two: *par facies nobilitate... par animo quoque forma* (804–5). More than this she is also *casta* (802), a Roman noblewoman of traditional virtue.

808. ***'laudamus magnas hac quoque parte deas'***: 'in this respect (beauty) we praise the great goddesses.' This line enables the poet to close one of several ring compositions. Ovid's 'apology', that even goddesses can be appreciated for their physical beauty, evokes the Judgement of Paris, a point of notorious sensitivity with Juno, which recurs three times in the proem: first to identify Juno: *quas Priamides in aquosae vallibus Idae... ex illis fuit una* (15, 17), next, as a reason for her lasting enmity towards the Roman descendants of Aeneas (*forma victa*, 44), and finally, as the poet's excuse for not taking sides with either Juno, Iuventas, or Concordia. Moving from Juno the warrior goddess to her wounded vanity, Ovid ends the proem in an elegiac register, and this is picked up in this line of the epilogue. The presence of the other two deities of the proem is perceptible in this passage. The harmony represented by Concordia is evident in the Muses (*adsensere sorores*, 811), while the poet's unexpected eulogy of *matertera Caesaris* reintroduces the Domus Augusta, which appeared in the proem in the guise of Augustus' Actian laurels which adorned Concordia. Iuventas' husband Hercules reappears, now closely aligned with the Muses in the temple of Hercules Musarum and sets the seal of divine approval on Ovid's literary endeavour in the final line of the extant poem: *adnuit Alcides increpuitque lyram* (812).

809. ***'nupta fuit quondam matertera Caesaris illi'***: the younger L. Marcius Philippus was married to the younger sister of Augustus' mother Atia, who was also called Atia. The Atia sisters thus married, respectively, a father and his son. The younger Atia's daughter, Marcia, was an intimate friend of her cousin's wife, Livia (*P* 3. 1. 77–166) and an acquaintance of Ovid's third wife, who may have been a relation of Paullus Fabius Maximus (*P* 1. 2. 136–40). Through these channels Ovid clearly hoped that he might win some mitigation of his exile. Marcia's mother was *matertera Caesaris.* The word *matertera* recalls the cult of Mater Matuta, who was traditionally invoked for nephews and nieces. Before her apotheosis Ino is addressed by Hercules as *matertera Bacchi* (523).

810. *'o decus, o sacra femina digna domo!'*: the honorific *decus* is used of Maecenas by Virgil (*G* 2. 40) and Horace (*Carm.* 1. 1. 2). When Ovid uses it to describe Marcia, he means that she is an ornament to the imperial family. The words *sacra domo* imply the royal Trojan ancestry of the Gens Iulia as well as Marcia's own descent from the royal line of Numa and Ancus. It is not, perhaps, over-imaginative to detect, by a slightly different route, the same resonance in Ovid's very similar description of Augustus in his *Tristia*: *o decus, o patriae per te florentis imago* (*Tr.* 5. 2*b*. 5).

811. *sic cecinit Clio, doctae adsensere sorores*: less than unanimous agreement would be an inappropriate response from Clio's learned sisters to her encomium of Marcia.

812. *adnuit Alcides increpuitque lyram*: for metrical convenience and poetic emphasis Ovid frequently chooses this *sedes* for *adnuit* (cf. *Met.* 4. 539, 12. 597, 14. 816, 15. 683, *Fast.* 5. 359, 6. 384, 549). This final, succinct pentameter presents two distinct ideas, separated by a central caesura. First Hercules indicates his agreement with Clio (*adnuit Alcides*), then, since he holds a lyre, he strikes a chord. Whilst this is obviously a natural gesture of closure, Ovid has also created a variation on the literary history of the word *increpuit* in final poems: it has been used to signal divine reaction to the poet's endeavours in both Ovid *Am.* 3. 15. 17 and Horace *Carm.* 4. 15. 2. In the first of these Bacchus whips the poet (*increpuit* implies sound) with his thyrsus to direct him to new themes. In the second Apollo strikes his lyre to distract Horace from ill-advised notions of writing of war, which he had in his previous poem, so that he celebrates instead the benefits of the Pax Augusta. In both these examples *increpuit* is associated with divine guidance. The appearance of *increpuit* in the final line of Ovid's *Fasti* must be interpreted in the light of the preceding examples. Hercules himself does not possess the powers of Bacchus or Apollo to inspire a new poetic direction, but he shares this temple with the Muses, the very source of poetic inspiration. When he strikes his lyre in the final line of *Fasti* 6, he gives a final endorsement to Clio's, or rather Ovid's, words which have been directly inspired by the Muses.

Bibliography

(a) Texts and commentaries

ALTON, E. H., WORMELL, D. E. W., and COURTNEY, E. (1978), *P. Ovidi Nasonis Fastorum Libri Sex*, 4th edn. 1997 (Leipzig).

BÖMER, F. (1957–8), *P. Ovidius Naso, Die Fasten*, 2 vols. (Heidelberg).

BOYLE, A. J. and WOODARD, R. (2000), *Ovid: Fasti*, translated and edited with Introduction and notes (Harmondsworth).

FANTHAM, E. (1998), *Ovid: Fasti Book IV*, (Cambridge).

FRAZER, J. G. (1929), *P. Ovidius Naso Fastorum Libri Sex*, 5 vols. (London).

GREEN, S. J. (2004*a*), *Ovid, Fasti I: A Commentary* (Leiden).

LE BONNIEC, H. (1969–70), *Les Fastes*, 2 vols. (Catania and Bologna).

MERKEL, R. (1841), *P. Ovidii Nasonis Fastorum Libri Sex* (Berlin), 2nd edn. (1850–2), 3rd edn. (1884) (Leipzig).

NAGEL, B. R. (1995), *Ovid's Fasti: Roman Holidays*, translated with Notes and Introduction (Indianapolis).

PEETERS, F. (1939), *Les Fastes d'Ovide, histoire du texte* (Brussels).

PETER, H. (1874), *P. Ovidii Nasonis Fastorum Libri Sex* (Leipzig), 4th edn. (1907).

PIGHI, I. O. (1973), *P. Ovidii Nasonis Fastorum Libri, Annotationes* (Turin).

SCHILLING, R. (1993), *Ovide: Les Fastes* (Paris).

(b) Books and articles

AHL, FREDERICK (1985), *Metaformations* (Ithaca, NY, and London).

ALFÖLDI, A. (1974), *Die Struktur des voretruskische Römerstaates* (Heidelberg).

ALTON, E. H., WORMELL, D. E. W., and COURTNEY, E. (1973), 'Problems in Ovid's *Fasti*', *CQ* 23: 144–51.

AXELSON, B. (1945), *Unpoetische Wörter* (Lund).

BARCHIESI, A. (1991), 'Discordant Muses', *PCPhS* 37: 1–21.

—— (1997*a*), *The Poet and the Prince: Ovid and Augustan Discourse* (Berkeley).

—— (1997*b*), 'Endgames: Ovid's *Metamorphoses* 15 and *Fasti* 6', in D. Roberts, F. M. Dunn, and D. Fowler (eds.), *Classical Closure* (Princeton), 181–208.

—— 'The Statue of Athene' in Peter Knox and Clive Foss (eds.), *Style and Tradition, Studies for Wendell Clausen* (Stuttgart), 130–40.

Barrett, A. A. (2002), *Livia, First Lady of Imperial Rome* (Yale, New Haven, and London).

Bayet, J. (1926), *Les Origines de l'Hercule romain, BEFAR* 132.

—— (1971), *Croyance et rites dans la Rome antique* (Paris).

Beard, M. (1980), 'The Sexual Status of Vestal Virgins', *JRS* 70: 12–27.

—— (1987), 'A Complex of Times: No More Sheep on Romulus' Birthday', *PCPhS* 33: 1–15.

—— (1994), 'The Roman and the Foreign: The Cult of the "Great Mother" in Imperial Rome', in N. Thomas and C. Humphrey (eds.), *Shamanism, History and the State* (Ann Arbor, Mich.), 164–90.

—— (1995), 'Rereading Vestal Virginity', in R. Hawley and B. Levick (eds.), *Women in Antiquity: New Assessments* (London), 166–77.

Bettini, M. (1991), *Anthropology and Roman Culture: Kinship, Time, Images of the Soul* (Baltimore).

Bispham, E., and Smith, C. (eds.) (2000), *Religion in Archaic and Republican Rome and Italy* (Edinburgh).

Blank-Sangmeister, U. (1983), 'Ovid und die Aitiologie des Juni in Fasti 6.1–100', *Latomus* 42: 332–49.

Boardman, J. (1972), 'Herakles, Peisistratus and Sons', *Rev. Arch.* 1: 57–72.

Boëls, N. (1973), 'Le Statut religieux de la Flaminica Dialis', *REL* 51: 77–100.

Boëls-Janssen, N. (1993), *La Vie religieuse des matrones dans la Rome archaïque* (Rome).

Bömer, F. (1987), 'Wie ist Augustus mit Vesta verwandt?', *Gymnasium* 94: 525–8.

—— (1988), 'Über das zeitliche Verhältnis zwischen den *Fasten* und den *Metamorphosen* Ovids', *Gymnasium* 95: 207–21.

Bonfante-Warren, L. (1970), 'Roman Triumphs and Etruscan Kings: The Changing Face of the Triumph', *JRS* 60: 49–66.

Bowersock, G. (1990), 'The Pontificate of Augustus', in K. A. Raaflaub and M. Toher (eds.), *Between Republic and Empire: Interpretations of Augustus and his Principate* (Berkeley and Oxford), 380–94.

Boyce, G. K. (1937), *Corpus of the Lararia of Pompeii, MAAR* 14 (Rome).

Boyle, A. J. (1997), 'Postscripts From the Edge: Exilic *Fasti* and Imperialist Rome', *Ramus* 26: 7–28.

Braun, L. (1981), 'Kompositionskunst in Ovids *Fasti*', *ANRW* II. 31. 4: 2344–83.

Cameron, A. (1995), *Callimachus and His Critics* (Princeton).

Capdeville, Gerard (1995), *Volcanus: recherches comparatistes sur les origines du culte de Vulcain, BEFAR* 288.

CARDAUNS, B. (1976), *M. Terentius Varro: Antiquitates Rerum Divinarum* (Mainz).

CASTAGNOLI, F. (1979), 'Il Culto della Mater Matuta e della Fortuna nel Foro Boario', *StudRom* 27: 145–52.

CHAMPEAUX, J. (1982; 1987), *Fortuna: le culte de la Fortune à Rome dans le monde romain des origines à la mort de César*, 2 vols., *Mémoires de l'École Française à Rome* 64 (Rome).

COARELLI, F. (1983), *Il Foro Romano: I. periodo arcaico* (Rome).

—— (1988), *Il Foro Boario* (Rome).

COLE, SUSAN (1984), Theoi Megaloi: *The Cult of the Great Gods at Samothrace. Études préliminaires aux religions orientales dans l'empire romaine* (Leiden).

CONTE, G. (1986), *The Rhetoric of Imitation* (Cornell).

CORNELL, T. J. (1986), 'The Value of the Literary Tradition Concerning Archaic Rome', in K. A. Raaflaub (ed.), *Social Struggles in Archaic Rome* (Berkeley, Los Angeles, and London), 52–76.

—— (1995), *The Beginnings of Rome* (London).

CRISTOFANI, M. (1990), *La Grande Roma dei Tarquini: Catalogo della mostra* (Rome).

DAVIS, P. J. (1999), ' "Since my part has been well played"; Conflicting Evaluations of Augustus', *Ramus* 28: 1–15.

DONAHUE, J. F. (2003), 'Towards a Typology of Roman Public Feasting', *AJPh* 124: 423–41.

DOUGLAS, E. M. (1913), 'Juno Sospita of Lanuvium', *JRS* 3: 60–72.

DUMÉZIL, G. (1970), *Archaic Roman Religion*, 2 vols., trans. P. Krapp (Chicago).

—— (1975), *Fêtes romaines d'été et d'automne* (Paris).

—— (1980), *Camillus* (Berkeley, Los Angeles, and London).

DUNBABIN, KATHERINE M. D. (2003), *The Roman Banquet: Images of Conviviality* (Cambridge).

DURY-MOYAERS, G., and RENARD, M. (1978), 'Aperçu critique de travaux relatifs au culte de Junon', *ANRW* II. 17. 1, 142–202.

ECKSTEIN, A. M. (1982), 'Human Sacrifice and Fear of Military Disaster', *AJAH* 7: 69–95.

EDWARDS, C. (1993), *The Politics of Immorality in Ancient Rome* (Cambridge).

—— (1996), *Writing Rome: Textual Approaches to the City* (Cambridge).

ELSNER, J. (1991), 'Cult and Sculpture: Sacrifice in the *Ara Pacis Augustae*,' *JRS* 81: 50–61.

—— (1996), *Art and Text in Roman Culture* (Cambridge).

ERSKINE, ANDREW (2001), *Troy Between Greece and Rome* (Oxford).

EVANS, E. C. (1939), *The Cults of the Sabine Territory* (New York).

FANTHAM, E. (1983), 'Sexual Comedy in Ovid's *Fasti*: Sources and Motivation', *HSCPh* 87: 185–216.
—— (1985), 'Ovid, Germanicus and the Composition of the *Fasti*', *Papers of the Liverpool Latin Seminar* 5: 243–81.
—— (1992*a*), 'The Role of Evander in Ovid's *Fasti*', *Arethusa* 25: 155–71.
—— (1992*b*), 'Ceres, Liber and Flora: Georgic and Anti-Georgic elements in Ovid's *Fasti*', *PCPhS* 38: 39–56.
—— (2002*a*), 'The Fasti as a Source for Women's Participation in Roman Cult', in G. Herbert-Brown (ed.), *Ovid's* Fasti: *Historical Readings at its Bimillennium* (Oxford), 23–46.
—— (2002*b*), 'Ovid's *Fasti*: Politics, History and Religion', in B. W. Boyd (ed.), *Brill's Companion to Ovid* (Leiden), 197–233.
FAUTH, W. (1978), 'Römische Religion im Spiegel der *Fasti* des Ovid', *ANRW* II. 16. 1: 104–86.
FAVRO, D. (1996), *The Urban Image of Augustan Rome* (Cambridge).
FEENEY, D. (1984), 'The Reconciliations of Juno', reprinted in S. J. Harrison (ed.), *Oxford Readings in Vergil's aeneid* (Oxford and New York 1990), 339–62.
—— (1992), '*Si licet et fas est:* Ovid's *Fasti* and the Problem of Free Speech under the Principate', in A. Powell (ed.), *Roman Poetry and Propaganda in the Age of Augustus* (Bristol), 1–25.
—— (1998), *Literature and Religion at Rome: Cultures, Contexts and Beliefs* (Cambridge).
FELDHERR, ANDREW, and JAMES, PAULA (2004), 'Making the Most of Marsyas', *Arethusa* 37: 75–104.
FLORY, M. B. (1984), '*Sic exempla parantur*: Livia's Shrine to Concordia and the Porticus Liviae', *Historia* 33: 309–30.
FLOWER, H. I. (1995), '*Fabulae Praetextae*: When Were Plays on Contemporary Subjects Performed in Republican Rome?', *CQ* 45: 170–90.
—— (1996), *Ancestor Masks and Aristocratic Power in Roman Culture* (Oxford).
FOWLER, DON (1998), 'Opening the Gates of War', in H. Stahl (ed.), *Vergil's Aeneid: Augustan Epic and Political Context* (London), 155–74.
FOX, M. (1996), *Roman Historical Myths* (Oxford).
—— (2004), 'Stars in the *Fasti*: Ideler (1825) and Ovid's Astronomy Revisited', *AJPh* 125.1: 91–125.
FRASCHETTI, A. (1988), 'Cognata numina: culti della Città e culti della Casa del Principe in epoca Augustea', *StudStor* 29: 941–65
FRAZEL, THOMAS D. (2003), 'Priapus' Two Rapes in Ovid's *Fasti*', *Arethusa* 36: 61–97.
FRÉCAUT, J. (1972), *L'Esprit et l'humeur chez Ovide* (Grenoble).

GABBA, E. (1991), *Dionysius of Halicarnassus and the History of Archaic Rome* (Berkeley).

GALINSKY, K. (1996), *Augustan Culture: An Interpretive Introduction* (Princeton).

GEE, E. R. (2000), *Ovid, Aratus, and Augustus: Astronomy in Ovid's Fasti* (Cambridge).

—— (2002), '*vaga signa:* Orion and Sirius in Ovid's *Fasti*', in G. Herbert-Brown (ed.), *Ovid's* Fasti*: Historical Readings at its Bimillennium* (Oxford), 47–70.

GENETTE, G. (1980), *Narrative Discourse* (Ithaca, NY).

GORDON, A. E. (1938), 'The Cults of Lanuvium', *Univ. California Publ. Class. Arch.* (Berkeley), 2.2: 21–58.

GORDON, R. (1990), 'From Republic to Principate: Priesthood, Religion and Ideology' and 'The Veil of Power: Emperors, Sacrificers and Benefactors', in M. Beard and J. North (eds.), *Pagan Priests* (London), 179–98 and 199–231.

GOTTLIEB, GUNTHER (1998), 'Religion in the Politics of Augustus', in H.-P. Stahl (ed.), *Vergil's* Aeneid*: Augustan Epic and Political Context* (London), 21–36.

GRADEL, ITTAI (2002), *Emperor Worship and Roman Religion* (Oxford, Stuttgart, and Leipzig).

GRAY-FOW, M. J. G. (1988), 'The Wicked Stepmother in Roman Literature and History: An Evaluation', *Latomus* 47: 741–57.

GREEN, S. J. (2004), 'Playing with Marble: Monuments of the Caesars in Ovid's *Fasti*', *CQ* 54: 224–39.

GRIFFIN, JASPER (1984), 'Augustus and the Poets: *Caesar qui cogere posset*', in F. Millar and E. Segal (eds.), *Caesar Augustus: Seven Aspects* (Oxford), 189–218.

GRUEN, E. (1985), 'Augustus and the Ideology of War and Peace,' in Rolf Winkes, *The Age of Augustus* (1985), 51–72.

—— (1990), *Studies in Greek and Roman Culture and Policy* (Leiden).

GUARDUCCI, M. (1964), 'Vesta sul Palatino', *MDAIR* 71: 158–69.

HABINEK, T. (2005), *The World of Roman Song: From Ritualised Speech to Social Order* (Baltimore).

HALBERSTADT, MANFRED (1934), 'Mater Matuta', *Frankfurter Studien zur Religion und Kultur der Antiquität* 8 (Frankfurt).

HARDIE, P. R. (1986), *Virgil's* Aeneid: *Cosmos and Imperium* (Oxford).

—— (1990), 'Ovid's Theban History: The First Anti-*Aeneid*', *CQ* 40: 24–35.

—— (1991) 'The Janus Episode in Ovid's *Fasti*', *MD* 26: 47–64.

—— (ed.) (2002), *The Cambridge Companion to Ovid* (Cambridge).

HARMON, D. P. (1986), 'Religion in the Latin Elegists', *ANRW* II. 16. 3: 1909–73.

HARRIES, B. (1989), 'Causation and the Authority of the Poet in Ovid's *Fasti*', CQ 38: 164–85.
—— (1991), 'Ovid and the Fabii: *Fasti* 2. 193–474', *CQ* 41: 150–68.
HARRISON, STEPHEN (1997), 'The Survival and Supremacy of Rome: The Unity of the Shield of Aeneas', *JRS* 87: 70–6.
—— (2002), 'Ovid and Genre: Evolutions of an Elegist', in P. Hardie (ed.), *The Cambridge Companion to Ovid* (Cambridge), 79–94.
HEINZE, R. (1919), 'Ovids elegische Erzählung', repr. in Heinze, *Vom Geist des Römertums*, ed. E. Burck (Stuttgart, 1960), 308–403.
HERBERT-BROWN, G. (1994), *Ovid and the Fasti: A Historical Study* (Oxford).
—— (2002), 'Ovid and the Stellar Calendar', in id. (ed.), *Ovid's Fasti: Historical Readings at its Bimillennium* (Oxford), 101–28.
HERSHKOWITZ, D. (1998), *The Madness of Epic* (Oxford).
HINDS, S. (1987), 'Generalising About Ovid', *Ramus* 16: 4–31.
—— (1992), 'Arma in Ovid's Fasti', *Arethusa* 25: 81–153.
—— (1998), *Allusion and Intertext: Dynamics of Appropriation in Roman Poetry* (Cambridge).
HOLLAND, L. A. (1961), *Janus and the Bridge*, Papers and Monographs of the American Academy in Rome 21 (Rome).
HOLLEMAN, A. W. J. (1973), 'Ovid and the Lupercalia', *Historia* 22: 260–8.
HÖLSCHER, TONIO (1999), 'Augustus und die Macht der Archäologie', in *La Révolution romaine après R. Syme*, Fondation Hardt XLVI (Geneva), 237–73.
—— (2004), *The Language of Images in Roman Art* (Cambridge), translated from the German (Heidelberg, 1987).
HOLZBERG, N. (1995), *Ovid, Festkalendar* (Zurich).
—— (2002), *Ovid, the Poet and his Work*, tr. G. M. Goshgarian (Cornell).
IDELER, LUDWIG (1825), 'Über den astronomischen Theil der Fasti des Ovid', *Abhandlungen der königlichen Akademie der Wissenschaften zu Berlin aus den Jahren 1822–3* (Berlin), 137–69.
JAEGER, M. (1997), *Livy's Written Rome* (Ann Arbor, Mich.).
JOHNSON, W. R. (1978), 'The Desolation of the *Fasti*', *CJ* 74: 7–18.
KELLUM, BARBARA (1985), 'Sculptural Programs and Propaganda in Augustan Rome: The Temple of Apollo on the Palatine', in Rolf Winkes (ed.), *The Age of Augustus* (Louvain), 169–76.
—— (1990), 'The City Adorned: Programmatic Display at the *Aedes Concordiae Augustae*', in K. Raaflaub and M. Toher (eds.), *Between Republic and Empire: Representations of Augustus and his Principate* (Berkeley), 276–308.
—— (1997), 'Concealing/Revealing: Gender and the Play of Meaning in the Monuments of Augustan Rome', in T. Habinek and A. Schiesaro (eds.), *The Roman Cultural Revolution* (Cambridge), 158–81.

KENNEY, E. J. (1969), 'Ovid and the Law', *YClS* 21: 242–63.

—— (2002), 'Ovid's Language and Style', in B. W. Boyd (ed.), *Brill's Companion to Ovid* (Leiden), 27–89.

KNOX, P. (1985), 'Wine, Water and Callimachean Poetics', *HSCPh* 89: 107–19.

—— (2002), 'Representing the Great Mother to Augustus', in G. Herbert-Brown (ed.), *Ovid's Fasti: Historical Readings at its Bimillennium* (Oxford), 155–74.

KORTEN, CHRISTINA (1992), *Ovid, Augustus und der Kult der Vestalinnen* (Frankfurt).

KÖTZLE, M. (1991), *Weibliche Gottheiten in Ovids Fasten* (Frankfurt).

KRAUS, C. S. (1994), *Livy: Ab urbe condita, Book VI* (Cambridge).

KUTTNER, A. (1995), *Dynasty and Empire in the Age of Augustus: The Case of the Boscoreale Cups* (Berkeley).

LE BONNIEC, H. (1989), *Études ovidiennes: introduction aux Fastes d'Ovide* (Frankfurt).

LEFÈVRE, É. (1976), 'Die Lehre von der Entstehung der Tieropfer in Ovids Fasten 1. 335–456', *RhM* 119: 39–64.

LEVENE, D. S. (1993), 'Religion in Livy', *Mnemosyne Supplement* 127 (Leiden, New York, and Cologne).

LEVICK, B. (1972), 'Tiberius' Retirement to Rhodes in 6 BC', *Latomus* 31: 779.

—— (1976) 'The Fall of Julia the Younger', *Latomus* 35: 301–39.

—— (1978), 'Concordia at Rome', in R. A. G. Carson and C. M. Kraay (eds.), *Scripta Nummaria Romana: Essays Presented to Humphrey Sutherland* (London), 217–33.

LIEBERG, G. (1969), 'Iuno bei Ovid. Ein Beitrag zu Fasten 6. 1–100', *Latomus* 28: 923–43.

LIEBESCHUETZ, J. H. W. G. (1979), *Continuity and Change in Roman Religion* (Oxford).

LIOU-GILLE, BERNADETTE (1998), *Une lecture 'religieuse' de Tite-Live I: Cultes, rites, croyances de la Rome archaïque* (Éditions Klincksieck).

LITTLEWOOD, R. J. (1981), 'Poetic Artistry and Dynastic Politics: Ovid at the Ludi Megalenses (*Fasti* 4. 179–372)', *CQ* 31: 381–95.

—— (2001), 'Ovid Among the Family Dead: The Roman Founder Legend and Augustan Iconography in Ovid's *Feralia* and *Lemuria*', *Latomus* 60. 4: 916–35.

—— (2002), 'An Ovidian Diptych: *Fasti* 6. 473–648. Servius Tullius, Augustus and the Cults of June 11th', *MD* 49: 191–211.

LOEHR, J. (1996), *Ovids Mehrfacherklärungen in der Tradition aitiologischen Dichtens* (Stuttgart and Leipzig).

LULOF, PATRICIA (1996), *The Ridgepole Statues from the Late Archaic Temple at Satricum* (Amsterdam).

McKay, Alexander (1998), 'The Shield of Aeneas and the Triple Triumph', in H.-P. Stahl (ed.), *Vergil's Aeneid: Augustan Epic and Political Context* (London) 199–221.

McKeown, J. (1979), 'Augustan Elegy and Mime', *PCPhS* 25: 71–84.

—— (1984), '*Fabula proposito nulla tegenda meo*': Ovid's *Fasti* and Augustan Politics', in A. J. Woodman and D. West (ed.), *Poetry and Politics in the Age of Augustus* (Cambridge), 169–87.

Meadows, A., and Williams, J. (2001), 'Moneta and the Monuments: Coinage and Politics in Republican Rome', *JRS* 91: 27–49.

Mertens-Horn, Madeleine (1996), 'Herakles, Leucothea e Palaimon', in P. S. Lulof and E. M. Moormann (eds.), *Deliciae Fictiles II: Proceedings of the Second International Conference on Archaic Architectural Terracottas from Italy held at the Netherlands Institute in Rome, June 1996* (Rome), 143–8.

Michels, A. K. (1967), *The Calendar of the Roman Republic* (Princeton).

Miles, Gary (1995), *Reconstructing Early Rome* (Ithaca, NY).

Millar, F. (1993), 'Ovid and the *Domus Augusta*: Rome Seen from Tomoi', *JRS* 83: 1–16.

Miller, J. F. (1980), 'Ritual Directions in Ovid's *Fasti*: Dramatic Hymns and Didactic Poetry', *CJ* 75: 204–14.

—— (1982), 'Callimachus and the Augustan Aetiological Elegy', *ANRW* II. 30.1: 371–417,

—— (1983), 'Ovid's Divine Interlocutors in the *Fasti*', in C. Deroux (ed.), *Studies in Latin Literature and History, III* (Brussels), 156–92.

—— (1991), *Ovid's Elegiac Festivals* (Frankfurt and Bern).

—— (1992), 'The *Fasti* and Hellenistic Didactic', *Arethusa* 25: 11–31.

—— (1997), 'Meter, Matter and Manner in Ovid, *Ars Amatoria* 1. 89–100', *CW* 90: 333–9.

—— (2002), 'The *Fasti*: Style, Structure and Time', in B. W. Boyd (ed.), *Brill's Companion to Ovid* (Leiden), 167–96.

Momigliano, A. (1942), 'Camillus and Concord', *CQ* 36: 111–20.

Morgan, Llewellyn (1998), 'Assimilation and Civil War: Hercules and Cacus', in H.-P. Stahl (ed.), *Vergil's* Aeneid*: Augustan Epic and Political Context* (London), 175–97.

Myers, S. (1999), 'The Metamorphoses of a Poet: Recent Work on Ovid', *JRS* 89: 190–214.

Mynors, R. A. B. (1990), *Virgil, Georgics* (Oxford).

Murgatroyd, Paul (2005), *Mythical and Legendary Narrative in Ovid's Fasti* (Leiden).

Neraudau, J.-P. (1979), *La Jeunesse dans la littérature et les institutions de la Rome republicaine* (Paris), 183–241.

Newlands, C. E. (1992), 'Ovid's Narrator in the *Fasti*', *Arethusa* 25: 33–54.

Newlands, C. E. (1995), *Playing with Time: Ovid and the Fasti* (Ithaca, NY).
—— (2000), 'Connecting the Disconnected: Reading Ovid's *Fasti*', in Helen Morales and A. Sharrock (eds.), *Intratextuality* (Oxford), 171–202.
—— (2002), '*Mandati memores*: Political and Poetic Authority in the *Fasti*', in P. Hardie (ed.), *The Cambridge Companion to Ovid* (Cambridge), 200–16.
Newman, J. K. (1967), *The Concept of Vates in Augustan Poetry* (Brussels).
Nisbet, R. G. M., and Hubbard, M. (1970), *A Commentary on Horace: Odes Book 1* (Oxford).
—— —— (1978), *A Commentary on Horace: Odes Book 2* (Oxford).
—— and Rudd, N. (2004), *A Commentary on Horace: Odes Book 3* (Oxford).
North, J. A. (1995), 'Religion and Rusticity', in T. Cornell and K. Lomas (eds.), *Urban Society in Roman Italy*, (London), 135–50.
Nugent, S. G. (1990), '*Tristia* 2: Ovid and Augustus', in K. A. Raaflaub and M. Toher (eds.), *Between Republic and Empire* (Berkeley), 239–57.
Oakley, S. R. (1997), *A Commentary on Livy, Books 6–10* (Oxford).
Ogilvie, R. M. (1965), *A Commentary on Livy, Books 1–5* (Oxford).
Pallottino, M. (1977), 'Servius Tullius à la lumière des nouvelles découvertes archéologiques et épigraphiques', *CRAI* 216–36.
Palmer, R. E. A. (1970), *The Archaic Community of the Romans* (Cambridge).
—— (1974), *Roman Religion and Roman Empire: Five Essays*, The Haney Foundation Series No. 5, 3–56.
Parker, H. C. (1997), *Greek Gods in Italy in Ovid's Fasti* (Lewiston, Queenston, and Lampeter).
—— (1999), 'The Romanisation of Ino (*Fasti*. 475–550)', *Latomus* 58: 336–47.
Parker, Holt N. (2004), 'Why Were the Vestals Virgins?', *AJPh* 125.4: 565–601.
Parry, H. (1964), 'Ovid's *Metamorphoses*: Violence in a Pastoral Setting', *TAPhA* 95: 268–82.
Pasco-Pranger, M. (2000), '*Vates operosus*: Vatic Poetics and Antiquarianism in Ovid's *Fasti*', *CW* 93.3: 275–93.
—— (2002) 'A Varronian Vatic Numa: Ovid's *Fasti* and Plutarch's Life of Numa', in D. S. Levene and D. P. Nelis (eds.), *Clio and the Poets, Augustan Poetry and the Traditions of Ancient Historiography* (Leiden), 291–312.
Pfiffig, A. J. (1980), *Herakles in der Bilderwelt der etruskischen Spiegel* (Graz).
Phillips, C. Robert (1992), 'Roman Religion and Literary Studies of Ovid's *Fasti*', *Arethusa* 25: 55–79.
Porte, D. (1985), *L'Étiologie religieuse dans les Fastes d'Ovide* (Paris).
Powell, A. (ed.) (1992) *Roman Poetry and Propaganda in the Age of Augustus* (London).

Purcell, N. (1986), 'Livia and the Womanhood of Rome', *PCPhS* 32: 78–105.
—— (2003), 'Becoming Historical: The Roman Case', in David Braund and Christopher Gill (eds.), *Myth, History and Culture in Republican Rome: Studies in Honour of T. P. Wiseman* (Exeter), 26–33.
Raaflaub, K. A., and Toher, M. (eds.) (1990), *Between Republic and Empire* (Berkeley and Oxford).
Radke, G. (1965), *Die Götter Altitaliens* (Münster).
—— (1981), 'Die *Dei Penates* und Vesta in Rom', *ANRW* II.17.1: 343–73.
Richard, J.-C. (1987), 'Recherches sur l'interprétation populaire de la figure du roi Servius Tullius', *RPh* 61: 205–25.
Richlin, A. (1992), 'Reading Ovid's Rapes', in A. Richlin (ed.), *Pornography and Representation in Greece and Rome* (Oxford and New York), 158–79.
Ridley, R. T. (1975), 'The Enigma of Servius Tullius', *Clio* 57, 147–77.
Robertson, Noel (1996), 'Athene and Early Greek Society: Palladium Shrines and Promontory Shrines', in Matthew Dillon (ed.), *Religion in the Ancient World: New Themes and Approaches* (Amsterdam), 205–25.
Ross, D. O. (1975), *Backgrounds to Augustan Poetry: Gallus, Elegy and Rome* (Cambridge).
Ross Holloway, R. (1994), *The Archaeology of Early Rome and Latium* (London).
Rüpke, Jörg (1995), *Kalendar und Öffentlichkeit: Die Geschichte der Repräsentation und religiösen Qualifikation von Zeit in Rom* (Berlin).
Sabbatucci, Dario (1988), *La religione di Roma antica: dal calendario festivo all'ordine cosmico* (Milan).
Salvadori, E. (1982), 'La Struttura narrativa dei Matralia: Ovidio, *Fasti* 6. 473–562', *Sandalion* 5: 205–21.
Scheid, J. (1992), 'Myth, Cult and Reality in Ovid's Fasti', *PCPhS* 38: 118–31.
—— (1993), 'Cultes, mythes et politique au début de l'empire', in F. Graf (ed.), *Mythos in mythenlosen Gesellschaft: Das Paradigma Roms* (Stuttgart and Leipzig), 109–27.
Schilling, R. (1954), 'La Religion romaine de Vénus', *BEFAR* 178 (Paris).
—— (1979), *Rites, cultes, dieux de Rome* (Paris).
Smith, C. J. (1995), *Early Rome and Latium: Economy and Society, c.1000–500 bc* (Oxford).
—— (2000), 'Worshipping Mater Matuta: Ritual and Context', in E. Bispham and C. Smith (eds.), *Religion in Archaic and Republican Rome and Italy* (Edinburgh), 136–55.
Somella Mura, A., (1993), 'Ancora sulla decorazione plastica del tempio arcaico del foro boario: statue e acroteri', in E. Rystedt, C. Wikander, and Ö. Wikander (eds.), *Deliciae Fictiles: Proceedings of the First International Conference on Etruscan Terracottas*, Swedish Institute at Rome (Stockholm).

STAHL, H.-P. (1998) (ed.), *Vergil's Aeneid: Augustan Epic and Political Context* (London).

STAPLES, A. (1998), *From the Good Goddess to the Vestal Virgins: Sex and Category in Roman Religion* (London and New York).

SYME, R. (1978), *History in Ovid* (Oxford).

THOMSEN, R. (1980), *King Servius Tullius* (Copenhagen).

VAN TRESS, HEATHER (2004), *Poetic Memory: Allusion in the Poetry of Callimachus and the Metamorphoses of Ovid* (Leiden).

VERNOLE, VITTORIO EMANUELE (2002), *Servius Tullius* (Rome).

VERSNEL, H. S. (1970), *Triumphus: An Enquiry into the Origin, Development and Meaning of the Roman Triumph* (Leiden).

VIDAL-NAQUET, PIERRE (1986), *The Black Hunter: Forms of Thought and Forms of Society in the Greek World* (Baltimore and London).

VOLK, K. (1997), '*cum carmen crescit et annus*: Ovid's *Fasti* and the Poetics of Simultaneity', *TAPhA* 127: 287–313.

WALLACE-HADRILL, A. (1982), '*Civilis Princeps*: Between Citizen and King', *JRS* 72: 32–48.

—— (1987), 'Time for Augustus: Ovid, Augustus and the *Fasti*', in M. Whitby, P. Hardie, and M. Whitby (eds.), *Homo Viator: Classical Essays for John Bramble* (Bristol), 221–30.

—— (1997), '*Mutatio morum*: The Idea of a Cultural Revolution', in T. Habinek and A. Schiesaro (eds.), *The Roman Cultural Revolution* (Cambridge), 2–22.

WEINSTOCK, S. (1960), 'Two Archaic inscriptions from Latium', *JRS* 50: 112–18.

—— (1971), *Divus Julius* (Oxford).

WHITE, P. (1993), *Promised Verse: Poets in the Society of Augustan Rome* (Cambridge, Mass.).

—— (2002), 'Ovid and the Augustan Milieu', in B. W. Boyd (ed.), *Brill's Companion to Ovid* (Leiden).

WIEDEMANN, T. (1975), 'The Political Background to Ovid's Tristia 2', *CQ* 25: 264–71.

WILLIAMS, G. D. (1991), 'Vocal Variations and Narrative Complexity in Ovid's *Vestalia*: *Fasti* 6. 249–468', *Ramus* 20: 183–204.

—— (1994), *Banished Voices: Readings in Ovid's Exile Poetry* (Cambridge).

WILLIAMS, R. D. (1972), *The Aeneid of Virgil I–VI* (London).

WILLS, J. (1996), *Repetition in Latin Poetry: Figures of Allusion* (Oxford).

WINKES, R. (1985) (ed.), *The Age of Augustus*, An Inter-disciplinary Conference held at Brown University, April 30th – May 2nd 1982 (Louvain).

WISEMAN, T. P. (1983), 'The Wife and Children of Romulus', *CQ* 33: 448–52.

—— (1984), 'Cybele, Vergil and Augustus', in A. J. Woodman and D. West (eds.), *Poetry and Politics in the Age of Augustus* (Cambridge), 117–28.

—— (1994), *Historiography and Imagination* (Exeter).

—— (1998), *Roman Drama and Roman History* (Exeter).

—— (2002), 'Ovid and the Stage', in Geraldine Herbert-Brown (ed.), *Ovid's Fasti: Historical Readings at its Bimillennium* (Oxford), 275–99.

ZANKER, P. (1988), *The Power of Images in the Age of Augustus* (Ann Arbor, Mich.).

ZIOLKOWSKI, A. (1992), *The Temples of Mid-Republican Rome and their Historical and Topographical Context* (Rome).

ZORZETTI, N. (1990), 'The Carmen Convivalia', in Oswyn Murray (ed.), *Sympotica: A Symposium on the Symposion* (Oxford), 308–20.

—— (1991) 'Poetry and the Ancient City: The Case of Rome', *CJ* 86: 311–29.

Index nominum

Index rerum

Index verborum